When should I travel to get the best airfare?

Where do I go for answers to my travel questions?

What's the best and easiest way to plan and book my trip?

frommers.travelocity.com

Frommer's, the travel guide leader, has teamed up with **Travelocity.com**, the leader in online travel, to bring you an in-depth, easy-to-use resource designed to help you plan and book your trip online.

At **frommers.travelocity.com**, you'll find free online updates about your destination from the experts at Frommer's plus the outstanding travel planning and purchasing features of Travelocity.com. Travelocity.com provides reservations capabilities for 95 percent of all airline seats sold, more than 47,000 hotels, and over 50 car rental companies. In addition, Travelocity.com offers more than 2,000 exciting vacation and cruise packages. Travelocity.com puts you in complete control of your travel planning with these and other great features:

> **Expert travel guidance from Frommer's** - over 150 writers reporting from around the world!
>
> **Best Fare Finder** - an interactive calendar tells you when to travel to get the best airfare
>
> **Fare Watcher** - we'll track airfare changes to your favorite destinations
>
> **Dream Maps** - a mapping feature that suggests travel opportunities based on your budget
>
> **Shop Safe Guarantee** - 24 hours a day / 7 days a week live customer service, and more!

Whether traveling on a tight budget, looking for a quick weekend getaway, or planning the trip of a lifetime, Frommer's guides and Travelocity.com will make your travel dreams a reality. You've bought the book, now book the trip!

D0109222

Here's what the critics say about
Frommer's Exploring America by RV:

"When you're ready to go, Slater and Basch provide grand itineraries . . . . Each itinerary includes maps, attractions, campgrounds, dining and shopping recommendations, and side trips. It would be difficult to find a better travel guide than *Exploring America by RV.*
—*Houston Chronicle*

"The husband and wife team of Shirley Slater and Harry Basch have assembled a nifty guide for RV aficionados that features sections on getting prepared, where to sleep and tips on buying and renting an RV, and most importantly, deciding which one is the best choice for you."
—*Chicago Tribune*

"Everything you need to know from buying a motor home . . . to great itineraries is included. The trips are very well done, providing not just information on the destinations but on [the authors'] experiences while driving to those places."
—*Boston Globe*

"Shirley Slater and Harry Basch weigh in on the best itineraries, campgrounds, parks, and attractions, as well as budget tips and unusual sights."
—*Condé Nast Traveler*

2ND EDITION

EXPLORING AMERICA by RV

Text and Photographs
by Shirley Slater & Harry Basch

Hungry Minds™

Best-Selling Books • Digital Downloads • e-Books • Answer Networks
e-Newsletters • Branded Web Sites • e-Learning
New York, NY • Cleveland, OH • Indianapolis, IN

To Janet and Alex Withers

Published by:

Hungry Minds, Inc.

909 Third Ave.
New York, NY 10022

Copyright © 2002 Text and Author Created Materials, Harry Basch and Shirley Slater

Maps © by Hungry Minds, Inc.

ISBN 0-7645-6595-8
ISSN 1527-165X

Editor: Kathleen Warnock
Production Editor: Donna Wright
Design by Madhouse Studios
Digital Cartography by Roberta Stockwell
Historical photos in chapter 1 courtesy of the David Woodworth Collection
Author photo by Donna Carroll

Special Sales

For general information on Hungry Minds' products and services, please contact our Customer Care department within the U.S. at 800-762-2974, outside the U.S. at 317-572-3993 or fax 317-572-4002. For sales inquiries and reseller information, including discounts, bulk sales, customized editions, and premium sales, please contact our Customer Care department at 800-434-3422.

Manufactured in the United States of America

5 4 3 2 1

CONTENTS

LIST OF MAPS

Major Interstate Highways

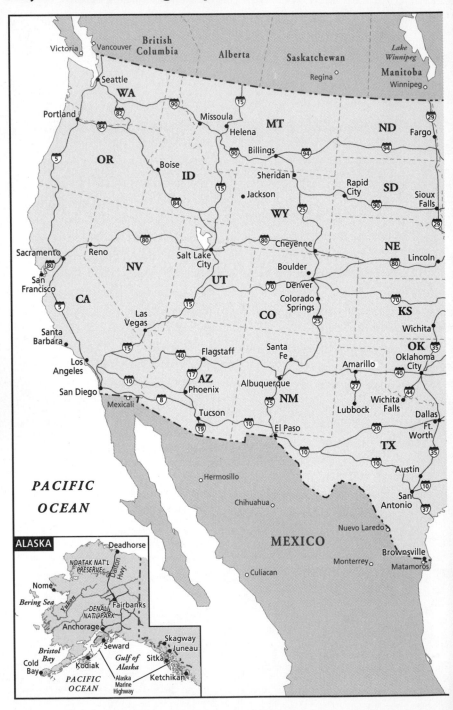

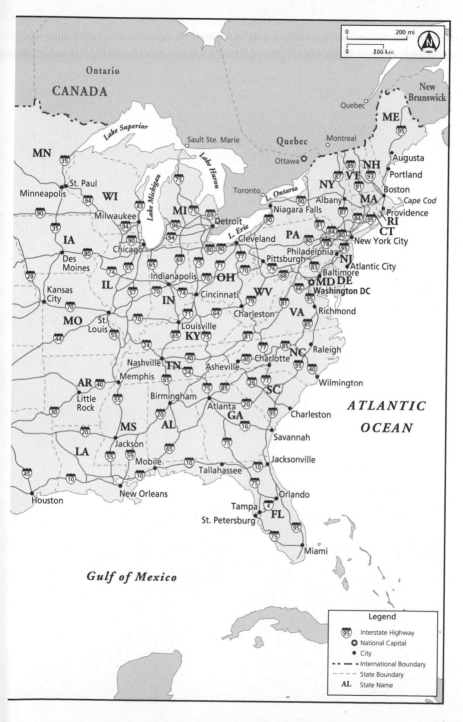

Legend

95 Interstate Highway
⊛ National Capital
● City
- · - · - International Boundary
- - - State Boundary
AL State Name

xi

ABOUT THE AUTHORS

Shirley Slater and Harry Basch are a husband-and-wife travel-writing team whose books, articles, and photographs have been published internationally over the past 25 years. Former stage, film, and television actors, they have written their syndicated column "Cruise Views" for the *Los Angeles Times* and other major newspapers for more than 18 years, produced six annual editions of the *North American Ski Guide* for Prodigy Computer Services, and written *Shirley and Harry's RV Adventures* (a monthly newsletter) plus four books on worldwide cruising.

In 1990, at the 60th World Travel Congress in Hamburg, Germany, the authors were only the third writers (and the first freelancers) to receive the prestigious Melva C. Pederson Award from the American Society of Travel Agents for "extraordinary journalistic achievement in the field of travel."

On assignment for publications as diverse as *Bon Appétit* and *Travel Weekly,* they have covered 188 countries by barge, elephant back, hot-air balloon, luxury cruise ship, cross-country skis, paddle-wheel steamer, and supersonic aircraft, but their favorite method of transportation is by RV. In their former 27-foot Winnebago Brave motor home and their new 36-foot Itasca Sunflyer, they have logged more than 80,000 miles traveling all over the United States, Canada, and Mexico. Aboard other RVs—from minimotor homes to 36-foot wide bodies with slide-outs—they have traveled an additional 60,000 miles exploring the back roads and campgrounds of America. These journeys are all based on the authors' personal experiences.

Shirley Slater and Harry Basch inside their RV.

Introduction: The RV Life & the Best of the Road

THERE'S SOMETHING QUINTESSENTIALLY AMERICAN ABOUT HITTING the road. You can almost hum along as the wheels eat up the highway— "King of the Road," "Hit the Road, Jack," "On the Road Again," "I've traveled each and every highway . . . I did it my way."

In an RV, you're free of airports, schedules, reservations, shuttles, and public transport. RVers can go anywhere without any advance reservations or preparations and always have a good time discovering something else new, interesting, or weird about the world around us.

"On the road" is shorthand for freedom, independence, discovery, self-reliance—but only if you search out routes that are off the beaten track, with an occasional jaunt over to an interstate to speed through less interesting terrain. As TV's *On the Road* guru, the late Charles Kuralt, once warned, "Thanks to the interstate highway system, it is now possible to travel from coast to coast without seeing anything." Leave the freeways to the truckers, the information highway to the computers, and virtual reality to the almost alive. With a folding camping trailer, van, travel trailer, truck camper, or motor home, an RVer can explore firsthand the famous, infamous, and off-the-wall attractions scattered all over North America, from the legendary Alaska Highway to Key West, the southernmost point in the United States.

This guidebook picks and chooses overnight oases, from private RV parks with heated swimming pools and golf courses to quiet, forested campgrounds in state and national parks. You'll also find offbeat places to eat or pick up tasty treats, including picking your own farm-fresh fruits and vegetables.

Big cities and world-famous commercial attractions do not fit our travel style—anyone can find them. Instead, we may opt to retrace the route of the Klondike Gold Rush, trying a hand at gold-panning; drop by the California desert museum dedicated to the art of striptease; shuffle off to see the buffalo in Custer State Park; or place a bet at Diamond Tooth Gertie's Casino in the Yukon's Dawson City.

In winter, RVers can learn rock climbing at Joshua Tree National Park or take in the sizzling Terlingua Chili Cook-off in West Texas. In the spring, we set out to catch the dogwood in bloom in the Blue Ridge Mountains. Late summer is the time to watch an Alaskan grizzly bear as it fishes for spawning salmon, or go river rafting on the Colorado. RVers can hang around New Hampshire in the autumn to sample fresh lobster or the dazzling display of red and gold leaves, or head south for stone crab season in the Florida Keys.

For some of us, discovering America may happen only after we've had a chance to explore Europe, Asia, Africa, or South America, and that makes the discoveries even richer. While we'd like to think this book is so riveting you'll read it cover to cover at one sitting like a mystery novel, we know you'll dip in and out of chapters at random.

And if we seem partial to KOA-member campgrounds, it's because we've learned through our years of travel that we can rely on a certain standard of excellence, toll-free reservations numbers, and a membership card discount.

The important thing, as Robert Louis Stevenson said, is "to travel for travel's sake. The great affair is to move."

John Lennon said, "Life is what happens while you are making other plans."

You Set the Lifestyle

Our introduction to RVs was during our many years as actors in film and television programs shot in Hollywood and on location, where the self-contained vehicles are used as dressing rooms. So when we leased a Winnebago motor home in 1992 to research an online ski guide we were producing for Prodigy Services Company, it was the first time we had been in an RV that actually moved, let alone under our own nervous control.

But what made us even more nervous than operating the machine itself was what we had always heard termed "the RV lifestyle." The suggestion was that by acquiring a recreation vehicle, you bought into a lifestyle—we pictured communal campfire visits, campground pancake breakfasts, and tours of each other's "rigs," culminating in an annual group caravan tour to some scenic area.

Instead, we quickly learned that while you can participate in group and club activities if you're so inclined, you can also use your recreation vehicle to continue whatever lifestyle you already practiced.

> **RV TRIVIA**
> RV campers drive an average of 4,585 miles a year, spend 46 nights on the road, and spend an average of $187 a day, including meals, gas and campground fees, on a 13-day vacation.

Because of our intense, high-pressure work as travel writers and performers, constantly on the move and in social situations, when on vacation we prefer what we call "The Garbo Gourmet Lifestyle." We "want to be alone" with the best food and wine and scenery, to read, go bird-watching or hiking, or listen to music. This doesn't mean we don't enjoy exchanging views with fellow RVers, only that we don't want to feel we have to.

It came as a tremendous relief to learn that we were free to do as we pleased. In our first RV journey, 6 weeks on the road all across the United States, nobody came over to urge us to join a club or otherwise identify with some larger group. We did, however, meet some very hospitable individuals, from a campground manager in Independence, Missouri, who taught us, with a flashlight after dark, how to dump the holding tanks we'd been trying to ignore for 3 days, to an exuberant group of hockey fans who shared a keg of beer with us at a campground in LaCrosse, Wisconsin.

The truth of the matter is, there's not one RV lifestyle; there are as many lifestyles as there are people who travel in RVs.

Here are only a few.

TWELVE PERSONALITIES IDEAL FOR RVS

1. **Garbo Gourmets.** They like to be alone together luxuriating in the best life can offer. They dislike tiptoeing through creaky B&Bs or suffering second-rate food and service at expensive hotels and resorts, preferring to carry their own wines and food, sleep in their own beds, and select their own surroundings by serendipity.

2. **Sportsmen.** Skiers, fishermen, surfers, golfers, and mountain bikers want to be in the heart of the action with all the comforts of home, including heating, air-conditioning, and hot showers, plus plenty of storage space to carry fishing rods, skis, golf clubs, and bikes.

3. **Weekenders.** The stressed-out want to get out of the rat race and into the countryside to delete the pressures of the work week from their hard drives. Their RV is always packed for a quick getaway, with only a shopping stop to load up on perishables on the way out of town. TGIF!

4. **Families on Vacation.** They offset that visit to a pricey amusement park by traveling with their own budget hotel, with self-serve restaurant at hand. A comfortable journey for the kids means no more, "Are we there yet?," "I have to go potty!," or "I'm hungry!" Everything they need is in the vehicle. They'll even sit still for an educational journey.

5. **Ecotourists.** Go back to nature the easy way, with dawn bird-watching, twilight wildlife spotting, photography, and hiking, laying less burden on Mother Earth than heavy hotel and resort infrastructures.

6. **The Ultimate Shoppers.** Hit all the antiques shops, estate sales, and the world's biggest swap meets in comfort and style, with room to take all the treasures back home.

7. **Relatives, Retirees, and Empty Nesters.** An RV is ideal for family visits because you bring your own bedroom and bathroom and can even entertain your hosts in your own home on wheels. Conversely, when parked at home, the RV doubles nicely as a guest room and bathroom.

8. **Pet Lovers.** Take Fifi and Fido along for the ride, enjoy their company, and avoid facing rebellious and destructive pets after a spell of boarding them out. Many (but not all) campgrounds welcome pets.

9. **Travelers with Disabilities.** If they get impatient with the well-meaning but often bungled accommodations in hotels, from hanging shelves too high to reach to bathroom doors too narrow to navigate, a customized RV can open up the world with familiar and accessible surroundings. (For more information, see "RVing for Travelers with Disabilities," later in this chapter.)

10. **Special Events Attendees.** Day or overnight RV trips to jazz festivals, weekend art shows, outdoor dramas, garlic festivals, tailgate parties, jumping frog jubilees, and Civil War reenactments let you sidestep overbooked hotels and restaurants. RVers can take off, even on the spur of the moment, and have bed, bathroom, and breakfast and lunch facilities on the spot.

11. **Snowbirds.** Escaping from -10° in Minnesota to the balmy Rio Grande Valley of Texas or heading for the high country to get out of summer's heat, an RV makes you a man (or woman) for all seasons.

12. **Full-Timers.** Whether quitting the rat race for a season or forever, chasing a dream, or discovering America, an RV is the only way to go.

RVS FOR EVERYONE

Of course, for these dozen lifestyle types there are 100 more that are perfectly accommodated by one of the types of RVs available. We've heard about RVers who follow a clothing-optional campground itinerary (yes, Virginia, there are nudist campers); travel newsletter editors who use their RVs as a combination home, office, and research vehicle; spa-goers who tootle from one hot spring to another; singles of both sexes who opt for the wandering life of a loner without a look back; and leaf peepers who live from one fall foliage tour to the next.

The vehicle adjusts to you and becomes an extension of your own life and travel style. It is simply a means to an end, a very well-designed and comfortable way to access the wilderness, nature, sightseeing, going to the sun, heading for the beach, the mountains, the woods—whatever will make you happy and enhance your life. It's your dream; you call the shots.

Campers have always found a sense of accomplishment in day-to-day survival: cooking food over a fire, finding a comfortable place to sleep, protecting yourself from the sun, rain, heat, or cold. With RVs, everything is much less work-intensive, without taking away the sense of self-reliance, of having everything you need for survival along with you.

Celebrities from Loretta Lynn to Danny DeVito, Michael Douglas to Pat Boone, John Madden to Bruce Willis are RV owners who use their vehicles for business and pleasure. More than one film megastar has had a contract sweetened with the perk of a big-bucks motor home, used as a private location dressing room during the shoot and given as a gift at the end of filming.

Our own favorite RV celebrity is senior golf champion Larry Laoretti, who was interviewed in his motor home on television during the U.S. Senior Open. After Laoretti won the tournament, sportscaster Brent Musberger asked him if now that he'd won $130,000 at the tournament, he would give up his motor home to "travel first class." Laoretti retorted that in his opinion, traveling by motor home *is* going first class, and a six-figure payday wasn't going to change that. We heartily concur.

But much as we love RVing, something we had never really anticipated before we tried it, we also will admit that perhaps not everyone is an ideal candidate for life on the road. If your idea of the perfect vacation is to check into a luxury resort and phone for room service, you may not be ready for an RV—that is, unless you have a mate who loves to wait on you.

A QUICK DO-IT-YOURSELF QUIZ TO TEST YOUR RVC (RECREATIONAL VEHICLE COMPATIBILITY)

1. Do you ever sing along with "My Way," "On the Road Again," or "King of the Road"?

2. Have you ever considered getting a second vacation home but can't decide between the mountains or the seashore?

3. Do you like to putter around the house or spend an entire Saturday morning browsing the shelves of a hardware store?

4. Did you ever envy Jack Kerouac, William Least Heat Moon, or Charles Kuralt, even a little bit?

5. Do you dislike timetables and schedules, the hurry-up-and-wait routine of catching a flight, and bumper-to-bumper commutes?

6. Are you tired of dress codes in restaurants that want men to wear a jacket and tie and women to wear a skirt, or vice versa?

7. Do you dislike using public toilets and showers, or wonder who slept in that motel bed just ahead of you?

8. Could you find paradise with *"a loaf of bread, a jug of wine and thou / Beside me in the wilderness"*?

9. Does the smoky smell of a campfire, a charred hot dog, or a burned marshmallow turn you on?

RVING FOR TRAVELERS WITH DISABILITIES

RVing, like sailing on cruise ships, makes an enjoyable and easy vacation for travelers with disabilities, particularly those who use a wheelchair, as long as the camping units are configured to take care of the chair's width and turning radius and are free of steps or level differences inside. Among manufacturers providing equipment for RVers with disabilities are Foretravel, Play-Mor, and Winnebago. For a complete list, contact the **Recreation Vehicle Industry Association (RVIA)**, P.O. Box 2999, Disabled LST, Reston, VA 20195-0999 (☎ 703/620-6003), which publishes a free booklet listing manufacturers of RVs or RV accessories for the physically challenged traveler.

Clubs for RVers with disabilities include **Handicapped Travel Club**, 667 J Ave., Coronado, CA 92118, and **Accent on Information**, P.O. Box 700, Bloomington, IL 61702 (☎ 309/378-2961). The latter publishes booklets and magazines for travelers with disabilities. 🚐

10. Are you susceptible to serendipity, doing things on a whim like turning down a side road that seems to call to you, buying something offbeat that instantly becomes a favorite possession, or striking up a conversation with an interesting-looking stranger who turns out to be a friend forever after?

If you answered yes to any one of the 10 questions, you might consider trying out an RV by rental. See chapter 14, "To Rent or Buy?" for details.

If you answered yes to 5 or more of the 10 questions, check out chapter 13, "RV Types & Terms."

If you answered yes to all 10 questions, what are you waiting for? Hit the road, Jack!

If you answered no to all 10 questions, you still haven't wasted your money. Thumb to one of the following chapters, grab your car keys and a lodging guide, or settle down in an easy chair, and set out on one of our roving RV adventures for a fast and funny look at weird, wonderful America.

PART I
Getting Ready to Hit the Road

Words of wisdom on preparing for life on the road and in the campgrounds

1

Life on the Road: A Personal & Public History of RVing

AMERICANS ARE A RESTLESS PEOPLE, CONSTANTLY ON THE MOVE, always expecting greener grass and greater opportunities over the next hill, beyond the horizon. For our predecessors, the covered wagon gave them a traveling home despite its lack of luxury. Tent camping provided a little more comfort for exploring America, but still slowed down the footloose.

Once the automobile came into everyday use, pioneering RVers didn't wait for specialty camping vehicles to be invented—they were creating their own motor homes just after the turn of the 20th century, in 1901. We discovered RVing in the early 1990s and, after an initial shakedown period, learned to love our life on the road. Our only regret now is that we didn't start earlier.

Excerpts from a Road Diary; or, If We Can Do This, Anyone Can

After nearly 20 years on the road as travel writers, we've traveled by just about every mode of transportation known to man, including hot-air balloons, elephants, and dugout canoes. But our lives changed when we set out for the first time in an RV, a leased 27-foot Winnebago Brave motor home, on a 6-week trip to visit more than 100 remote ski areas all over the United States for a computer service guidebook.

In an earlier life, as film and television actors, we had spent many long days in RVs changing clothes and studying scripts—they are used as dressing rooms on film locations and studio sound stages—but we had never been in one that moved. The size we selected was a compromise between how large an inside and how small an outside we could deal with. Here are some notes from that first time, all of them written in the passion of the moment.

August 12

At the California dealer where we are leasing the motor home, a young man named Daryll, with sun-bleached shoulder-length hair and a Persian Gulf War T-shirt, walks us through it, saying how easy everything is and how nothing can go wrong. We nod wisely and make frantic scribbled notes like "circuit breaker and fuses in bedroom" and "generator runs off gas tanks" and "water pump—switch off while moving." When he leaves us alone for a while, we go into a frenzy of measuring and diagram drawing.

August 14

The day before we are scheduled to leave, we lay out newspaper sections on the floor of our apartment folded to fit the measurements of the RV's cupboards, then set out the items we intend to put there and pack only those items in a box labeled for that section.

August 15

Unfortunately, life isn't that rational and orderly. On packing day, we are forced to double-park in our crowded urban neighborhood and relay boxes of books, cartons of pots and pans, and hangers of clothes back and forth from our apartment to the street, one of us keeping a constant eye out so nothing is stolen, and dumping things anywhere there is space, most of it on the plastic-wrapped mattress and in the bathroom shower.

When Daryll saw us off at the dealer's, he turned on the generator so the rooftop air conditioner could cool down the interior and chill the refrigerator and freezer, but neglected to tell us whether to keep it on while we're driving, or turn it off. Somewhere we remember him saying it's capable of running 16 hours straight with no problem, so we leave it on.

The soothing noise from the air conditioner drowns out many of the small crashes and thuds from the back as our possessions settle in on their own, with only an occasional loud thunk causing us to glance furtively backward.

August 15 (from the Driver's Seat)

The first impression is that you're way above the traffic and at the same time divorced from the road itself. Suddenly you realize you're looking down at the middle of the lane and half your vehicle is in the next lane. To keep from slipping over into an adjacent lane, you have to hug the left-lane line. The back of the vehicle seems to have a mind of its own and wants to turn at a shorter distance than the front end. We soon learn to make wide turns, particularly to the right. Another problem is that at any bump or rut, the vehicle leans to the right or left, then rolls back to the other side. Our fingers and arms are stiff after a couple of hours from white-knuckling the wheel.

August 15 (Nightfall)

It is after dark when we stop for gas in Kingman, Arizona, and Harry goes into a state of shock as he watches the numbers on the tank turn and turn and turn, as gallon after gallon flows in, until the pump turns off automatically at $50 and the tank still isn't full.

Exhausted, we agree it's time to stop. In front of us, between the gas station and the freeway, is an RV campground—we can see the sign—but we can't figure out how to get to it since a used car lot and a mall are in the way.

(It is about now that we give up the fantasy of waking to bird song and the breeze wafting through the pine trees.)

Not far away we find a second campground and something better than bird song—a space called a "pull-through," which means we can drive the motor home in one side, plug it in, then drive out the other side the next morning without backing up—something we haven't learned how to do yet.

We begin to speed-read the instruction manual and learn that it is necessary to turn off the generator before plugging in the electricity. That part is a snap—our plug fits into the campground's receptacle.

We make a long, fruitless search by flashlight through the outdoor storage bins for a hose so we can hook up the water connection. (Harry is positive Daryll pointed one out, but Shirley thinks he has remembered the sewage hose instead, and Harry thinks that maybe we should get a divorce, or at least go check into a motel with running water. As it turns out, we have plenty of water in the storage tanks without having to use the external hookup.)

We studiously ignore the sewage hookup. The refrigerator has been turned down to the coldest setting—obviously Daryll wanted it to get chilled quickly—and we find frozen romaine, eggs, and chicken breasts inside. Instead of a gourmet dinner, we settle for soup warmed in the microwave.

Stunned, almost stupid with exhaustion, we wash the dishes, close the blinds and curtains, and move back to the bedroom to make up the bed. Clearing it is easier than we expect, since most of the gear piled on the bed has already fallen onto the floor.

We raise the mattress to remove its plastic cover, and the hinged supports lock into the open position, leaving the bed set at a rakish 45° angle. By this time we're so tired we probably could have slept in it anyhow, but we get out the toolbox and unscrew the supports so we can flatten the mattress. Somehow we manage to simultaneously make up the bed and fall asleep in it!

August 16

The skies have opened up in the high desert of western New Mexico, dumping so much water in the streets of Socorro that the intersections are flooded ankle-deep. Although our campground guidebook promises there is an RV park in town, we spot the flickering light of a Motel 6 just ahead and, with no discussion, pull in behind a battered truck camper from Texas. If the veterans can't weather the storm, we amateurs can't be expected to.

August 17

The sun comes out. We stop at a hardware store and buy a water hose, which we hook up, but for some reason it never fills the tank. Later we realize we hooked the water hose to the outside connection that feeds water directly into the system. While we're still not able to make the TV work, we've gotten very good at plugging in the electric, once we realize our large three-prong plug has to fit into a three-prong 30-amp receptacle.

We studiously ignore the sewage hookup.

August 18

While checking out the ski resort at Crested Butte, we make a left turn uphill into the parking garage of the Grande Butte Hotel, which causes the tow-bar connection at the rear of the motor home to drag and stick fast in the asphalt. The concierge arrives and says a Greyhound bus got stuck there only last week, and should she call the tow truck again? Harry congratulates himself on taking out Auto Club emergency insurance, and the tow truck duly frees us. We vow never again to turn into a hotel driveway that heads uphill.

August 19

In the ski town of Breckenridge, we spot a locksmith standing beside his truck talking to a pretty blonde, and ask if he could help us get into our outdoor storage area because either the lock is broken or the key doesn't fit. The locksmith takes one look at the key and says we're using it upside down. At Dillon Reservoir, we settle down to lunch beside the lake, opening a couple of the roof vents for air, when a sudden gust of wind tears across the roof of the motor home and takes off one of the white plastic roof vents. Harry chases it down and climbs on the roof to replace it, just as the rain begins. At a nearby gas station, we buy a roll of silver duct tape and batten the vent down. We vow never again to open the roof vents on a windy day.

August 20

We get lost in Kansas City looking for Arthur Bryant's famous barbecue restaurant, so it is once again after dark when we check into a small RV campground in Independence, where a kindly campground manager with a flashlight loans us a sewage hose (ours is too short for the hookup) and talks us step-by-step through the dumping procedure for the holding tanks, which have reached their capacity. The same helpful manager shows us where to push a black button that activates the TV set.

Harry, I don't think we're in Kansas anymore.

August 27

It is almost with a sense of relief that we return to Winnie (for some reason we have begun calling the vehicle that lately) after staying overnight in some friends' lavish West Virginia country cottage. Their gardens are lovely, their hospitality warm, but Winnie has become home.

August 29

It has taken us 2 weeks to discover why the bedroom in the back of the motor home would get so hot while we're traveling, then cool down once we've stopped for the night. It turns out that Harry had kept a control switch on the dash to the left side on, thinking it was off, when the left side actually activates the low fan of the bedroom heater.

September 1

There is a great comfort in riding along listening to the sounds in the motor home behind us. We recognize the sharp clatter of the cutlery drawer suddenly swinging open, the more subdued sounds of the mug of wooden utensils spilling onto the stove top, the rolling thud of the canned food swaying back and forth in its bin, the rattle when the bedroom blinds come unhooked from their pins and are swaying, the bump when a camera forgotten and left on a chair falls onto the floor and breaks its wide-angle lens, the swishing sound of the cardboard box with its water jugs sliding on the plastic floor covering. (We did not remove the plastic over the carpeting, figuring that was one way to keep it cleaner inside.)

After we have the bed supports repaired, the bed develops a mind of its own and pops up occasionally, as if to have a look around.

September 15

We drive into Yellowstone, suddenly aware of how special it is to travel in a motor home with wide scenic views through the big windows and high seats, as if looking down from a bus. Herds of bison shamble around in the roadway, in no hurry, and our vantage point is ideal for photographing them. We stop for lunch by the Yellowstone River in a grove of trees, their leaves turned golden, and for the first time discuss buying a motor home of our own.

September 27

Partly because we despair of ever having to unpack Winnie, we buy her from the dealer. That was more than 50,000 miles ago. When not on the road, she resides at a Winnebago dealer's storage area in Carson, California, not far from the Goodyear blimp.

How to Give Backing-Up Directions Without Destroying Your Marriage

Whenever possible, request a pull-through campsite and postpone as long as possible the agony of a back-in site.

When no drive-throughs are available, we prefer to start with a quick confab about the broad general aims of the driver, particularly in regard to where the RV will end up, along with some general observations about the presence of boulders, picnic tables, and low-hanging tree limbs. Unfortunately, if the vehicle is blocking campground traffic, the prologue step has to be eliminated.

It is critical to establish a mutual signal that means "Stop immediately before you back into that _____" (fill in as applicable: truck, tree, utility post, fence, fire grate, and so on).

The first step is for the signaler to learn to stand where he or she can be seen by the driver in the side mirror. The same rule applies here as for cameras: If you can see the mirror, the mirror can see you.

Next, the signals should be clear and decisive. The fewer signals that are used, the simpler it usually becomes. We use a two-hand beckoning signal for "keep coming back," a right-hand signal to move toward the right, a left-hand signal to move toward the left, and a dramatic thrust of hand up and palm open toward the driver that means, "For God's sake, stop!"

If all else fails, you still have a couple of options: Invest in a closed-circuit TV backup system that shows the driver exactly what is behind him as he backs—expensive but effective (although these, too, have their limitations)—or a CB radio system with one unit in the cockpit and the second hand-held. Motorola also makes a two-way radio with a two-watt transmitter good for a 2-mile line of sight ($299 at Camping World). Less expensive walkie-talkies can be had from Radio Shack, but get one with more than one channel. It seems like everybody and his brother has the same one-channel system, and you'll find yourself having overlapping conversations with your neighbors.

RV History: The Tin Can Tourists

They called themselves "Tin Can Tourists." They braved the dust and mud to drive their tin lizzies across the United States before transcontinental roads were paved, camping by the side of the road, heating tin cans of food on a gasoline stove, and bathing in cold water.

They dressed in their Sunday clothes in the days before jogging suits and running shoes. A photograph of one 1920s camping club shows owners in front of their Weidman Camp Body vehicles, the men in fedoras, suits, and ties, and the women in dresses, cloche hats, stockings, and high-heeled shoes.

It took ingenuity to travel across the country in those days before the first motel, which opened in 1925 in California. In 1921, for instance, Lee Scoles of Fort Wayne, Indiana, converted his 1916 Federal truck to "a house on wheels" and drove it on an 8-month, round-trip journey to San Francisco with 11 relatives aboard. Such additions as solid rubber tires, a canvas awning, cots, a stove, and washtubs added to their comfort, according to his granddaughter Alice Worman, herself a motor home owner, who chronicled the story in *Lifestyles,* one of many such publications dedicated to RVing.

According to a story in *RV West* magazine, the family of Charles Ulrich set out for California in 1929 in a General Motors truck body mounted on a Ford chassis, with built-in bunks, overhead wardrobe storage, and a dining table with six folding chairs. The interior was polished mahogany and on the rear

"Tin Can Tourist" at Mammoth, 1920.

was a caboose-type open platform with iron railings. After their "once-in-a-lifetime" trip, which continued on to Hawaii aboard a Matson Line cruise ship, the Ulrichs stored the camper until the 1960s, when it was purchased by a group of hunters to serve as a forest base camp.

A fire-engine red 1929 Ford Model A converted to a minimotor home camper complete with pop-up top still carries the Ray Glenn family on trips around the Seattle area, according to *MotorHome* magazine.

Originally, auto camping was regarded as a rich man's hobby. The well-publicized outings of auto manufacturer Henry Ford, inventor Thomas Edison, naturalist John Burroughs, and tire manufacturer Harvey Firestone, who called themselves "the four vagabonds" as they camped in America's parks, had paved the way. Interestingly, it was the affordability and popularity of Henry Ford's Model T, which made its debut in 1909, that helped bring auto camping to the average American.

Nobody knows more about the early history of recreation vehicles than David Woodworth of Tehachapi, California, who owns the largest collection of antique camping equipment, photography, and literature known to exist. Much of his material appeared in the 1986 Smithsonian Institution's show "At Home on the Road," which he helped produce.

Alaska-born Woodworth attributes his fascination with RVs to his childhood memories, when his family traveled around the country in a Detroiter travel trailer following his carpenter father from job to job.

At RV shows and state fairs, he exhibits vehicles like his Art Deco–style 1937 Hunt House Car, designed and manufactured by a Hollywood cinematographer and inventor named J. Roy Hunt. (Among Hunt's many credits was the classic 1929 film *The Virginian*, starring Gary Cooper.)

The sleek, 19-foot, teardrop-shaped motor home, crafted on a Ford truck chassis and powered by a Ford flathead V-8 engine, includes a bathroom with hand-pumped shower, lavatory, and toilet (which has to be manually removed to empty); a stove with two burners; an icebox; a sofa and a dinette (both of which convert to beds); and even a kitchen sink.

Woodworth proudly claims membership in the Tin Can Tourists, whose last surviving affiliates have appointed him "Grand Can Opener."

Among the 30 or so antique camping vehicles in Woodworth's collection are 1928 and 1931 Covered Wagon Travel Trailers, manufactured in Detroit; a 1935 York Rambler built in York, Pennsylvania; a Hays from Grand Rapids, Michigan; and a Harley Bowless, created by the builder who oversaw the construction of Charles Lindbergh's historic transatlantic aircraft, the *Spirit of St Louis*. Airstream later used the Harley Bowless as an inspiration for its famous aerodynamic travel trailer back in 1936, Woodworth says.

He can also spout nonstop historic information about auto camping and the early campers. Here are some of his revelations:

- The first campgrounds were free, built and maintained by cities and towns hoping to attract affluent travelers who would spend money while they were in town. In the days before World War I, only the affluent had the time and money to go auto camping. When Ford's Model T made auto camping affordable for everyone, campgrounds started charging fees to discourage some of the overflow crowds.

- One early pair of auto campers was a couple who were fearful their new travel trailer might pull the rear end off their car, so the husband

1929 Ford with Weidman Camp Body.

THIRTEEN NOTABLE DATES IN RV HISTORY

ca. 1901: The first motor homes are built as special-order units by auto body builders.

1907: Henry Ford introduces the first mass-produced Model T Fords, automobiles with a 2.9-liter, four-cylinder engine that make auto camping affordable for most Americans for the first time.

1910–15: The first manufactured, mass-produced RVs—folding camping trailers—start coming off the line from Los Angeles Trailer Works, Auto-Kamp Trailers in Saginaw, Michigan, and other pioneers.

1917: The first fifth-wheel trailer is built by airplane manufacturer Curtiss-Wright; its name probably originated from the trailer hitch, which is located in the center of the towing truck's bed and could be considered a "fifth" wheel after the four on the trailer unit bottom.

1919: The Tin Can Tourists gather for their first rally, in a Florida campground near Tampa called DeSoto Park, with 20 members present, most of them Model T owners; by the mid-1930s, the club numbered 150,000.

1922: Fifteen million auto campers hit the road, according to the *New York Times*, most of them sleeping on cots, in tents, or in "newfangled houses on wheels."

1923: There are 7,000 free campgrounds in the United States, including Denver's Overland Park, with 800 campsites, piped water, a garage, restaurant, beauty shop, billiards hall, soda fountain, and eight electric washing machines.

1926: Fords equipped with Weidman Camp Bodies are first produced in Tonawanda, New York; the 1929 model sells for $1,900.

1962: John Steinbeck publishes *Travels with Charley* about his RV journey around America with his elderly poodle.

1966: Winnebago becomes the first mass-production motor home assembly line, turning out its early models (with moldings above the windshield that resembled eyebrows) in lengths of 17, 19, and 22 feet.

1966: David Garvin begins selling RV parts and camping accessories at his family's campground in Bowling Green, Kentucky; by 1993, his chain of Camping World stores (which he calls "Toys R Us for grown-ups") has become the world's largest retailer of camping supplies with 29 stores, 10 million mail order catalogs distributed annually, and a sales base of $150 million.

1967: Charles Kuralt rents a Dodge motor home to begin broadcasting "On the Road," his famous series of CBS-TV news features that brought small-town Americans and their stories into the living rooms of people everywhere. During his 27 years on the road, Kuralt used six different motor homes; the last, a 29-foot FMC motor coach, is installed at the Henry Ford Museum near Detroit.

1976: Winnebago Industries introduces the Heli-Home, a helicopter camper for off-road exploration that could sleep six; we note it's no longer included in their published brochures.

drove the car and the wife sat in the trailer for the entire journey watching the car's rear end to make sure nothing happened to it.

- Highways were notoriously bad in the early days. Woodworth quotes from the memoirs of some 1924 auto campers who termed themselves "Modern Gypsies" and wrote about a local resident telling them, "That's a good road; somebody just made it through there yesterday." Later, he says, the travelers commented, "When we left New York for Chicago, we were motorists. When we left Chicago for California, we were pioneers."

Six Common Misperceptions About RVs & Their Owners

As Gary Cooper said in the movie *The Virginian,* "When you call me that, smile!" Because we enjoy our freewheeling life on the road so much, we shudder at every false stereotype that some uninformed person perpetuates. Here, then, are a few common errors, followed by the way it really is.

- **Misperception no. 1:** We find misperceptions particularly hard to take when the perpetrator is a fellow travel writer who should know his nomenclature. A writer in a popular travel magazine writing about driving in Utah said Arches National Park "makes even the most remote rock formations visible to wheezing geezers willing to take a short walk from motor home to overlook." (The same writer spent much of his story bragging about how much speed his $40,000 Nissan Infiniti made on the empty highways and complaining about the dearth of gas stations

Early camping club.

INSIDER TIP

The **Museum of Family Camping** in Bear Brook State Park (turn off Route 28 and turn right on the road after the toll booth), Allenstown, New Hampshire (☎ **603/485-3782**), includes "typical campsites" of each decade of camping, as well as photo and taped reminiscences of old-timers and a Hall of Fame commemorating such pioneers as Airstream's Wally Byam, who organized and led camping caravans all over the world.

and fast-food outlets in southern Utah.) **Reality:** Puh-leeze, wheeze us no geezers! According to a 1994 University of Michigan study, the average RV owner is 48 years old, married with children, owns his own home, and has a household income of around $40,000 a year. During the next decade, the highest RV ownership category by age will be college-educated baby boomers just reaching the age of 45.

• **Misperception no. 2:** Another writer, describing a lonely highway he drove, says he met "only a few Winnebagos" along the way. **Reality:** While he might have met a series of RVs that were produced by Iowa-based Winnebago Industries, he probably used the term *Winnebago* to mean *recreation vehicles*. While all Winnebagos are RVs, not all RVs are Winnebagos. Out of today's 64 million campers, nearly half use a recreation vehicle. When Death Valley tabulated its overnight campground stays in 1988, a total of 61,743 overnights were made in tents, 249,726 in recreation vehicles.

• **Misperception no. 3:** A real-estate developer friend inquiring politely about our RV passion asked about our "mobile home" and was startled to be so instantly and vehemently corrected. **Reality:** Our motor home is not a "mobile home." The latter is not a recreation vehicle but manufactured residential housing that is infrequently moved after initially being set in place.

• **Misperception no. 4:** Well-meaning environmentalists like to say that unlike backpacking and tent camping, RVing pollutes the environment and guzzles gas and water resources. **Reality:** Having graduated from the ranks of backpackers and tent campers, we're acutely aware of this "purist" attitude. A recent Recreation Vehicle Industry Association (RVIA) poll shows that 98% of all RVers practice one or more forms of "green" RVing. In our case, our low-water toilet and quick showers use much less water than public facilities in the parks. We put all waste water into holding tanks, which are then properly disposed of at dump stations, rather than pouring anything on the ground or into streams. We never build a campfire that leaves layers of pollution hanging in the atmosphere, never dig up the ground or tie anything to trees and bushes, and recycle everything possible.

- **Misperception no. 5:** According to the University of Michigan study, some 14% of all potential RVers believe their state requires a special license to drive an RV. **Reality:** No state requires a special license to operate an RV; your normal driver's license is all you need. At present, 1 of every 10 motor-vehicle-owning families in the United States has an RV. In the 35-to-54 age group, it's 1 out of every 9. In fact, the RVers between 35 and 54 outnumber the over-55s.

- **Misperception no. 6:** When city officials of the former naval base town of Port Hueneme in Southern California proposed to bolster the town's sagging economy by building an ocean-side luxury RV resort, the proposal passed, despite a handful of residents at a town meeting that claimed "typical" RVers are "homeless, jobless, use drugs, commit crimes, belong to gangs, and desecrate any area they happen to park in," according to a journalist on the scene. Wow! And we thought our neighbors in the next campsite were just toasting marshmallows!

2

Getting Prepared: RVing Tips & Hints

THE FIRST TIME WE SET OUT IN AN RV, WE DEVOTED AS MUCH ATTENTION to it as the Allies planning D-Day, and had about as much success as Napoléon at Waterloo. Now, we can decide on the spur of the moment to go away for a few days, pick up the RV keys, and set out. In this chapter we'll discuss some of the nuts and bolts of life on the road so that you, too, can overcome disorganization and have the courage to just hit the road.

Driving Schools

While most confident (or overconfident) drivers pick up RV-wrangling fairly quickly, if you want to acquire some certifiable professional RV driving skills, contact the **RV Driving School,** P.O. Box 470, Applegate, CA 95703 (☎ 530/ 878-0111; www.rvschool.com). Instructor Dick Reed has more than 20 years of RV driving experience as well as being a teacher of truck and RV driving. He and his associates cover use of mirrors, driving defensively, courtesy, backing into campsites, safety checks, and braking and control. Students may learn on their own rigs or his. He also offers driving seminars at the Los Angeles RV Show each October at the Fairplex in Pomona. Classes are taught at his training locations in southern, central, and northern California, Arizona, Arkansas, Oregon, and Texas. Lessons run around $200 for a 4- to 6-hour lesson.

Your local RV dealer may also provide such instruction or be aware of an RV driving school in your area.

Every year RV writer Gaylord Maxwell offers his **Life on Wheels RV conference** at places such as the University of Idaho, Harrisburg Area Community College in Pennsylvania, and Western Kentucky University in Bowling Green, Kentucky. Seminars cover everything from RV maintenance, safety, money making, photography, computing, and anything else you might want to know about RVing. In addition, Dick Reed will be conducting his driving lessons at the conference. For information and reservations, call ☎ 866/569-4646; www.lifeonwheels.com.

Learning Your Vital Statistics

As beginners, our lack of technical knowledge was most frightening the first time we encountered a narrow, rickety, one-lane bridge near New Harmony, Indiana, with a small sign noting its weight limit was 5 tons. But how much did we weigh? We didn't know. Finally, since there was no way to turn around and go back, and the traffic was beginning to build up behind us, we gingerly inched our way across, holding our breath until we made it.

Later we studied the brochure that detailed our floor plan and learned that our maximum weight, fully loaded and with passengers, could be just over 12,000 pounds, or 6 tons.

The moral is, memorize your height, weight, and width before getting behind the wheel.

Before August 2000, the following terms were used on the weight information sheets provided with new vehicles:

- **GVW (Gross Vehicle Weight):** Total weight of a fully equipped and loaded RV with passengers, gas, oil, water, and baggage; must not be greater than the vehicle's GVWR.

- **GVWR (Gross Vehicle Weight Rating):** The amount of total loaded weight a vehicle can support; determined by the manufacturer, this amount must not be exceeded.

- **Dry Weight:** The weight of the RV without fluids such as gas, oil, and water added.

Beginning in August 2000, new terms were added:

- **UVW (Unloaded Vehicle Weight):** The weight with full fuel, water, propane, driver, and passengers.

- **CCC (Cargo Carrying Capacity):** The maximum permissible weight of all pets, belongings, food, tools, and other supplies you can carry in your motor home. This is the GVWR minus the UVW.

- **GAWR (Gross Axle Weight Rating):** The maximum permissible weight that can be carried by an axle with weight evenly distributed throughout the vehicle.

- **GCWR (Gross Combination Weight Rating):** The maximum allowable loaded weight of the motor home with towables.

Making a List, Checking It Twice . . .

It's a good idea for beginning RVers to make up a checklist to follow when packing for a trip, preparing the vehicle, or when setting up and breaking up camp. Some veterans laminate the list, then check off the items in grease pencil or erasable felt pen so it can be wiped clean to use again.

What Kind of Wardrobe Is Right?

Like most RVers, we have a wardrobe always stowed in our motor home that can cover any situation we may encounter on the road, from an impromptu dinner in a fine restaurant to an outfit for cold-weather camping or white-water rafting.

Since wardrobe and drawer space is fairly limited except on the largest motor homes and fifth-wheels, you'll want to confine your carry-along wardrobe to a few carefully selected basics, adding seasonal or special apparel when the journey requires it.

We concentrate on basic clothing that is machine washable, stretchable with elastic waists, and a comfortable fit, in styles and colors that will harmonize with the other items in the closet. For cold-weather camping, even in parts of the California desert in winter, a set of silk long underwear is invaluable under sweatshirts and pants. A loose cotton gauze or linen shirt and a pair of shorts are always on hand for unusually hot weather, like the heat wave we encountered in New England last summer.

A spare pair of hiking or jogging shoes is handy, along with a comfortable pair of slippers for the evenings after outside chores are finished. We each take one pair of slightly worn but acceptable dress-up shoes, along with one business or evening outfit, in case of an important appointment en route. Anyone planning to use the public showers in the campground should also take a pair of shower shoes.

Several changes of underwear, socks, and pajamas, along with a bathrobe, are folded and tucked into nightstand drawers beside the bed. We even carry spare bottles of prescription medication and a full supply of toiletries so we can slip away on the spur of the moment yet still have everything we need.

Knit clothes that can be folded and stacked rather than put on a hanger take up less room and don't need ironing. We often take travel- or sample-size toiletries, stowing them at home in a special RV box that's ready to be taken along on the next trip.

On our initial 6-week journey, we took far too many clothes, forgetting that a lot of campgrounds have laundromats and that items of clothing can be worn more than once. The other thing to remember is that in a campground, nobody pays much attention to what anyone wears anyhow.

Stocking the Larder

Because we use our RV all year, we keep it stocked with nonperishables that are always ready to go and need only be supplemented with fresh food, ice, and water before we set off for a weekend. But since even canned goods should not be stored for a long period of time, we mark the date of purchase on top of each can with an indelible marker and use them in order of age.

Particularly in warm weather, we avoid leaving open cardboard packages of crackers, flour, or cornmeal in the RV. We store small amounts of dried beans, rice, and grains in screw-top jars or resealable plastic bags, along with coffee beans and sugar. Open bottles of olive oil, mustard, or mayonnaise are brought back home at the end of each outing, to be replaced by another small, unopened container on the next trip. All wines are returned home at the end of every trip, but liquors can usually be stored in the vehicle between trips.

Because we both enjoy cooking for ourselves, we include among our permanent equipment a food processor, spice rack, and pots of fresh herbs (which go back home between journeys).

A large, French enameled cast-iron soup pot, which doubles as a spaghetti pot, is the biggest item in our cookware collection. It is accompanied by several smaller, nonstick enameled cast-iron skillets and pans, a small whistling teakettle, an earthenware teapot that travels in an old-fashioned, padded tea cozy, and several microwaveable measuring cups and dishes. We've recently added a pressure cooker, which cuts down cooking time, thereby saving propane. In hot summer weather, or to keep cooking odors outside when we have a hookup at the campground, we plug a single electric burner hot plate into the outlet by the counter of the outdoor entertainment center if we're cooking something like Southern fried chicken or a long-simmering stew, again saving on the propane consumption.

For eating, we have a set of sturdy French bistro plates, soup bowls, and wine glasses, plus two oversized ceramic mugs that fit nicely into the beverage-carrier on the cockpit dash. New dishtowels double as place mats and/or napkins, then become dishtowels after a few washings. We try to avoid using disposable paper products, preferring to recycle.

A cook's kitchen on the road may have fresh herbs and a food processor.

A large wooden cutting board, padded with a rubberized mat on the bottom, doubles as a cooktop cover when we're traveling; it keeps the burners from rattling and has a slide-out drawer that stores four sharp knives safely. We store in overhead cabinets or drawers under the cooktop a food processor, electric can opener, utensils that include tongs, funnel, and a long-handled cooking fork, and measuring cups. On nonskid matting the same color as our countertop, we put a spice rack, a jar of coarse salt, paper towels on a wooden spindle, and vacuum-topped canisters to keep dry items like cereals, chips, and snacks crisp.

Optional appliances we've taken with us include a toaster oven (indispensable if you don't have a regular oven, handy if you dislike bending to light the regular oven), sorbet maker (you need a freezer that can be set extralow), and bread maker (as easy to use on the road as at home).

AN ODE TO BUBBLE WRAP

Mel Brooks, in the classic comic routine "The 2000-Year-Old Man," lauded plastic wrap as the greatest invention of the past 2 millenniums, but we'd say bubble wrap is a close second in the wonderful world of RV cupboards.

It's not realistic to expect to stack dishes and glasses in an RV cupboard without some protection to keep them from chipping or breaking if you hit a rough stretch of highway. The cylinder-shaped bubble wrap containers that come around bottles in airport duty-free shops make great sleeves for mugs and glasses, while the flat sheets that come in packing boxes are easy to slide between plates or pots and pans to protect them. You can also buy plastic foam sleeves for glasses and pan and plate protectors in camping supply stores such as the Camping World chain.

Alternately nesting baskets and metal bowls keeps down the clatter from the cupboards as well. And lining the bottoms of drawers and cupboards with waffle-patterned rubber matting, available by the yard at RV dealers and camping stores, makes a nonskid surface for dishes.

We store fragile items like tulip-shaped champagne glasses in their original boxes and use other boxes or shaped Styrofoam packing protectors that come around appliances to wedge them firmly in the cupboard. Whenever possible, we use real dishes and utensils and cloth napkins instead of disposable paper and plastic products. If we're having guests for dinner, we like to surprise them with a dinner party comparable to one we'd have at home, including china, crystal, linens, and candles, when they were probably expecting paper plates and hot dogs on a stick.

DELICIOUS, QUICK & EASY ONE-POT MEALS

The following are some of our favorite quickly assembled meals after a day of driving or hiking, made with ingredients that are easy to keep on hand. Each involves one pot and a few simple preparation steps. On some, there are vegetarian and/or low-fat adaptations of the original recipe.

Quick Tortilla Soup

The cook controls the spiciness in this dish with the ratio of enchilada sauce to chicken broth. Makes 2 to 4 servings.

> 1 8-ounce can mild enchilada sauce
>
> 1 to 2 14-ounce cans of low-sodium, low-fat chicken broth (for milder flavor, use more broth)
>
> 1 15-ounce can of beans, drained and rinsed (black, red, or pinto beans)
>
> 2 seeded and chopped fresh tomatoes
>
> Cut kernels from 2 ears shucked fresh corn

Combine enchilada sauce, chicken broth, beans, and tomatoes in a saucepan. Heat thoroughly, then stir in the kernels cut from two ears fresh corn that have been shucked and washed. Stir and let warm through briefly. Remove from heat, garnish with tortilla chips and serve with any or all of these toppings: grated cheese, sliced green onions, fresh cilantro, cooked chicken breast slivers, or wedges of fresh lime to squeeze over the soup.

Easy Fried Rice

With planned-ahead leftover cold cooked rice, this is a tasty hot main dish that takes less than 15 minutes. Makes 2 main- or 4 side-dish portions.

> 4 slices bacon chopped in 1-inch pieces
>
> 1 green pepper, seeded and chopped
>
> 2 green onions, washed, trimmed, and chopped
>
> 2 tbsp. fresh Italian parsley, washed and chopped (optional)
>
> 2 cups cold cooked rice
>
> 2 beaten whole eggs
>
> 2 tbsp. bottled soy sauce

Arrange bacon in large nonstick frying pan. Cook over medium heat until the bacon browns, then remove to drain on paper towels, leaving the fat in the pan. Still over medium heat, in the same pan, sauté green pepper, green onions, and parsley until tender but not browned. Stir in rice. Continue stirring until heated through. Blend eggs with soy sauce, then pour evenly over the top of the mixture. Cook over medium heat, stirring constantly, until eggs are no longer runny. Sprinkle the cooked bacon on top and serve at once.

Variation: Low-Fat Fried Rice

Omit the bacon from the recipe above. Instead, lightly spray the pan with no-stick cooking oil or heat ¼ cup vegetable or chicken broth in the pan. Sauté the vegetables and follow the recipe above until the addition of the eggs. Or, instead of two whole eggs, add one whole egg and two egg whites beaten with the soy sauce.

Three-Bean Tuna Salad

For lunch on a warm day after a hike, this is ideal. Makes 4 to 6 portions.

> 1 15-ounce can kidney beans or white cannellini beans
>
> 1 15-ounce can black beans
>
> 1 15-ounce can garbanzo beans
>
> 1 6-ounce can of solid tuna in water, well drained
>
> ¼ cup finely chopped red or green onions
>
> 2 tbsp. minced parsley, basil, oregano, or other fresh herb (optional)
>
> Juice of 1 large lemon or lime
>
> 1 to 2 tbsp. olive oil
>
> Lettuce leaves

Drain and rinse beans in cold water. Combine beans in a mixing bowl. Add tuna, onions, parsley, lemon or lime juice, and olive oil. Toss gently and serve on lettuce leaves. Can be prepared as much as a day ahead and refrigerated, tightly covered, until serving time.

Easy Low-Fat Oven-Fried Chicken

This is good hot or cold or in sandwiches. We sometimes make a double recipe and refrigerate part of it for another meal. Makes 4 portions.

> 4 boneless, skinless chicken breasts (about 1 lb.)
>
> ½ cup vermouth, dry white wine, or chicken broth
>
> 1 minced clove of garlic
>
> ½ cup bread crumbs
>
> 2 tbsp. cornmeal
>
> ½ tsp. each cumin, ground cayenne pepper, and crumbled dry sage or thyme

Rinse chicken and pat dry. Marinate for 30 minutes in a mixture of vermouth (or wine or chicken broth) and garlic.

Remove from marinade and dip each piece in a mixture of bread crumbs, cornmeal, and a mixture of cumin, cayenne, and sage or thyme. Arrange in baking pan that has been sprayed lightly with no-stick cooking oil and bake at 450°F about 20 minutes or until no longer pink inside.

Microwave Fish Dinner

We like this when we're driving along the coast and spot a fish market. Makes 2 main-dish portions.

> 2 boneless, skinless fresh fish fillets or steaks
>
> 1 cup diced, unpeeled red potatoes, parboiled until almost tender, then drained

1 cup thin spears of fresh asparagus or zucchini

Salt

White pepper

Juice of ½ to 1 fresh lemon

1 to 2 tbsp. olive oil

Arrange fish fillets side by side in the center of an ovenproof pie plate. Arrange diced red potatoes around the edges of the dish. On top of the fish, place asparagus or zucchini. Sprinkle lightly with salt and pepper and lemon juice, to taste. Drizzle olive oil across the top. Cover tightly with plastic wrap and microwave on high for 11 minutes. Serve with slices or chunks of fresh sourdough bread (optional) to mop up the delicious juices.

Rest Area Huevos Rancheros

On a driving day, we like to start early in the morning with only some fruit or juice and a cup of tea, then stop later at a highway rest area for something more substantial. This dish takes less than 30 minutes from the start of cooking through cleanup after the meal. Makes 2 portions.

2 to 4 corn tortillas

½ tbsp. butter

2 to 4 eggs

¼ to ½ cup prepared salsa or canned enchilada sauce

Sauté tortillas in a nonstick skillet sprayed with no-stick cooking oil. When hot, remove to serving plates. Melt butter in the same pan. Fry eggs over easy or as preferred. Put the cooked eggs on top of the tortillas. Then add salsa or canned enchilada sauce to the same pan. Heat through and spoon on top of eggs.

Variation: Low-Fat Huevos Rancheros

Warm the tortillas without oil in a nonstick skillet, at the same time poaching the eggs in water with a tablespoon of vinegar in a second pan. Remove tortillas, put drained poached eggs on top, and spoon over the heated salsa as directed above.

Quick Posole

This low-fat version of a full-meal, traditional winter soup from Mexico and New Mexico is easy to put together and good enough for guests. It's even better reheated the next day. Makes 4 to 6 portions.

2 pounds of boneless, skinless chicken thighs, cut into 1-inch pieces

2 quarts chicken broth (may use canned or a mix made from bouillon cubes or powder with water)

3 cloves minced garlic (optional)

1 yellow onion, peeled and chopped

1 tbsp. ground New Mexico chile or commercial chile powder

1 sprig fresh or 1 tsp. dried thyme or oregano

2 14-ounce cans of white or yellow hominy, drained and rinsed

Mix chicken, chicken broth, garlic, onion, chile, and thyme or oregano in a large soup pot. Simmer for an hour or so, then add hominy. Simmer until heated through. Serve in soup bowls with any or all the following toppings:

Thinly sliced raw radishes

Thinly sliced green cabbage

Diced avocado

Prepared corn chips

Lime wedges

Chopped red or green onions

Sprigs of fresh cilantro

Eggplant Parmesan

This dish can be prepared in a regular oven or a 650-watt microwave. Makes 2 to 3 main-dish servings, 4 to 6 side-dish servings.

1 medium eggplant cut into ½-inch slices, then diced

2 seeded, diced fresh tomatoes

1 to 2 cloves minced garlic

2 tbsp. chopped fresh basil or parsley (optional)

1 tbsp. olive oil

½ cup grated mozzarella cheese

2 tbsp. freshly grated Parmesan cheese

Combine eggplant, tomatoes, garlic, basil or parsley, and olive oil in a baking dish. Cover tightly with foil and bake in a 400°F oven for 1 hour.

Uncover and sprinkle with mozzarella and Parmesan. Return to oven and bake 5 minutes or until cheese has melted.

To prepare in a microwave oven, put the cheeses on top of the eggplant/tomato mixture, cover tightly with plastic wrap, and microwave on high for 5 minutes.

One-Pot Garlic Spaghetti

This vegetarian dish contains heart-healthy olive oil and garlic. Spraying the cooking pot before adding the water keeps the spaghetti from sticking to the bottom, making the pan much easier to wash. Makes 2 to 4 portions.

1 to 2 tbsp. salt

¼ pound dry spaghetti for each serving

¼ cup olive oil for two portions, ½ cup for four

4 to 6 cloves minced garlic

Minced fresh parsley, basil, and/or oregano

Freshly grated Parmesan cheese

Spray a very large cooking pot with no-stick cooking oil, fill with water, and add salt. When water is boiling rapidly, add spaghetti. Cook until al dente (just soft enough to bite through easily but not soft and flabby), then drain and rinse with hot water. Wipe out the spaghetti pot with a paper towel and return to the heat. Put in olive oil and garlic. Cook until garlic begins to sizzle, then stir in minced fresh parsley, basil, and/or oregano to taste. Return spaghetti to the pot and toss over heat until warmed through. Serve at once with freshly grated Parmesan cheese. A big green salad goes well with this, along with fruit and cheese for dessert.

French Vegetable Soup

This soup from the south of France is incredibly delicious, although it is simple and easy to make. It is even better with a spoonful of pesto stirred in just before serving. Makes 6 to 8 portions.

2 quarts water or chicken broth

2 cups unpeeled red or new white potatoes chopped into ½-inch cubes

2 cups fresh green beans, cut into 2-inch pieces

2 to 3 zucchini, washed and sliced

2 cups fresh tomatoes, preferably plum, seeded and chopped into small pieces

4 ounces dry spaghetti, broken into short pieces

1 15-ounce can garbanzo beans or cannellini beans, drained and rinsed

Salt

Pepper

Freshly grated Parmesan cheese or pesto sauce (optional)

In a large soup pot, combine water or chicken broth, potatoes, green beans, zucchini, and tomatoes. Bring to a boil, lower heat, cover and simmer for 1 hour, then add spaghetti and beans. Cook until spaghetti is tender, season to taste with salt and pepper, then serve in wide soup bowls. Top each portion with optional grated Parmesan cheese or pesto sauce.

Pesto Sauce

3 cloves peeled garlic

1 cup fresh basil leaves (can use a blend of basil and fresh parsley)

2 tbsp. olive oil

Finely chop the garlic and basil together, using a blender or food processor for convenience or a knife or mortar and pestle for authenticity, then drizzle in olive oil, beating with a fork or mixing with the blender until combined.

Microwave Polenta with Mushrooms

This trendy Italian dish technically takes two pots, one for the microwave and one for the top of the stove. We like this when we find fresh wild mushrooms in farmers' markets or supermarkets. The microwave eliminates the stirring from the traditional recipe, as well as cutting down the time considerably. Any leftovers can be put in a dish or small loaf pan and refrigerated to slice and sauté later for a side dish. Makes 2 to 4 portions.

4 cups water

1 cup yellow cornmeal

1 tsp. salt

1 pound wild or cultivated mushrooms (preferably a mix of several, such as oyster, portobello, chanterelle, or shiitake)

1 tbsp. unsalted butter or margarine

1 tbsp. olive or other cooking oil

1 clove garlic, peeled and minced

2 to 3 tbsp. fresh sage leaves, chopped, or 1 tsp. dry sage

To make the polenta, mix water, cornmeal, and salt in a large microwave-able bowl. Microwave uncovered for 12 minutes, stirring once about halfway through. Remove from microwave and let stand 3 minutes, then spoon onto serving plates.

While the polenta is cooking, prepare the mushroom sauce. Clean, trim, and slice the mushrooms. In a large nonstick skillet, melt butter and olive or cooking oil. Over medium heat, sauté the mushrooms until tender and lightly browned, about 5 to 8 minutes. Remove and keep warm. Sauté the garlic and sage in the same pan.

Spoon polenta on warm serving plates, and top with mushroom sauce and herbs.

Don't Drink the Water

When there's no bottled water available in the fishing villages of Fiji or the mountainside inns of the Himalayas, we brush our teeth with whiskey. We veto street food vendors in Madras, Mazatlán, or Manhattan, and always skip summer shellfish salads, rare hamburgers, and anything with custard in it.

As veteran world travelers, we're cautious—some of our friends say overly cautious—but with a schedule that requires us to be on the road 60% of the time, we can't risk getting sick even for a day.

So we decided long ago that whenever we're on the road, we'd stick with **bottled water** for drinking and cooking, and always use **bags of commercial ice,** using the campground water supply and the surplus stored in our tank only for washing and flushing. While most of the city water in North America is probably safe to drink, a constantly changing mineral content when you're making 1-night stands can throw your system off. We pick up 2 or 3 gallons at a time at a supermarket, convenience store, or campground store, put one in the galley and the others below in outside storage, and store a 7-pound plastic bag of ice cubes in the freezer.

People who have a restricted sodium intake would also be wise to use **sodium-free bottled water,** available in most supermarkets, since the sodium content of water varies widely from one campground area to the next.

A solution for RVers who don't want to buy ice and water is to use a **water filter**—either one that's permanently installed in the kitchen sink or one you hook up to the hose system when filling the tank initially.

Even more thorough is a water purifier that not only removes sediment from the water the way a filter does, but also takes out bacteria and delivers clean, good-tasting drinking water. When we bought our new Istasca Sunflyer, one of the options we ordered was a water filter and ice maker for the sink and refrigerator. If you don't have an RV with these extras, you can simply do as we used to, stay with bagged ice and bottled water for daily use.

We also saw, at the Los Angeles RV Show, a Rexhall motor home that was equipped with an optional water exchange, with which you could separate your own fresh water source for drinking and cooking and use the campground plug-in source for washing and flushing only.

It's wise to use **biodegradable toilet paper** and **holding-tank chemicals,** both available from camping stores and many campground stores. Follow the RV instruction booklet or the directions on the chemical container.

When you're driving every day, you rarely need to use your **water heater,** since the engine keeps the water hot. If you have an electric water heater, you may want to operate it only when necessary or during the night, since it draws a lot of power you may need for the air conditioner, TV, or microwave.

Trimming Costs: Eight Money-Saving Tips for the Road

1. **Buy local produce.** Shopping at roadside fruit stands or farmers' markets will usually net the freshest and the cheapest local produce and give you a chance to chat with the locals.

2. **Watch for pick-your-own farms and orchards in season,** where a few minutes of work can save a lot of money on luxuries like fresh raspberries and cherries. One national park campground in Utah is set in the midst of fruit orchards where campers pick their own. (See chapter 5, "Utah's Parks & Canyons.")

3. **Clip coupons locally.** Pick up local newspapers or free throwaways in towns where you overnight and use the ads and supermarket discount coupons to save grocery money.

4. **Take advantage of capitalism.** If you see a gas station having a price war with a neighboring station, go back and fill up your tank. While price wars are uncommon during these days of high gas prices, every penny counts when you have a 75-gallon gas tank on a vehicle that gets under 10 miles to the gallon.

5. **Cash or charge?** Some gas stations charge more when you use a credit card than when you pay cash. Keep your eye out for stations that list the same price for credit or cash. If there's no sign that says so, ask before filling the tank.

6. **Don't skimp on service.** Spend that extra money for regular engine and vehicle upkeep on a long haul. This saves a lot of money in the end.

7. **Be rational about your campground needs.** When overnighting in campgrounds that charge based on hookups and facilities used, opt for the most basic, since RVs are designed to be self-contained. Instead of paying extra for a sewer connection, use the free (for registered campers) dump site at a campground as you're pulling in for the night or out in the morning. Opting for water and electric only may save as much as $5 a night. (For more campground money-savers, see chapter 3, "Where to Sleep: Campgrounds & RV Parks.")

8. **Buy out of season (antifreeze, for instance, in summer) and in quantity.** When canned or paper goods are on sale in bulk, buy two or three for the house and two or three for the RV.

Safety, Sanity & Insurance

DRIVING TIPS

To combat glare, fog, snow, or oncoming headlights when driving after dark, slip on a pair of yellow glasses (sold in ski shops as ski goggles) or clip a pair over your regular glasses.

Binoculars for the navigator solve that ever-present problem of changing lanes with a large vehicle when approaching an on-ramp for an interstate. It's easy to look ahead to see if the entrance is from the left lane or the right lane, or to read the street names at intersections.

Defensive driving is always important. Many drivers pausing at an intersection when we have the right-of-way don't seem to realize that motor homes are like big tractor-trailer rigs; they can't stop on a dime. Many also make the erroneous assumption that RV drivers are elderly slowpokes, when most of us drive at the prevailing speed limit with the rest of the traffic. So we're always half-expecting a driver to pull out of a side road in front of us, and are rarely disappointed. One rule of thumb: If you see a pickup truck waiting at a side road to pull into traffic, you can count on him pulling out in front of your RV.

SPEEDERS BEWARE

While exceeding the speed limit is never laudable, it can also be extremely inconvenient for residents of California, Alaska, Hawaii, Montana, Oregon, Michigan, and Wisconsin—states that are not signatories to the Non-Resident Violators Compact.

What it means is that drivers with license plates from these seven states are subject to having their driver's license confiscated and being required to go to the nearest office of a judge, sheriff, or justice of the peace to appear before an officer, post bond, and/or pay a fine. If said officer is not available, the individual may be jailed until a court appearance can be arranged, which may be several hours later.

Keep your headlights on. More and more states are requiring the use of headlights in the daytime. We think it should be mandatory throughout the country. It's amazing how some cars can blend into the roadway and suddenly appear headed your way, particularly when you're planning to pass another car. Headlights on in the daytime can be a life-saving factor.

We also try to avoid driving at night, preferring to get an early morning start when leaving and stopping for the day by midafternoon.

GENERAL RV SAFETY & SECURITY TIPS

Remember that you are driving a vehicle that has a propane tank that, while it simplifies your daily life by allowing heating and refrigeration to take place when your RV is not hooked up to shore power, also complicates things by being flammable. Modern RVs also have propane gas-leak detectors to warn you with a sound signal if there is a propane leak. If you hear the signal, get out of the RV, turn off the propane valve at the tank (reached from an outside door), and leave the RV open to let the gas escape. Some experts recommend that it is safest to drive with the propane tank turned off. Many long highway bridges and tunnels require that the tank be turned off before entering.

Occasionally your gas-leak detector will signal when you're cooking garlic in an open pan, because the odor is similar to the odor added to propane to make it easy to detect a leak. If this happens, turn off the burner, remove the pan of garlic, turn off the detector, turn the burner back on, and finish cooking the dish, then reactivate the detector.

Always check the gas leak detector and smoke detectors installed in your RV to make sure the batteries are fresh.

Carbon monoxide detectors are also mandatory in RVs. You want to inspect your unit regularly to make sure the floor, sidewalls, doors, and windows have no holes or openings that would allow the gas to come into the vehicle while you're driving; if you find any, seal them up with silicone adhesive or have repairs made before driving again.

Never run your generator while you're sleeping, and always open one of the roof vents when the generator is operating. And don't stay long when

AIN'T MISBEHAVIN': ROAD ETIQUETTE

1. **Don't hog the highway;** pull over at turnouts or into slow-moving lanes to let vehicles behind you have a chance to pass. In some states it's against the law for a slow-moving vehicle not to allow following vehicles to pass at the first opportunity when five or more are trailing.

2. **Keep in the right lane except when passing a car,** and when you do pass, make sure you have the speed and space to do it quickly and easily. Some motor homes don't have the power to easily overtake vehicles on an uphill route, especially if the driver speeds up as you attempt to pass.

3. **As with your car, dimming your RV headlights for an approaching car is a must.** It is also a good idea to do the same when driving into a campground after dark.

4. **It seems customary to make a friendly wave to an oncoming RV as you meet,** particularly if it's a make and model similar to your own.

5. **Always signal your intention to turn or change lanes well ahead of time** so the driver in back of you has plenty of warning. Your vehicle is not as agile as those around you.

6. **Use binoculars to check out the road signs ahead** to make it easier to change lanes in traffic. They are especially useful when trying to determine whether the interstate entry ramp will require being in the right or left lane, since changing lanes in a big vehicle takes additional time and distance. 🚐

you're parking in a roadside rest area in the vicinity of a tractor-trailer running its motor to keep the refrigeration operating.

When packing an RV, or adding more items to an already-outfitted motor home, be aware of the vehicle's load limit and the necessity to balance the weight equally. You can check the weight at a public scale, sometimes found at big truck stop complexes. Get a reading for each wheel and, for a trailer, the tongue weight, which is the weight the trailer coupler puts on the tow hitch. Check that against the net carrying capacity listed on the weight information label installed somewhere inside the RV.

SHOULD YOU CARRY A GUN IN YOUR RV?

If you want to start a lively argument around a campground, try this as an opener. We personally would never carry a firearm in our motor home, but then we would never have one at home, either. While many frequent and full-time RVers agree, just as many others disagree, sometimes vociferously.

Entering Mexico with a firearm of any sort can land an RV owner in jail—and did, in a case in 1993. A veteran RVer had bought a semiautomatic rifle at an Arizona gun show and stowed it, along with 500 rounds of ammunition, in his travel trailer. Mexican police found the AK-47 in the trailer and a pistol in his truck, and confiscated the vehicle, firearms, and ammunition, and put him in jail. He spent months incarcerated with no bedding or regular meal service, both optional luxuries the prisoner's family members are expected to pay for, before his attorney could bring the case to trial. Canada also prohibits entering the country with guns.

Despite our feelings that our motor home is indeed our home, the law in many states considers the RV a motor vehicle when moving and a home only when parked in camp. Therefore, any firearms carried must be unloaded and the bullets kept separately from the weapon when in transit.

Firearms are also prohibited in many state parks.

If we did choose to carry a firearm, we would make it a point to keep abreast of the regulations in every state, which can differ radically the minute you cross a state line.

SHOULD YOU CARRY A CELLULAR PHONE IN YOUR RV?

We always do, but it provides almost as much frustration as assistance. The places we like to drive and camp are frequently, if not always, in a borderline or "no service" area, even though we have (and are willing to pay a sizable sum for) a Follow Me Roaming system that theoretically can forward our calls to almost anywhere in the United States and Canada. Our editors have been able to reach us in the wilds of British Columbia or when we're driving down an interstate in west Texas, but can't seem to get through to us when we're on a 2-day outing in a national park in San Diego or Santa Barbara, only a hoot and a holler from our Los Angeles base.

We find cell phones most helpful for dialing ahead for a campground reservation or for returning business calls we've picked up from our answering machine when the campground or highway pay phones are too noisy. And we are certainly happy to have one in case of an emergency, which we have had to deal with on occasion.

The technology leaves something to be desired, with voices fading in and out when you're in a fringe reception area. The cost is almost prohibitive because you pay for connecting to the roamer system as well as the elapsed time for any calls. Some new pricing plans include long distance and roaming charges throughout the United States for a flat fee for a certain number of minutes, but these plans are costly unless you plan to make a lot of calls.

A cellular travel guide promising **all you need to know about roaming** is available for $19.95 from Telecom Publishing, 2607 Perth Court SE, Olympia, WA 98501-6642 (☎ **360/794-9800;** www.telecompublishing.com). It includes areas with maps, instructions on sending and receiving for many cities, and roaming agreements.

If you are reluctant to invest in a cell phone, most private campgrounds and many public campgrounds have a pay phone on the premises.

SIX OFF-THE-WALL TIPS FOR RV AILMENTS

1. **To remember to lower your TV antenna** before pulling out of the campground, put some sort of label or tag—one RVer suggests a spring-loaded clothespin—on the antenna crank in the travel position. When the antenna is up, put the same tag or device on the gearshift or steering wheel. Then as you prepare to move out, the item will remind you the antenna is still raised.

2. **To get unstuck** when mired in snow, mud, or sand, one Canadian RVer suggests using two strips of metal plasterer's lath, available in hardware stores, approximately 10 by 30 inches each, either in front of or behind the drive axle wheels to extricate the vehicle. The lath can be hosed off and stored flat to be reused as many times as needed.

3. **To get rid of mice,** tuck sheets of Downey fabric softener around the sofa, under the sinks, and near the furnace.

4. **When lights or turn signals on a tow vehicle fail to work,** spray white vinegar on the electrical connectors.

5. **When sensors on holding tanks for gray and black water do not read properly,** a Prodigy online bulletin board subscriber suggests filling the problem tank half full of water and adding a half cup of Dawn liquid dish detergent before leaving home, then emptying the tank on arrival at the campground. He suggests repeating the technique if the first effort doesn't fix it.

6. **To do the wash,** a Nevada man reminds us of the hero in *The Accidental Tourist* with his suggestion: Put hot water, dirty clothes, soap, and a tennis shoe (to act as an agitator) in a large beverage cooler and strap the whole thing to the rear bumper of the motor home. At lunchtime, empty the soapy water in an appropriate spot, refill the cooler with clean water, and drive on into the afternoon. In camp, set up a clothesline and hang the clean laundry out to dry.

RV INSURANCE

We were pleasantly surprised to find our RV insurance was very affordable, even in costly Southern California. Safe driving records, a shorter use period during the year, and slightly older drivers on the average mean less risk for the insurer. Before buying, check your own automobile insurance carrier as well as specialized RV insurance carriers, such as **Good Sam Club's National General** (☎ 800/234-3450; www.goodsamclub.com), **Foremost Insurance Company** (☎ 800/545-8608; www.foremost.com), **AARP Insurance** (☎ 800/541-3717; www.aarp.com), **RV Alliance America** (☎ 800/521-2942; www.rvallianceamerica.com), and for Mexican insurance, **Sanborn's** (☎ 800/222-0158; www.sanbornsinsurance.com), or **Oscar Padilla** (☎ 800/258-8600; www.mexicaninsurance.com). Towing insurance in case of a breakdown is a good idea; in many cases, AAA members can extend that company's towing coverage to their RV. For a more extensive discussion of coverage and insurers, see *The RV Money Book*, by Bob Howells, a Trailer Life book, $29.95 (see "Financing," in chapter 14, "To Rent or Buy?").

The Community of Man: Getting Together with Other RVers

CARAVANS & RALLIES

RVers who would prefer to travel or camp with a group can join up with any number of like-minded people for a paid vacation tour in their own rig instead of a tour bus, or a friendly get-together with other owners of the same brand of RV. Caravans are the RV equivalent of a group tour with structured itineraries, sightseeing, communal meals, and many group social functions.

Popular caravan destinations include Mexico, Alaska, and New England at autumn foliage time. To find out about caravan and club tours, read general monthly RV publications such as *Trailer Life* and *MotorHome,* available by subscription or from most magazine racks; *Family Motor Coaching Magazine* (for FMCA members); *Highways* (for Good Sam Club members); or other club or RV manufacturing company publications.

RV CLUBS

American Sunbathing Association. For nudist RVers; has RV parks in many states (☎ 407/933-2064; or www.aanr.com).

Baby Boomers. For RV enthusiasts born between 1940 and 1960 (P.O. Box 23, Stoneham, CO 80754).

Escapees Incorporated. Founded in 1978 by veteran RV writers Joe and Kay Peterson, Escapees is a support system for full-timers. Membership numbers more than 33,000. Members have pooled resources to build their own nonprofit RV parks across the country, as well as create a new CARE program that provides parking facilities and support services for temporarily or permanently incapacitated full-timers (100 Rainbow Dr., Livingston, TX 77351; ☎ 888/757-2582; www.escapees.com).

Family Motor Coach Association. For owners of self-propelled, self-contained vehicles with cooking, sleeping, and sanitary facilities in which the living quarters can be accessed directly from the driver's seat. Members number around 170,000 families, each with its own ID number. The group provides a monthly magazine and other benefits, including insurance. Costs are $35 for a family, including initiation fee and first year dues (8291 Clough Pike, Cincinnati, OH 45244; ☎ 800/543-3622; www.fmca.com).

Flying J Real Value Club. A free membership provides fuel (gasoline or diesel) discounts of 1¢ a gallon at all Flying J stations plus 5¢ a gallon discount on propane. Additional credit can be gained from non-fuel purchases in their restaurants and convenience stores. Insurance, roadside assistance, and prepaid calling card programs are also available (P.O. Box 150210, Ogden, UT 84415; ☎ **888/438-3537;** www.flyingJ.com).

Good Sam Club. A broad-range club with insurance, campground affiliates, financing, and other services. Members number nearly a million, and the club also has special interest chapters for hobbyists, computer aficionados, singles, hearing impaired, and others (c/o Susan Bray, 2575 Vista Del Mar Dr., Ventura, CA 93001-3920; ☎ **800/234-3450;** www.goodsamclub.com).

Handicapped Travel Club. For disabled individuals who enjoy traveling and camping; also welcomes the nonhandicapped. For membership requirements, send SASE with first-class postage to 5929 Ourway, Citrus Heights, CA 95610 (☎ **916/961-1611**).

Loners on Wheels. Now 25 years old, Loners on Wheels is a club for single RVers, numbering around 3,000 widowed, divorced, or never-married members. While members who subsequently give up traveling alone turn into nonmembers, they are welcomed back at special anniversaries and rallies (1060-WB, Cape Giradeau, MO 63702). For a sample newsletter, call ☎ **888/ 569-4478;** fax 573/651-8601; www.lonersonwheels.com.

Motorhome America Club. A membership fee of around $15 a month provides a variety of services including discounts in campgrounds, roadside assistance, magazine subscriptions, new RV product testing program, emergency messaging service, toll-free technical assistance hotline, legal help, travel accident policy, and other discounts and services (64 Inverness Dr. East, Englewood, CO 80112; ☎ **800/986-5366**).

Passport America. A $39 yearly membership provides 50% discounts at over 400 campgrounds throughout the U.S., Canada, and Mexico. Some restrictions apply, depending on the individual campground, the time of year, and the length of stay (18315A Landon Rd., Gulfport, MS 39503; ☎ **800/681-6810,** 228/832-9199).

RV Elderhostel. Offers study groups for RV owners at universities or on the road in caravans along a historic route (80 Boylston St., Suite 400, Boston, MA 02116; ☎ **617/426-7788;** www.elderhostel.org).

Vagabundos del Mar. A club of RV travelers who spend a lot of time in Mexico. Also provides Mexican auto insurance and information on RV parks south of the border (190 Main St., Rio Vista, CA 94571; ☎ **800/474-BAJA** or 707/374-5511; www.vagabundos.com).

COMPUTER ONLINE SERVICES

Online RV bulletin boards on computer services such as AOL allow RV enthusiasts or "wannabe" RVers to exchange dialogue, give helpful hints, and discuss the pros and cons of the various vehicle brands.

The greatest use of onboard computers is for e-mail connection. More and more campgrounds provide phone jacks to connect to your Internet service, some for free, some for a modest charge if it is a local call to connect. Some upscale campgrounds now have phone connections at the site for those newer motor homes that have phone lines built into the wiring system.

3

Where to Sleep: Campgrounds & RV Parks

THE ANSWER TO THE QUESTION OF WHERE TO SLEEP IN YOUR RV IS "almost anywhere." There are more than 16,000 campgrounds in the United States that can accommodate RVs, some offering hookups, others for self-contained or "dry" camping.

A few are free, but many more are lavish resorts that may cost $25 a night and up for full hookups, cable TV, phone service, spas, swimming pools, tennis courts, playgrounds, and miniature or par-3 golf courses.

If you prefer ranger hikes and scenery to horseshoe pits and pancake breakfasts, head for one of the 29,000 campsites in our national parks and monuments. The national forest service has 4,000 developed campgrounds in 155 forests, and the Bureau of Land Management oversees 270 million acres of scenic outdoor sites, many with free camping.

For watery wonderlands, check out the Corps of Engineers projects, with 53,000 campsites near oceans, rivers, and lakes, with fishing, boating, swimming, and water-skiing on tap.

Bird-watchers can overnight in many of the nation's wildlife refuges to get the drop on feathery friends, and game-watchers can take advantage of the optimum spotting times of dawn and dusk. (See "The Best Campground Directories," below, for how to get a full listing of wildlife refuge camping, as well as guides for all the other campgrounds.)

Campground Glossary

Black water: Waste water from the toilet.
Boondock: To camp without electrical or other hookups.
Dual electrical system: An RV system in which lights and other electrical systems can run on 12-volt battery power, 110 AC electrical hookup, or gas generator.
Dump station: Also called sanitary dump, disposal station, and so on; this is where an RV dumps the gray water and black water from its holding tanks.

Minimotor home in a tree-shaded campsite near Anacortes, Washington.

Gray water: Waste water from the sinks and shower.

Hookups: Umbilical cords that connect your RV with electrical power, water, and sewer service. (Full hookups are sites furnished with all three connections. Partial hookups are sites furnished with one or two of the three connections.)

Propane or LPG: Liquefied petroleum gas used for heating, cooking, and refrigeration in RVs.

Pull-through: A campsite that allows the driver to pull into the site to park, then pull out the other side when leaving, without ever having to back up—a boon for beginners.

Spirit level: A device for determining true horizontal or vertical directions by the centering of a bubble in a slightly curved glass tube or tubes filled with alcohol or ether. Some RVs come with built-in levels. If yours does not, small spirit levels can be purchased in hardware stores or RV supply centers.

Three-way refrigerator: An RV refrigerator/freezer that can operate on LPG, electrical hookup, or gas generator.

Should You Sleep by the Side of the Road?

While more than half the states permit some overnight parking in highway rest areas, except where posted, we feel there have been too many recent incidents of violence in these areas and would not consider parking overnight in our RV in a rest area, mall parking lot, truck stop, or by the side of the road. Some of our friends do, however, and consider us money-wasting wimps for overnighting at a secure private or public campground.

The thing that amazes us is how many owners of expensive motor homes take the risk of sleeping free in a parking lot or by the side of the road when the cost of their vehicle advertises how much in cash, credit cards, and expensive electronics might be inside. All this to save $12 or $15? Campground fees are a modest enough investment in security and peace of mind. Besides, unlike RVers, the truckers with whom you share the road have few other options when they need to rest. Why take up their space?

Campsites: The Good, the Bad & the Ugly

As backpackers, we would set up camp at any clearing that didn't have too many rocks and spread out the ground cloth and sleeping bags.

As tent campers, we looked for scenery, shelter, and seclusion, but not too far away from the water source and facilities.

Now, as RV campers, we have a long list of Ls:

- **Location:** We want to be away from the highway and campground entrance and not too near the swimming pool, bathroom facilities, garbage Dumpster, playground, or dog-walking area.

- **Large:** It must be big enough to back our 27-foot motor home in and park it, and still have space for chairs, table, and charcoal grill.

- **Level:** There's a lot of running back and forth to check spirit levels inside and outside the vehicle; sometimes we have to wedge wooden blocks under the tires until that pesky little bubble hits the center. Hydraulic jacks make this procedure much easier. (What happens if it's not level? Something dire and expensive befalls the refrigerator.)

- **Length:** The umbilical cords from the vehicle to the electric, water, and sewer connections (where applicable) must reach comfortably.

- **Look out:** Watch for any low-hanging branches or wires that could damage the roof air conditioner or TV antenna; for a potentially noisy neighbor; and for wet or marshy ground that could mire you down if it should rain all night.

- **Width:** It's not an "L," but it's important; with most newer vehicles containing one or more slide-outs (portion of the living and/or bedroom that slide out to expand the interior area) the width of the site becomes more important. Some older campgrounds can't handle a slide-out and will say so. Others may have room for the slide but there will be nothing left to use as recreation area. Any campsite width under 15 feet will limit comfortable use of the site unless you're just stopping overnight.

INSIDER TIP

A good way to begin is to get a free videotape about RV camping by calling the **GO-RVing Coalition** (a group of RV manufacturers, retailers, campground owners, and parts manufacturers) toll-free at ☎ **888/GO-RVING.**

A campsite may or may not contain a picnic table, grill, or fire ring. What is critical for tent campers becomes an added luxury for an RVer, who already has a table, chairs, and stove. While we all want to overnight in the best campgrounds, we find that campground ratings—for example, those in the popular *Trailer Life Campground/RV Park & Services Directory*—do not always seem to relate to us. The guide, issued annually, rates campgrounds according to a detailed form that scores in three areas: facilities, cleanliness (particularly of toilets and showers), and visual or environmental appeal.

Since we always use our own toilet and shower facilities, we are not concerned with the campground's, and we rarely if ever take advantage of a TV lounge, swimming pool, Saturday night dance, or children's playground.

Therefore, for us, a highly rated campground may have less appeal than a remote area in a national forest, or a simpler family-run park in the country.

Occasionally, in both private and state park campgrounds, you may encounter what we call a "parking lot" design, with rows of paved spaces fairly close together. The up side is that you're usually level and don't have to spend time checking spirit level bubbles and putting ramps (otherwise known as wedges) under tires. (Newer vehicles have hydraulic jacks that will automatically level the vehicle as well as stabilize it at the touch of a button.) The down side is that your dining room window may be 2 feet away from your neighbor. The saving grace is that with an RV, you can close your curtains or blinds, turn on some soft music, and be all alone in the universe.

On the other hand, we are always thrilled to find those enlightened campground owners who have spent extra time and money to create terraced areas with landscaping that gives a sense of space, light, and privacy.

Using the Directories to Find a Campground

While we frequently are at odds with campground ratings, we find the directories, especially the one from *Trailer Life,* invaluable when traveling, particularly when we're making 1-night stands and need to find a place to overnight. Being able to call ahead for reservations is also helpful; you won't have to drive 5 miles off the route only to find there are no campsites left. This is where a cell phone comes in handy (see discussion in chapter 2, "Getting Prepared: RVing Tips & Hints").

Careful reading of an entry can also tell you the site width (important if you have an awning or slide-out); if there are pull-throughs; if you can expect any shade trees; if the campground is open year-round or only seasonally; and if there's a dump station on the premises.

THE BEST CAMPGROUND DIRECTORIES

Bureau of Land Management, 270 million acres of public land. Ask for camping information from BLM, Department of Interior–MIB, 1849 C St. NW, Room 5600, Washington, DC 20240. Free. (www.blm.gov).

The authors' Itasca Sunflyer in Jamestown, North Dakota, KOA campground.

KOA, 615 campgrounds in the United States, Canada, and Mexico. You can receive a guide free, or send $3 for an annual guide from Kampgrounds of America Executive Offices, P.O. Box 30558, Billings, MT 59114-0558 (☎ **406/ 248-7444;** www.koa.com).

National Association of RV Park and Campgrounds has a directory with listings of more than 3,000 RV parks and campgrounds. National ARVC, 113 Park Ave., Falls Church, VA 22046 (☎ **703/241-8801;** www. gocampingamerica.com).

National Forest Service, 4,000 campgrounds. For a free guide, write to U.S. Department of Agriculture Forest Service, Public Affairs Office, P.O. Box 96090, Washington, DC 20090-6090 (www.fs.fed.us).

National Park Camping Guide, 440 campgrounds. U.S. Government Printing Office, Superintendent of Documents, Washington, DC 20402-9325. Ask for stock no. 024-005-01080-7 ($4; www.gpo.gov).

National Wildlife Refuges, 488 refuges. For free publications write to U.S. Fish and Wildlife Services, Public Affairs Office, 1849 C St. NW, MS-5600/MIB, Washington, DC, 20240 (☎ **202/452-5125;** www.refuges.fws.gov).

Trailer Life Campground/RV Park and Services Directory, 2575 Vista del Mar Dr., Ventura, CA 93001 (☎ **800/234-3450;** www.tldirectory.com),

CAMPGROUND COSTS

A family of four can vacation in a family campground for less than $200 a week, and a snowbird can spend the entire winter in a full-service warm-climate resort for less than $2,000, according to the National Association of RV Parks and Campgrounds.

covers 12,500 campgrounds in the United States, Canada, and Mexico. Available for $20 at bookstores and camping stores, or write to above address.

U.S. Army Corps of Engineers, 53,000 campsites near oceans, rivers, and lakes. For free publications write to U.S. Army Corps of Engineers, OCE Publications Depot, 2803 52nd Ave., Hyattsville, MD 20781-1102 (☎ **301/394-0081;** www.usace.army.mil).

Wheelers RV Resort & Campground Directory, Print Media Services, 1310 Jarvis Ave., Elk Grove Village, IL 60007; $12.95.

Woodall's Campground Directory, 28167 North Keith Dr., Box 5000, Lake Forest, IL 60045-5000; www.woodalls.com; $16.95.

Yogi Bear's Jellystone Park Campground Directory, Leisure Systems, Inc., 6201 Kellogg Ave., Cincinnati, OH 45230; free (☎ **800/558-2954;** www.campjellystone.com).

Ten Ways to Save Money on Campgrounds

1. **Never pay for more park than you'll use.** Posh playgrounds with swimming pool, spas, tennis courts, and miniature golf are usually

pricier than simple, clean mom-and-pop campgrounds. The latter are adequate for an overnight stay. If there is a charge per hookup, take the electric and water and forgo the sewer unless you really need it.

2. **Remember, you can camp without hookups comfortably for several nights** as long as you don't insist on using the TV, air conditioner, or microwave. Read a book or listen to a tape for entertainment, and cook on your gas cooktop or outdoors on a grill. You'll still have running water, lights, refrigeration, heat, and hot water for dishes and shower.

3. **If you're on a tight budget, watch out for campground surcharges** such as extra fees for running your air conditioner or hooking up to cable TV, a surcharge for 50-amp electricity, or "extra person" charges for more than two people when you're traveling with your kids. Some of the campgrounds that accept pets may also levy a fee on Fido's head.

4. **Join membership clubs that offer a discount to member campgrounds,** such as KOA (Kampgrounds of America) and Good Sam, which usually discount 10%. KOA promises the discount whether you pay by cash or credit card; Good Sam usually grants the discount only if you pay cash. In most cases, you can join up right at the campground when you register.

5. **Take advantage of age.** If one of you is over 62 and applies for a free Golden Age Passport with proof of age at a national park visitor center, your vehicle enters the park, national monument, recreation area, or wildlife refuge free, and gets a 50% discount on overnight camping areas administered by the federal government.

6. **Look for free campgrounds,** such as those in the southwestern desert, administered by the Bureau of Land Management.

A private RV park in Bend, Oregon.

7. **Invest in a current campground guide** (such as the *Unofficial* series, above) or request a state tourism office's free campground listings. County, city, and national forest campgrounds range from free to considerably less expensive than most privately owned campgrounds, although they do not often offer the luxury of hookups.

8. **If you arrive late at a campground, ask about staying overnight self-contained in an overflow area at a reduced price.** Some owners are amenable, some are not.

9. **Stay longer than a week and you can negotiate discounts,** usually from 10% to 20% or more, depending on the season and length of stay.

10. **Consider volunteering as a campground host** if you're interested in staying a long time in one area. You can camp free and may pick up a bit of pocket change for performing specified duties on the premises. (See "How to Become Campground Hosts," later in this chapter.)

Membership Campgrounds

Membership campgrounds and resorts are sort of like time-share condos; once an RVer is a member, he can stay at any of the areas participating with the group. Joining something of this sort has to be weighed carefully against the initial cost, the amount of time you'll stay in the various resorts (note the locations and your access to them), and the amenities they offer.

For example, we recently checked out two upscale membership RV resorts affiliated with Outdoor Resorts of America in the Palm Springs area (see chapter 4, "The California Desert & Las Vegas," for details), the older of which is owner-operated and mostly owner-occupied. We were quite impressed with the cleanliness and security, as well as the landscaping. A great many expensive motor homes and fifth-wheels, as well as a few more modest travel trailers and minimotor homes, are parked seasonally or permanently on the sites, many of them owned by Southern Californians who use them as a weekend home in the desert.

BEWARE OF MEMBERSHIP SCAMS

A recurring scam you should be aware of preys on people who want to sell their memberships in campgrounds or resorts: An individual contacts the seller, says he has a buyer, then sends an official-looking contract with buyer name and purchase price by Federal Express. All the eager seller has to do is send back a certified check for $500 or so by return FedEx. You can guess what happens next—nothing.

INSIDER TIP: GATHERING INFORMATION

Always stop at the tourist information offices or welcome centers when you enter a new state on an interstate highway. You can pick up everything from maps to campground booklets to individual flyers for private RV parks that may offer a discount for visitors—all of it free.

While a few owners make their sites available for overnighters or transient RVers, most seem to keep their vehicles based there. The base lot price in the newer park limited to motor homes is $36,900 to $51,900 for a 35-by-69-foot site, plus a monthly fee of $180.

There are about 450 membership resorts nationwide for RV travelers who want a range of indoor and outdoor activities. Most sell memberships for a one-time fee, much like a country club, plus an annual or monthly fee. One company, **Thousand Trails/NACO,** based in Bellingham, Washington, owned by U.S. Trails in Dallas, Texas, estimates it has 150,000 members in North America, with about 10,000 using the campground chain year-round as full-timers. Members who use the campgrounds for fewer than 50 nights a year pay no surcharge, said a spokesman for Thousand Trails, while those who use them more than 50 nights a year pay a $2 fee for each additional night. Except during peak travel seasons, RVers can usually find a spot without reservations. Contact Thousand Trails at ☎ **800/328-6226** (www.thousandtrails.com) for details and reservations, which can be made up to 90 days in advance.

In general, the spokesman said, the cost of joining a membership campground has dropped considerably from a peak of $5,000 to $10,000 a few years ago. Thousand Trails members currently pay $2,500 membership with annual fees of $499. Thousand Trails/NACO membership campgrounds offer potential members a chance to try out their product with no obligation to buy or attend a sales presentation. A 2-night stay in any of the company's 62 campgrounds costs $29.95.

On all membership campgrounds, memberships can be sold after a specified period of time, but it appears to be a buyer's market with a lot of members opting to sell.

Because some membership resorts in the past have been plagued by bankruptcies and undelivered promises, potential buyers should check with the local Better Business Bureau, the state attorney general's office, and members of the prospective resort before signing up or making a payment.

Avoid resorts that use high-pressure sales tactics and promise big prizes for buyers who sign up right away. And be wary of resorts that seem reluctant

<u>INSIDER TIP: CALIFORNIA CAMPING</u>

California state parks have instituted something called **Enroute Camping,** in which self-contained RVs may stay overnight, from sunset until 9 or 10am the next morning, in the day parking lot for the park's basic camping fee. These parks are located primarily along the coast and designated with RV profile signs.

to provide information unless you make a personal visit. If you're interested in buying someone's membership, check the classified ads each month in RV magazines such as *Trailer Life* and *MotorHome.*

Special Camping Situations

CAMPING WITH KIDS

Children make great campers.

Veterans of family camping suggest involving children in the preliminary planning, assigning regular duties at the campsite, assigning seats in the car or RV en route to the campsite, and curfew and campfire times, taking into consideration any special evening events from ranger talks to movies and dances at the campground. Older children might also be assigned a last-minute duty at home before leaving, whether locking doors and windows or removing perishable food from the refrigerator.

Even infants can happily go camping. Experts recommend taking along a backpack for a toddler or a chest pack for an infant for hikes, as well as a folding stroller and playpen, mosquito netting, and a baby guardrail for the bed to use in camp. A baby seat that clamps to a picnic table will also allow the child to participate with the rest of the family at meals or game time.

Sunscreen to protect a baby's delicate skin is essential, along with a gentle insect repellent like Avon's Skin So Soft skin lotion. (That works for adults as well; we've used it in buggy places like the jungles of Honduras.)

CAMPING WITH PETS

Six percent of all traveling dog owners take their pets with them on vacation, but only 1% of cat owners do, according to the Travel Industry Association of America. Here are 10 tips that'll keep you and your campground neighbors from wishing that figure were lower.

- **Keep the cat's litter box in the shower or tub, encased inside a 30-gallon plastic trash bag.** Put the bottom of the box in the trash bag, dump a 10-pound bag of kitty litter inside, and snap on the litter box cover. The same cat owner who suggested this to us carries a folding cat cage so her pets can enjoy the outdoors.

- **Put a throw rug or two on top of the carpeting** in a motor home to protect it from cat (or dog) feet. They can be taken out and shaken when necessary, and washed and dried in the campground laundry.

- **Decide whether or not to use a kennel crate.** Owners get into debates about whether to keep dogs and cats in airline-type kennel crates when the RV is in motion, or let them lie on the floor, furniture, or dash. The lie-about school suggests the pet could protect itself better from possible injury in an accident if it's free, while the kennel crowd (many of them professional dog handlers) assert just as doggedly that the pet (and driver) are much safer enclosed en route.

- **Always carry resealable plastic bags to pick up after your pet,** even in camping and hiking areas (or should we say especially in camping and hiking areas?).

- **Never leave your pet alone in the RV for more than 10 minutes** in any weather, and less than that in summer when heat can cause great discomfort or even death.

- **Feed pets at night only** (especially if they're susceptible to motion sickness), so they will have digested the food before the next day's drive. Give only water during the day, preferably bottled water, which you have introduced at home several days before leaving.

- **Check in a campground guide to ascertain whether the campground will accept pets.** While many do, some assess a surcharge, and all require that dogs be kept on a leash. When in doubt, call ahead. (See "The Best Campground Directories," above, for a list of campgrounds.)

- **Bring familiar bedding and toys for the pet,** and spend some time regularly for about a week ahead of setting off on its first trip just sitting with your pet in the RV to help accustom it to it.

- **Bring along your pet's shot records and extra leashes and collars,** as well as flea treatment products that will kill not only live fleas but eggs and larvae as well.

- **Good Sam Club members can take advantage of the club's Lost Pet Service.** They provide a tag imprinted with a toll-free number to call so your pet can be returned during, rather than after, the trip.

WINTER CAMPING

Some of our best RVing adventures have been in winter in snow-covered campgrounds in national parks such as the Grand Canyon and Bryce Canyon, as well as at various ski resorts. Skiers on a budget will find that many good ski areas permit free, or low-cost, self-contained RV parking overnight in their parking lots—Killington and Aspen Highlands, for example—while other resorts such as Breckenridge, Deer Valley, and New

York's Holiday Valley have RV hookups or year-round RV campgrounds at or near the site. California's Sierra Summit has free RV hookups for skiers.

AIN'T MISBEHAVIN': CAMPGROUND ETIQUETTE

1. **No claim jumping.** Anything marking a campsite, from a jug of water on a picnic table to a folding chair in the parking space, means that site is occupied and the campers are temporarily away in their car or RV. You may not set it aside and move into the site.

2. **Mind your fellow campers' personal space.** Teach your kids never to take a shortcut across an occupied campsite, but to use the road or established pathways to get where they're going.

3. **Keep your pets from roaming.** Never let your dog roam free in a campground. It should be walked on a leash and exercised in a designated pet area.

4. **Avoid using your generator whenever possible,** even within designated generator-use hours, to keep from disturbing other campers with the noise and fumes. If using electrical appliances such as microwaves and TV sets is that important, go camping in a private campground with hookups.

5. **Avoid loud and prolonged engine revving** in the early morning and late evening hours.

6. **Don't play radios, TVs, or boom boxes loudly at any time in a campground.** Many of your fellow campers are there to enjoy the peace and quiet.

7. **Never ever dump waste water from holding tanks, even gray water, on the ground.** While some old-timers claim it's good for the grass, it can also contain virulent salmonella bacteria if raw chicken has been rinsed in the sink, or bits of fecal matter from diapers. This matter can be transferred to anyone touching or stepping on contaminated ground. Gray water, like black water, belongs only in a dump station.

8. **Do not cut trees for firewood.** Most campgrounds sell firewood at special stands or the camp store. Even picking up or chopping dead wood is forbidden in many parks.

9. **Watch what you throw in the fire.** Never leave aluminum foil, aluminum cans, bottles, or filter-tipped cigarette butts in a campground fire ring or grill. They do not burn but remain as litter. And never crush out cigarettes on the ground without picking up the butts and putting them in the garbage.

10. **Don't leave porch or entry lights on all night in camp;** they may shine in someone else's bedroom window. 🚐

Many RVers enjoy snowmobiling, sledding, cross-country skiing, skating, and ice fishing in winter. Besides being able to stay toasty warm with a propane heater that does not require a hookup, winter RVers can enjoy hot meals, hot showers, and a snug, cozy feeling despite ice and snow all around.

We've found winter a good time to visit and photograph national parks, particularly in the Southwest, where a light dusting of snow highlights the vivid red canyons and green pines. Another bonus is the wildlife, especially deer and elk, that comes down into lower elevations in winter for better feeding. (See chapter 5, "Utah's Parks & Canyons.")

Ten Tips for Cozy Winter Camping

1. **Don't connect your water hose to an outdoor faucet overnight** unless you want to create a 25-foot Popsicle. Use water from the RV's supply and refill when necessary.

2. **Add antifreeze to holding tanks** to keep drains from freezing.

3. **Don't park under trees** where branches heavily weighted with snow and ice could break off and fall on your RV.

4. **Watch battery strength;** the colder it gets, the faster it will discharge.

5. **Open one window slightly for fresh air when using a propane heater;** we use the window above the kitchen sink.

6. **Leave the bathroom door open at night** so the heat from the main living area can circulate inside this normally unheated room.

7. **Keep a pair of après-ski boots handy** for good traction on even short walks through the snow, especially to a photo opportunity.

8. **Carry chains** or have snow tires for your tow vehicle or motorized RV.

9. **Don't let snow accumulate** on the refrigerator roof vent or exhaust ports.

10. **Drive with extreme care.** Even an experienced driver will find handling a motor home or pulling a towable trickier in snow and ice. A heavy motor home can be difficult to stop on an icy surface.

MAKING CAMPSITE RESERVATIONS BY PHONE

You can call ☎ **800/280-2267** for campsite reservations in national forests and U.S. Army Corps of Engineers Campgrounds—although the line is usually busy or applicants wait on hold for a long time. The line is operative daily from 7am to midnight eastern standard time. Their website is www. reserveusa.com.

How to Become Campground Hosts

Energetic retirees or full-timers on a budget can camp free and sometimes pick up a little extra income as well by volunteering as campground hosts or work campers. In theory, it's a great idea—living in your RV in a lovely campground with free hookups, maybe even with your pick of sites.

In practice, however, veterans of a season's work seem to either love it or hate it. Some mutter darkly of being treated like migrant labor, while others describe it as a highlight of their lives. A lot depends on how thoroughly you check out the campground and its management ahead of time and how realistic you are about doing hard and sometimes unpleasant chores like cleaning toilets and showers or telling a noisy camper to turn off his generator at curfew.

If campground hosting sounds like something you may want to do, here's how to get started:

- **Apply well ahead of time.** Veterans of the program suggest a year in advance is not too early.

- **Learn about job openings in RV publications** under "help wanted" or from a newsletter called *Workamper News,* published six times a year in Heber Springs, Arkansas, by Greg and Debbie Robus. Call ☎ **800/ 446-5627** weekdays between 9am and 5pm, central standard time, for more information or a subscription.

- **Good Sam Club members** can also apply through that organization's Campground Host Program, P.O. Box 8540, Ventura, CA 93001, ☎ **805/ 667-4426.** The application form requires your name, Good Sam Club membership number, address, telephone, type and size of RV, first, second and third choice of states as a work area, months available for work, and the period of stay, a minimum of 60 days. In addition, they ask if you would consider working the entire season, what RV hookups you require, and any special considerations you wish to add.

- **You can also volunteer in campgrounds** by contacting the **National Forest Service,** U.S. Department of Agriculture, P.O. Box 2417, Washington, DC 20013; the National Parks Service, 18th and C Street NW, Washington, DC 20240; or the Bureau of Land Management, Public Affairs Office, 1800 C Street NW, Washington, DC 20240.

You should apply to several campgrounds, using a résumé that should include both personal and business references. Some ads ask for a recent photograph, which many applicants think shows possible discrimination because of age, physical appearance, or condition. Many campgrounds prefer a couple to a single person, or require a single person to work 30 to 40 hours a week rather than the 15 or 20 a couple would work.

If you get a positive response, ask for references from the campground managers so you can interview people who have worked previously for them. Check privately owned campgrounds with the local chamber of commerce or Better Business Bureau.

One cautionary note: Out-of-state workers who volunteer for California campgrounds are required to register their motor vehicles, including RVs, in California since live-in volunteers are considered to be gainfully employed.

Plugging in Your Rig

ELECTRICAL HOOKUPS

Many older campgrounds, especially in state parks, may have 15- or 20-amp electrical hookups, for which modern RVs with a three-prong plug will need an adapter. When we first encountered this, we were at a Texas state park that loaned out adapters, but we soon got one of our own. You can use the lower amperage as long as you remember not to run the air conditioner, microwave, and TV set at the same time. Otherwise, you'll blow a fuse.

Each manufacturer issues a list of the amperage used by the various appliances, such as TV, refrigerator, microwave, and air conditioners. The total amperage of those units in use should not exceed your campground hookup amperage limitation, which is 15-, 20-, 30-, or 50-amp. If you do exceed it, the power goes off, which is not so much a problem if you are in a campground with circuit breakers. But older campgrounds still using fuses will make resetting more difficult. Learn when to turn off one appliance when turning on another to keep from going over the limit.

CABLE TV

Many private RV parks offer cable TV connections as an option, sometimes with an added dollar or two on the nightly fee. If you don't have a built-in exterior cable connection, you can use a length of coaxial cable hooked to the campground connection at one end, then routed through a window to your RV's TV set. You can also use an alternative outdoor entertainment area hookup as the connector. It's best if you carry your own cable, since the campground often does not provide it. Don't forget to turn off the switch to your roof antenna. (It usually has a little red light beside it.) It is also wise to have a male and female connector since campground cable connections vary.

SATELLITE TV

Newer models of RVs now have satellite dishes on the roof with internal wiring to the control box, usually installed near the TV set. The software for whatever system you use is usually included with the package. (The two major systems are DISH and DirecTV.) One disadvantage of the mounted dish is that in many campgrounds there is inevitably a tree in the direct path of the satellite signal, requiring you to move the vehicle. If you have such a system, mention it when checking in so the registrar can assign you a site that might be tree-free.

We carry a portable dish on a tripod using a secondary control box from our home, which means we don't have to have a separate account for the RV. We've found that it is a simple matter to make a connection to the satellite by being able to move the dish to an open viewing area. Satellite dishes are particularly advantageous when you travel in rural areas with little or no local TV reception, or when you plan to stay in one area for several days.

Remember, your dish programming is set on your home time, so as you move to other time zones, programs are still based on your home time.

PART 2
RV Adventures

Hitting the road on 9 great RV excursions

4

The California Desert & Las Vegas

ACTUALLY, THERE'S NOT ONE DESERT IN CALIFORNIA, BUT MANY—
Death Valley's low desert with its sizzling heat records, the **Mojave's** high
desert with its ghost towns and mines, and vast **Anza Borrego,** the biggest
state park in California with 600,000 acres of cactus and canyons. Death
Valley and Joshua Tree, previously designated national monuments, have
been turned into national parks by Congress.

And then there's The Desert: **Palm Springs** and vicinity, where Beverly
Hills goes to desiccate, safe and circumspect once again after its own Desert
Storm action when the late celebrity-mayor Sonny Bono outlawed teen
spring-break frivolities and put Palm Canyon Drive back in the hands of the
Waxworks (the area's senior celebrity residents). It's where 10,000 swimming
pools and countless lawn sprinklers, water slides, and misting outdoor air
conditioners turn once bone-dry air damp; where cows are allotted 1,000
acres of feeding area apiece to browse on vitamin-rich desert spinach.

The California deserts gave us trail mix and date milkshakes, the state's
first nudist bed-and-breakfasts, the world's first broken sound barrier, 20-
Mule-Team Borax, and the Twentynine Palms Outhouse Race.

It's where Wyatt Earp retired, where Al Capone took the waters, where
Lawrence of Arabia rode his camel across the dunes, where General Patton
left his tank tracks, and where Paul Newman, Steve McQueen, and James
Garner learned how to drive race cars.

It's where Elvis and Priscilla Presley honeymooned, where Frank Sinatra
lived on Frank Sinatra Drive, and where old-time radio favorites Jack Benny,
Amos and Andy, and Fibber McGee and Molly beamed their shows out to a
simpler nation.

RVers can find the Hullabaloo World Tobacco Spitting Championships in
Calico every Palm Sunday, visit an endangered desert pupfish in Anza
Borrego State Park, attend camel and ostrich races in Indio during the
National Date Festival in mid-February, and go sand-sailing on a dry lake at
speeds up to 70 mph—with no brakes.

California Desert Highlights

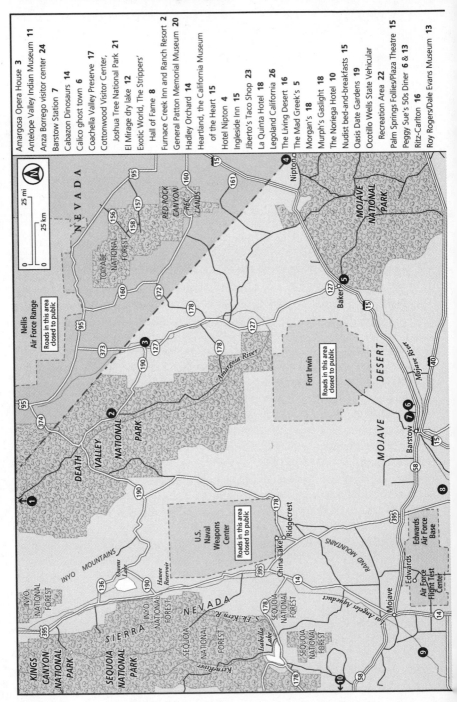

Amargosa Opera House **3**
Antelope Valley Indian Museum **11**
Anza Borrego visitor center **24**
Barstow Station **7**
Cabazon Dinosaurs **14**
Calico ghost town **6**
Coachella Valley Preserve **17**
Cottonwood Visitor Center,
   Joshua Tree National Park **21**
El Mirage dry lake **12**
Exotic World, The Strippers'
   Hall of Fame **8**
Furnace Creek Inn and Ranch Resort **2**
General Patton Memorial Museum **20**
Hadley Orchard **14**
Heartland, the California Museum
   of the Heart **15**
Hotel Nipton **4**
Ingleside Inn **15**
Jiberto's Taco Shop **23**
La Quinta Hotel **18**
Legoland California **26**
The Living Desert **16**
The Mad Greek's **5**
Morgan's **18**
Murph's Gaslight **18**
The Noriega Hotel **10**
Nudist bed-and-breakfasts **15**
Oasis Date Gardens **19**
Ocotillo Wells State Vehicular
   Recreation Area **22**
Palm Springs Follies/Plaza Theatre **15**
Peggy Sue's 50s Diner **6 & 13**
Ritz-Carlton **16**
Roy Rogers/Dale Evans Museum **13**

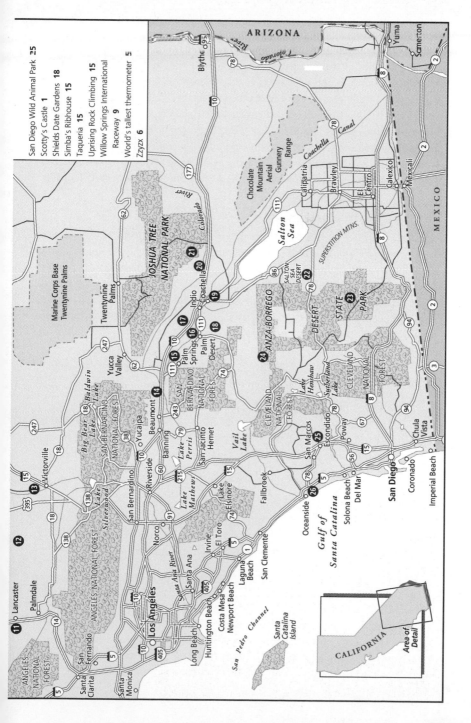

San Diego Wild Animal Park **25**
Scotty's Castle **1**
Shields Date Gardens **18**
Simba's Ribhouse **15**
Taqueria **15**
Uprising Rock Climbing **15**
Willow Springs International
 Raceway **9**
World's tallest thermometer **5**
Zzyzx **6**

ARIZONA

MEXICO

CALIFORNIA

Area of Detail

RVing in the California Desert & Las Vegas

A lazy loop around California's deserts can be made in one long haul or on a series of shorter drives from a central base. From the Palm Springs area, the route fans south and east as far as the Arizona and Mexico borders. From San Bernardino, it radiates east to the Colorado River, northeast to Las Vegas, and north to Death Valley. From Lancaster/Palmdale, it runs north into the Owens Valley east of the Sierra Nevada. The whole circuit is about 1,000 miles, plus side trips, but can be divided into a number of shorter trips.

Stay on roads and trails at all times, whether driving or walking. The desert terrain is fragile and slow growing, and one careless off-road driver can destroy vegetation decades old.

HITTING THE HIGHLIGHTS

If you divide your time between Death Valley, the Palm Springs area, Joshua Tree National Park, and Anza Borrego State Park, you should get to know the California desert fairly well. Allow 4 days in Death Valley, and then drive south through Baker, Barstow, and Calico or detour into Nevada for a fling at the gaudy casinos of Las Vegas or Laughlin. Allow 2 or 3 days in Joshua Tree, longer if you want to make day trips over into nearby Palm Springs. Anza Borrego State Park is south from Indio and Coachella, then west on Route 78 through Ocotillo Wells.

If you're flying in and renting an RV, either Los Angeles or San Diego makes a good base.

GOING FOR THE LONG HAUL

If you want to spend a winter among the snowbirds in the California desert, you could explore all three major desert areas, take a leisurely attack on the side trips, then settle in around Palm Springs if you're affluent or on the BLM Lands (see "Trimming Costs" in chapter 2, "Getting Prepared: RVing Tips & Hints") if you're strapped.

Most recreation areas, state parks, and forest service campgrounds have posted camping limits, often around 14 days, but you can check out and then check in again on a later day. Or you could become a VIP (Volunteer in Parks) and camp free all season long as a campground host.

Travel Essentials

WHEN TO GO

Winter is ideal in California's desert country: balmy and warm days with cool nights. Early spring and late autumn are also good. Summer in the low desert is only for mad dogs and Englishmen, as well as Germans, Swiss, and Japanese, who dote on traveling in Death Valley in August when the temperature can top 115°.

WHAT TO TAKE

Bring binoculars, a camera and plenty of film, and a tripod if you plan to shoot cactus, wildflower portraits, or dazzling sunsets. Carry a strong sunscreen and a canteen or water carrier for hikes.

WHAT TO WEAR

In the desert, lightweight and light-colored natural fiber fabrics are best. Stout-soled hiking shoes and tough-fabric pants are essential to repel cactus spikes if you're hiking in cactus country. Winter evenings cool quickly once the sun sets, so be prepared with a down vest or jacket, windbreaker, or heavy sweatshirt. A wide-brimmed hat, preferably one that can be tied down, is best in the strong desert sun.

TRIMMING COSTS ON THE ROAD

Ask any snowbird turned desert rat how to live off the land—or rather, the Bureau of Land Management—and he'll tell you about "the Slabs" or one of the other Long-Term Visitor Areas (LTVAs) in the southern desert.

Here's how it works: You can buy a Golden Eagle Passport for $50 that gives you a camping discount good for 1 year. Prices and discounts vary depending on season, state, and camping area. To make an advance purchase, call one of the district offices listed below and they'll supply a permit by mail. If you want to spend only a few days, you can buy a short-term permit from campground hosts in each camp area.

Don't expect hookups, paved parking (except at "the Slabs," which were once cement pads for military buildings), water, or sanitary dump sites. What you get is plenty of desert, some solitude if you wish, and all the warm sunshine you can handle.

Calico's bottle house.

The sites are generally located off I-8 or I-10 west of Yuma and in Arizona at Quartzsite on U.S. 95 off I-10. The most established areas are Hot Spring, off I-8 east of El Centro at Highway 115; Imperial Dam, off I-8 at Winterhaven, then west on Senator Wash Road; Pilot Knob, off I-8 at Sidewinder Road 5 miles west of Yuma; Dunes Vista, off I-8 at Ogilby Road, 10 miles west of Yuma; La Posa at Quartzsite, Arizona, on both sides of Route 95; Midland, off I-10 at Lovekin Boulevard; and Mule Mountain, off I-10 at Wiley's Well Road, then north 9 miles. To get more information, call the **California Desert District Office of BLM** in Riverside (☎ **909/697-5200;** www.blm. gov), or the **Yuma District Office** in Arizona (☎ **602/726-6300**).

WHERE TO GET TRAVEL INFORMATION

The following organizations can supply you with any visitor info you need for your desert trek.

- **The Borrego Springs Chamber of Commerce,** 622 Palm Canyon Dr., Borrego Springs, CA 92004 (☎ **800/559-5524;** www.borregosprings.com).
- **California Division of Tourism,** 801 K St., Suite 1600, Sacramento, CA 95814 (☎ **916/322-2881;** www.gocalif.ca.gov).
- **Inland Empire Tourism Council** (providing info for Riverside and San Bernardino counties), 301 E. Vanderbilt Way, Suite 100, San Bernardino, CA 92408 (☎ **909/890-1090;** www.ieep.com).
- **Las Vegas Convention and Visitors Authority,** 3150 Paradise Rd., Las Vegas, NV 89109 (☎ **702/892-7575;** www.lasvegas24hours.com).
- **Palm Springs Desert Resorts,** 69–930 Highway 111, Suite 201, Rancho Mirage, CA 92270 (☎ **800/41-RELAX** or 760/770-9000; www.desert-resorts.com).
- **Palm Springs Tourism,** 333 North Palm Canyon Dr., Suite 114, Palm Springs, CA 92262 (☎ **800/34-SPRINGS;** www.palm-springs.org).

DRIVING & CAMPING TIPS

- **Leave an itinerary with friends.** Never head out on back roads in the desert without telling someone where you're going and when you expect to return.
- **Carry water**—at least 1 gallon per person per day.
- **Carry good detailed local maps.** Desert access guides are available for $2.50 each from the Bureau of Land Management, California Desert District Office (☎ **909/697-5200;** www.blm.gov).
- **Never trespass on private desert land**—some of the "desert rats" don't take kindly to strangers.
- **Be aware of where you set up camp.** Set up at least 200 yards away from a man-made water source for wildlife and no more than 300 yards from the road. Don't set up camp in a wash where flash floods could literally wash you away.

The Best Desert Sights, Tastes & Experiences

OFF-THE-WALL ATTRACTIONS

The Palm Springs Follies. Retired chorus girls aged 50 to 80 with great gams still kick 'em high at the city's nostalgic Plaza Theatre, 128 S. Palm Canyon Dr. Call ☎ **760/864-6516;** www.palmspringsfollies.com for information, 760/327-0225 for tickets (around $25). Daily matinees at 1:30pm, nightly performances at 7pm, winter season only.

Nudist bed-and-breakfasts, Palm Springs. We haven't run across many of these anywhere, but Palm Springs has a selection. **The Terra Cotta Inn,** 2388 E. Racquet Club Rd., is a clothing-optional, 17-room resort for couples, open year-round. From $79 summer, $115 winter (☎ **800/SUNNY FUN;** www.sunnyfun.com). **Desert Shadows Inn,** 1533 Chaparral Rd., also welcomes naturists with 74 year-round units (☎ **800/292-9298;** www. desertshadows.com). Other small, clothing-optional boutique hotels in Palm Springs cater to gay male or female clientele. For a full hotel list, contact Palm Springs Tourism at ☎ **800/347-7746.**

The Roy Rogers/Dale Evans Museum, Victorville. An eclectic compendium of everything the cowboy film stars ever saw, received, or touched. A collector's set of 1950s Western tableware; a Pontiac decorated with horns, pistols, and silver dollars; and dioramas about the family's life are only a minuscule part of the assortment. Roy's horse Trigger and Dale's horse Buttermilk, along with several family dogs, survive as models of taxidermy.

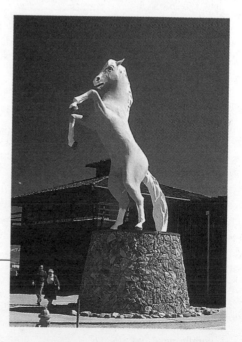

Roy Rogers's horse Trigger announces the location of the Roy Rogers/Dale Evans Museum in Victorville.

Adults $8, seniors and students $7, children 6 to 12, $5. 15650 Seneca Rd. in Victorville. Exit Interstate 15 at Roy Rogers Drive, keep left, and make a left on Civic Drive (☎ 760/243-4547).

Exotic World, The Strippers' Hall of Fame, Helendale. At 29053 Wild Rd. in Helendale, former headliner Dixie Evans, better known as "the Marilyn Monroe of Burlesque," commemorates the days when disrobing seductively was a work of art for once-famous stars like Lili St. Cyr, Blaze Starr, and Tempest Storm. See Gypsy Rose Lee's cape, Jayne Mansfield's dressing room ottoman, and an urn with the ashes of Jennie Lee, who started this museum before she died of cancer. $10 admission. Call ahead for an appointment (☎ 760/243-5261; www.exoticworld.org).

The moving rocks of Death Valley. They skitter along the desert floor at Racetrack Playa, leaving behind a trail of their route. Scientists suspect rain-slick clay allows the wind to push the rocks back and forth at speeds of up to 2 mph, but no one has ever seen them in motion. Death Valley National Park, at state highways 127 and 190 (☎ 760/786-2331; www.nps.gov).

Amargosa Opera House. The ballerina dances for an audience of painted figures if no live ones show up at the Amargosa, at the intersection of Highways 127 and 190, where dancer Marta Becket painted in 250 spectators for her dances and pantomimes scheduled on winter weekends. Call ahead for tickets at ☎ 760/852-4441; www.amargosafilm.com.

The roadside dinosaurs at Cabazon. About 40 to 45 miles northeast of Palm Springs on I-10, the dinosaurs appeared in the film *PeeWee's Big Adventure* and serve to promote a chow stop at the Wheel Inn, where no less a gourmet authority than Gault-Millau praises the huge helpings of homemade desserts, from strawberry shortcakes to bread puddings. While we were not lured by their "famous" cream pies, we adored the gift shop in the belly of the biggest dinosaur. Since a pair of fast-food purveyors moved into the neighborhood, you have to look twice to spot the dinosaurs.

Long-eared owls and short-eared owls. If you've ever wondered what the difference is (beside the obvious), take a winter's day drive on the dry side to Harper Lake, 25 miles east of Barstow via Highway 58, then 5 miles north to the dry lake. The long-eared owls hang out in woodland thickets, while the short-eared owls stay close to the marsh. One veteran birder reports seeing 300 short-eared owls feeding in a single field. Bureau of Land Management (☎ 909/697-5200; www.blm.gov).

The world's tallest thermometer, Baker. It soars above the Bun Boy restaurant in the Mojave Desert town of Baker, showing 1 foot for each degree of temperature, up to the hottest recorded day in history at Death Valley (July 10, 1913, when it hit 134°). You can see it as you drive along I-15, with the current temperature recorded both day and night. The restaurant dates from 1926, and has a minimuseum about Death Valley in the entrance. The intriguingly named Bun Boy Motel is next door. Baker Area Chamber of Commerce (☎ 760/733-4469).

Scotty's Castle, Death Valley. A $2 million Moorish mansion built by a Chicago insurance executive and his radio evangelist wife (but named for a former performer in Buffalo Bill's Wild West Show who also lived there), the castle has an unfinished 270-foot swimming pool, 25 rooms with tapestries and fireplaces, and a 26-foot clock tower. Johnson and his friend Walter Scott (Scotty) rejected designs submitted by Frank Lloyd Wright in favor of an unknown architect who did not go on to fame and fortune. Guided tours led by costumed docents are so popular you can expect a wait of an hour or two in season. Scotty died in 1954, and his estate consisted of one well-worn cowboy hat. On Scotty's Castle Road in Death Valley National Park. You can get there from Highway 190. Look for a sign. You can also take Highway 95 to 267-S and take Scotty's Castle exit (☎ **760/786-2392**).

Coachella Valley Preserve covered-wagon tours. If you've always yearned for the rugged pioneer life, hop into a genuine bone-crusher of a prairie schooner, drawn by draft mules, with an optional campfire and barbecue also on the agenda; $55 for adults, $27.50 for kids. Located north of I-10 and about 6 miles east of Thousand Palms at the north end of Washington Street on the Coachella Valley Preserve (☎ **800/367-2161** or 760/347-2161).

Antelope Valley Indian Museum, Lancaster. This whimsical and eclectic place, built in the style of a Swiss chalet, is filled with giant kachina dolls, bird claw fishhooks, grass skirts, and some unlikely illustrated Indian legends; a second-story cave is open on weekends only, October through mid-June, at 15701 E. Ave. M in Lancaster. It was hand-built by a romantic, self-taught artist in 1928 (☎ **661/942-0662** or 661/946-3055; www.avim.av.org).

Barstow Station. East of Barstow on East Main Street (off I-15), the station looks like several small railway cars by the station from the outside, but inside it's one huge, rambling shop with an astonishing collection of great tacky souvenirs, from life-sized plaster of Paris howling coyotes to plastic cacti and personalized mugs for every Tom, Dick, and Lupe that happens by. Things dangle from the ceilings and are stacked precariously on random shelves and counters around the premises. A tour bus rest stop, the station also has a McDonald's and take-out food counters. We were fascinated with the 42 jelly bean flavors, not to mention the life-sized plaster American eagles and the Marilyn Monroe cookie jars. Barstow/Mojave Desert Convention and Visitors (☎ **760/253-4782;** Bureau/www.visitmojavedesert.com).

Heartland, the California Museum of the Heart, Palm Springs. Walk through a giant model of a human heart, record your heartbeat, or step into a pulsating coronary artery to observe plaque formation, all in a wing of the Heart Institute of the Desert at 39-600 Bob Hope Dr. in Palm Springs. While there, you can catch a healthy snack at the Heart Rock Cafe or watch a heart-warming film at the Happy Heart Cinema. Free admission, but voluntary donations suggested. From Highway 111, take the Country Club exit and make a left on Bob Hope Drive; the first right takes you to the Heart Institute (☎ **760/778-4639**).

Barstow Station.

Naked hiking. Take a moonlight desert hike au naturel with Desert Safari's Moonlight Hiking Expedition. Contact ☎ 888/TO-SAFARI or www.desertsafari. com. The hikes are conducted in "secret remote locations" outside Palm Springs each month on the night of the full moon and the day before and after it.

PUTTING YOURSELF IN PERIL, AT SPEED

Aside from heat, desert daytimes offer just about any extreme you could dream up. Here are three of the better ones.

Willow Springs International Raceway. Willow Springs Raceway offers an appointment in the fast lane, a chance to watch or take part in fast track racing. You can watch a race, take a lesson on handling your own car from an expert at any of several schools, or book a formula car racing session, just as many movie star drivers like Paul Newman and James Garner have in the past. 3500 75th St. West, in Rosamond. From Highway 14 north, exit west on Rosamond Boulevard. Continue for 5 miles to the track (☎ 661/256-2471; www.willowspringsraceway.com).

El Mirage dry lake. El Mirage, in the eastern Mojave, is a haven for sand sailors on windy weekend afternoons. With the right wind, their sand sail craft—T-shaped tubular frames 6 feet wide and 10 feet long with a triangular sail on a 17-foot mast—let them get speeds of up to 70 mph—but there are no brakes. Get there via Avenue P in Lancaster, which turns into El Mirage Road, then turn north on El Medio road (unpaved) 5 miles to the lake.

Flyaway Indoor Skydiving. A 21-foot vertical wind tunnel lets you learn skydiving the easy way, flying without wings with all the gear and lessons included in the $45 class price. Open 10am weekdays, 11am on Sundays,

until 6pm weekdays, 4pm Sundays year-round (☎ **877/545-8093;** www.
flyawayindoorskydiving.com).

Uprising Rock Climbing Center. Palm Springs is home to the only outdoor
rock climbing gym in the United States, with a canopy-covered, mist-sprayed
climbing wall open daily and evenings. Lessons cost $25 to $36, with a
promise you should master the basics in less than an hour, then can spend
the rest of the day practicing at no extra charge. Come back to practice for
$15 a day, $7 to rent gear. It's at 1500 South Gene Autry (☎ **760/320-6630;**
www.uprising.com).

THREE DESERT SPLURGES

1. **Furnace Creek Inn and Ranch Resort.** Furnace Creek, Highway 190
   in Death Valley National Park, has a dazzling, cerulean swimming pool
   and palm garden that look like a mirage from the 1930s, with stone
   arches framing distant views of snow-capped mountains beside a lush
   oasis shaded by palms. From $95 a night for two (☎ **760/786-2514;**
   www.furnacecreekresort.com).

2. **Desert Adventures of Palm Springs.** A bouncy Jeep ride along private
   dirt roads with this outfit lends insights into everything from lifestyles
   and rituals of the local Cahuilla tribes to fascinating facts about desert
   flora and fauna. Try to catch a ride with Morgan Wind-in-Her-Hair
   Levine, a mile-a-minute talker and one of the company's co-owners.
   Tours range from 1 to 4 hours and cost $35 to $99 for adults. Call
   ☎ **760/324-5337** to book. Reservations are required.

3. **Ingleside Inn in Palm Springs.** Sit under the shade trees on the
   grassy lawn by the pool at the circa-1935 Inn, 200 W. Ramon Rd., in
   Palm Springs, on the corner of Highway 111 and Ramon, where
   Howard Hughes used to check in under the name "Earl Martyn," along
   with Ava Gardner as "Mrs. Clark." In the hotel's Melvyn's Restaurant,
   you can still dine on 1950s-style martinis, shrimp cocktails, and steak
   while overhearing remarks like, "Sheila, you look wonderful; not even
   in the light can you tell!" From $100 for two (☎ **800/772-6655** or
   760/325-0046; www.inglesideinn.com).

GREAT TAKE-OUT (OR EAT-IN) TREATS

Murph's Gaslight, Bermuda Dunes. The pan-fried chicken with all the
trimmings—black-eyed peas, mashed potatoes, cornbread, hot biscuits,
country gravy, and fruit cobbler—can be ordered to take out if you call
ahead. Murph's is open 11am to 3pm and 5 to 9pm daily except Sundays,
when the hours are 3 to 9pm, and Mondays, when the restaurant is closed.
You can also feast family style at a table inside on a first-come, first-served
basis; the platters of chicken keep on coming. 79–860 Ave. 42, by the airport
in Bermuda Dunes (☎ **760/345-6242**).

The Mad Greek's, Baker. The hummus and homemade pita bread and falafel sandwich with tahini are good choices to go at The Mad Greek's at 72112 Baker Blvd. in Baker, where an unautographed photo of Zsa Zsa Gabor hangs over the door. Truckers like the $5 ham-and-three-egg breakfast pictured on the wall. Take Highway 127 to Baker exit (☎ 760/733-4354).

Hadley Orchard, Cabazon. The original recipe for trail mix, concocted 20-some years ago by an employee of Hadley Orchard, is still for sale in the freeway farm stand, along with dried fruits and nuts and what appears to be the world's largest assortment of fruit-and-nut gift packs. Take the Apache Trail exit from I-10 near Palm Springs (☎ 800/854-5655; www.hadleyfruitorchard.com).

Morgans, La Quinta. The peanut-butter pie at Morgans in the La Quinta Hotel, 49–499 Eisenhower Dr., La Quinta, is surprisingly light and delicate, with a brushing of chocolate on the crisp crust before the filling is piled on, then topped with whipped cream and sliced almonds. Even in a take-out carton, the pie slice is nestled on a base of chocolate stripes, which helps justify its $3.95 tariff. Open 6am to 10pm (☎ 760/564-5720).

Taqueria, Palm Springs. The vegetarian enchiladas, burritos, tamales, and tacos at Taqueria, 125 E. Tahquitz Canyon Way, Palm Springs, come with your choice of refried, black, or ranch beans and a big dollop of rice. This charming cantina with its bright colors and big patio also features a selection of margaritas. Open daily from 11:30am to 10pm (☎ 760/778-5391).

Fresh dates, Indio. Dates are harvested between September and mid-December around Indio; check **Shields Date Gardens,** 80–225 Highway 111, dating from 1924, for Royal Medjool-Super Jumbo dates, the world's biggest. Open daily (☎ 760/347-0996; www.shieldsdates.com). The **Oasis Date Gardens** in Thermal on Highway 111 gives you a date milkshake at the end of its free 20-minute tour and an enlightening video on the sex life of the date (☎ 800/414-2555).

Simba's Ribhouse, Palm Springs. The best barbecued ribs in the desert can be found at Simba's, located in a former bank building at 190 N. Sunrise Way in Palm Springs, along with down-home versions of chicken and dumplings, black-eyed peas, barbecued beans, cornbread, hush puppies, and sweet potato pie. Call ahead at ☎ 760/778-7630 for takeout or reservations.

Peggy Sue's 50's Diner, Victorville and Yermo. Two branches of a great roadside eatery brighten the night with salads, pizzas, malts, and burgers, plus kitschy souvenirs, old movie-star photos (what is it about the desert that brings out old movie-star photos?), and souvenir dolls. In Victorville, it's located east of I-15 at 16885 Stoddard Wells Rd. (☎ 760/951-5001). In Yermo, it's off I-15 at the Ghost Town Rd. exit at 35654 Yermo Rd. (☎ 760/254-3370).

The Noriega Hotel, Bakersfield. A family-style Basque restaurant, the Noriega Hotel is always worth a detour. Founded in 1893 by Faustino Noriega and operated since 1931 by the Elizalde family, it's open daily except Mondays, with breakfast ($7) served between 7 and 9am, lunch ($8) served promptly at noon, and dinner ($15) at 7pm. Breakfast, tailored to the appetites of the Basque sheepherders who've always eaten here, includes fried eggs or omelets; Basque sausage; bacon or ham; California jack cheese; sheepherder bread; salsa; coffee; and wine. At lunch and dinner, the long tables are set with tureens of hot soup, platters of salad, beans, meats (chicken, lamb, pork chops, liver and onions, corned beef and cabbage), vegetables, bottles of house red wine, loaves of sheepherder's bread with butter, and dishes of blue cheese. It's located at 525 Sumner St., near the intersection of Golden State Avenue and Union Avenue. Call ☎ 805/ 322-8419 for reservations, even only a few minutes ahead of time. The hotel has a medium-sized parking lot; large RVs will also find adequate street parking within a block or two.

Jiberto's Taco Shop, Borrego Springs. Ensenada-style fish tacos, carne asada burritos, or Sonoran chimichangas can be found at Jiberto's, 655 Palm Canyon Dr. in Borrego Springs. Call ahead for takeout. It's open daily 7am to midnight (☎ 760/767-1008).

WILDLIFE-WATCHING

Dusk and dawn are the best wildlife-watching times in the desert, especially where there's a water source. Stay downwind so the animals can't smell you.

Besides the **bandit coyotes** that lurk around all day, you might spot the elegant little **desert kit fox** or the malevolent **sidewinder** in the sand dunes around Stovepipe Wells at dawn or dusk. **Roadrunners** are everywhere, looking exactly like the cartoon version.

California's endangered state reptile, the **desert tortoise,** can often be seen in its Mojave Desert sanctuary near California City. Chances of sighting one are best from mid-March to mid-June, but if you spot one moving slowly across the highway, don't touch him or pick him up. He'll panic and pee, losing the precious water he's been hoarding from those rare winter showers.

One of the best places to see **desert bighorn sheep** is on the manicured lawns of the posh Ritz-Carlton Hotel in Rancho Mirage. They hoof down from their adjacent hilltop wildlife sanctuary to feast on the foliage, and don't seem to mind tourists and cameras.

Another good spot to look for bighorns, especially rams, is in Anza Borrego State Park on road S22 between markers 12.5 and 13.5. The best time is in the morning; pull your vehicle off the road and do not disturb them.

In Death Valley, you can spot the endangered **desert pupfish** from a boardwalk at Salt Creek Interpretive Trail off 190 south of Stovepipe Wells.

Both the pupfish and the rare **fringe-toed lizard,** which can shut off all its body orifices and "swim" through sand dunes, can be found in the Coachella Valley Reserve and may be glimpsed on one of several easy walking trails radiating out from the visitor center. Take Thousand Palms Canyon Road off Ramon Road north of I-10 near Palm Springs.

The Living Desert is a 1,200-acre wildlife and botanical park located at 47–900 Portola Ave., off Haystack Road in Palm Desert, showcasing captive and wild-roaming desert species year-round. Look for roadrunners, quail, desert tortoises, desert pupfish, rattlesnakes, desert kangaroo rats, Peninsular bighorn sheep, coyotes, golden eagles, Mexican wolves, bobcats, mountain lions, javelina, and rare naked mole rats. It's open daily 9am to 5pm (☎ 760/346-5694; www.livingdesert.org).

On the Road

ACTIVE ADVENTURES IN ANZA BORREGO

In the 600,000 acres of California's largest state park, tent campers can set up almost anywhere as long as they follow the park's guidelines, spelled out in a free publication at the visitor center in Borrego Springs. Campers will have to carry their own water in and all trash and garbage back out.

The earth-covered "underground" **visitor center,** on S22 (aka Palm Canyon Drive) 2 miles west of the town of Borrego Springs, provides an introduction to the park, including the endangered desert pupfish.

More organized camping is available at **Borrego Palm Canyon Campground,** part of the state park system, with full hookups and 30-amp electrical capacity. Sites are unshaded and not particularly attractive, but the surroundings are pretty. Hot showers and flush toilets are on-site, and a self-guided nature trail sets out from the campground area. It's located on S22 2 miles west of Borrego Springs (☎ 760/767-5311).

The best time to visit is during the winter months. With good January rains, expect to see blossoms in February when the flowering Mojave yucca breaks out in cream-colored bursts from spiny stalks, ocotillos take on sprays of tiny red flowers, and beavertail cactus are topped with big jaunty pink blooms. And don't be surprised to see 10,000 other like-minded visitors. Check on conditions in advance by calling the visitor center.

East of Anza Borrego on the north side of Highway 78, just west of the San Diego County border with Imperial County, is the **Ocotillo Wells State Vehicular Recreation Area,** where owners of 125s with knobbies can play pretend-moto and new owners of 4x4s can check out the equipment without offending the neighbors.

Campground Oases Around Anza Borrego

Palm Canyon Resort and RV Park. Palm Canyon Resort in Borrego Springs makes a good family getaway, except on major winter holiday weekends when so many RVs are so close together it looks like gridlock. With 130 full hookups (30-amp), cable TV, modem capability, heated pool and spa, and an Old West–style resort hotel adjoining, the park is appealing despite its fairly narrow 20-foot sites. Located at 221 Palm Canyon Dr., Borrego Springs. From Highway 86, take S22, then make a right on Palm Canyon Drive. Call ☎ 800/242-0044 for reservations.

Fountain of Youth Spa Campground. On Coachella Canal Road near Salton Sea, 15 miles north of Niland off Highway 111, Fountain of Youth Spa Campground has 546 RV sites with full hookups, flush toilets, showers, artesian steam rooms, hydrojet pools, masseur, laundry, barber shop, beauty parlor, propane, groceries, and church services for Catholics, Protestants, Mormons, and Adventists. Huge and almost mind-boggling, Fountain of Youth says it's for over 55s. If it sounds like your speed, call ☎ 760/354-1555 for information, or 888/8000-SPA for reservations. $20 and up.

ELSEWHERE IN SAN DIEGO COUNTY

Kids and their parents adore the new **LEGOland California** theme park off of I-5 in Carlsbad, 1 hour south of Disneyland, 30 minutes north of San Diego. Created by the Danish company that makes the brightly colored interlocking plastic building blocks called LEGO, the 128-acre family theme park has 40 interactive rides and attractions. Admission $39 adults and $33 kids 3 to 16. Most attendees make a day of it and enjoy the low-key, relaxed sense of fun and creativity. It's particularly good for smaller children who are sometimes intimidated by bigger, noisier theme parks (☎ 760/918-5346; www. legoland.com).

San Diego Wild Animal Park makes another good family getaway for a day. Located in Escondido at 15500 San Pasqual Valley Rd., just off Route 78, the park is an offshoot of the famous San Diego Zoo, with safari trails through the forest, savanna, and wetlands to see more than 200 exotic animals in their natural habitats (☎ 760/747-8702; www.sandiegozoo.org/wap).

PALM SPRINGS

Every other one of Palm Springs's checkerboard lots belongs to the Agua Caliente band of Cahuilla Indians, who control 42% of the land in the Coachella Valley and are the richest tribe in North America. The **Spa Hotel & Casino & Mineral Springs,** at 100 N. Indian Canyon Dr., is one of the tribal ventures, offering 24-hour poker, slots, and Spa-21, which we interpret as a healthy version of blackjack.

While many of Palm Springs's senior celebrity residents are irreverently referred to as The Waxworks, there's nothing sedentary about the area. You can catch a polo match or try a version of golf cart polo at **Eldorado Polo Club,** 5950 Madison, Indio (☎ 800/525-7634); splish-splash in California's largest wave-action pool or ride an inner tube down a 600-foot white-water river at the **Oasis Waterpark,** on Gene Autry Trail between Ramon Road and East Palm Canyon Drive in Palm Springs (☎ 760/325-7873); float above the cactus with **Balloon Above the Desert** (☎ 760/776-5785; www. pshotairballoons.com), or ride the **Aerial Tramway** from the desert floor to the cool crest of 8,516 feet in 15 minutes (take I-10 west to Indian Avenue exit, turn left at exit, then make a right on San Rafael; ☎ 888/515-TRAM or 760/325-1391; www.pstramway.com).

Desert Campgrounds

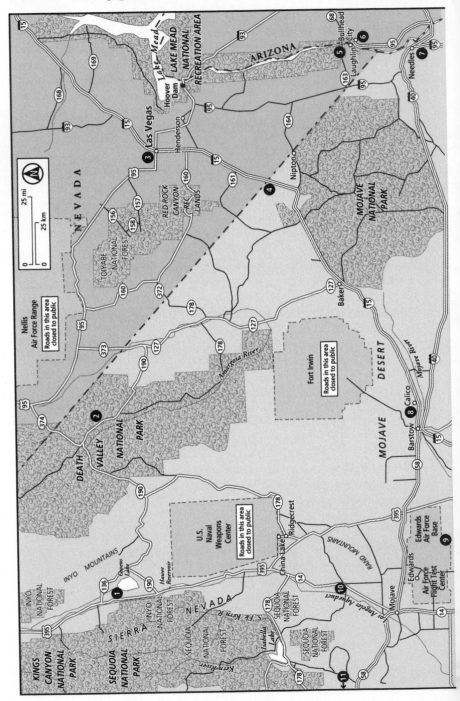

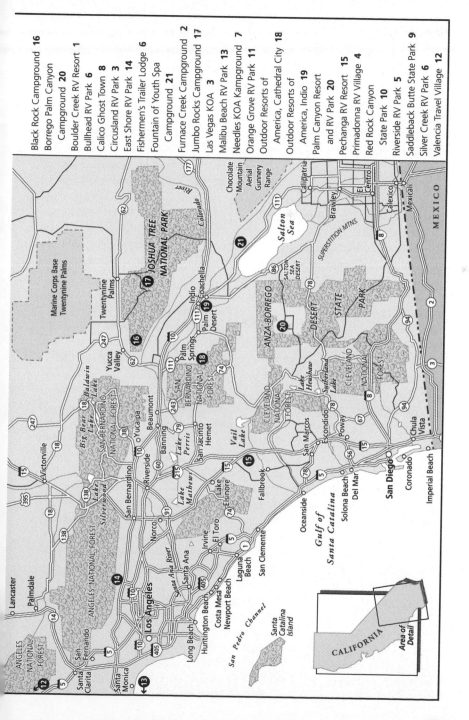

Black Rock Campground **16**
Borrego Palm Canyon Campground **20**
Boulder Creek RV Resort **1**
Bullhead RV Park **6**
Calico Ghost Town **8**
Circusland RV Park **3**
East Shore RV Park **14**
Fishermen's Trailer Lodge **6**
Fountain of Youth Spa Campground **21**
Furnace Creek Campground **2**
Jumbo Rocks Campground **17**
Las Vegas KOA **3**
Malibu Beach RV Park **13**
Needles KOA Kampground **7**
Orange Grove RV Park **11**
Outdoor Resorts of America, Cathedral City **18**
Outdoor Resorts of America, Indio **19**
Palm Canyon Resort and RV Park **20**
Pechanga RV Resort **15**
Primadonna RV Village **4**
Red Rock Canyon State Park **10**
Riverside RV Park **5**
Saddleback Butte State Park **9**
Silver Creek RV Park **6**
Valencia Travel Village **12**

69

For couch potatoes, we'd recommend more sedentary amusements. Watching **Fun in the Sun Candies** make Nutcorns at its factory store is riveting (68–845 Perez Rd.; ☎ **800/922-6390;** closed in summer). You can sample microbrews at the **Palm Springs Brewing Company,** 5055 Calle San Raphael, by appointment on Tuesdays through Thursdays (☎ **760/327-BREW**). **Ruddy's 1930s General Store Museum** on the Village Green makes nostalgic browsing for anyone who remembers Uneeda Biscuits, Rinso, sarsaparilla, and silk stockings. It's open weekends only in summer, Thursday through Sunday in winter 10am to 4pm (☎ **760/327-2156**).

Wind Farm Tours, 62–950 20th Ave., west of the Indian Avenue exit on the north side of I-10, North Palm Springs, takes tourists around in electric vehicles powered by the wind to see the forest of giant windmills that dominate the desert landscape around Palm Springs. One-and-a-half-hour tours leave four times a day in winter—9 and 11am and 1 and 2pm—and sometimes less frequently in summer. Reservations are encouraged, although they do accept walk-ins, space providing (☎ **760/251-1997**). Admission $22 adults, $20 seniors, $15 youth, $10 child.

"How could you travel to California and not see the San Andreas Fault?" your neighbors back home might well ask. Two different companies hawk tours of it in Palm Springs. **Jurassic Expeditions** (☎ **760/862-5540**) sells a 3-hour "Indiana Jones" motor coach ecoadventure tour with guide Murray Rodkin and his dog Seismo, while **Eco Tours** (☎ **760/322-6029**) takes a more educational approach and requires reservations for the once-daily, Monday-through-Thursday excursions. The 3-hour tour is $65 per person.

RVing golfers who carry along their clubs (and even their carts, in some cases) can book a round at one of the nearly two dozen **golf courses** in the Palm Springs area. Tee times are obviously easier to come by in summer than in the winter high season, and as long as you get on the course by 6am to play 18 holes, you'll survive before the worst of the dry heat hits.

Most private golf courses require you play with a member; however, the following do not: **Palm Springs Country Club,** 2500 Whitewater Club (☎ **760/323-2626**); **Rancho Mirage Country Club,** 38–500 Bob Hope Dr. (☎ **760/324-4711**); **The Golf Center at Palm Desert,** 74–945 Sheryl (☎ **760/837-9553**); **Date Palm Country Club,** 16–200 Date Palm, Cathedral City (☎ **760/328-1315**); and **Indian Wells Golf Resort,** 44–500 Indian Wells (☎ **760/346-4653**).

A 1-hour **Celebrity Bus Tour** (☎ **760/770-2700**) drives past 30 to 40 homes where the rich and famous once lived, while a 2½-hour tour adds the Eisenhower Medical Center, the Sinatra and Annenberg Estates, and The Springs and Rancho Mirage Country Clubs plus a rest-and-refreshment stop at Edwards Date Shoppe. Reservations are required and no credit cards accepted. Admission is $15 adults, $13 seniors, $7 students under 16 for the hour tour; $20, $17, and $9 for the 2½-hour tour.

To see stars in a different light, the **Desert Memorial Cemetery** offers a free guide to their graves, listing locations and birth and death dates for such big names as Frank Sinatra, Sonny Bono, songwriters Jimmy van Heusen and Frederick Lowe, director Busby Berkeley, actors William Powell (*The Thin Man*) and Cameron Mitchell (*How to Marry a Millionaire*), and actor/bon vivant Charlie Farrell, who founded the Palm Springs Racquet Club. The cemetery is open daily 7am to 7pm; ask in the office for the guide or refer to a copy posted outside when the office is closed. It's located at 69–920 Ramon Rd. at Da Vall Road; enter from Da Vall (☎ 760/328-3316).

Special events in the desert worth planning ahead for include the **Indio Date Festival camel and ostrich races** in mid-February (☎ 760/863-8247); the **Desert Swing 'n Dixie Jazz Festival** in mid-March at the Doral Resort Hotel, Vista Chino at Landau (☎ 760/778-7718); the **Nude Recreation Week** in early July at the Terra Cotta Inn, a 17-room, clothing-optional couples resort (☎ 760/322-6059); and the **Indio International Tamale Festival** the first weekend in December (☎ 760/347-0646).

Palm Springs Nightlife

The **Rat Pack Room** in Mayo's Supper Club on El Paseo is a private dining room with a Sinatra soundtrack, larger-than-life photographs of Sinatra and his buddies Dean Martin, Sammy Davis Jr., Joey Bishop, and Peter Lawford, and a digitally enhanced photo of Bob Mayo, the club owner, "singing" with the guys at the Sands in Las Vegas. The bistro is at 73–990 El Paseo Dr. in Palm Desert. (☎ 760/346-2284; www.mayos.com). Closed in summer.

The hottest club in town is **Muriel's Supper Club** at 210 S. Palm Canyon Dr. Reminiscent of a vintage New York supper club, the new spot offers "eclectic world cuisine"—desert talk for "whatever our chef knows how to

Lush greens and fairways in the middle of a desert.

cook"—along with nationally known entertainers like Nancy Sinatra. They actually serve dinner as late as 11:30pm, a desert first. Call ☎ **760/325-8839** for reservations.

Just like Branson and Pigeon Forge, Palm Springs promises a respite to performers who are tired of touring but don't want to give up show biz. Noted entertainer Jim Bailey appears as Barbra Streisand, Peggy Lee, Judy Garland, and Phyllis Diller, among others, at whichever seasonal venue he redubs the **Jim Bailey Theater** during the winter season. And **Frankie Randall** sings his heart out in a musical tribute titled "Sinatra, My Way," also at a local theater in season. Check listings in the current copy of the *Desert Guide,* free at information racks all over town.

Campground Oases in & Around Palm Springs
Outdoor Resorts of America. Outdoor Resorts of America has two Palm Springs–area RV parks, one for motor homes only, that are well-landscaped, individually owned sites made available to travelers when space is open. With lavish spa facilities from swimming pools to par-3 golf courses, the full-hookup sites cost around $45 a night. Call ☎ **800/453-4056** (or 800/841-3131 in California) for the Cathedral City property, 69411 Ramon Rd. (use the Date Palm Drive exit south from I-10), open to both motor-driven and towable RVs. Call ☎ **800/892-2992** for the Indio location, off Jefferson Street on Avenue 48 (reached from the Jefferson Street exit south 3.3 miles from I-10), open only to type A and type C motor homes (www.outdoor-resorts.com).
Pechanga RV Resort, 45000 Pala Rd. in Temecula (☎ **877-99-RVFUN;** www.pechangarvresort.com), has 170 full-service sites with 25 pull-throughs, cable TV, and complimentary Internet hookup. The resort is adjacent to a 24-hour casino and restaurant.

THE MOJAVE DESERT & JOSHUA TREE NATIONAL PARK
The Mojave is dotted with twisted green Joshua trees, which explorer John C. Fremont, never a happy camper, considered "the most repulsive trees in the vegetable kingdom."

Explorers, immigrants, and miners alike endured rather than adored the high desert, but latter-day desert rats get rapturous about such ersatz doings as chili cook-offs, tobacco-spitting contests, and burro biscuit tossings.

Cynics forget that **Calico,** for example, was a real ghost town before it became an artificial ghost town re-created by Walter Knott of Knott's Berry Farm. Silver was mined there in the late 1880s, and a dog named Dorsey used to carry the mail from Calico to Bismarck, a half mile away. Take the Calico exit off I-15 between Barstow and Yermo (www.calicotown.com).

You may notice the exit markers from I-15 for **Zzyzx,** where Dr. Curtis Howe Springer, a radio evangelist and health-food vendor, developed a health resort for refugees from Los Angeles's Skid Row. After 30 years of tending the urban ill free of charge, the Springers were suddenly evicted by

Palm Springs

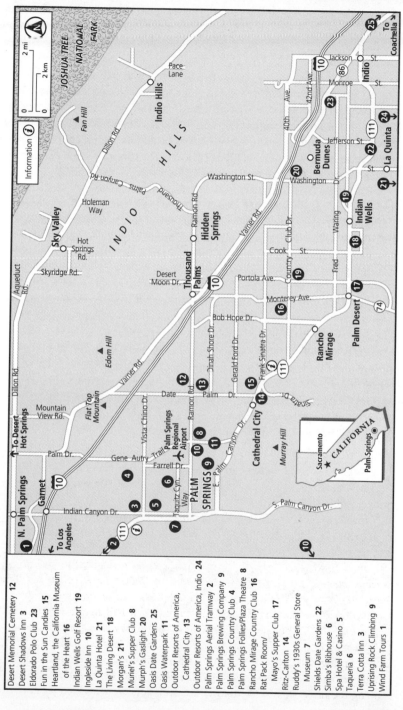

Desert Memorial Cemetery **12**
Desert Shadows Inn **3**
Eldorado Polo Club **23**
Fun in the Sun Candies **15**
Heartland, the California Museum of the Heart **16**
Indian Wells Golf Resort **19**
Ingleside Inn **10**
La Quinta Hotel **21**
The Living Desert **18**
Morgan's **21**
Muriel's Supper Club **8**
Murph's Gaslight **20**
Oasis Date Gardens **25**
Oasis Waterpark **11**
Outdoor Resorts of America, Cathedral City **13**
Outdoor Resorts of America, Indio **24**
Palm Springs Aerial Tramway **2**
Palm Springs Brewing Company **9**
Palm Springs Country Club **4**
Palm Springs Follies/Plaza Theatre **8**
Rancho Mirage Country Club **16**
Rat Pack Room/ Mayo's Supper Club **17**
Ritz-Carlton **14**
Ruddy's 1930s General Store Museum **7**
Shields Date Gardens **22**
Simba's Ribhouse **6**
Spa Hotel & Casino **5**
Taqueria **6**
Terra Cotta Inn **3**
Uprising Rock Climbing **9**
Wind Farm Tours **1**

the Bureau of Land Management in the 1970s for trespassing. The site, which was nearly destroyed by vandals over the years, was rescued and restored not long ago by the California Desert Studies Consortium, which welcomes visitors.

At nearby **Nipton** (pop. 26), the four-room **Hotel Nipton,** 107–355 Nipton Rd. (☎ **760/856-2335;** rooms from $60), recalls the days when silent film star Clara Bow and cowboy-actor husband Rex Bell had a ranch nearby. An outdoor hot tub lets you soak under the stars while listening to the whistle of a passing freight train. Nipton is about 70 miles from Las Vegas near the California-Nevada border. Take I-15 east to Nipton Road. Continue for 10.1 miles to the railroad tracks, then make a right to the hotel.

Joshua Tree National Park is a wonderland of bizarre boulders and glorious gardens of cactus ideally visited by RVers who can tent or stay overnight in a self-contained recreational vehicle; there are no hookups or water available. At all but two of the park's campgrounds (Cottonwood and Black Rock Canyon), campers must bring in all the water and firewood they plan to use, and toilet facilities are primitive. Jumbo Rocks, our favorite campground, is also a top draw for rock climbers. (See "Campground Oases in the Mojave Desert," below, for details.) Joshua Tree is one of the world's most popular climbing areas, with more than 3,500 climbing spots for every degree of ability (www.nps.gov/jotr).

Parts of the park still bear scars from four lightning-ignited fires that swept through during the 1999 Memorial Day weekend, the largest wildfire in the park's history. The 13,894 acres damaged by the fires are in the park's northwestern corner, between the West Entrance Station past Hidden Valley Campground to Ryan Campground and Keys View road and a smaller area around Covington Flat off the main roadways.

Calico in the late afternoon sun.

JOSHUA TREE CAMPSITE TIP

If you visit Joshua Tree in early to mid-winter or on a weekday, you'll be able to choose a great site on a first-come, first-served basis, but if you arrive on weekends or during the prime rock-climbing season in early spring, you'll have to take any vacancy you can find. See "Campground Oases in the Mojave Desert," below, for campground listings.

Cottonwood Visitor Center is 7 miles north of the Joshua Tree National Park exit from I-10 (☎ 760/367-7511; www.nps.gov/jotr).

While vehicles of all sorts can negotiate the main roads in the park, four-wheel-drive vehicles, motorcycles, and bicycles are best for exploring unpaved roads. Rules require all bicycles and motor vehicles to stay on established roadways. Good **backcountry roads** include Pinkham Canyon Road, 20 miles from Cottonwood Visitor Center to an I-10 service road; Covington Flats, which accesses some of the best Joshua tree stands, 4 miles from Covington Flats picnic area to Eureka Peak; Geology Tour Road, 5.4 miles from Jumbo Rocks to Squaw Tank; or Black Eagle Mine Road, up through the canyons in the Eagle Mountains. Alert freewheelers may spot roadrunners, coyotes, kangaroo rats, golden eagles, and sidewinders.

Birders will find good watching at Cottonwood Spring, while photographers and wildflower enthusiasts will want to walk Lost Palms Oasis Trail in early spring to find dozens of native desert wildflowers.

The **General Patton Memorial Museum** at 2 Chiriaco Rd. in Chiriaco Summit, a marked exit just off I-10 about 50 miles east of Palm Springs, is built on the site of Camp Young, the World War II desert training center. While you won't see George C. Scott lurking around in his Patton uniform, you will see memorabilia, boots, and saddles, and plenty of tanks and war film footage. Open daily 9:30am to 4:30pm; $4 adults, $3.50 seniors, under 12 free (☎ 760/227-3483).

Campground Oases in the Mojave Desert

Black Rock Campground. Located at the northern end of Joshua Tree National Park, Black Rock Campground has 100 sites with piped water and flush toilets. Sanitary dump available. $10 for RVs up to 32 feet long. Good hiking. Open October to May only. Take I-10 east to Highway 62 east to Yucca Valley. Turn right on Joshua Lane. Follow signs 5 miles to the campground (☎ 800/365-CAMP for reservations; www.nps.gov/jotr).

Jumbo Rocks Campground. Located in the middle of Joshua Tree National Park near Twentynine Palms, Jumbo Rocks Campground has 125 sites, pit toilets, some evening ranger programs, and rock climbing (sites are surrounded by huge boulders). No hookups, no water, no fee. It's easiest to find space in winter when nights are nippy; early spring weekends are chock-ablock with rock climbers and desert flower photographers. Take Highway 62 to Park Boulevard exit. Enter at west entrance. Continue for 23 miles to campground. Call ☎ **760/367-5525** (www.joshuatree.org) to contact the Joshua Tree National Park Association, an educational support group.

Calico Ghost Town. This San Bernardino County campground, located in the canyons just steps from the commercialized but genuine silver mining town of Calico, near Baker, has 220 sites, 46 with full hookups (30- and 50-amp), some grills, picnic tables, showers, flush toilets, and sanitary dump. Up to $22 a night with hookups. Reservations essential on weekends (☎ **760/254-2122;** www.calicotown.com). Take Calico exit off I-15 between Barstow and Yermo. There are restaurants, shops, and attractions in Calico, and groceries, propane, and laundry facilities nearby. Families with children, ghost town collectors, and rock hounds will especially like the area.

Saddleback Butte State Park. Located off Highway 14, 17 miles east of Lancaster; use Avenue J turnoff. Once called Joshua Tree State Park, it has well-preserved stands of Joshua trees, rocky buttes, and excellent hiking trails. Fifty sites accommodate self-contained RVs up to 30 feet and have piped water, flush toilets, and a sanitary dump, but no hookups. No reservations except for groups. $10. (☎ **661/942-0662;** www.calparksmojave.com).

Red Rock Canyon State Park. Red Rock Canyon park has 50 primitive sites with no hookups. Water and sanitary dump available. No reservations. Ranger campfire programs in summer and fall, hiking trails, dramatic geologic formations, and archaeological displays at visitor center are available. Expect occasional winter snowfalls, cool to cold nights, and nesting falcons, hawks, owls in spring. Take Highway 14 for 25 miles. The turnoff to the campground is well marked (☎ **661/942-0662;** www.calparksmojave.com).

Campground Oases Around Los Angeles & Elsewhere

East Shore RV Park. East Shore RV Park, in San Dimas, is perched atop a hill overlooking Pomona's Fairplex, site of the Los Angeles County Fair, with cool breezes even on the hottest days. Large, grassy sites, mature shade trees, and some lakefront locations make East Shore a reliable getaway year-round. Reserve ahead, especially on weekends or holidays, by calling ☎ **800/809-3778.** Exit I-10 via Fairplex Drive and follow the signs.

Malibu Beach RV Park. Located on Pacific Coast Highway in Malibu, Malibu Beach RV Park overlooks the sea, and the beach is only a short walk downhill and across the road from your campsite. In winter, you may see whales migrating along the coast. Sites are small but the views are great (☎ **800/ 622-6052** for reservations; www.maliburv.com).

Valencia Travel Village. Valencia Travel Village, on Route 126 off I-5 north of Los Angeles near Magic Mountain, has 250 sites, cable and satellite TV, and offers shade trees, swimming pools, a large convenience store, and a quiet, convenient location less than an hour from Los Angeles (☎ **888/ 588-8678** or 661/257-3333 for reservations; www.valenciatravelvillage.com).

Orange Grove RV Park. Off Highway 58 east of Bakersfield at Edison Road, 122 sites are nestled in an orange grove, with pick-your-own privileges, a pool, recreation room with big-screen TV, playground, country store, hot showers, air-conditioned restrooms, cable TV, laundry, propane. $23 a night (☎ 800/553-7126; www.orangegrovervpark.com). Nearby: Bakersfield's famous Basque restaurants.

DEATH VALLEY NATIONAL PARK

If publicists had been around during wagon train days, Death Valley would have been named Golden Sands or Shimmering Haze. Instead, it took nearly a century to shake off the bad-mouthing the pioneers gave it. It wasn't until stalwart, sincere Ronald Reagan brought TV's *Death Valley Days* into our living rooms that it became a tourist destination.

Now, as a national park with an additional 1.3 million acres, it's busy even in summer, when European tourists flock here to experience the hottest, driest, lowest, loneliest, and so on.

Tent campers and self-contained RVs (no hookups available) will find comfortable spots to spend a winter weekend at **Furnace Creek Campground,** which has shade trees and some privacy, flush toilets, hot showers, and dump station. (See "Campground Oases in & Around Death Valley National Park," below.) Bigger, less attractive camping areas include **Stovepipe Wells** and **Sunset Campground** (☎ 800/365-2267), near the **Furnace Creek Visitors Area,** Highway 190, 30 miles east of Death Valley Junction at State Road 127 at Highway 190 (☎ 760/786-3244; www.nps.gov/deva).

Bicyclists can tour the mostly flat terrain of Death Valley quite comfortably in winter. Rain is rare, but winds can come up to hinder your progress. Use touring bikes on paved roads, mountain bikes on sandy or rocky routes. The 13-mile, paved **Artists Palette Road** is particularly scenic—a winding, narrow one-way with a lot of up and down. A 9-mile paved route from Furnace Creek to Zabriskie Point is best at daybreak, but a 7-mile loop to the sand dunes from Stovepipe Wells is easy any time of day.

Campground Oases in & Around Death Valley National Park

Furnace Creek Campground. Located in the community of Furnace Creek in Death Valley, the grounds have 136 sites, most large enough for an RV, at $16 a night. Spacious campsites look across open desert terrain. No hookups, but flush toilets, hot showers, fire grates, drinking water and sanitary disposal station, general store, restaurant, and propane available nearby. Get there early on winter weekends or holidays or you'll be banished to the overflow campground across the road, which has much less ambience. Take Highway 190 to Furnace Creek Visitors Center; the campgrounds are less than a mile north of the center (☎ 800/365-2267).

Boulder Creek RV Resort. At 2550 S. Highway 395, a few miles south of Lone Pine, this handsome modern campground has campsite views toward Mount Whitney and makes a great year-round stop for travelers driving to

<u>COYOTE TIP</u>

Keep an eye out for the bandit coyotes of Stovepipe Wells, a trio (when we last visited) of brazen animals that come out at midday alongside the highway to stop traffic in hopes of scrounging food handouts. Don't encourage them by giving them food or the rangers will banish them to the far-off regions of the park.

Death Valley or Yosemite. Buffet breakfasts and dinners are available on occasion. It's the RV headquarters for the Lone Pine Film Festival every October, saluting the Western films shot in Lone Pine's scenic Alabama Hills (☎ 800/648-8965 for reservations; www.395.com/bouldercreek).

LAS VEGAS

Las Vegas welcomed 30.6 million visitors in 1998, issued 1.2 million marriage licenses, and raked in $5 billion in gross gambling revenue, representing an average gambling budget of $469 per person per trip—and for that very reason, we always feel a little guilty about the place because if it were anywhere else and financed by any other activity, its eccentric, over-the-top architecture would bring us joy and delight. But gambling holds no appeal for us, hotel pyrotechnics and gee-whiz magic shows leave us cold, and huge buffets, however cheap, fail to tempt our palates. We liked it a little better back in the days when people dressed to go to shows and restaurants rather than donning shorts and tank tops or jogging suits and shoes.

New York, New York Hotel, Las Vegas.

The average nightly room rate in Las Vegas makes the typical RV camp-ground hookup site look like a real bargain. Plus, by visiting Vegas in your own RV you can come home to peace and quiet rather than crossing a jan-gling hotel lobby casino filled with secondhand smoke.

Because Las Vegas traffic is heavy on the under-reconstruction I-15, the traffic-clogged downtown, and the often-gridlocked strip, RVers will proba-bly want to leave their rigs on hookup IVs in the campground and commute by city bus, casino shuttle, towed car, or rental car (some campgrounds—Las Vegas KOA, for instance—have car rentals available on the premises). Shuttle buses are provided by the campgrounds and/or casinos. Hours vary, but some run all night. Inquire locally.

Las Vegas Hotel Casinos

Since you're in your RV and don't need a hotel room, you're free to wander along the Strip and enjoy the fantasy venues. In addition to those we've listed below, an imaginative company was planning, pending zoning approval, a **Titanic Resort** to be built in the shape of the tragic luxury liner (but twice the size) with a 1,800-seat showroom encased in an iceberg. We'll see.

- **Bellagio** is lush and lavish, with an art gallery starring millions of dollars worth of masterpieces by such artists as Monet, van Gogh, and Picasso; a glassed-in garden conservatory; a stunning blown-glass chandelier centerpiece by Dale Chihuly; and 1,200 fountains splashing to synchro-nized classical music.

- **The Venetian** offers gondola rides along a canal in a Venice replica, complete with singing gondolier.

- **New York, New York** has the Manhattan Express roller coaster that zips you around past the Statue of Liberty and the city skyline.

- **The Las Vegas Hilton Star Trek Experience** offers a future fantasy that includes being beamed up into the starship *Enterprise* to blast across the galaxies and battle the Klingons in the 24th century. You can even arrange a wedding ceremony on the spaceship's bridge with a couple of Star Trek characters for witnesses.

- **Circus Circus** is roller coaster heaven, with the world's only indoor, double loop, double corkscrew coaster and an unlimited-rides wrist-band admission.

- **Stratosphere Tower,** the tallest free-standing observation tower in the United States at 1,149 feet, offers a thrill ride to the top. In daytime you get a panoramic view of the desert, at night the bright lights of Vegas.

- **Rio** has a free Mardi Gras parade daily. You can also don a costume and ride a float for only $10.

- **Treasure Island** has a free Mutiny Bay pirate battle with sailing ships, pirates, and firing cannons every 90 minutes from 4 until 10pm, later on weekends.

- **Paris** presents the Eiffel Tower, L'Opera, the back streets of old Paree, and a pop-rock version of *The Hunchback of Notre Dame.*

- **Mirage** has an erupting volcano that spews nightly every 15 minutes from 6pm to midnight. Feel the blast when the volcano erupts, with flames leaping into the air.

- **The Mandalay Bay Resort and Casino** has a sandy beach—but it's open only to hotel guests.

- **Luxor** features the Sphinx, a glass pyramid, and King Tut's tomb, just like Howard Carter found it in 1922, along with an IMAX theater.

Off-the-Wall Las Vegas

The Liberace Museum displays a king's ransom in sweetly innocent rhinestone-beaded capes, piano-shaped knickknacks, ornately gilded bibelots, mirror-covered pianos, and one-of-a-kind decorated automobiles. "Donations" to enter (their phrasing) are $6.95 adults, $4.95 seniors and students, and $2 children 6 to 12. The museum is at 1775 E. Tropicana (☎ **702/798-5595;** www.liberace.org).

The **Elvis-a-Rama Museum** displays $3 million in artifacts and memorabilia, including a 1955 Cadillac limousine, the King's winter dress army uniform, his Social Security card, a peacock jumpsuit, his customized purple Lincoln, and a whole lot of shakin' goin' on in interactive games and concert clips. It's open daily from 9am to 7pm at 3401 Industrial Rd., 1 block off the Strip via Spring Mountain Road (☎ **702/309-7200;** elvisarama.com). Admission: $9.95 adults, $7.95 seniors, residents, and students, free for children under 12.

Luxor Hotel, Las Vegas.

Las Vegas

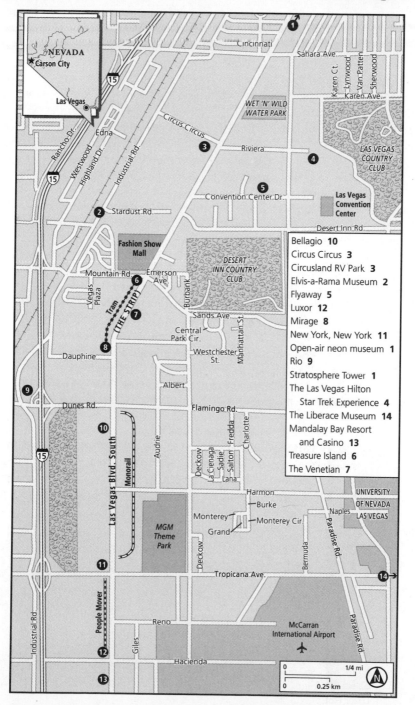

NEVADA
Carson City
Las Vegas

Cincinnati

Sahara Ave.

Karen Ct.
Lynwood
Van Patten
Sherwood
Karen Ave.

WET 'N' WILD
WATER PARK

LAS VEGAS
COUNTRY
CLUB

Circus Circus

Riviera

Edna

Rancho Dr.
Westwood
Highland Dr.
Industrial Rd.

Convention Center Dr.

Las Vegas
Convention
Center

Stardust Rd.

Desert Inn Rd.

Fashion Show
Mall

DESERT
INN COUNTRY
CLUB

Mountain Rd.

Emerson
Ave.

Burbank

Bellagio **10**
Circus Circus **3**
Circusland RV Park **3**
Elvis-a-Rama Museum **2**
Flyaway **5**
Luxor **12**
Mirage **8**
New York, New York **11**
Open-air neon museum **1**
Rio **9**
Stratosphere Tower **1**
The Las Vegas Hilton
 Star Trek Experience **4**
The Liberace Museum **14**
Mandalay Bay Resort
 and Casino **13**
Treasure Island **6**
The Venetian **7**

Vegas
Plaza

Tram
(THE STRIP)

Sands Ave.

Manhattan St.

Central
Park Cir.

Dauphine

Westchester
St.

Albert

Dunes Rd.

Flamingo Rd.

Fredda

Charlotte

Las Vegas Blvd. South

Monorail

Audrie

Deckow
La Cienaga
Sadie
Salton
Lana

Harmon

Burke

UNIVERSITY
OF NEVADA
LAS VEGAS

Monterey
Grand

Monterey Cir.

Naples

Paradise Rd.

MGM
Theme
Park

Deckow

Bermuda

People Mover

Tropicana Ave.

Industrial Rd.

Reno

Giles

McCarran
International Airport

Paradise Rd.

Hacienda

0   1/4 mi
0   0.25 km

N

Ethel M Chocolates fulfills that childhood fantasy of touring a chocolate factory, then getting to pick out a free sample. The tour is self-guided and free, both in the chocolate factory and in the adjacent cactus gardens. The factory is open daily from 8:30am to 7pm with spacious parking lots able to handle RVs easily. Take exit 64 at Sunset Road to the junction with Mountain Vista Street and follow the signs (☎ 888/627-0990; www.ethelm.com).

The **open-air neon museum,** best seen at night, preserves the vintage signs that no longer have a hotel to cling to—Chief Hotel Court from 1940, The Flame from 1961, Aladdin's Lamp from 1966, the Hacienda horse and rider of 1967, and dairy mascot Andy Anderson from 1956. Other signs are in the process of being restored; look for them near the Fremont Street Experience between 4th Street and Las Vegas Boulevard.

The **Clark County Heritage Museum** shelters indoor and outdoor collections of railway cars, vintage furnished bungalows from the 1930s and 1940s, ranching displays, and a ghost town. It's at 1830 S. Boulder Hwy. in Henderson, just north of where Highway 582 meets Route 93/95, with plenty of RV parking space. Open daily from 9am to 4:30pm, the museum charges $1.50 adults, $1 children and seniors (☎ 702/455-7955).

You can fly like Peter Pan without the wires, like a full-sized Tinkerbell, at **Flyaway.** You go into a chamber where a covered and protected airplane engine is mounted below a grid floor, then flap about suspended in the vertical blast of air. Prices begin at $45; it takes 20 minutes of instruction to train, then you can fly. Your height and weight must be in proportion. Open daily at 200 Convention Center Dr. near the Stardust (☎ 702/731-4768; www. flyawayindoorskydiving.com).

Campground Oases in & Around Las Vegas

Circusland RV Park. Located behind Circus Circus Casino, Circusland is the only RV park on the Strip, but with so much construction and renovation going on, you can't expect much peace and quiet. The 384 spaces are served with 30- and 50-amp electric (you'll need it in summer for the air-conditioning), a swimming pool, sauna, and hot tub (☎ 800/444-CIRCUS or 702/734-0410 for reservations; www.circuscircus-lasvegas.com).

Las Vegas KOA. Located away from the casino noise at 4315 Boulder Hwy., off Route 93/95 at exit 170, the Las Vegas KOA is a busy year-round park with a lot of pavement, which makes a hot day seem even hotter, but it's courteously run with frequent shuttle service to the Strip. Rental cars are available. Rates are on the high side ($30–$35 for two adults with hookup; ☎ 800/KOA-7782 for reservations; www.koa.com).

Primadonna RV Village. 35 miles south of Las Vegas on I-15, adjacent to Buffalo Bill's and Whiskey Pete's Casinos at the California-Nevada border in Primm Valley. Essentially a paved parking lot with hookups, the RV park is only steps from these two casinos, a roller coaster, Fashion Outlet mall, and two 18-hole championship golf courses, and is only 35 miles from Las Vegas.

With 198 30- and 50-amp hookups, 24-hour security, showers, dump, heated pool, and spa, it's a bargain stopover at $12 or so. Just don't expect a quiet, scenic state park (☎ **800/FUN-STOP** for reservations; www. primmvalleyresorts.com).

Campground Oases in Laughlin, Needles & Bullhead City

Riverside RV Park. Riverside RV Park in Laughlin is another huge parking lot RV park with 900 full hookup sites (30-amp electric). There's a 24-hour shuttle to the Riverside Resort Casino, but advance reservations are required. Located at 1650 Casino Dr., Laughlin (☎ **800/227-3849**).

Bullhead City, Arizona. Bullhead has a number of RV parks across the river from Laughlin with a little less flash and noise and a lovely distant view of the bright lights from the casinos. Three good choices: **Fishermen's Trailer Lodge,** on the river at 491 Moser St. off Route 95 (☎ **520/754-3846**); **Silver Creek RV Park** at 1515 Gold Rush Dr. off Route 95 (☎ **520/763-2444**); and **Bullhead RV Park,** 3 miles south of the junction of highways 95 and 68 on 95 (☎ **520/763-8353**).

Needles KOA Kampground. This park bills itself as the closest KOA to Laughlin, Nevada. It's at I-40 and the West Broadway River Road exit, then north a half mile on Old Trails Highway. Some 81 of the 95 sites are pull-throughs, and there are some 50-amp hookups, so it's definitely a big-rig-friendly campground. In winter, the Cactus Kafe serves meals for times you don't feel like cooking (☎ **800/562-3407** for reservations; www.koa.com); average price around $24.

Ten Scenic Side Trips

1. **The California poppy trail** (about 50 miles). When the winter has the right amount of rain, early spring looks like Dorothy's dream in *The Wizard of Oz,* except the poppies are orange instead of red. Drive California 138 between Gorman and Lancaster, turning south on Avenue I to the Antelope Valley California Poppy Reserve (☎ **805/ 724-1180;** www.totalescape.com/active/leisure/wildflwr.html). While there's an admission fee, you may, as we did one year, see more poppies in bloom along the roadsides than in the reserve itself. Call ahead to determine bloom time, usually best March through May.

2. **The Alabama Hills Loop, Lone Pine** (about 10 miles, unpaved). Make a circle through this wacky terrain where countless good guys in white hats have headed off bad guys at endless passes, not to mention where Cary Grant's 1939 classic *Gunga Din,* Humphrey Bogart's *High Sierra,* and James Stewart et al's *How the West Was Won* were shot. The rounded, sculpted outcroppings that resemble animals, castles, temples, and skyscrapers are best viewed in early morning or late afternoon. If you leave signposted Movie Road, pay attention to your route or you could

get lost forever in this weird place. North of Lone Pine off Highway 395. Contact Lone Pine Chamber of Commerce (☎ **760/876-4444;** fax 760/876-9205; www.cris.com/lpcc).

3. **The road to Bodie** (13 miles, some of it unpaved). Bodie was one of the rip-roaringest gold towns in California, with some 12,000 residents in its heyday between 1876 and 1880. Today the remaining houses, school, and mines exist in a state of arrested decay preserved by the state park system. Schoolbooks lie open on wooden desks and rusting tins of food line the grocery store shelves. It's best not to attempt the road in bad weather, since the last 3 miles become a dirt washboard road. Best time to go is summer or early fall. Take Highway 270 east off U.S. 395, 7 miles south of Bridgeport. Bodie State Historic Park (☎ **760/647-6445;** www.ceres.ca.gov/sierradsp/bodie.html).

4. **The bristlecone pine forest.** From late June through October, a narrow, winding road is often (but not always) open to an enclave of the world's oldest living creatures, the oldest more than 4,300 years old. The tough, twisted trees have only a few limbs but sturdy trunks that grow about an inch a century. From U.S. 395 at Big Pine, turn east on Route 168; a sign will be posted within half a mile that will tell you whether the 25-mile road to the trees is open. If you're in a motor home or towing a travel trailer, you should go no farther than Schulman Grove, where the pavement ends. From here, a ranger station offers maps and self-guided walking trails leading into the pines. Call Inyo National Forest in Bishop (☎ **760/873-2500;** www.thesierraweb.com).

5. **Along the Salton Sea** (41 miles plus side trips). From Niland to the evocatively named Mecca, Route 111 skirts the Salton Sea National Wildlife Refuge, great for spotting Canada geese, snowy egrets, snow geese, and pelicans, with an occasional glimpse of the endangered Yuma clapper rail. Thousands of migratory birds winter here, filling the air with noise as they chatter or argue back and forth. You'll have to leave the main road at marked intervals and proceed on short, sometimes rough, unpaved stretches to the observation areas. Salton Sea National Wildlife Refuge (☎ **760/348-5278**).

6. **The desert rat's road to Randsburg.** This offbeat mining town never quite became a ghost town, and today still has a small but hardy population, a museum, and some antiques shops. The Hard Rock Cafe is a piker compared to the Hard Rock Dinner in the town's museum—eggs, pie, sausage, cauliflower, potatoes, even (yes!) hamburgers—all of it actually natural rocks and minerals that just look like food. You can swing 5 miles northeast of California City (itself about 10 miles from Highway 14 at the California City exit), following Randsburg Mojave Road to the marked entrance, 5.5 miles from town, to pay homage to

the endangered desert tortoise at a 38-square-mile sanctuary. The best time for sightings is mid-March to mid-June.

A loop of roughly 100 miles from the Lancaster area on Route 14 could include Red Rock Canyon State Park and Mojave Airport, with its huge grounded fleet of resting or retired jets from commercial airlines near the junction of highways 14 and 58. The town of Mojave was also the terminus of the 20-mule-team borax wagons from Death Valley. Randsburg "Living" Ghost Town (www.randsburg.com).

7. **Along the Lower Colorado River.** A 150-mile loop from Needles can snare you a camping, gaming, and watersports excursion. First go north by U.S. 95 and Route 163 to bustling Laughlin, Nevada, where every casino welcomes RVers. Then head south on State Road 95 via Oatman, Arizona, on old Route 66, where wild burros roam the colorful main street. Farther south is Lake Havasu City, Arizona, where London Bridge spans the Colorado. Go west again on Parker Dam Road to Route 62 into Earp, a minuscule California desert town where the famous marshal retired to try his hand at mining instead of shooting.

8. **The Barstow Triangle.** Despite certain similarities to the more infamous Bermuda Triangle, you won't have to worry about dropping out of sight here so long as you stay off the desert's back roads. Start in the town of Barstow and its Desert Information Center, on Barstow Road between Virginia Way and Kelly Drive (☎ 760/256-8617), for a quick read of the Mojave Desert, then check out the Barstow Station, the ultimate curiosity shop built in and around a 1900s railway station. Head east on I-15 to Yermo and the thriving ghost town of Calico (see "Campground Oases in the Mojave Desert," earlier in this chapter), where mining lore shares the spotlight with archaeology and the Early Man site excavated by Dr. Louis Leakey. A few miles east of Barstow on I-40 is the 1860s town of Daggett where you can take a self-guided walking tour. Then head west on Route 58 into the triangle, brushing Edwards Air Force Base (where space shuttles often land—and some say UFOs as well) at Four Corners before dropping south to Victorville and the ever-popular Roy Rogers/Dale Evans Museum. (For more about the Roy Rogers Museum and Barstow Station, see "Off-the-Wall Attractions," earlier in this chapter) Barstow/Mojave Desert Convention and Visitors. (☎ 760/253-4782; www.visitmojavedesert.com). Roy Rogers Museum (☎ 760/243-4547).

9. **The I-8 to Yuma.** The 171 miles between San Diego and the California-Arizona border could whiz by in a blur, but not if you take these detours: Desert View Tower at the In-Ko-Pah Park Road exit near Jacumba gives you a great view of what's ahead, plus some eccentric carved stone animals lining the trail; Calexico, separated by a fence

from its Mexican neighbor Mexicali, is mysteriously chockablock with Chinese restaurants; and the Imperial Sand Dunes Recreation Area, where retakes of the film *Lawrence of Arabia* were shot, draws off-road-vehicle types between October and May. Allow some sightseeing time for the Yuma Territorial Prison, now a state park but once "the hellhole of Arizona." Imperial Sand Dunes, Yuma County Chamber of Commerce (☎ 520/782-2567).

10. **East Mojave National Scenic Area.** This "wannabe" failed to get full national park honors in the recently passed California Desert Protection Act, ending up with a "preserve" status, a designation lobbied for by the National Rifle Association because it will allow hunting to continue in this 1.2-million-acre high desert reserve. Cattle grazing, as well, will go on. In Kelso, visit the singing dunes—the sand you dislodge when you walk on a dune makes moaning and humming sounds as it slides. Head north from Kelso on Kelbaker Road to see the cinder cones and lava beds where astronauts trained for the 1969 moon landing. When you join I-40, drive east to the Essex Road exit, then north 16 miles to Mitchell Caverns in Providence Mountain State Recreation Area, where rangers lead tours into the caves and self-contained camping is available. North on Black Canyon Road, Mid Hills and Hole-in-the-Wall campgrounds, with 63 sites between them, are connected by 11-mile Wild Horse Canyon Road, a scenic unpaved backcountry byway. Mojave National Preserve, Barstow (☎ 760/733-4040).

Utah's Parks & Canyons

UTAH CONTAINS FIVE NATIONAL PARKS, SEVEN NATIONAL MONUMENTS, seven national forests, two national recreational areas, one national historic site, and forty-five state parks.

Utah is where Butch Cassidy and Etta Place rode a bicycle in *Butch Cassidy and the Sundance Kid,* where Thelma and Louise drove off the cliff into the canyon, and where Max von Sydow delivered the Sermon on the Mount in *The Greatest Story Ever Told.*

It's where the California gull is the state bird, the world's most famous automobile commercial was filmed, and Brigham Young took his 27th wife.

America's first department store was unveiled in Salt Lake City in 1868, Philo T. Farnsworth (the inventor of television) was born in Beaver in 1906, and the first licensed franchise for Kentucky Fried Chicken—still serving up finger-lickin' chicken today—is located on State Street in Salt Lake City.

Mountain man Jim Bridger tasted the waters of the Great Salt Lake and thought he'd reached the Pacific; mountain man Robert Redford, shooting the film *Jeremiah Johnson,* sniffed the clear, clean air of the Wasatch Mountains and thought he'd reached Nirvana; and countless wandering hobos dreamed of licking the Big Rock Candy Mountain.

"This is the most beautiful place on earth."
—Edward Abbey,
Desert Solitaire, 1968

Early tourists flocked to take the waters at Schneitter's Hot Pots, later turned into The Homestead Resort, and to gawk at the wild man of Borneo, a pair of Siamese twins, and an alligator pit at the fantasy towers of Saltair, the Coney Island of Salt Lake, whose ghost pavilion still lurks off I-80 some 17 miles west of Salt Lake City.

This is where dinosaurs roamed 500 million years ago, where the Anasazi, or Ancient Ones, planted corn 2,000 years ago, and where Chinese miners

Utah Highlights

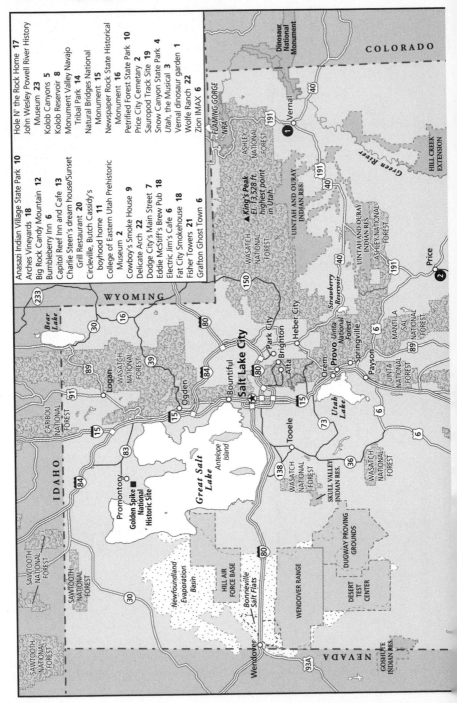

Anasazi Indian Village State Park **10**
Arches Vineyards **18**
Big Rock Candy Mountain **12**
Bumbleberry Inn **6**
Capitol Reef Inn and Cafe **13**
Charlie Steen's dream house/Sunset
    Grill Restaurant **20**
Circleville, Butch Cassidy's
    boyhood home **11**
College of Eastern Utah Prehistoric
    Museum **2**
Cowboy's Smoke House **9**
Delicate Arch **22**
Dodge City's Main Street **7**
Eddie McStiff's Brew Pub **18**
Electric Jim's Cafe **6**
Fat City Smokehouse **18**
Fisher Towers **21**
Grafton Ghost Town **6**

Hole N' the Rock Home **17**
John Wesley Powell River History
    Museum **23**
Kolob Canyons **5**
Kolob Reservoir **8**
Monument Valley Navajo
    Tribal Park **14**
Natural Bridges National
    Monument **15**
Newspaper Rock State Historical
    Monument **16**
Petrified Forest State Park **10**
Price City Cemetary **2**
Sauropod Track Site **19**
Snow Canyon State Park **4**
Utah, the Musical **3**
Vernal dinosaur garden **1**
Wolfe Ranch **22**
Zion IMAX **6**

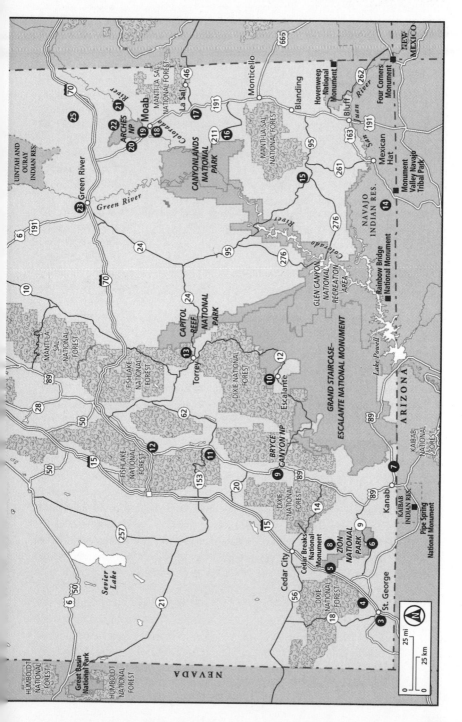

Countryside around Zion National Park.

at Silver Reef put food on family graves a century ago (giving local Paiutes a taste for Chinese cuisine).

Utah has the highest literacy rate, largest average household size, second highest birth rate, and second lowest death rate in the 50 states. More than 70% of the state's population are members of the Church of Jesus Christ of Latter-day Saints, also known as Mormons.

THE MORMONS

In the spring of 1830, Joseph Smith, a devout young man in Fayette, New York, published the Book of Mormon and founded the Church of Jesus Christ of Latter-day Saints, a charismatic religion claiming to be a restoration of the original church. Among its tenets were polygamy and an active program of proselytism, neither of which found favor in the neighborhood.

Chased from New York and then Ohio, Smith and his followers settled in Nauvoo, Missouri, where they developed a city of 20,000. But the new neighbors were no more hospitable than the old ones, burning and killing until Smith decided in 1844 it was time to move again. In the meantime, however, he declared himself a candidate for president of the United States and said that if elected he would not move West.

> *"This is the right place!"*
> —Brigham Young in 1847, on first seeing Salt Lake Valley

When members of the church smashed a printing press they believed was publishing libel against them, Smith and his brother were jailed, then taken from prison by a mob and killed.

The man who succeeded Smith as church leader was Brigham Young. At the end of 1845, when the state of Illinois repealed the city charter for Nauvoo, he organized an advance party to go West looking for a new settlement. Beginning in early 1846, church members loaded their goods onto covered wagons, hitched up their horses, and led them down to ferries on the Mississippi River. The great Mormon exodus had begun.

That year they got as far as Iowa. Then, on July 24, 1847, Brigham Young and his pioneers entered the Salt Lake Valley. The migration continued, with thousands of the devout literally walking and pulling their possessions in handcarts, until by 1900 the Mormons had established 500 settlements in and around Utah, many of them in arid, inhospitable desert.

Certainly the most dramatic moment was at Hole-in-the-Rock in 1879, when 230 Mormons blasted a hole through a 50-foot cliff at Glen Canyon and lowered their 80 wagons by chains and ropes to the river 1,800 feet below, where homemade rafts waited. They went on to found the town of Bluff, which today claims a population of 250—20 more than its founding fathers. Today boaters and four-wheel-drive travelers can see the spot where the hole was blasted in the rock.

The Mormon cause was severely set back in 1857 when some xenophobic members, fearful of federal interference and anxious to keep out both miners and eager new settlers, triggered the infamous Mountain Meadows Massacre, where Mormon militia members and local Indians slaughtered 120 of the 137-member Fancher wagon train party bound for California. The only survivors were 17 children under the age of 7. A marker off Route 18 near the town of Central in southwestern Utah identifies the massacre site.

It took almost 50 years and the church's outlawing of polygamy before Utah achieved statehood in 1896.

RVing Utah's National Park Country

Early on an October morning, the snowcapped Henry Mountains glisten against a blue sky. Down every wash, a stalwart line of cottonwoods has turned a glowing gold. Flocks of tiny Berwick's wrens, exuberant after the rain, flutter up past our windshield and across the Bicentennial Highway. Water shines from holes and grooves in slickrock, and snow dusts the red mesas and buttes and throws twisted black junipers into sharp relief. As we begin to climb toward Natural Bridges National Monument, the whole desert forest of piñon pines and sagebrush is covered with puffy white clumps of snow. Everything is breathtakingly beautiful.

Because so much of Utah is public land, it makes an ideal getaway for RVers, especially those who enjoy self-contained camping in parklands and the wilderness. Driving through the state, we always imagine the pioneers and early Mormon settlers moving through the eerie terrain with plenty of time on their hands and a little creative daydreaming. It's the only way some of the geological landmarks could have been named. We stare at spots like Capitol Reef's Capitol Dome or Zion's Great White Throne and wonder who could have thought that particular rock really looks like a dome or a throne.

The state tourism people have divided southern Utah into four different areas—**Color Country** in the south central and southwest, including Zion and Bryce Canyon National Parks; **Canyonlands** to the southeast, including Canyonlands and Arches National Parks; **Panoramaland** in the west central region, including Capitol Reef National Park; and **Castle Country** in the east central sector, the terrain where Butch Cassidy used to ride.

Northern Utah is divided into **Golden Spike Empire,** named for the spot where the first transcontinental railroad was finished in 1869, the extreme northwest corner reaching from the Nevada border east to Ogden; **Bridgerland,** named for mountain man Jim Bridger, the northeastern corner surrounding Logan; **Great Salt Lake Country,** which includes Great Salt Lake, the Bonneville Salt Flats, and Salt Lake City; **Mountainland,** with Utah's best ski country and Sundance Resort; and **Dinosaurland,** notable for dinosaur digs, Green River rafting, and dude ranches. You'll need to remember the divisions when using the state travel guides.

One of the newest recreation areas in Utah is **Grand Staircase–Escalante** National Monument, the first to be administered by the Bureau of Land Management instead of the National Park Service. Gateways to the new national monument are Escalante and Boulder on Route 12 and Kanab on Route 89, in the south central area of Utah. With world-class paleontological sites and a panoramic geologic sampler, Escalante attracts adventuresome hikers and four-wheel-drive explorers. Few services and facilities are available yet inside the monument.

I-70 is the only paved road accessing the spectacular scenery of the **San Rafael Swell,** Utah's most inaccessible wilderness area. We've done the drive in both directions, and strongly urge you to go west to east for the most dramatic impact. There are numerous scenic turnouts on the 100-mile route between Salina and Green River, but no services, so be sure to top off the gas tank before crossing the reefs.

Utah state parks accept advance reservations. Call ☎ **800/322-3770** or 801/322-3770 weekdays between 8am and 5pm mountain time. For Utah national forests reservations, call ☎ **800/280-2267;** www.reserveusa.com.

HITTING THE HIGHLIGHTS

The roads are generally very good in Utah, so you'll be able to move along as briskly as necessary, except when the first snow begins to fall in late October or early November. The highlights could be covered in as little as 7 days, but you'd have very little time to hike and explore.

Zion and Bryce Canyon National Parks require a minimum of a full day each, with 2 days in each allowing time to hike a bit as well.

RVers who choose not to take the tunnel route from Zion to Bryce can return to I-15, make the short detour into Kolob Canyons from the interstate, then exit at Cedar City to drive through Cedar Breaks and along Route 143 past Panguitch Lake, a very scenic route, before turning south on U.S. 89 to connect with Route 12 to Bryce.

Although geology buffs will enjoy the dead-end scenic drive that delves more deeply into **Capitol Reef National Park,** travelers pressed for time can skip it. But everyone should take the time to drive into the orchards and campground area at **Fruita,** as well as make roadside stops along the way at the old schoolhouse and the cliff petroglyphs.

If time permits, swing south from the junction at Hanksville to drive **Bicentennial Highway,** which allows you a good look at Glen Canyon National Recreation Area at Hites Crossing and a visit to Natural Bridges National Monument. Otherwise, head north to I-70 and take U.S. 191 south at exit 180 to drop down in Moab, Arches, and Canyonlands.

Allow a full day each for **Arches, The Needles,** and **Islands in the Sky,** adding to the latter a side detour into Dead Horse Point State Park.

GOING FOR THE LONG HAUL

We ran across quite a few people in Utah who came out on a vacation and never went home, so consider yourself warned. One could certainly spend a long, happy season RVing, hiking, and biking in and around the public lands with an occasional hop into town to restock the larder, fill up with gas, top off the water, and dump the holding tanks.

Two weeks in each park or national monument, taking into consideration the 14-day camping limit, would give plenty of time to explore, and a week or two on a houseboat in **Lake Powell** would provide pure pleasure. Add another 2 weeks at particularly scenic BLM areas, such as the **Colorado River** outside Moab, and you'll find an entire season filled with things to do.

The temporary employment scene in Moab is usually active, so full-timers can find seasonal shops looking for clerks and restaurants hiring waiters. In winter, ski areas are good sources of seasonal employment.

Travel Essentials

WHEN TO GO

Any time of year, some part of Utah is in its prime. In winter, skiers flock to "the greatest snow on earth," Utah's champagne powder. Most of its dozen major ski areas are clustered to the east of Salt Lake City, but Brian Head ski resort, nearly 10,000 feet with a long snow season, is 12 miles off I-15 at Parowan, near Cedar City. St. George in the southwest's Dixie area is mild in winter. Fall and spring are the ideal times for RVers to visit Utah's national parks; summer is hot in the lower elevations, but cooler at Brian Head, Cedar Breaks, and Bryce Canyon. All the national parks, however, are jam-packed in summer with Americans and Europeans.

WHAT TO TAKE

Sunblock, a sun hat, good walking or hiking shoes, an adequate supply of favorite spirits, a camera, and at least twice as much film as you'd expect to use (it's that photogenic!).

WHAT TO WEAR

Take layered clothing for all of Utah's parks. In late fall and winter, you'll want heavy parkas and boots or shoes with snow-safe treads. We encountered considerable snow in mid-October at Bryce Canyon and Cedar Breaks, while Zion, Canyonlands, Arches, and Capitol Reef still had sunny, shirtsleeve weather. In summer's heat, natural fibers help absorb perspiration.

TRIMMING COSTS ON THE ROAD

As a state, Utah is much less expensive than many, although sparsely settled southern Utah does not offer frequent or varied shopping opportunities. Keep your larder well stocked and your gas and water tanks topped off when venturing into less-traveled territory.

With so much of southern Utah's most scenic terrain under Bureau of Land Management (BLM) administration, RVers will find some no-fee undeveloped campsites where camping is permitted under the following conditions: Camping in one site is limited to 14 days; campers must pack out all trash; campfires may not be left unattended; and camping is not permitted within 300 feet of springs or ponds so that water is accessible to wildlife. Self-contained RVs meet with BLM's regulations as long as dumping of gray or black water takes place only in designated sanitary dump stations and never on the ground. Call the **BLM** in Salt Lake City for information at ☎ **801/539-4001;** www.blm.com.

WHERE TO GET TRAVEL INFORMATION

All of the following park offices will be able to provide you with travel information:

- **Arches National Park:** ☎ 435/259-8161; www.nps.gov/arch
- **Bryce Canyon National Park:** ☎ 435/834-5322; www.nps.gov/brca
- **Canyonlands National Park:** ☎ 435/259-7164; www.nps.gov/cany
- **Capitol Reef National Park:** ☎ 435/425-3791; www.nps.gov/care
- **Cedar Breaks National Monument:** ☎ 435/586-9451; www.nps.gov/cebr or www.utahsplayground.org
- **Dead Horse Point State Park:** ☎ 435/259-2614; www.go-utah.com
- **Glen Canyon National Recreation Area:** ☎ 520/608-6404; www.go-utah.com
- **Grand Staircase of the Escalante National Monument:** ☎ 435/826-4291; www.blm.gov/utah//monument
- **Natural Bridges National Monument:** ☎ 435/692-1234; www.gov/nabr
- **Utah Travel Council:** ☎ 800/200-1160; fax 801/538-1399; www.utah.com
- **Zion National Park:** ☎ 435/772-3256; www.nps.gov/zion

DRIVING & CAMPING TIPS

- **Use the plat system.** Brigham Young directed Utah's early Mormons to lay out street plats with streets running true north and south and true east and west from a central point. If an address is 500 South 700 East, for instance, you drive 5 blocks south from the center and then 7 blocks east. Blocks are laid out in increments of 100. Whether you're in Salt Lake City or Moab, the plan holds true. They were also instructed to make streets "wide enough for a team of four oxen and a covered wagon to turn around."

- **Bring along tapes or CDs.** Otherwise you'll have to listen to the car radio, and in Utah you can get only three sounds day or night: the Mormon Tabernacle Choir, country music, and Rush Limbaugh.

- **Be aware of Utah's mysterious liquor laws.** Utah's liquor laws allow purchases of wine and spirits by the bottle in state liquor stores in many areas except on Sundays and holidays. Beer with 3.2% alcohol can be purchased in grocery and convenience stores 7 days a week. Licensed restaurants may serve alcohol by the drink, but neither drinks nor a wine list can be offered by the server; the patron must request them. In some areas, alcohol by the drink can be served only if patrons "join" a private club by paying a small fee. Lounges and taverns serve only beer. "Brown-bagging," bringing your own alcohol for consumption in a location, is no longer permitted.

- **Don't break the cryptobiotic crust.** The direst thing you can do in southern Utah is to walk, bike, drive on, or otherwise break the cryptobiotic crust, a fragile and ancient covering that looks dark brown and crumbly and nurtures virtually all desert life, both flora and fauna. One careless step can destroy crust that will take 50 to 100 years to recover. Always stay on the trail or roadway. As locals say, "tiptoe through the crypto."

The Best Utah Sights, Tastes & Experiences

OFF-THE-WALL ATTRACTIONS

The Big Rock Candy Mountain. Located on Highway 89 south of Richfield, off I-70, exit 23 to Sevier, it really does look a little like a mound of caramel. Neither folk singer Burl Ives nor songwriter Harry McClintock ever saw it, but that didn't stop them from making money out of a hit song about it. Folk experts John Lomax and Charles Seeger said the original version, with its "lemonade springs" and "lakes of stew," was sung by old-time hobos to lure young farm boys into a life on the road.

The Vernal dinosaur garden. Sculpted by Elbert Porter at the Utah Field House of Natural History State Park in Vernal, the garden displays 13 critters, from woolly mammoths to triceratops. The park is at 235 E. Main St. in Vernal (☎ 435/789-3799). Utah is also home to the largest dinosaur egg found, discovered at the Cleveland-Lloyd Dinosaur Quarry south of Price and exhibited in the **Prehistoric Museum** of the College of Eastern Utah, 200 E. 100 North, in Price (☎ 435/637-5050; www.ceu.eov/museum.com).

Hole 'n the Rock Home, South of Moab. Not to be confused with where the Mormons crossed Glen Canyon, the Hole 'n the Rock Home in Moab is a 5,000-square-foot drilled-out cavern that was home to Albert and Gladys Christensen beginning in 1952. It has 14 rooms, a 65-foot chimney, and a bathtub carved from a rock. During the 12 years Albert spent creating it, he also painted a Sermon on the Mount and carved the head of Franklin D. Roosevelt in the rock above the house. After Albert died, Gladys continued to run their cafe and gift shop until her death in 1974. Now their family operates it as a museum and memorial, and the gift shop sells souvenirs. It's on U.S. 191 south of Moab; admission $2.50 adults (☎ 435/686-2250).

The Zion IMAX big-screen theater. It's hard to believe, but near the entrance to Zion National Park is a new IMAX big-screen theater purporting to show "the Zion you came to see—the real Zion." Since we didn't succumb to the come-on and pay $6.50 a ticket for a 37-minute film, we are not sure what it shows that we missed by driving into the park itself. If your curiosity causes you to stop by when leaving the park by the Springdale exit, the theater promises to refund your park admission if you buy a movie ticket. (☎ 435/772-2400).

The John Wesley Powell River History Museum, Green River. This has to be the only museum in America dedicated to river-rapids runners, with some 15 Hall of Fame members to date. Admission is free but donations are appreciated. The handsome new museum commemorates Powell, the one-armed Civil War veteran who first mapped the Grand Canyon and navigated the Colorado River seated in a chair lashed atop a pine rowboat. Located at 885 E. Main St. in Green River (☎ 435/564-3427).

Circleville, boyhood home of Butch Cassidy. Circleville, on U.S. 89 about 25 miles south of I-70, was the boyhood home of Butch Cassidy, and where he came on his return from Bolivia (if, indeed, he ever went there), to meet with his mother for the last time in 1925. The family shared a blueberry pie, said Butch's sister, Lula Parker Betenson, who wrote a book about her brother. The outlaw's real name was Robert LeRoy Parker. What remains of their two-room log cabin is still standing south of town on U.S. 89.

Charlie Steen's dream house, Moab. Now the Sunset Grill Restaurant, the dream house sits atop the tallest hill in Moab, north of town on Route 191. (Locals opine that the view surpasses the food, mostly steaks, pasta, and seafood.) Charlie was, you may remember, the Texan who became a millionaire in the uranium market during the Cold War days of the 1950s. He struck pay dirt in 1952, and the rush of miners that followed quadrupled the population of Moab. His mine, named Mi Vida, brought him $60 million in a few short years. The house became a restaurant in 1974 when Charlie ran into bad tax and mining luck. Call the restaurant at ☎ 435/259-7146.

Newspaper Rock State Historical Monument. Located 12 miles off U.S. 191 via Route 211 west, Newspaper Rock is an Indian-era billboard made up of petroglyphs (carvings incised on rock surfaces). Most of the drawings date back 1,000 years, attributed to prehistoric Indians and early Utes, with additions by white pioneer settlers and, unfortunately, a few contemporary vandals. A primitive, attractive, 10-site campground is here among the aspens, with two spaces for RVs up to 40 feet, along with grills and picnic tables but no water or hookups. Call the Bureau of Land Management for camping information: ☎ 435/259-6111; www.desertusa.com/newut/du_newut_vvc.html.

HOT ROCKS

Moab's bounty of uranium was first noted by France's Madame Curie when she used ore from Moab to develop radium in 1896 (some say she traveled to Utah and conducted experiments on-site). The supply finally bottomed out in the late 1960s.

Indian petroglyphs at Newspaper Rock State Historical Monument.

Price City Cemetery. The Price City Cemetery is the final resting place for a body shot by a posse in 1898, identified as Butch Cassidy, and laid out with great fanfare before burial. One of the many visitors couldn't stop laughing when viewing the corpse. Later, when a Wyoming lawman made a positive identification of the body as another outlaw, people realized the stranger had been Cassidy himself. The whole story is carved on the stranger's tombstone. Price is at the junction of U.S. 6 and U.S. 191 in the center of the state.

The Sauropod Track Site. Eight miles south of I-15 on U.S. 191 and north of the Arches National Park entrance, then 2 miles down a dirt road, is where four dinosaurs tramped through a damp river channel some 150 million years ago, leaving only footprints (but probably not taking pictures). Discovered in 1989, the footprints of the single brontosaurus are 2 feet wide, and one of the carnivores, probably an allosaurus, leaves evidence of having a limp. Don't attempt the trip in an RV during or after a rain or you may end up as a sightseeing attraction yourself for some future tourists.

Wolfe Ranch, in Arches National Park. Civil War veteran John Wesley Wolfe came here with his son Fred searching for a place to raise cattle. His wife and three younger children remained in Etna, Ohio. Eventually, in 1906, his daughter Flora, with her family, came to stay, and talked her father into gentrifying the ranch. For her sake, he built a new cabin with a wood floor (the one you see today), ordered a 100-piece set of china dishes from the Sears Roebuck catalog because she disliked tin plates, and bought her a camera and developing kit, with which she made one of the earliest known photographs of Delicate Arch. To get there, turn east off the main road onto

Wolfe Ranch Road and continue to the parking area. A short walk leads to what's left of the ranch. Farther up the trail you'll see some Ute petroglyphs.

SEVEN SITES OFFERING *DEJA VU* ALL OVER AGAIN

1. **Grafton.** This picturesque ghost town, set against the towering rock walls of Zion National Park, is where Paul Newman and Katherine Ross rode a bicycle to the music of "Raindrops Keep Fallin' on My Head" in the film *Butch Cassidy and the Sundance Kid*. Turn south (200 East) on Bridge Road in Rockville, near the entrance to Zion National Park on Route 9, cross an old iron bridge, and follow a 4-mile dirt road to the old cemetery and town. Larger motor homes and trailers might find it a tight squeeze in some spots, so we'd recommend pulling off at the tunnel information/scenic view turnout on Route 9 west of Rockville for an overview of the area.

2. **Fisher Towers.** History's most famous TV car commercials were shot outside Moab at a pair of 1,500-foot looming spires called Fisher Towers. A Chevrolet, lowered by helicopter, was shown sitting all alone atop a tall, narrow pinnacle, surrounded only by desert and craggy red rocks in all directions. The first commercial was such a big hit in 1964, that a second one was shot in 1974. The towers are on Scenic Route 128 east from Moab at mile 21, with a road sign identifying them. A hiking trail to the towers and a picnic table are also at the site.

3. **Delicate Arch, Arches National Park.** All the book covers and posters you've ever seen about Utah leap to life at Delicate Arch. Early cowboys called the much-photographed 45-foot-high red sandstone arch "The Schoolmarm's Drawers," but to us it most closely resembles the bottom half of a bow-legged cowboy wearing chaps. The hike, the park's most popular walk, is a strenuous 480-foot ascent over a huge rock mountain similar to Australia's Ayers Rock; it seemed to us much longer than the 3-mile round-trip the park literature claims, especially on the uphill part. Once there, many visitors sit and stare in awe at the arch (trying, perhaps, to catch their breath) while photographers clamber over precarious rocks for an ever-better angle. Late afternoon is best to photograph the golden light against the stone. The walk sets out from the Wolfe Ranch parking lot off the park's main road.

4. **Movie location in Moab.** Pick up a free "Moab Movie Locations" brochure in the Moab Information Center, Center and Main streets, and you can head for all your favorite movie locations in the area. See where scenes for *Indiana Jones and the Last Crusade* (1988) were shot in Arches National Park. At Canyonlands' Island in the Sky, Max von Sydow as Christ delivered the Sermon on the Mount in *The Greatest Story Ever Told* (1963); he stood facing the Green River at the Green River Overlook on a rock to the left of the fence. Two thousand years

later in cinema time, Thelma and Louise, in the film of the same name (1990), drove off the cliff under Dead Horse Point 10 miles down the Shafer Trail (also called Potash Road), an unpaved road off Route 279, located 19 miles south of Moab. Earlier in the film, at Arches' Courthouse Towers, they locked a pursuing police officer in his patrol car trunk, and several chase scenes were filmed in the La Sal Mountains outside the town of La Sal off Route 46.

For Western movie fans, in Rio Grande (1950), John Wayne rescued kidnapped cavalry children from a pueblo just off Utah Scenic Byway 128, a half mile up a dirt road from milepost 19, and located the hide-out in The Comancheros (1961) 9/10 mile east of milepost 21. In Cheyenne Autumn (1963), cavalryman Richard Widmark chased the Cheyenne across a flat area south of the Arches' South Park Avenue. And Devils Garden in Arches served as the site where an Indian ambush trapped the U.S. cavalry in the truly terrible Taza, Son of Cochise (1953), starring Rock Hudson and Barbara Rush.

5. **Monument Valley Navajo Tribal Park.** Located in southeastern Utah on the Arizona border, Monument Valley Park is bisected by Highway 163. Famous for its appearances in a host of John Ford films, Monument Valley stood in for Texas in *The Searchers,* Arizona in *My Darling Clementine,* and New Mexico in *Stagecoach.* Visit the Visitor Center, east on Monument Valley Road off Route 163, open daily for a self-guided driving map and information (☎ 801/727-3287; www.desertusa.com/monvalley/index.html). The **Navajo Tourism Department** will mail a guide for tours from 2 hours to a full day (☎ 520/871-6436; http://rednations.com).

   Goulding's Monument Valley Campground & RV Park has nightly shuttle service to the company's historic lodge and trading post for a sound-and-light show. Open mid-March to the end of October, the park's 66 RV sites provide satellite TV, full hookups with 30-amp electric, and a heated pool. Take 163 south to Monument Valley west; go 2 miles. Call ☎ 435/727-3235 for reservations; www.gouldings.com.

6. **Snow Canyon State Park.** Northwest of St. George, Snow Canyon State Park is where Robert Redford in *The Electric Horseman* (1979) freed his stallion at the end of the film; Jane Fonda and Willie Nelson costarred in the contemporary Western set in Las Vegas.

7. **The Main Street of Dodge City.** The very main street where Marshall Dillon in TV's long-running series *Gunsmoke* faced gun battles weekly still stands in Johnson Canyon, 9 miles east of Kanab off Highway 89 on Johnson Canyon Road. Sometimes the set is open to visitors for a fee; otherwise, you can see it from the roadway with binoculars.

Lake Powell at Hites Crossing.

TEN MACHO THINGS TO DO IN UTAH

1. **Go mountain biking.** The tiny town of Brian Head, reached via Route 143 from exit 78 on I-15, offers 12 different routes rated "easy" to "advanced." Because the area is at 10,000 feet, it's cool enough in summer to enjoy biking, but snow-covered from November through May. Expect a rich variety of flora and fauna in the four life zones: alpine, subalpine, Canadian, and transitional. You can get essential detailed maps locally. There are bike-rental shops in town: **Brian Head Sports,** 329 S. Brian Head Blvd. (☎ **435/677-2014;** www.brianheadtown.com); and **George's,** 612 S. Brian Head Blvd. (☎ **435/677-2013;** www. brianheadtown.com). Reservations: **Brian Head Resort (☎ 800/27-BRIAN** or 435/677-2035).

   Local shuttle services or chairlifts can ferry you to the top of the hill, and you can ride down. The nearest camping is in Cedar Breaks.

2. **Go white-water rafting and four-wheeling.** One-day expeditions that combine white-water river rafting and four-wheel-drive land tours are offered by **Navtec Expeditions of Moab (☎ 800/833-1278;** www.navtec.com). A morning sports boat ride goes along the Colorado River gorge just underneath Dead Horse Point State Park, stopping to see dinosaur tracks, petrified wood, and Indian rock art. A buffet picnic lunch is served, then a transfer to 4x4s for a tour up Long Canyon and Gemini Bridges. Cost is around $75 for adults, $58 for kids up to 17.

TALKIN' UTAH: A GLOSSARY

Butte: An isolated hill or mountain rising suddenly out of flat land.

Desert varnish: A dark, glossy finish on rock created by heat-loving bacteria that draw iron and manganese from airborne dust.

Gentile: In Latter-day Saints usage, any non-Mormon.

Hoodoo: An eroded pillar of sandstone topped with a hard rock cap and sculpted into eerie shapes.

LDS: Church of Jesus Christ of Latter-day Saints, also called Saints or Mormons.

Mesa: A flat-topped, steep-walled land area; a table mountain.

Natural arches: Water-cut rock formations that stand on the skyline.

Natural bridges: Water-cut (including snow melting and refreezing) rock formations in the bottoms of canyons.

Petroglyphs: Carvings incised on rock surfaces.

Pictographs: Pictures drawn on rock surfaces.

Slickrock: A smooth, slippery rock formation burnished by "desert varnish."

Wash: The dry bed of a sometimes stream; never camp in these areas, and avoid them during rainstorms.

3. **Go trail riding.** Trail rides from Pack Creek Ranch near Moab can be as short as an hour or two or as long as a 4-night pack trip into the backcountry. Previous riding is not necessary for the short rides, which start at $25 and can accommodate kids 6 and over. Morning and evening rides into Courthouse Wash in Arches National Park are also available in summer for $20 an hour, $35 for 2 hours. Meals and cabin or bunkhouse lodging are also available at the ranch, but reservations need to be made well ahead of time. Call the ranch at ☎ 435/259-5505; www.packcreekranch.com.

4. **Go cross-country skiing or snowshoeing at Bryce Canyon.** Bryce Canyon in winter offers extraordinary views of bright red Navajo sandstone sprinkled with snow and sparkling in the sunlight against a clear blue sky. Cross-country skiing or snowshoeing are two excellent ways to see it. Self-contained RVs can stay in the park's North Campground near the visitor center during winter, although water is cut off and the sanitary dump closed down. There are no hookups. The 11-mile Rim Trail with its level terrain and sensational views down into the canyon is a good place to start. Snowshoer-wannabes can borrow a pair free from the rangers at the visitor center (at the north end as you enter the park), leaving a credit card or driver's license as a deposit, and set off in the snow (☎ 435/834-5322; www.nps.gov/brca).

5. **Go mountain biking on the Slickrock Trail.** From Moab, the North American capital of the sport, you can start on the 10-mile Slickrock Trail, tackled by 100,000 eager sprocket-heads a year. Beginners are

advised to start with Gemini Bridges or Hurrah Pass, each 14 miles long. In town, six bike shops, each with its obligatory espresso machine, rent or sell anything you might need, from maps to machines: **Chile Pepper Bike Shop,** 702 S. Main St. (☎ **888/677-4688** or 435/259-4643; fax 435/259-4643; chilebikes@aol.com); **Dreamrides,** 96 E. Center St. (☎ **888/662-2882** or 435/259-6419; fax 435/259-8196; www.dreamride.com); **Kaibab Mountain Bike Tours,** 391 S. Main St. (☎ **800/451-1133** or 435/259-7423; fax 435/259-6135; www.kaibabtours.com); **Nichols Expeditions,** 497 N. Main St. (☎ **800/648-8488** or 435/259-3999; fax 435/259-2312; www.nicholsexpeditions.com); **Poison Spider Bicycles,** 497 N. Main St. (☎ **800/635-1782** or 435/259-7882; fax 435/259-2312); www.poisonspiderbicycles.com); and **Rim Tours,** 1233 S. Hwy. 191 (☎ **800/626-7335** or 435/259-3349; www.rimtours.com).

6. **Take a 1-day river run through Gray Canyon.** A run on the Green River with **Moki Mac River Expeditions** in Salt Lake City is a quick, easy option for beginners. They'll pick you up at your campground in the Green River area off I-70 and take you through six or so splashy rapids and some rugged scenery on an oar-powered expedition that costs $45 for adults, $35 for children (☎ **800/284-7280;** www.mokimac.com).

7. **Run the Green in Desolation Canyon.** Desolation Canyon, with its calm waters and peaceful put-in point, is a favorite for first-timers and families. But with more than 60 rapids and an ultimate Class III rating, the river challenges experienced river rafters and kayakers as well. Contact **Adrift Adventures** in Canyonlands (☎ **800/874-4483;** www.adrift.com); **Adventure Bound Trips** (☎ **800/423-4668;** www.raft-utah.com); **Red River Canoe** (☎ **800/753-8216;** www.redrivercanoe.com); or **Western River** (☎ **800/453-7450;** www.westernriver.com).

8. **Take a snowmobile tour.** One-and-a-half-hour, half-day, or custom tours set out from Brian Head during ski season priced from $40. Kids 10 and under travel free. Cedar Breaks National Monument, gorgeous against a blue sky when decorated with snow, is nearby. Call **Crystal Mountain Recreation** at ☎ **800/BIKE-SKI** or 801/677-2012.

9. **Rent a houseboat and go exploring on Lake Powell.** Explore ancient Anasazi caves, photograph remote Rainbow Bridge, and swim and picnic at a deserted beach—all from the comfort of home. Houseboating on Lake Powell, second-largest man-made lake in North America, is something akin to having your RV walk on water. Houseboats ranging from 36 to 59 feet are available for rent year-round from four perimeter marinas in Glen Canyon National Recreation Area—Bullfrog, Hite Marina, Wahweap, and Halls Crossing. Between October and May, houseboats can be reserved for trips as short as 1 or

2 days. The rest of the year, minimum rental requirements are longer. Call **ARAMARK** well ahead of time in summer for reservations (☎ 800/ 528-6154; www.visitlakepowell.com).

10. **Go horseback riding along the scenic rim of Bryce Canyon.** Head through the Butch Cassidy country or a 1,600-year-old bristlecone pine forest. Any of these can be booked through the office in Ruby's Inn at the entrance to Bryce Canyon (☎ 800/679-5859 or 435/679-8761; fax 435/679-8778; www.brycecanyonhorseback.com). All rides are guided and range from an hour to all day. On the longer rides, there is an age and weight limit—no less than 8 years old and no more than 220 pounds on the all-day ride, 6 years and 250 pounds on the half-day. Big-game hunting is also available in season.

TAKE-OUT (OR EAT-IN) TREATS

Bumbleberry Inn, Springdale. Bumbleberry pie is the house specialty at the Bumbleberry Inn, 97 Bumbleberry Lane in Springdale (☎ 800/ 828-1534), gateway town to Zion National Park. While the house hands out a whimsical description of its fruit—"burple and binkel berries that grow on giggle bushes"—it's a black-red berrylike loganberry or boysenberry in a cornstarch-thickened sauce and fairly thick crust. A wedge to go costs $2.79 (☎ 435/772-3611 for restaurant).

Capitol Reef Inn and Cafe, Torrey. The Capitol Reef Inn and Cafe, at 360 W. Main St. in Torrey (☎ 435/425-3271), west of Capitol Reef National Park, may or may not be the only restaurant in southern Utah serving fresh vegetables, but it's the best bet in the area for vegetarians as well as carnivores. The former can feast on 10-vegetable salad and stir-fry vegetables atop steamed brown rice, while the latter can tuck into fresh local rainbow trout, grilled rib-eye steak, or charbroiled lemon hickory chicken. Beer and wine are available. Breakfast-eaters get hearty omelets with optional bacon or smoked trout, or an order of French toast or pancakes. It's a good idea to call ahead.

Fat City Smokehouse, Moab. Fat City Smokehouse, at 36 S. 100 W. in Moab (☎ 435/259-4302), not only dishes up pit-style barbecue ribs in what was once a turn-of-the-century dance hall, but also turns out fine vegetarian sandwiches from grilled eggplant, zucchini, onions, and green peppers with fresh tomato pesto. Prices are modest, and you can save time by calling ahead on orders to go. Open daily at 4pm.

Green River melons. The town of Green River is famous for its melons, which reach their peak in late summer and early fall. We tried Dunham's fruit stand on the east end of town and found their honeydew, Crenshaw, and cantaloupe were all delicious. They grow watermelons, too.

Bear Lake raspberries. Dark red Bear Lake raspberries, which grow in the tiny northeastern Utah town of Bear Lake, are the world's most delicious— aficionados arrive the last week of July and the first week or two of August

Southern Utah Campgrounds

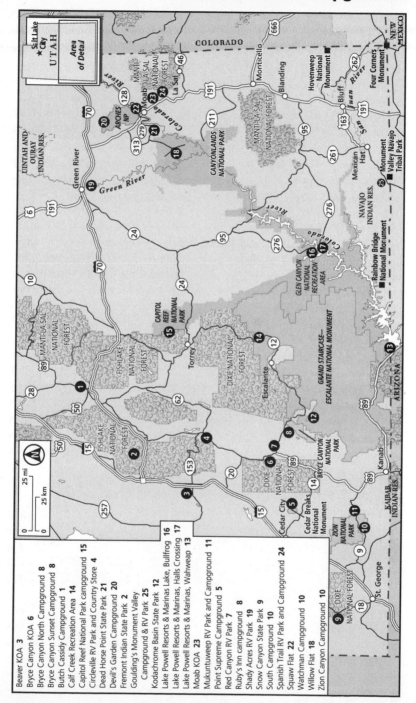

Beaver KOA **3**
Bryce Canyon KOA **6**
Bryce Canyon North Campground **8**
Bryce Canyon Sunset Campground **8**
Butch Cassidy Campground **1**
Calf Creek Recreation Area **14**
Capitol Reef National Park campground **15**
Circleville RV Park and Country Store **4**
Dead Horse Point State Park **21**
Devil's Garden Campground **20**
Fremont Indian State Park **2**
Goulding's Monument Valley
   Campground & RV Park **25**
Kodachrome Basin State Park **12**
Lake Powell Resorts & Marinas Lake, Bullfrog **16**
Lake Powell Resorts & Marinas, Halls Crossing **17**
Lake Powell Resorts & Marinas, Wahweap **13**
Moab KOA **23**
Mukuntuweep RV Park and Campground **11**
Point Supreme Campground **5**
Red Canyon RV Park **7**
Ruby's Inn campground **8**
Shady Acres RV Park **19**
Snow Canyon State Park **9**
South Campground **10**
Spanish Trail RV Park and Campground **24**
Squaw Flat **22**
Watchman Campground **10**
Willow Flat **18**
Zion Canyon Campground **10**

to eat them fresh from the vine at Hildt's Famous Bear Lake Raspberry Stand, or have them whirled into milkshakes at Le Beau's or Raspberry and Yummy Things Bakery. The climate limits the vines to one instead of the usual two annual crops, and locals believe that packs in more flavor intensity. If you can't make it to Bear Lake, taste the fresh Bear Lake raspberry ice cream at Snelgrove's local chain of ice-cream stores in Salt Lake City.

Electric Jim's Cafe, Springdale. The Virgin Burgers from Electric Jim's Cafe in Springdale by the entrance to Zion National Park are world-famous, the cafe claims, probably because the park attracts people from all over the world, some of whom undoubtedly get hungry after a hike. Jim's also claims the best shakes in the West. Since the Mormons are not supposed to drink coffee, tea, soft drinks, or alcohol, Utah is heaven for milkshake freaks.

Eddie McStiff's, Moab. Moab's Eddie McStiff's offers several unique boutique brews, including a jalapeño beer, a spruce beer with the foresty tang of spruce needles and bark, light blueberry and raspberry wheat beers, cream ale, amber ale, chestnut brown beer, and full-bodied stout. You'll find it at 57 Main St., and all food and beer are available to go (☎ 435/259-BEER).

The Cowboy's Smoke House, Panguitch. Closed during the winter but otherwise open from early morning for breakfast (we got the sausage biscuit, a huge biscuit with a spicy patty inside) till the last of the barbecued beef, chicken, and ribs is gone and the last customer leaves in the evening. Some of the mounted animal heads around the room were bagged by Smokehouse employees, like the elk "shot down by Panguitch Lake" by one of the waitresses. Located at 95 N. Main St. in Panguitch (☎ 435/676-8030).

Arches Winery, Moab. Arches Winery is Utah's oldest winery, and offers tastings of its red and white table and dessert wines daily from 11am to 7pm, but never on Sundays. It's at 420 Kane Creek Blvd. (☎ 435/259-5397).

WILDLIFE-WATCHING

Mule deer are almost everywhere in southern Utah, especially in Bryce Canyon, Capitol Reef around the Fruita campground, Dead Horse Point State Park, and Natural Bridges National Monument.

Unexpected glimpses of **Shiras moose,** as well as **elk** and Great Basin mule deer, are possible in the Hogan Pass area along Route 72 between I-70 at Fremont and the town of Loa 32 miles to the south, with the best possibility between the pass and Loa.

Buffalo have been reestablished in the Henry Mountains around Hanksville. A resident buffalo herd, some of them in enclosures and thereby guaranteed to be seen, can be visited on Antelope Island, reached by the Route 127 causeway off I-15 at Syracuse, north of Salt Lake City.

We saw lots of inquisitive Utah **prairie dogs,** a threatened species of this ubiquitous Western rodent, popping up from holes beside the road on Route 211 into the Needles area of Canyonlands.

Along the Colorado River, keep a lookout for river otter, beaver, and birds. **Bald eagles** winter in the area around Fremont Indian State Park, and Canyonlands offers glimpses of **peregrine falcons** and other birds of prey.

On the Road

ZION NATIONAL PARK

The national park, which began its official life as Mukuntuweap National Monument in 1909, dates from 1917 with the name Zion, given to it by Mormon settlers in the area who did not like the Paiute name. Its early description as an "extraordinary example of canyon erosion" fails to do justice to the rich palette of colors in the canyon, which range from creamy white to burnished copper and dark rose.

Dramatic, accessible, and beautiful, Zion is Utah's most-visited national park, with more than 2.5 million visitors a year. Some 800 species of wildflowers bloom here, and 75 species of mammals, 271 birds, 32 reptiles and amphibians, and 8 varieties of fish are native to the park, including the unique (and endangered) Zion snail. More than 100 varieties of plants in the park were introduced after European settlement began in the mid-1800s and are presently being eliminated. A wide range of elevations, temperatures, water, and sunlight create microenvironments that showcase diverse flora and fauna, from hanging gardens with "weeping" rocks watering cascading ferns to forested canyons and arid mesas.

Despite its hot summers, Zion's mild spring, autumn, and winter make the park a year-round destination. There may be some snow in winter, but the roads are plowed, and one campground is open at the south entrance.

Zion National Park's top attraction is the 7-mile **Zion Canyon Drive,** which has been notoriously traffic-clogged during the past decade and so is now served by a propane-fueled shuttle-bus system, meaning no private vehicles are allowed in the canyon between Easter and Halloween. Hikers and bicyclists are still permitted, as are visitors with confirmed reservations at Zion Lodge. But anyone else arriving between March and October will be expected to board buses into Zion Canyon. Motor vehicles, including RVs, are still permitted on the park's eastern side and in the campground area at the south entrance from Springdale. Parking is available at various areas in the town of Springdale and at the new visitor center, just inside the south park entrance at Springdale. The park entry fee is $20, which includes shuttle fees. If you want to visit Kolob Canyons, off I-15 in the northwestern part of the park, the fee is $10. Call ☎ **435/772-0312** for information.

Based on our experience, RVs, particularly trailers and large motor homes, never had adequate turnaround or parking space at popular points along the canyon road anyway, so we've always supported the shuttle system concept.

There are four **driving entrances** into Zion, only two of which connect— the Route 9 south entrance at Springdale and the east entrance on Zion-Mt.

Zion National Park

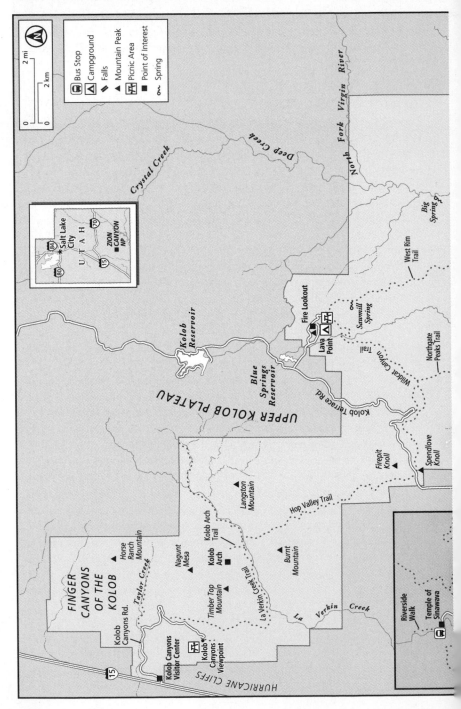

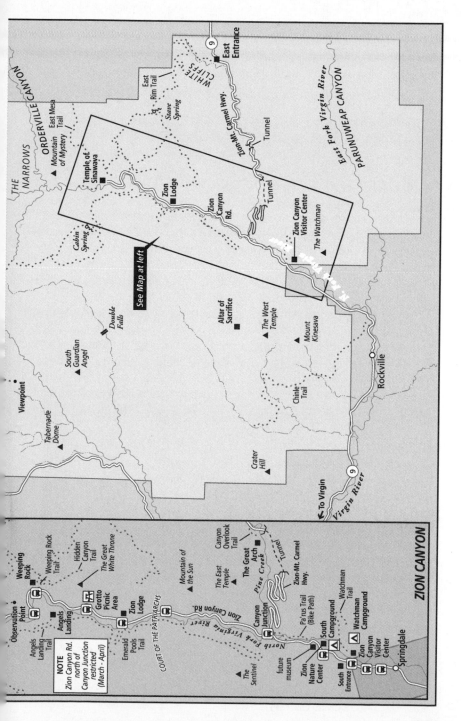

THE NARROWS

ORDERVILLE CANYON

▲ Mountain of Mystery

East Mesa Trail

East Rim Trail

WHITE CLIFFS

Stave Spring

Temple of Sinawava ■

Zion Lodge ■

Zion Canyon Rd.

Zion–Mt. Carmel Hwy.

Tunnel

Tunnel

Cabin Spring ○

Zion Canyon Visitor Center ■

The Watchman ▲

See Map at left

East Entrance ■

9

East Fork Virgin River

PARUNUWEAP CANYON

Double Falls

▲ South Guardian Angel

Altar of Sacrifice ■

▲ The West Temple

Mount Kinesava ▲

Chinle Trail

Viewpoint •

Tabernacle Dome ▲

Crater Hill ▲

To Virgin ←

9

Rockville ○

Virgin River

ZION CANYON

Observation Point •

Weeping Rock

Weeping Rock Trail

Hidden Canyon Trail

The Great White Throne ▲

Mountain of the Sun ▲

The East Temple ▲

Canyon Overlook Trail

The Great Arch

Pine Creek

Tunnel

Zion–Mt. Carmel Hwy.

Angels Landing Trail

Angels Landing ■

Grotto Picnic Area

Zion Lodge ■

Emerald Pools Trail

Zion Canyon Rd.

COURT OF THE PATRIARCHS

The Sentinel ▲

Canyon Junction

Pa'rus Trail (Bike Path)

North Fork Virgin River

future museum

Zion Nature Center ■

South Campground ⛺

Watchman Campground ⛺

Watchman Trail

South Entrance

Zion Canyon Visitor Center

Springdale ○

NOTE
Zion Canyon Rd.
north of
Canyon Junction
restricted
(March – April)

Carmel Highway. The 25-mile dead-end drive along Kolob Terrace Road from the town of Virgin to the Kolob Reservoir winds in and out of the park's western boundaries through varying terrain, and the not-to-be-missed Kolob Canyons Road enters the northernmost part of the park from I-15 south of Cedar City. For more about both, see "Ten Scenic Side Trips," later in this chapter.

The best way to see the canyon is to use **hiking trails.** Hikers should arrive early in the morning since most parking areas fill by midday. Permits are required for overnight hikes; you can get one at the visitor center after 8am the day before the hike begins. Permits require a fee of $5 per person.

Among the park's most popular hiking trails are several that are short and/or easy. **Weeping Rocks trail** is a steep quarter-mile climb leading to an enormous rocky ledge covered with mosses and plants with a stream of "tears" dripping from it. It's also a cool place to linger on a hot summer day.

The 2-mile **Emerald Pools** trail loop is not too demanding if you go uphill via the right-hand trail after crossing the footbridge by the parking lot, climb to the Middle Pool, and then take the other trail, somewhat rougher and steeper, back downhill.

The **Lower Emerald Pool trail** and the **Gateway to the Narrows trail** at the Temple of Sinawava are wheelchair-accessible if a companion is along to help with the rough spots along the cement paving. The latter trail is a fairly level 2-mile loop that goes through the hanging gardens area, bright with wildflowers in spring and early summer.

Dedicated hikers like to strike out along the 10-mile **West Rim trail** between the canyon and Lava Point, but those starting from the canyon are

ZION RV RESTRICTIONS

RVs entering Zion National Park are subject to parking and tunnel restrictions that do not cause any major inconveniences but must be adhered to. A fee of $10 is required for any RV wider than 7 feet, 10 inches (including side mirrors) or taller than 11 feet, 4 inches to drive through the 1.1-mile tunnel on the Zion–Mt. Carmel road. This is because the vehicle has to proceed through the middle of the tunnel without oncoming traffic, which is controlled by park rangers posted at either end. The tunnel is open to RVs under 13 feet high between 8am and 8pm March through October; to pass through any other time, call ☎ 435/772-3256 to make advance arrangements. The fee is collected at the park's entrance, where drivers are issued a yellow receipt to display on the windshield. It is not essential to go through the tunnel; simply arrive and leave the park by the same Springdale gate.

THE HISTORY OF UTAH—AND A TASTY DINNER, TOO

Down in St. George, southwest of Zion off I-15, the outdoor musical drama *Utah* is open summer nights between June and September, with a cast of 80, along with lightning bolts, floods and waterfalls, burning cities, Indian raids, galloping horses, coyotes that howl on cue, and a full-fledged fireworks display. Admission is $19.50 to $28.50 adults, $14 to $19 kids under 12. Call ☎ 800/746-9882 for reservations. An optional Western Dutch-oven dinner or "family feast" is served for $10.50 adults, $7.50 children, but must be reserved at the same time tickets are booked. The theater is 10 miles from St. George at Tuacahn, off Route 300 near Snow Canyon State Park. 🚐

cautioned not to try to make it uphill to Lava Point on a 1-day hike. The **Zion Narrows trail,** which splashes through the icy waters of the Virgin River at some points, requires a free hiking permit for the 2-day, 32-mile round-trip. (Permits can be obtained from a ranger station in the park, and you have to apply in person.) Fall is best, when water levels in the river are lowest; take along a dry change of clothing in a sealed plastic bag.

Bicyclists are limited to paved roads in the park, and are not permitted to ride through the Mt. Carmel tunnel. Rangers will transport your bicycle through the tunnel free of charge, however.

Photographers should try to visit the canyon in early morning and again in late afternoon to take advantage of the dramatic light that models the contours of the rocks.

Campground Oases in & Around Zion National Park

Watchman & South Campgrounds. The two campgrounds in Zion suitable for RVs can be found just beyond the park's Springdale entrance: Watchman Campground with Loops A, B, and C (229 sites), and adjacent South Campground (140 sites). The sites, without hookups except for 91 electrical connections in Watchman, are generally widely spaced with some shade trees. All have metal picnic tables and cooking grills; some of the nicest are along the Virgin River at the edge of Loop A. Campgrounds have flush toilets but no showers, and a 14-day limit on a first-come, first-served basis except for some sites at Watchman. Many sites are handicap-accessible. All spaces fill before noon in summer. One of the two sites is open in winter. A sanitary dump station and water are located at the entrance to Watchman. Reservations are available in Watchman in summer at ☎ 800/365-2267 or 435/772-3256; http://reservations.nps.gov.

Zion Canyon Campground. A hundred sites with 30- and 50-amp electricity, pull-throughs and back-ins, dataports for e-mail, cable TV, and wheelchair access are available just a half-mile from the entrance to the national park in the town of Springdale. You can walk to the shuttle or the town's restaurants. Call ☎ 435/772-3237 for reservations; www.zioncanyoncampground.com.

Mukuntuweep RV Park and Campground. Located near Mount Carmel in Orderville on Route 9 just outside the east entrance to Zion National Park, Mukuntuweep has more tent sites (120) than RV sites (30, all with full hookups and 20 or 30 amps). Call ☎ **435/648-2154** for reservations; zion park@xpressweb.com.

Beaver KOA. This KOA in Beaver is convenient to both Zion and Bryce and makes a handy stopover for travelers between Salt Lake City and Las Vegas. It's reached from I-15, exit 112, and is open March through October, with 65 pull-through sites offering water and 30-amp electric; 27 sewer connections available. Call ☎ **800/KOA-2912** or 435/438-2924 for reservations; www.koa.com.

Snow Canyon State Park. Snow Canyon, near St. George in Utah's Dixie district, has 14 sites with water and electrical hookups and picnic shelters lined up in a row, plus 22 nonhookup sites that are more spacious and tree-shaded. The park has flush toilets, showers, a sanitary dump station, and hiking trails through spectacular scenery. It's open year-round, and the weather is mild, although summer can be hot; the canyon was named for a pioneer family's surname, not the falling white stuff, which rarely falls here. Take exit 6 (Bluff St.) from I-15 and drive northwest of St. George on Route 18 10 miles, then 2 miles southwest on Route 8. The ¾-mile hike to Johnson's Arch is the park's most popular, although some visitors take flashlights and explore the lava caves near the north end of the park. Call ☎ **800/322-3770** or 435/628-2255 for reservations.

BRYCE CANYON NATIONAL PARK

Bryce Canyon—"a hell of a place to lose a cow," in the words of one early rancher—is a collection of needlelike red limestone hoodoos (see "Talkin' Utah: A Glossary," earlier in this chapter), jewel-like eroded spires seen at their best in early morning or late-day light or, best of all, after a snowfall, when puffs of white snow dust the bright red rocks. Local Paiute legend has it that they were men turned into stone by an angry god.

BRYCE CANYON RV RESTRICTIONS

RV restrictions abound in Bryce Canyon National Park, but should not inhibit RVers from sampling some of the park's best scenery. Vehicles towing trailers are not permitted beyond Sunset Point turnoff, but after a winter snowfall the road is usually closed off at this point, anyhow. Travel trailers may be left in designated parking areas at the visitor center or Sunset Campground. RVs longer than 25 feet are not allowed at Bryce Point or Paria Point because of extremely limited turnaround space.

Snow in Bryce Canyon.

Winter can be a rewarding time to visit if you enjoy cross-country skiing or snowshoeing; the park lends snowshoes to visitors free of charge at the visitor center (at the north end as you enter the park) if you leave a credit card or driver's license for deposit.

Mule deer are plentiful and easily spotted. Elk are also present but more rarely seen. With 172 species of birds identified in the park, you'll have a good chance of spotting some; a checklist is available at the visitor center.

A number of **hiking trails,** a total of 61 miles, wend their way into the canyons among the hoodoos. The most popular half-day trek is a combination of the Queens Garden and Navajo Loop trails, a 3-mile round-trip jaunt through the most dramatic part of the amphitheater. Just remember that every trail that goes down in the early part of the hike when you're fresh comes back up later when you may be tired; don't overestimate your ability.

Bristlecone Loop trail from Rainbow Point takes a 1½-mile circuit through a forest. If a level walk sounds ideal, the **Rim trail** follows an 11-mile route with paved walking areas accessible for wheelchairs between Sunrise and Sunset Points. Naturalists offer morning walks daily in summer, and moonlight hikes on the 3 evenings a month preceding a full moon.

The reconstructed **Bryce Canyon Lodge** (☎ 435/834-5361), a National Historic Landmark, echoes some of the 1920s feeling of the original. **Ruby's Inn,** north of the park entrance on State Highway 63, dates from 1919 but has suffered so many fires over the years it has lost its period look. There is a private campground at Ruby's Inn with hookups; closed in winter (☎ 435/834-5301).

Bryce Canyon National Park

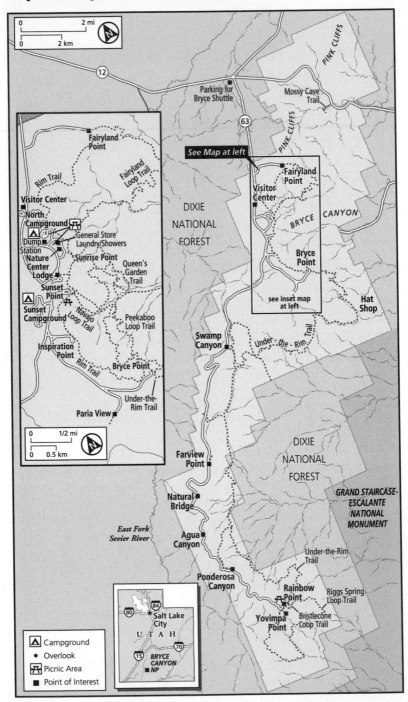

0   2 mi
0   2 km

12

Parking for
Bryce Shuttle

Mossy Cave
Trail

PINK CLIFFS

63

Fairyland
Point

Rim Trail

Fairyland
Loop Trail

See Map at left

Fairyland
Point

Visitor Center

Visitor
Center

BRYCE CANYON

North
Campground

General Store
Laundry/Showers

Dump

Bryce
Point

Station

Nature
Center
Lodge

Sunrise Point

Queen's
Garden
Trail

see inset map
at left

Hat
Shop

Sunset
Point

Sunset
Campground

Navajo
Loop Trail

Peekaboo
Loop Trail

Swamp
Canyon

Under - the - Rim Trail

Inspiration
Point

Rim Trail

Bryce Point

Paria View

Under-the-
Rim Trail

0   1/2 mi
0   0.5 km

DIXIE

NATIONAL

FOREST

DIXIE

NATIONAL

FOREST

GRAND STAIRCASE-
ESCALANTE
NATIONAL
MONUMENT

Farview
Point

Natural
Bridge

East Fork
Sevier River

Agua
Canyon

Under-the-Rim
Trail

Ponderosa
Canyon

Rainbow
Point

Riggs Spring
Loop Trail

Yovimpa
Point

Bristlecone
Loop Trail

Salt Lake
City

80

84

UTAH

15

70

BRYCE
CANYON
NP

△ Campground
● Overlook
🎪 Picnic Area
■ Point of Interest

114

SAFETY TIPS

Be careful to allow a day or two to acclimatize to the area's elevation—in Bryce, 6,500 to 9,100 feet—before setting out on a major hike. And if a lightning storm comes up, stay away from the canyon rims, particularly the iron railings.

The most direct connection to Bryce Canyon is from Zion National Park north on U.S. 89, then east on Route 12—one argument in favor of paying the $10 RV tunnel fee on the Zion–Mt. Carmel Road. Otherwise, you can access U.S. 89 from the west via Routes 14 or 20 from I-15, or from the north via I-70. Red Canyon on Route 12 is a particularly scenic approach, with rock tunnels and bridges framing the road ahead.

Campground Oases in Bryce Canyon National Park

Bryce Canyon National Park. Bryce has two campgrounds, both near the entrance, open from late spring to early fall, with some limited winter camping. **North Campground** offers 105 sites, and **Sunset** has 111, none with hookups. A sanitary dump station (fee), showers (fee) at Sunset, and flush toilets are available. Picnic tables, fireplaces, and piped water are supplied. Bring your own firewood. There's a 14-day camping limit; pets are permitted on leash. Reservations are not taken, but to check ahead if there's space for the night. Visitor center: Bryce Canyon National Park, P.O. Box 170001, Bryce Canyon, UT 84717 (☎ **435/834-5322**).

Bryce Canyon KOA. This fairly new RV park, at 555 S. Main St. in the town of Panguitch, about 25 miles from Bruce Canyon, has big level sites, 30- or 50-amp hookups, and lots of camping cabins. Call ☎ **800/KOA-1625** or 435/676-2225 for reservations; www.koa.com.

Red Canyon RV Park. Red Canyon, a Good Sam member in Panguitch, has 31 sites, many suitable for big rigs. Located 15 miles from Bryce Canyon on Highway 12, 1 mile east of the junction with 89; open mid-March through mid-November. Call ☎ **435/676-2690** for reservations; fax 435/676-2765.

Kodachrome Basin State Park. Named by the National Geographic Society for its colorful, phallic rock formations called chimneys, Kodachrome Basin is off Route 12 on an unnamed road 7.3 miles south of the junction of Highway 12 and Main Street in Cannonville (look for the sign for Kodachrome Basin), with 27 sites for RVs and a sanitary dump station but no hookups. Call ☎ **435/679-8562** for reservations.

CEDAR BREAKS NATIONAL MONUMENT & CEDAR CITY

The "breaks" in the park name comes from early settlers in the region, who called any terrain too steep for wagon travel "breaks" or "badlands." The

Snowy overlook at Cedar Breaks National Monument.

same folks thought the junipers and ancient bristlecone pine trees growing on the rim of the red rock amphitheater were cedars.

Similar to Bryce Canyon but even more vivid in color, Cedar Breaks is less visited, despite its location only 23 miles from I-15 via Route 14.

A huge rock amphitheater with trails leading 3,400 feet down into the gorge, it offers a special challenge to hikers in good shape. Two special 2-mile walks for those already acclimated to the elevation are the **Alpine Pond Trail,** a fairly easy jaunt to a pond and forest glade, and the **Spectra Point Trail,** a good place to see bristlecone pines. There are also ranger-led nature walks, geology talks, and campfire programs in summer. Information on these activities is listed in the free newspaper you get on entering the park.

Although roads are closed by snow in winter, visitors can come into the park by cross-country skis or snowmobile, entering via Brian Head ski resort. A campground is open June through September only. The **Rim Drive** along Scenic Byway 148 goes through the monument when weather permits.

The **Utah Shakespearean Festival** in nearby Cedar City, going strong for more than 30 years, presents three classic plays in repertory every summer in the outdoor Shakespearean theater, as well as three contemporary plays in a smaller indoor theater. The season runs from early July through September, and playgoers come early to enjoy the evening's Greenshow of jugglers, puppeteers, and vendors dressed in Elizabethan costume. They can also dine at a lively Renaissance Feaste. For information on the festival and reservations, call ☎ **800/PLAY-TIX.**

Campground Oases in the Cedar Breaks/Cedar City Area & North off Interstate 15

Point Supreme Campground. Located in the Cedar Breaks National Monument 1 mile north of the visitor center on Highway 148, Point Supreme Campground offers 30 sites suitable for RVs, with picnic tables, piped water, and flush toilets. Because the elevation is above 10,000 feet, the campground is open mid-June through mid-September only. No reservations are taken, there are no hookups, and a fee is charged (☎ 435/586-9451).

Circleville RV Park and Country Store. Located a half mile south of Circleville on Highway 89, the park is in the heart of Butch Cassidy country and has paved sites, some pull-throughs, and full hookups with 30- and 50-amp electric. Call ☎ 435/577-2437 for reservations; crvpark@aol.com.

Fremont Indian State Park. Near Loa/Richfield, this former Fishlake National Forest campground, previously called Castle Rock and located a couple of miles off I-70 near the junction of I-15, was shifted over to state park status to supplement the park, where part of a large Fremont River Indian village has been excavated. The little-known Fremont River Indians, who preceded the Anasazi, vanished before the first Spanish arrived. We found the campground quiet and uncrowded (we shared its 15 sites with one other RV one moonlit October night). The camping fee also includes admission to the museum. Sites are well spaced out, many shaded by aspens, all with tables; there are flush toilets but no hookups or dump station. Open year-round to RVs 30 feet or under (☎ 800/322-3770 or 435/836-2811).

Butch Cassidy Campground. A Good Sam member, Salina's Butch Cassidy Campground is reached by taking exit 54 from I-70 and driving north 7/10 mile on Route 89. With 50 tent sites and 40 RV sites, the year-round campground offers 20-, 30-, and 50-amp electric hookups and a heated swimming pool. Call ☎ 800/551-6842 or 435/529-7400 for reservations.

CAPITOL REEF NATIONAL PARK

Little-known and little-visited Capitol Reef lies about halfway between Bryce Canyon and Canyonlands on Route 24. The park is notable primarily for its unique **Waterpocket Fold,** a 100-mile wrinkle in the earth's crust formed by enormous pressures deep inside the earth that caused ancient rock beds to buckle. After a rain, pockets in the fold hold water and serve as residence and nursery for the unique spadefoot toad, which lays eggs in the water as soon as it rains so they can hatch into tadpoles, perhaps even make it to adulthood, before the puddles dry up.

Early settlers thought a white sandstone formation in the park resembled the Capitol Dome in Washington and that the Waterpocket Fold looked like a coral reef (although few of them had ever seen either). Ergo, the park is named Capitol Reef (www.nps.gov/care).

A 10-mile, one-way **scenic drive** is accessible to small to medium-sized RVs; pick up a self-guided trail map at the beginning of the drive to follow

Capitol Reef National Park

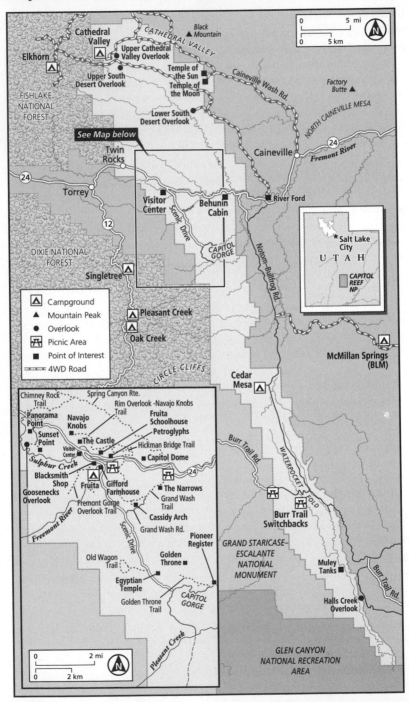

Cathedral Valley

Elkhorn

CATHEDRAL VALLEY

Black Mountain

Upper Cathedral Valley Overlook

Upper South Desert Overlook

Temple of the Sun

Temple of the Moon

Caineville Wash Rd.

Factory Butte

NORTH CAINEVILLE MESA

FISHLAKE NATIONAL FOREST

Lower South Desert Overlook

See Map below

Twin Rocks

Caineville

24

Fremont River

24

Torrey

Visitor Center

Behunin Cabin

River Ford

12

DIXIE NATIONAL FOREST

Scenic Drive

CAPITOL GORGE

Notom-Bullfrog Rd.

Salt Lake City

UTAH

CAPITOL REEF NP

Singletree

Pleasant Creek

Oak Creek

CIRCLE CLIFFS

Cedar Mesa

McMillan Springs (BLM)

Legend

- ⛺ Campground
- ▲ Mountain Peak
- ● Overlook
- 🏕 Picnic Area
- ■ Point of Interest
- ⌗⌗ 4WD Road

Chimney Rock Trail

Spring Canyon Rte.

Panorama Point

Navajo Knobs

Rim Overlook -Navajo Knobs Trail

Fruita Schoolhouse

Sunset Point

The Castle

Petroglyphs

Hickman Bridge Trail

Visitor Center

Capitol Dome

Sulphur Creek

Blacksmith Shop

Fruita

Gifford Farmhouse

24

The Narrows

Goosenecks Overlook

Fremont Gorge Overlook Trail

Grand Wash Trail

Cassidy Arch

Fremont River

Grand Wash Rd.

Pioneer Register

Burr Trail Rd.

WATERPOCKET FOLD

Old Wagon Trail

Golden Throne

Egyptian Temple

Scenic Drive

Golden Throne Trail

CAPITOL GORGE

Burr Trail Switchbacks

GRAND STAIRCASE–ESCALANTE NATIONAL MONUMENT

Muley Tanks

Burr Trail Rd.

Halls Creek Overlook

Pleasant Creek

GLEN CANYON NATIONAL RECREATION AREA

the layers of rock that tilted, folded, and eroded to create today's dramatic formations. While we confess to a certain shortsightedness in recognizing every Egyptian Temple, Golden Throne, Castle, and Chimney dotted on the map, we admire the structure of them. Let's face it—the old-timers had more leisure to sit and contemplate what they resembled than we do.

Fifteen **hiking trails**, from ⅒ mile to 4½ miles, are designated as very easy, easy, moderate, and strenuous. A trail to **Hickman Bridge**, a natural bridge, is 1 mile each way and termed moderate, while a strenuous climb to **Cassidy Arch** is 1¾ miles each way.

Petroglyphs on the canyon walls on the main drive near the visitor center are only a few short steps from the turnout.

In 1900, eight to 10 Mormon families lived here, planting orchards, operating a blacksmith shop, and teaching in a one-room log schoolhouse. The last of the community's residents moved away in 1960, and now the park maintains the village as a restored historic site known as the **Fruita settlement.** The park campgrounds are built in and around the orchards, which are open for visitors to pick their own fruit—you pay by weight at a scale and honor cash box. Browsing mule deer are common in the campgrounds, especially at dawn and dusk.

Butch Cassidy and his gang used to hang out in the neighborhood. Cassidy Arch, on the Grand Wash road off the Scenic Drive, was named for the famous outlaw.

Even more fascinating is the **Behunin Cabin,** a tiny one-room rock cabin where an early Mormon settler raised 10 children. The historical plaque beside it says they ate their meals outdoors, which is only logical, since it would be hard for all of them to be inside at the same time. We can't imagine where they all slept.

Campground Oases in & Around Capitol Reef National Park

Capitol Reef National Park campground. The only RV campground in the park is among the orchards at the Fruita settlement, less than a mile from the visitor center. The 70 RV sites are mostly level, grassy, and tree-shaded, with gorgeous red rock cliffs on all sides and grazing mule deer at dawn and dusk. It's open year-round. There are no hookups, no reservations, a 14-day limit, flush toilets, and a sanitary dump station. One wheelchair-accessible campsite in Loop B is held until 6pm nightly. Capitol Reef National Park, HC70, Box 15, Torrey, UT 84775 (☎ **435/425 3791;** www.nps.gov/care).

TRAVEL TIP

Always take drinking water with you, especially in summer, when hiking or exploring in Capitol Reef National Park. There's no reliable source of water outside the Fruita settlement.

Calf Creek Recreation Area. This campsite, near Escalante, lies in a river bottom canyon surrounded by red cliff walls and has 11 well-spaced sites, some of them adequate for RVs up to 25 feet. Trout fishing is nearby. There are no hookups, a 14-day camping limit, and primitive toilets. A 5-mile trail leads to Calf Creek Falls. Operated by the Bureau of Land Management and closed late November to mid-March, the park is 15 miles northeast of Escalante off Route 12 (☎ **435/826-5499** or 435/826-4291; www.blm.com).

CANYONLANDS NATIONAL PARK

The pristine serenity of Canyonlands has been protected for more than a century, largely because early white settlers deemed the land totally worthless. The Anasazi had lived and farmed the region until 1200, when they mysteriously left, perhaps because of drought, tribal warfare, or the arrival of hostile strangers.

Canyonlands National Park is divided into three separate areas, each self-contained and reached only by exiting one area of the park and reentering elsewhere. **The Maze,** a dense, impenetrable mass of convoluted rock described as "a 30-square-mile puzzle in sandstone," lies southwest of the confluence of the Green and Colorado rivers. **The Needles** is southeast of it, and **Island in the Sky** is north of it. A trail leads to the confluence of the rivers from the road's end at Big Spring Canyon Overlook in The Needles.

Only experienced hikers with good topographic maps and compasses should venture into The Maze, the most remote and forbidding part of Canyonlands, a dense and complex system of chasms and ravines. Two roads suitable only for four-wheel-drive vehicles enter it from the west, but only after a long and rough journey from Route 24 near Goblin Valley State Park.

Spired sandstone walls, some as high as 400 feet, characterize The Needles in the southern part of Canyonlands, 75 miles from Moab, 49 miles

CAMPING AT GLEN CANYON NATIONAL RECREATION AREA

If you're heading into the Glen Canyon National Recreation Area, **Lake Powell Resorts & Marinas** provide RV camping with full hookups at Wahweap, Bullfrog, and Halls Crossing in Glen Canyon. Reservations can be made at ☎ **800/528-6154;** www.visitlakepowell.com. A national park campground at Lees Ferry has no hookups but does have a dump station, showers, and a coin laundry, with sites available on a first-come, first-served basis. Bullfrog Campground has a laundry and showers; Halls Crossing Campground has a dump station, laundry, and showers; and Wahweap Campground, a laundry and showers.

ABOUT EDWARD ABBEY

You won't travel far in southeastern Utah without running across the ghost of the late Edward Abbey, a tough-minded, combative outdoor writer and environmentalist who spent several seasons as a park ranger in Arches.

He was best known for comments like, "You can't see anything from a car; you've got to get out of the goddamned contraption and walk, better yet crawl, on hands and knees, over the sandstone and through the thornbush and cactus. When traces of blood begin to mark your trail, you'll see something, maybe. Probably not." Nevertheless, he wasn't above poking fun at himself as he railed against overuse of his beloved Utah desert. On an early trip into The Maze, the most remote part of Canyonlands, he and a friend stopped to look at an almost-new hiker register.

"Keep the tourists out," a tourist from Salt Lake City had written, to which Abbey added, "As fellow tourists we heartily agree."

Later, still at The Maze, he wrote in the log, "For God's sake leave this country alone—Abbey," to which his friend added, "For Abbey's sake leave this country alone—God."

Pick up a copy of his book, *Desert Solitaire,* at any of the park visitor centers. It makes a good companion on the journey. 🚐

from Monticello, and 31 miles off U.S. 191 via Route 211. Less visited than its northern counterpart, The Needles has a particularly scenic drive outside park perimeters as an introduction.

Island in the Sky, the mesa that composes much of the northern part of Canyonlands, is outlined in a V-shape as the Colorado and the Green rivers meet at the park's belly button. This area is reached by Route 313 off U.S. 191 north of Moab (www.nps.gov/cany).

Views are memorable, especially in early morning or late afternoon when the landscape is gilded with red and gold. **Upheaval Dome,** a short walk from the parking lot at the end of the road at Holman Spring Canyon Overlook, may have been formed when struck by a meteorite—at least that's the explanation we prefer of the two possibilities offered by the information sign at the overlook. The other, much less sexy reason is underground salt buildup that eroded until a crater appeared.

Here at the edge of Canyonlands' Island in the Sky, not at what most viewers assumed was Grand Canyon, is where Thelma and Louise, in the film of the same name, drove their Thunderbird convertible off the cliff.

Both bobcats and mountain lions are occasionally seen in the park, as well as mountain sheep in the White Rim area.

Four-wheel-drive vehicles and backpackers can get much more deeply into the park than RVs and family cars, and there are primitive campsites at intervals along the routes. Throughout Canyonlands, campers are expected to carry their own water and firewood. The only water supply in the park is at the Squaw Flat campground in The Needles, and it is not operative in winter.

Canyonlands National Park

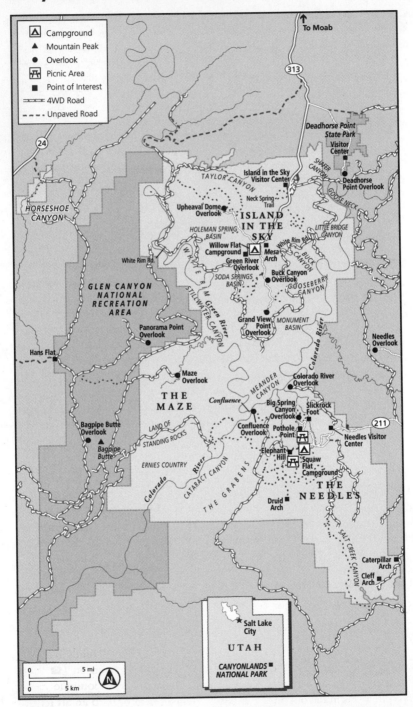

Campground Oases in Canyonlands National Park

Squaw Flat. Squaw Flat, in The Needles section of Canyonlands, has 26 well-separated sites, many snuggled into rock-surrounded coves with trees, and some, but not all, are adequate for RVs up to 28 feet. Each site has fire grates and a table, and there are pit toilets and water available by the bucketful from a water wagon. If you need to top off your RV tank, follow signs to a water hose connection on Cave Spring Road near Wooden Shoe Arch. The campground is located at 2282 S. W. Resource Blvd. in Moab. From U.S. 191 take Utah 211 west to The Needles.

Willow Flat. The only campground in the Island in the Sky area of Canyonlands accessible to most RVs is Willow Flat, down a rough washboard dirt road off Highway 313, with 12 primitive sites for smaller RVs only (under 25 ft.). Unfortunately, gnats are a problem much of the summer. There are pit toilets and fire grates but no water (☎ **435/259-7164;** www.nps.gov/cany).

MOAB, THE MOUNTAIN BIKE CAPITAL OF THE WORLD (& MORE)

Suddenly this faded uranium-prospecting town, best known as a Western-movie location area, has become the mountain bike capital of the world, attracting as many European yuppies as American outdoorsmen to its gentrified streets. The **Moab Slickrock Bicycle Trail,** which begins on Sand Flats Road, 2.3 miles from the intersection of the Sand Flats Road and Millcreek Drive in Moab, and follows a 12.7-mile loop through orange Navajo sandstone, is for experienced bikers with only a little time to spare. The big deal, though, is the 128-mile **Kokopelli's Mountain Biking Trail,** still under construction, between Moab and Grand Junction, Colorado. Ask locally when you get there to see if it's been finished.

The mid-October **Fat Tire Festival** brings hundreds of bikers to join both fun and semicompetitive events. Leading manufacturers of bikes and equipment are there to show off their products and host parties. The weekend before the Festival, Granny Gear Productions organizes an endurance race for four-person teams called "24 Hours of Moab" (☎ **304/259-5533;** www.grannygear.com). For more information, contact **Moab Information Center,** Center and Main streets in Moab (☎ **435/259-8825**).

An itemized list of things to do in the Moab area, detailed in the town's visitor guide, includes aerial tours, backpacking, camp outs and cookouts, dirt biking, hiking, horse and llama pack rides, hot-air balloon rides, helicopter rides, boating, cross-country skiing, four-wheel-drive and all-terrain tours, among many other activities. You can also watch the local sound-and-light show called "Canyonlands by Night."

The uranium miners wouldn't recognize the town with its trendy business names, everything from **Poison Spider Bikes,** 497 N. Main St. (☎ **800/635-1792**), with its espresso bar, to the **Moab Brewery,** a boutique brewery with a dozen flavors on tap at 686 S. Main St. next door to an art gallery promising "an eclectic mix of fun, folk art, and funk" (☎ 435/259-6333). Also in town is a tasting room for Utah's oldest winery, **Arches Vineyards,** at 420 Kane Creek Blvd. It is currently turning out a vintage chardonnay as well as a cabernet, merlot, and pinot noir (☎ 435/259-5397).

Campgrounds in & Around Moab

Dead Horse Point State Park. Dead Horse Point park makes an excellent alternative to the campgrounds at Canyonlands or Arches when they are full, which is most of the time. There are 21 campsites with 20-amp electric hookups, covered cooking/eating areas and windbreaks, metal picnic tables, and concrete pads for RVs. A sanitary dump station is available. A family of mule deer is often seen grazing in the area. The campground is open year-round. The park is located off Route 313 northwest of Moab. Park office at ☎ 435/259-2614 (☎ 800/322-3770 for reservations; www.go-utah.com).

Spanish Trail RV Park and Campground. South of Moab on U.S. 191, Spanish Trail RV Park offers 60 sites with 20-, 30-, and 50-amp electric, cable TV, and city water (☎ 800/787-2751 or 435/259-2411 for reservations; www.moab.net/spanishtrail).

Moab KOA. Also south on U.S. 191, Moab KOA has 103 spaces with 20- and 30-amp electric, city water, and cable TV, as well as an innovative miniature golf course (☎ 800/KOA-0372 or 435/259-6682 for reservations; www.koa.com or www.moab-utah.com).

ARCHES NATIONAL PARK

Arches National Park boasts the world's largest concentration of stone arches, perhaps as many as 2,000 by the most recent tally. To qualify as an arch, the formation has to pass light through an opening at least 3 feet wide.

Some are visible from the paved roadway, others are reached by short or medium hikes from ⅒ mile to 7 miles long. Daily **ranger-guided hikes** are also available; check schedules at the visitor center, located just inside the entrance gate. The Fiery Furnace, for instance, in a labyrinth of red sandstone cliffs and narrow passageways, can be visited only with a ranger; hikes are scheduled twice a day in season and must be reserved in person ahead of time at the visitor center.

See "Seven Sites Offering Deja Vu All Over Again," earlier in this chapter, for the park's most popular long hike, a half-day trip to **Delicate Arch.**

Rock climbers also love the Arches for its cliffs, walls, towers, and cracks in the rock, coupled with incredible views. Modern techniques in rock climbing often avoid the old system of pounding pitons into the rock, then ascending by nylon ladders. Today the goal is to do "free" climbing, either face climbing, in which the climber grasps or steps on natural holds in the rock, or crack climbing, by wedging part of the body into cracks in the rocks. Women can often outdo men in their dexterity in rock climbing.

If you're hiking or camping here, be sure your gas tank is adequately full, and take along your own water, food, and firewood, since nothing is available in the park. Check the website at www.npg.gov/arch.

Campground Oases in & Around Arches National Park

Devil's Garden Campground. Located in Arches National Park, Devil's Garden is situated amid red rocks and green pines near the end of an 18-mile road, with 53 first-come, first-served sites. We suggest that if campground space is still available when you enter the park, no matter what the time of day, that you drive straight to the campground, pick out a spot, and register, then go out to do your sightseeing. The fee is $10 a night, and sites include tables and grills, with flush toilets and piped water. While all the pads are paved, RVs owners will need to check the level, since many are uneven. There is no camping fee when the water is turned off, usually from the end of October until mid-March. Call the park office at ☎ 435/259-8161.
Shady Acres RV Park. Located in the town of Green River at 360 E. Main St. (Business Route 70), it's a favorite of river rafters, fishermen, and melon aficionados (for the festival in late September). Some 68 paved pull-throughs, an RV car wash, cable TV, and 30- and 50-amp electric make this popular with big rigs (☎ 800/537-8674 or 435/564-8290 for reservations; www.shadyacresrv.com).

SALT LAKE CITY

In the early 19th century, itinerant fur traders trapped beavers along the waterways of the Wasatch Mountains, but by midcentury Mormon colonists, following the commands of Brigham Young, had established farms and settlements in the "vast desert" of the Great Salt Lake Valley with irrigation and a lot of hard work. Many of the colonists who walked to Utah, pulling handcarts filled with their possessions, were immigrants recruited in Europe by Mormon missionaries. Settlers fought off hostile Indians, bad weather that destroyed the crops, and clouds of locusts. A flock of seagulls flew in and devoured the locusts, and to this day you'll see large numbers of California gulls, the state bird of Utah, all around the Great Salt Lake.

In **This Is the Place State Park** in Emigration Canyon, west of Salt Lake City on Sunnyside Avenue, a monument marks the spot where Brigham Young stopped on July 24, 1847, and proclaimed he'd found the haven that would shelter his 148 weary followers from persecution because no outsider would covet this barren basin with its saltwater lake.

RVers will enjoy Salt Lake City's wide streets and easy layout. Primary tourist goals are **Temple Square,** where the Mormon Tabernacle Choir's Thursday night rehearsals and Sunday broadcasts are open to the public, as well as daily organ recitals. Two **visitor centers** are on the square with tours of the Temple Square area starting by the flagpole every few minutes.

You can even search out your family roots at the **Family Search Center** in the famous genealogy files of The Church of Jesus Christ of Latter-day Saints. For more information on tours and events call ☎ **800/537-9703.**

Winter visitors to Salt Lake City, site of the Winter Olympics in 2002, can take advantage of Utah's champagne powder snow at smaller ski resorts like **Brighton** (☎ **800/873-5512**) and **Solitude Mountain** (☎ **800/748-4754**), both in Big Cottonwood Canyon 30 miles east of town by exit 7 from I-215.

Taste bud treats abound in this legendary sweet-tooth town, from **Snelgrove's ice cream** at locations all over town to **Cumming's Studio Chocolates,** 679 E. 900 S. (☎ **801/328-4858**), from **Peppermint Place candy factory** tour at 155 E. 200 N. in Alpine (☎ **801/756-7400**) to the **Deli Lama Tony Caputo's** downtown, 308 W. 300 S. (☎ **801/531-8669**).

Campground Oases in Northern Utah

Century Mobile Home & RV Park. Located off I-15 at exit 346 in Ogden, near three local ski areas. It's open year-round and offers pull-throughs, big-rig, and full-hookup sites with 30- and 50-amp electric and cable TV (☎ **801/731-3800** for reservations).

Bear Lake KOA. This KOA is on U.S. 89 in Garden City in Utah's northeast corner, en route to Yellowstone and adjacent to Bear Lake, home of the world's most delicious raspberries. Only a mile north of town, the campground is open from May 1 through October 31, but book well ahead for the end of July raspberry season. There are 100 pull-through sites with 30-amp electric and water hookups; 56 of them also have sewer hookups (☎ **800/KOA-3442** or 435/946-3454 for reservations; www.koa.com).

Antelope Island State Park. Antelope Island is in the Great Salt Lake, accessible by the Route 127 causeway, and has several parking-lot RV "campsites" by the beach and at White Rock Bay. No hookups. Fees are $6 for day use and $8 for overnight stays (☎ **801/773-2941** for reservations).

Cherry Hill. Cherry Hill, 20 minutes north of Salt Lake City in Kaysville, provides splashy summer fun for the family between early April and early November with its water park, miniature golf, hamster haven, aeroball, and batting cages, plus 240 RV campsites with 30- and 50-amp electric hookups. Note, however, that the amusements are closed on Sunday. From the junction of I-15 and U.S. 89, take exit 326 and drive 2 miles north on 89. The campground is on the left (☎ **888/4-GO-CAMP** for reservations; fax 801/451-2267; www.cherry-hill.com).

Camp VIP. Within walking distance of Temple Square in downtown Salt Lake City, Camp VIP is open year-round and has 226 full hookups offering 30- and 50-amp electric, an RV wash, and heated spa. Only half an hour from many of the ski areas, this park attracts long-term visitors and big rigs (☎ **800/226-7752** or 801/328-0224 for reservations; www.campvip.com).

Northern Utah Campgrounds

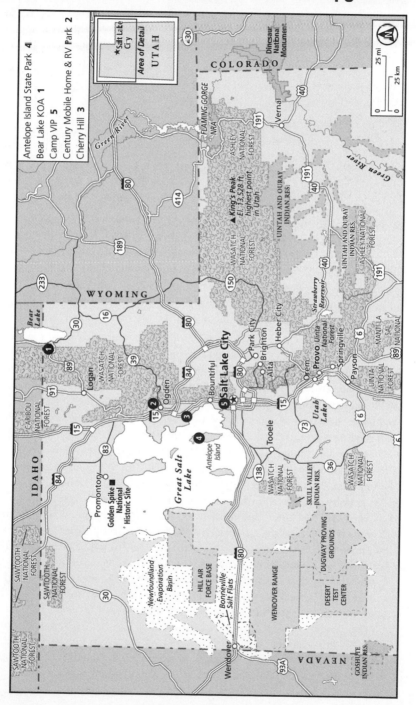

Antelope Island State Park **4**
Bear Lake KOA **1**
Camp VIP **5**
Century Mobile Home & RV Park **2**
Cherry Hill **3**

Ten Scenic Side Trips

1. **Kolob Terrace Road to Kolob Reservoir.** Kolob Terrace Road strikes out to the north for 25 miles from the town of Virgin (like the river) on Route 9 west of Zion National Park. From farms with lush grass and trees it climbs up through ranch land terrain amid rich red rocks, into groves of aspen and oaks, and into the secluded high country. If the dirt road to Lava Rock looks passable, take the short detour out to an over-look down into Zion Canyon. The lightly traveled Kolob Terrace Road, paved for most of its length, is not recommended for long travel trailers and RVs over 32 feet because there are few pullouts and no good turn-arounds along the way. Allow 1½ to 2 hours for the round-trip.

2. **Kolob Canyons.** The northern end of Zion National Park, Kolob Canyons is only 5 minutes away from I-15 at exit 42, and cannot be reached by vehicle from the rest of the park. The beautiful 5-mile drive winds its way between the red Navajo sandstone Finger Canyons to a forested overlook among groves of piñon pine and aspen. Several hik-ing trails set out from the overlook area, including a moderately stren-uous 5-mile trek along Taylor Creek and a strenuous 14-mile hike to Kolob Arch, believed to be the world's largest freestanding arch.

3. **Scenic Byway Route 12.** Running between Escalante and Boulder, Scenic Byway Route 12 climbs a narrow hogback ridge near Calf Creek Recreation Area amid breathtaking views and sheer drop-offs. The Civilian Conservation Corps built the road here in the early 1940s; until then, the mail was delivered by mule into Boulder. Mountain bikers and four-wheel-drive vehicles can take the original Hell's Backbone dirt road into Dixie National Forest and Box Death Hollow Road, scourge of the mule-riding mailmen. **Petrified Forest State Park** at Escalante dis-plays colorful specimens of petrified wood (☎ 520/524-6228; www. go-utah.com). **Anasazi Indian Village State Park** at Boulder exhibits a reconstructed pueblo where you can try your hand at grinding corn (☎ 435/355-7308). The former also has a campground, but a more attractive spot, if there's space, is **Calf Creek Recreation Area** (see listing under "Campground Oases in & Around Capitol Reef National Park," earlier in this chapter). The 32-mile road between Boulder and Grover, the last of it not paved until 1985, passes through elegant groves of aspen, past several forest service campgrounds, and over a 9,600-foot pass (☎ 435/826-5499; www.blm.com).

4. **Bicentennial Highway.** So-named because it was built in 1976, the Bicentennial Highway opens up one of the most sensational stretches of countryside in the West. From Hanksville south on 95 to Blanding in the Four Corners country, the terrain unfolds with one spectacular vista after another. The Henry Mountains, snow-capped and framed with red rock buttes and golden fields of hay, stand out against a vast

blue sky. Washes are delineated with narrow stripes of cottonwood, leaves bright green in summer and gold in autumn. After a rain, birds flock to the water shining from holes and grooves in the rock. At Hites Crossing on Lake Powell, a delicate arched bridge crosses the Colorado River while houseboats bob at anchor all around the nooks and crannies of the lake.

5. **Natural Bridges National Monument.** For RVers in a hurry, there are three natural bridges easily seen from roadside viewpoints along the Route 275 circle loop through the monument; they're accessible by hiking trails for travelers who want to explore. A small visitor center details the differences between natural bridges and arches. The campground here, while dotted with trees and very attractive, is too small for any RVs over 21 feet long. Don't even attempt to drive a big rig into it (☎ 801/692-1234; www.nps.gov/nabr).

6. **The 50-mile loop around Brian Head and Cedar Breaks National Monument.** Beautiful any time of year, but especially in winter when snow sets off the bright red rock formations of the huge natural amphitheater. Many photographers feel it's even more dramatic than Bryce Canyon. The roads are usually clear into Brian Head but might sometimes be closed in winter into Cedar Breaks. Exit 78 at Parowan from I-15 leads to Route 143 and Brian Head; from there, take Route 148 through Cedar Breaks and Route 14 back downhill into Cedar City. Call Cedar Breaks at ☎ 801/586-9451; www.nps.gob.cebr.

7. **Kodachrome Basin State Park.** The aptly named Kodachrome Basin State Park, 7 miles off Highway 12 at Cannonville, makes a dramatic detour by paved road into more stunning rock formations. Hiking trails and horseback riding are available, as well as a campground with 24 concrete pad sites, tables, grills, piped water, flush toilets, and showers. You'll find a sanitary dump station and camper supply store but no hookups. The National Geographic Society, by the way, is the group that named this colorful basin (☎ 435/679-8562; www.go-utah.com).

8. **The Bullfrog Basin loop, Glen Canyon National Recreation Area.** Some 75 miles long, the Bullfrog Basin loop ventures more deeply into Glen Canyon than Route 95. Take the Route 276 cutoff north of Hite Crossing and rejoin Route 95 just before Natural Bridges National Monument. The Bullfrog Marina provides rentals for power- and houseboats, as well as an 86-unit campground and some beach area for swimmers. To complete the loop, you'll have to take the toll ferry called the John Atlantic Burr that goes to Halls Crossing; it can handle all sizes of RVs. You could also take a houseboat out for a few days, towing a small powerboat behind, and explore Anasazi caves, discover remote rock arches, and go hiking. Call ARAMARK, the national park's concessionaire (☎ 800/528-6154; www.go-utah.com).

9. **The Riverway (Route 128).** North of Moab, Route 128, also called the Riverway, strikes east along the Colorado River for 45 miles, following a winding scenic drive into Negro Bill Canyon, named for William Granstaff, a prospector who ventured through in 1877, some said selling whiskey to the Indians. Along the route you can go camping; river running by raft, kayak, or canoe; mountain biking; hiking; or riding off-road vehicles on designated trails. Big Bend Recreation Site offers attractive nonhookup campsites by the river big enough for RVs and with tables and grills, a good alternative when Arches is full. The Bureau of Land Management suggests wearing a life jacket when swimming or boating in the river. Call them at ☎ 435/259-6111.

10. **Dead Horse Point State Park.** Dead Horse Point takes your breath away as you peer over the edge of a sheer 2,000-foot cliff into the double gooseneck loops of the muddy Colorado River cutting its way through red earth and green vegetation. Because of exposed cliff edges and a paucity of railings, we heard a local guide caution his group of chattering Japanese schoolgirls to "Be careful." They chorused back cheerfully in unison, "Be care-full." Wild mustangs were herded and broken here in the old days because a simple brush fence could close the narrow neck to the point. After taking the best of the horses, cowboys would leave the fence open to let the "broomtails" (culls) from the herd pick their way back to the open range. Unfortunately, one group of broomtails got confused and wandered in circles until they died of thirst, ironically while looking down at the waters of the Colorado far below. To get to the park, take 191 to 313 south, which ends at the park (☎ 435/259-2614; www.go-utah.com).

Driving the Alaska Highway

ALASKA IS WHERE PEOPLE RELISH SPAM AND LINE UP ON HIGHWAY roadkill lists for a chance at the next moose struck down by a car. It's where Warren G. Harding drove a golden spike to mark the completion of the Alaska Railroad in 1923, and where the most powerful earthquake ever to hit the North American continent struck on Good Friday in 1964—a 9.2 on the Richter scale, which lasted an incredible 5 minutes.

It's where you can stand in mud up to your knees and have dust blow in your face, where mosquitoes are as big as hummingbirds, and where you won't be considered a real Alaskan until—to paraphrase the locals in more polite terms—you've wrestled a grizzly, urinated in the Yukon, and had an amorous encounter with a bear.

The beginning of the Alaska Highway in Dawson Creek, British Columbia.

Alaska Highlights

MILEAGE CHART — Approximate driving distances in miles between cities.	Anchorage	Circle	Dawson City	Eagle	Fairbanks	Haines	Homer	Prudhoe Bay	Seattle	Seward	Skagway	Tok	Valdez
Anchorage		520	494	501	358	775	226	847	2234	126	832	328	304
Circle	520		530	541	162	815	746	1972	2271	646	872	368	526
Dawson City	494	530		131	379	548	713	868	1843	619	430	189	428
Eagle	501	541	131		379	620	727	868	1974	627	579	173	427
Fairbanks	358	162	379	379		653	584	489	2121	484	710	206	364
Haines	775	815	548	620	653		1001	1142	1774	901	359	447	701
Homer	226	746	713	727	584	1001		1073	2455	173	1058	554	530
Prudhoe Bay	847	1972	868	868	489	1142	1073		2610	973	1199	695	853
Seattle	2243	2271	1843	1974	2121	1774	2455	2610		1361	1577	1931	2169
Seward	126	646	619	627	484	901	173	973	1361		958	454	430
Skagway	832	872	430	579	710	359	1058	1199	1577	958		504	758
Tok	328	368	189	173	206	447	554	695	1931	454	504		254
Valdez	304	526	428	427	364	701	530	853	2169	430	758	254	

Chukchi Sea

Little Diòmede Island

Nome

Norton Sound

YUKON DELTA NWR

Bethel

Nunivak Island

YUKON DELTA NWR

Bering Sea

Pribilof Islands

Bristol Bay

Attu Island

Cape St. Stephen

Rat Islands

ALASKA PENINSULA

Aleutian Islands

Adak

Adak Island

Atka

Atka Island

Fort Glen

Dutch Harbor

Unimak Island

Unalaska

Cold Bay

3,600 billed caps/Toad River Lodge **4**
Action Jackson's Bar **11**
Alaska Wild Berry chocolates **21**
Alaskaland **15**
Alaskan Brewery and Bottling Company **8**
Baranof Hotel **8**
Bird House Bar **21**
Bonanza Meat Company **10**
Braeburn Lodge **6**

Dawson Peaks Resorts **12**
Denali National Park Visitor Access Center **18**
Denali State Park **20**
Diamond Tooth Gertie's **10**
ERA Aviation **22**
The Double Musky **21**
Goldfields Bakery **2**
Hyder ghost town **1**

0 100 mi
0 100 km

Ferry – – – –
Unpaved Road – – –

ARCTIC OCEAN

Beaufort Sea

Barrow

Prudhoe Bay

Deadhorse

CAPE KRUSENSTERN NM
BROOKS RANGE

NOATAK N PRES

Anaktuvuk Pass

ARCTIC NWR

KOBUK VALLEY NP

Kotzebue

BROOKS RANGE

UNITED STATES
CANADA

NORTHWEST TERRITORIES

GATES OF THE ARCTIC NP AND PRES

Dalton Hwy.

BERING LAND BRIDGE N PRES

Bettles

Fort Yukon

YUKON FLATS NWR

Dempster Hwy.

ARCTIC CIRCLE

8

Galena

Manley Hot Springs

Chena Hot Springs

Circle

YUKON-CHARLEY RIVERS NP

5

CANADA

Unalakleet

2 15

16

Fairbanks

6

Eagle

YUKON

Yukon River

17

14

Delta Junction

5 10

Dawson City, Yukon

DENALI NP

18

13 9

11

McGrath

19

ALASKA RANGE

8

Tok

12

6

Kuskokwim River

Mt. McKinley

3

4

9

4

20

Talkeetna

Glennallen

2

Willow

1

WRANGELL MTS.

Whitehorse, Yukon

1

Wasilla

Palmer

10

McCarthy

4 1

3

Anchorage

22 21

LAKE CLARK NP AND PRES

Kenai

Valdez

9

6

5

4

Soldotna

Whittier

Cordova

7

Skagway

1

Dillingham

Seward

Prince William Sound

7

BRITISH COLUMBIA

King Salmon

Homer

Halibut Cove

KENAI FJORDS NP

Yakutat

GLACIER BAY NP AND PRES

8 Juneau

2

Seldovia

KATMAI NP AND PRES

Alaska Marine Highway

Haines

Gustavus

ADMIRALTY ISLAND NM

Cook Inlet

Kodiak

Gulf of Alaska

Chichagof Island

Kodiak Island

Admiralty Island

ANIAKCHAK NM AND PRES

Baranof Island

Sitka

Petersburg

Prince of Wales Island

1 Wrangell

PACIFIC OCEAN

Craig

Ketchikan

MISTY FJORDS NM

Prince Rupert, B.C.

To Seattle

Kantishna Roadhouse **4**
Log Cabin Restaurant **4**
Lung Duck Tong restaurant **4**
Malamute Saloon **4**
Midnight Sun **4**
Nenana tripod **4**
North Pole **4**
Palace Grand Theatre/Gaslight Follies **4**
Pump House Restaurant **4**

Sign Post Forest, Watson Lake **4**
Sourdough Campground **4**
Taku Smokeries Market Place **4**
"Teslin taxi"/George Johnston Museum **4**
Turnagain Arm/Alyeska/Portage Glacier **4**
White Pass & Yukon Railway **4**
World's largest chopstick
   manufacturing plant **4**
Wrangell–St. Elias National Park and Preserve **4**

It's where Arco tapped a $10 billion oil reserve at Prudhoe Bay in 1968 and Exxon spilled 11 million gallons of it off Valdez in 1989, where Russia established an outpost in the 19th century, and where a historical marker at a creek-side bordello describes the area as a place where the salmon and the fishermen both came upstream to spawn.

It was where wannabe gold miners headed for the Klondike by any means they could, crammed into any boat that could float and some that couldn't, where salesmen brought their inventory, gamblers their cards and dice, women their bodies for sale or their scrub boards and sadirons for labor. And all of them intended to get rich.

Last, Alaska is where they keep the Alaska Highway, the road that helped prevent the Japanese from invading the North American mainland during World War II, aided Alaska in achieving statehood in 1959, and, more recently, set off a flourishing bumper sticker and T-shirt industry with lurid illustrations around the theme "I Drove the Alaska Highway."

BUILDING THE HIGHWAY

When Japan bombed Pearl Harbor in December 1941, it didn't take long for the U.S. government to look at a map and see that the narrow Bering Strait that separated the westernmost spot in North America—in Alaska—from the easternmost spot in Asia—in Siberia—was only 36 miles across. With the Japanese navy lurking close to North American shores (and even invading the Aleutians) and Russia an ally that desperately needed supplies, the United States decided its Corps of Engineers should construct an inland road to Alaska. Because timing was important, trainloads of U.S. soldiers and equipment began arriving in tiny, remote Dawson Creek before any agreement was signed with Canada. All told, 33,000 men would work on the road that year, 11,000 of them U.S. Army troops, and some 200 would die in the subzero temperatures and hazardous working conditions.

"They didn't build a city here; they found gold. That's the whole story of Alaska."
—Ruth Allman, Alaska pioneer

The surveyors were just steps ahead of the bulldozers that winter of 1942, sinking into the mud and the permafrost below it. Not much attention was paid to grades or curves. As the surveyors pointed to what they perceived as the horizon, the bulldozers followed in their footsteps. The original 1,422-mile road was built in only 8 months and 12 days.

Canadian construction crews cleaned up and straightened out the roadway for the next several years, but the Japanese threat in Alaskan waters had subsided. By 1949, the road was open to traffic, and paving continued sporadically until the last stretch was more or less covered by macadam in 1992. Drivers today still encounter rough stretches undergoing construction.

RVing Along the Alaska Highway

While the mighty Alaska Highway still strikes fear into the hearts of travelers, it's become more tame in recent years. The main attraction to the RVer is a combination of end-of-the-world roadways peeling off it at intervals and all the incredible scenery and wildlife waiting to be discovered along the way, from craggy peaks capped with perpetual snow, hanging and calving glaciers, golden midnight sunsets, and swirling acid-green northern lights to grizzly bears, moose, caribou, bald eagles, and sometimes wolves.

The **eastern access route** goes from Great Falls to Calgary, across Alberta to Edmonton and northwest to Dawson Creek. The **western access route** sets out from Seattle, north on I-5 to the Trans-Canada 1, east to Hope and north via either the new Coquihalla Highway or the slower Route 97 to Cache Creek, Quesnel, Prince George, and Dawson Creek.

The first challenge in driving the Alaska Highway is to get to the starting point, the famous **Mile 0,** located in Dawson Creek, British Columbia (B.C.), 817 miles north of Seattle on the western access route (or 867 miles northwest of Great Falls, Montana, on the eastern access route).

Eighty percent of the Alaska Highway is in Canada, which is why some people still call it by its nickname "the Alcan." While it sounds appropriate, even hip, to some citizens from the Lower 48, the very word *Alcan* makes Alaskans and Canadians of a certain age bristle because it was an acronym for the Alaska-Canada Military Highway, which did not permit civilian travel during the war years. Locals equate it to calling San Francisco "Frisco."

Rocky Crest Lake, near Muncho Lake on the Alaska Highway.

Despite losing their box office billing in the official name, the Canadians got a good deal because in 1946, after the war that created its construction, they bought their share at half what it cost to build.

The precise length of the Alaska Highway keeps changing as engineers straighten out its notorious curves. The original, or historic, mileposts are still used as addresses by the businesses and residents along the highway. Contemporary mileposts reflect the present distances, while in Canada kilometer posts are also in service.

Another point of contention is where the highway actually starts and stops. Historic Mile 0 is in **Dawson Creek, British Columbia,** and the true terminus is in **Delta Junction, Alaska,** because a road connecting Delta Junction and Fairbanks already existed. Most Alaska Highway travelers, however, consider **Fairbanks** the real end of the highway, after which they usually head south via **Denali National Park and Preserve** to **Anchorage.**

HITTING THE HIGHLIGHTS

With only a 2-week vacation, you can still see a lot of Alaska, especially if you fly in (say, to Anchorage) and pick up an RV there (see "To Bring Your Own RV or to Rent?" below, for rental information). From Anchorage, take Route 3 north to Fairbanks; Route 2 east to Delta Junction, where you pick up the official Alaska Highway; and continue southeast on Route 2, which becomes Highway 1 when you cross the Canadian border. Through the Yukon, continue southeast on Highway 1 to Whitehorse. From here, you could follow Route 2 north to Dawson or continue along the Alaska Highway, Route 1, to Watson Lake. If time permits, follow the Alaska Highway, now Route 97 in British Columbia, to Dawson Creek, the beginning of the Alaska Highway. If you want to vary your return route, take Route 1 (the Glenn Highway) southwest from Tok to Anchorage.

GOING FOR THE LONG HAUL

If you want to stretch out your Alaska RV adventure for a full summer, follow as many of the 10 side trips listed at the end of this chapter as you can squeeze in and weather permits. In spring and fall, check ahead on weather conditions since there could be a late thaw and some roads still closed by snowpack in spring. We were snowed in one August day in Dawson City when a storm dumped so much of the white stuff the roads were closed.

Travel Essentials

WHEN TO GO

While the highway is open and maintained year-round, RV visitors will find mid-May to late September best. The "season," according to the locals we met on our mid-May trip, had not yet begun, which meant we could find empty campsites late in the day. But a few lodges and service stations had not yet opened for the summer. Try to avoid July and August, when RVs are almost bumper-to-bumper along some stretches of the highway.

TO BRING YOUR OWN RV OR TO RENT?

To take your own RV to Alaska without amassing a lot of overland miles or doubling back over the same territory, consider taking it aboard one of the Alaska ferries from Bellingham, Washington, to Skagway, which connects by road with Whitehorse or Watson Lake. Call ☎ **800/382-9229** for reservations as soon as possible after January 1 of the year you want to travel—and be patient, the line is often busy. Or check the website: www.akms.com/ferry.

Alternatively, you can rent, starting out from Seattle, Skagway, or Anchorage. To rent an RV in British Columbia or Alaska, reserve as early as possible and determine whether you can pick up at one point and drop off at another. In Alaska, Anchorage is the center of RV rentals, with a number of companies such as these:

- **ABC Motorhome Rentals:** ☎ **800/421-7456;** www.abcmotorhome.com.
- **Alaska Motorhome Rentals:** ☎ **800/254-9929;** www.alaskarv.com, has one ways between Skagway and Seattle.
- **Alaska Panorama:** ☎ **800/478-1401;** www.alaskan.com/alaska panorama.
- **Alexander's RV Rental:** ☎ **888/660-5115;** rvman@gci.net.
- **Clippership Motorhome Rentals:** ☎ **800/421-3456;** www.custom cpu.com/commercial/clippership.
- **Cruise America:** ☎ **800/327-7799;** www.cruiseamerica.com.
- **Great Alaskan Holidays Inc.:** ☎ **888/225-2752;** www.greatalaskan holidays.com.
- **Murphy's RV:** ☎ **800/582-5123;** murphysrv@gci.net.
- **Sweet Retreat Motorhome Rentals:** ☎ **800/759-4861;** www.sweet retreat.com.

Ferries in Alaska carry RVs as well as cars.

Call for prices, making sure to weigh the unlimited mileage rate against per mile fees.

A Seattle-based company called **Alaska Highway Cruises** (☎ 800/ 323-5757; www.alaskarv.com/vacpac.html) markets a combination package that includes one of several overland itineraries in a type C motor home with paid reserved campsites nightly and an Alaska cruise aboard a Holland America Line luxury ship. Its 12-day program lets you fly to Anchorage, pick up an RV, drive to Denali and Fairbanks, take the Alaska Highway to Tok, the Taylor Highway and Top of the World Highway to Dawson City, and then the Klondike Highway to Whitehorse and Skagway. At Skagway you pick up a cruise ship that cruises Glacier Bay, calls in Ketchikan, and returns you to Vancouver for a flight home. The whole package starts at around $2,500 per person, double occupancy, plus airfare to Seattle, and includes the cruise with all meals and entertainment, a fully furnished rental RV, campground reservations and fees. You buy the gas and food.

Our 21-foot Fleetwood Jamboree rented from Alaska Highway Cruises averaged 6 to 7 miles per gallon on the Alaska Highway. We drove a total of 3,100 miles, spending approximately $600 on gas and about $500 on food and beverages for two a couple of years ago when gas was cheaper.

WHAT TO TAKE

Binoculars, cameras and plenty of film, a world-class mosquito repellent, sunscreen, and good maps. Fishermen will want to carry fishing gear for lake trout, northern pike, Dolly Varden, arctic grayling, and five species of Pacific salmon. Spin or bait-cast fishing and/or fly-fishing rods and tackle capable of handling fish up to 30 pounds are recommended by the experts.

For the RV, take spare parts such as a fan belt, oil filter, air filter, radiator hose, and heater hose. Mud flaps or "eyelashes" for the back are a good idea to keep gravel and mud from splashing all over the rear window. We took a basic tool kit and an emergency medical kit, neither of which we had to open.

WHAT TO WEAR

Although we took along ski-weight down parkas and heavy-soled hiking boots, we never donned either. Walking or jogging shoes were adequate on the short trails we hiked. But dedicated hikers and climbers should carry specialized equipment. A raincoat and umbrellas are a good idea, since it can rain or snow, but don't be surprised to find Fairbanks sunny and hot. Dress is casual all over Alaska, so typical RV outfits will pass muster anywhere (except on a cruise ship, if you take the Alaska Highway Cruise package).

TRIMMING COSTS ON THE ROAD

The type of RV you choose to drive can make a big difference in expense on the road. The best gas mileage and greatest route flexibility comes from a four-wheel-drive truck camper with a cab-over sleeping and cooking unit, but you'll sacrifice some of the comforts a type C or type A motor home can provide. (This quandary inspired a popular bumper sticker that says, "Sure it gets lousy gas mileage for a car, but it gets great mileage for a house.")

Staying in government campgrounds without facilities is much cheaper than private campgrounds with hookups. Parking by the side of the road is cheapest of all, if you're in an area where you feel safe. However, noting how many RV parks list security as a plus, we don't recommend it. (See "Should You Sleep by the Side of the Road?" in chapter 3, "Where to Sleep: Campgrounds & RV Parks.")

Food is expensive in the north, so **stock up with as many provisions as you can** in the gateway cities to the south.

WHERE TO GET TRAVEL INFORMATION

Contact the **Alaska Travel Industry Association,** Dept. 101, P.O. Box 196710, Anchorage, AK 99579. Call ☎ **907/929-2200;** www.travelalaska.com, for a free booklet, *Alaska State Vacation Planner.*

Tourism British Columbia, Parliament Buildings, Victoria, BC, Canada V8V 1X4 (☎ **800/663-6000;** www.hellobc.com), provides a lot of free material about the province, including maps, campground guides, and other specialized information.

Tourism Yukon, P.O. Box 2703-VG, Whitehorse, YT, Canada Y1A 2C6 (☎ **867/667-5340;** www.touryukon.com), can also provide material, including maps and campground guides.

Last, don't set out on the Alaska Highway drive without the road bible called *Milepost* ($23.95), published annually by Vernon Publications, Bellevue, Washington (☎ **800/726-4707**). It includes mile-by-mile logs of all the North Country highways, as well as updated road conditions, best places to spot wildlife, and every hiccup of life along the highway. You can order it from the company or buy it en route in many of the towns or roadside lodges, or at most major bookstores in the United States.

DRIVING & CAMPING TIPS

- **Expect to drive with your headlights on.** In this part of Canada the law requires it, and in times when dust is billowing, you'll be glad the oncoming traffic is visible (and you to it) through the clouds.

- **Don't try to "make time" on the road;** it can make you crazy. We saw too many RVers limping into camp exhausted at 9pm—they'd kept driving because the sun was still high, either not knowing or ignoring the fact that in summer it almost never sets this far north. Even if you drove your RV hell-for-leather, ignoring loose gravel, buckled roadways, and potholes, you'd miss a lot of the scenery and the wildlife, two of the most important reasons for being there.

- **Always top off your gas tank when you pass an open station.** Sometimes a station ahead may be closed for the day or gone out of business. Our closest call came on the Klondike Highway when we had to drive 269 miles between open stations and finally rolled into Dempster Corner on fumes. Another time, we turned around and drove 20 miles back to buy gas at a station we had passed up because the one we were headed for was closed.

- **Watch for frost heaves.** These are the biggest enemy your vehicle has: irregular bumps where the pavement has buckled or sunk because of permafrost melting and refreezing. Spots may be marked with red flags by the roadside, but sometimes the wind takes them away. If the white center or side lines look squiggly, slow down.

- **Don't drink the water.** We make it a habit never to assume any piped campground water is potable, using it only for the kitchen and bathroom. We drink bottled water and use prepackaged ice, which is available almost everywhere along the route in Alaska and northern Canada, where tap water sometimes comes out in shades of brown. Also, never drink water from a stream or lake. The parasite *giardia,* which can cause extreme intestinal upset and is impervious to antibiotics, is present in northern Canada and Alaska waterways.

- **Come prepared.** Stock up your RV with any esoteric items before you get into the woods. You'll be able to find basic groceries, towing services, RV repairs, and telephones along the road; but if you want to prepare a bouillabaisse with your freshly caught fish, take your own saffron and sauvignon blanc along with you.

The Best Alaska Highway Sights, Tastes & Experiences

OFF-THE-WALL ATTRACTIONS

A collection of 3,600 billed caps. They're stapled to the ceiling at Toad River Lodge, Mile 422, making an intricately textured soundproofing (☎ 250/232-5401).

The Sign Post Forest, Watson Lake. Located at Mile 612, the Sign Post Forest started in 1942 when a homesick GI from Illinois working on the highway put up a road sign to his hometown, and has grown to some 42,000 signs from all over the world.

The "Teslin taxi." Photographer George Johnston had a 1928 Chevrolet shipped up to the little Tlingit town of Teslin by barge, despite the fact there were no roads. He built a 3-mile road for summer use, then put chains on the taxi and drove it across the frozen lake in winter. See the restored vehicle in the George Johnston Museum, on the left of the highway as you head north. Open late May to early September (☎ 867/390-2550; www.yukon web.com/community/teslin/museum).

Action Jackson's Bar, Boundary. At the Top of the World Highway on the Alaska side of the Alaska/Canada border, Yukon Highway 9, Action Jackson's was one of Alaska's first roadhouses, manned by its eponymous owner, who kept six-shooters strapped to each hip. Restless citizens used to drive the 70 miles from Dawson City on a Friday or Saturday night for the action. Today it has no liquor license, but you can get gas, as a rule.

The Bird House Bar, Indian. Located in Indian, 27 miles southeast of Anchorage on the Seward Highway, the Bird House collapsed during the 1964 earthquake and is half-buried, with a giant blue bird head facing the highway and everything inside on a slant.

Chetwynd, the chainsaw-carving capital of the world. With its distinctive three bears, heroic loggers, and other rustic road sculptures, it sits on B.C.'s Highway 97 at the junction of Route 29.

North Pole. This town, at Mile 349 on the Richardson Highway, 13 miles south of Fairbanks, is where letters to Santa Claus are delivered by the U.S. Postal Service. See Mr. and Mrs. Claus at Santa Claus House (☎ 800/ 588-4678).

The big black-and-white tripod in Nenana. It's put out on the Nenana River ice in winter, connected to a clock. When the ice breaks up enough in the river to drag the tripod cable and stop the clock, lottery ticket holders who guessed the closest date and time share a prize that can run up to $180,000. A hint to would-be winners: The ice usually breaks up some time between mid-April and mid-May. Nenana is an hour's drive south of Fairbanks on the Parks Highway. Purchase in person only at Nenana Visitor Center, at the intersection of the highway and A Street (☎ 907/832-9953).

Hyder, "the friendliest ghost town in Alaska." Off the Cassier Highway straddling the Canadian border at Stewart, Hyder is where people traditionally pin a dollar to the wall in the Glacier Inn in case they pass through again in the future broke and in need of a drink. The bars here are open 23 hours a day.

TEN GREAT SPLURGES

1. **Dinner at the elegant Log Cabin Restaurant.** At the Log Cabin, on Tabor Lake near Prince George, B.C. (☎ 250/963-9515), host Richard Gunther will show you his astonishing collection of antique stoves and sewing machines, plus Indian artifacts, stuffed and mounted black bears and wolves, and everything else you could imagine. The food is Continental with a German accent (Gunther is from Berlin), and dinner begins with a bottomless tureen of homemade soup.

2. **An evening of gaming at Diamond Tooth Gertie's.** Named for Gertie Lovejoy, who had a diamond wedged between her two front teeth, Gertie's is located at the corner of Queen Street and 4th Avenue in Dawson City. It gets especially rambunctious at the end of the season when all the locals are trying to win enough money to head south for the winter. (No one under 19 admitted.) Contact the Klondike Visitors Association for information (☎ 867/993-5575).

A CRASH COURSE IN SPEAKING ALASKAN

The Bush: Any place reached by plane instead of road or Alaska ferry.
Cheechako: A newcomer.
Native: Not just anyone born in Alaska, only those belonging to one of the Native American peoples of Alaska: the Athabaskan, Yup'ik, Cup'ik, Inupiaq, St. Lawrence Island Yupik, Aleut, Alutiiq, Eyak, Tlingit, Haida, or Tsimshian peoples.
Outside: Anywhere that isn't Alaska; generally the lower 48 states.
Permafrost: The permanently frozen subsoil that covers much of the state.
Sourdough: Anyone who's been in Alaska longer than one season, as in "Sour on Alaska without enough dough to get out."

3. **An overnight or two at the Kantishna Roadhouse.** The Roadhouse is an appealing if archly rustic place at the end of the road inside Denali National Park. From here, you can go on guided hikes deep in the park. A special permit is necessary to drive in, but there's the park shuttle bus or, if you're in a hurry, a resort airstrip for a Denali air shuttle. Reserve well in advance (☎ 800/942-7420; www.kantishnaroadhouse.com).

4. **A performance of the Gaslight Follies.** Performed in Dawson City's 1899 Palace Grand Theatre, the Follies brings together a surprisingly professional cast; it's far less corny than the similar show in Whitehorse. Nightly except Tuesdays from mid-May to mid-September. Contact the Klondike Visitors Association (☎ 867/993-5575).

5. **A 3-hour excursion aboard the White Pass and Yukon Railway.** It takes you along the famous Trail of '98 from Skagway to the White Pass Summit and back. There's also daily afternoon service from Skagway to Whitehorse (via train to Fraser, B.C., then motor coach to Whitehorse) with a morning return. Built in 1899, the narrow-gauge train has one of the steepest railroad grades in North America. Summers only (☎ 800/343-7373; www.whitepassrailroad.com).

6. **A dinner of rare white King salmon at Simon & Seafort's Saloon & Grill.** It's all the rage in Anchorage during its very brief season. Start with fresh King crab and follow the salmon with the house's brandy ice, a concoction of vanilla ice cream, brandy, Kahlúa, and crème de cacao (420 L St.; ☎ 907/274-3502).

7. **Shopping for qiviut.** In northern craft shops, look for rare and costly qiviut, the soft underwool of the musk ox, gathered when it's shed each spring and woven into warm, feather-light gloves, scarves, caps, and sweaters. Alternatively, seek carved soapstone pieces, ceremonial wooden masks, or last season's trendy ulus (fan-shaped chopping knives with wood handles).

8. **Flying over Mount McKinley.** On a clear day you can fly over McKinley and the Susitna Valley, where you might catch glimpses of

moose, bear, foxes, and eagles, then land in Talkeetna, the staging area for climbers who tackle the high peaks of the Alaska Range. Call **FRA Helicopters Flightseeing Tours** (☎ 800/843-1947; www.eraaviation. com), **Talkeetna Air Taxi** (☎ 800/583-2219), **K2 Aviation** (☎ 800/764-2291; www.flyk2.com), or **Hudson Air Service** (☎ 907/733-2321; www.alaskan.com/hudsonair) for details.

9. **Dinner at the Pump House Restaurant.** The colorful Pump House, on the banks of the Chena River, 2 miles southwest of Fairbanks on Chena Pump Road, is now a national historic site crammed with Gold Rush–era artifacts (☎ 907/479-8452).

10. **Era Aviation, Anchorage.** Specially scheduled flights on vintage DC-3s recall the grand old days of flying, with period magazines, flight attendants in 1940s uniforms and Big Band music piped in. Figure around $150 per person for the scenic flight (☎ 800/866-8394 for information and reservations).

TAKE-OUT (OR EAT-IN) FAR NORTH TREATS

Goldfields Bakery, Barkerville. Grab some whole wheat or sourdough bread from Goldfields, in the historic gold rush town of Barkerville, near Quesnel, B.C. Call the Barkerville Reception Centre for information (☎ 250/994-3241).

Lung Duck Tong restaurant, Barkerville. Chinese dim sum in a gold rush town? Why not? Call the Barkerville Reception Centre for information (☎ 604/994-3332).

Bonanza Meat Company, Dawson City. At Bonanza Meat you can design your own sandwich. On 2nd Avenue in Dawson City (☎ 867/993-6567).

The Braeburn Lodge. Try the Braeburn's superburgers—one is big enough for two. They also serve something they call "gianormous" cinnamon buns. Big, yes, but not particularly tasty. Mile 55.6, Klondike Highway (radio phone ☎ 2M-3987, Fox Channel).

Dawson Peaks Resorts, south of Teslin. Try the grilled Teslin lake trout and rhubarb pie. Seven miles south of Teslin on the lake, Mile 769 (answering service ☎ 867/390-2310; radio phone, mobile 2M-3169, Teslin Channel).

Alaskan Brewery and Bottling Company. The Juneau-based Alaska Brewing Company has been around only since 1986, but its Alaskan Amber has already been twice voted the most popular brew at the Great American Beer Festival in Colorado. The brewery is at 5429 Shaune Dr., outside Juneau. To get there, turn right from Egan Drive onto Vanderbilt Hill Road, which becomes the Glacier Highway, and then right on Anka Street and right again on Shaune Drive. Tours leave every half hour between 11am and 5pm, Tuesday through Saturday May through September; Thursday through Saturday the rest of the year (☎ 907/780-5866; www.alaskabeer.com).

Malamute Saloon, west of Fairbanks. Try the reindeer stew and Alaska crab at the Malamute Saloon, 8 miles west of Fairbanks on Old Nenana Highway, at Ester Gold Camp. At night it includes the price of the Northern Lights Show (☎ 800/676-6925; www.alaskasbest.com/ester).

Taku Smokeries Market Place, Juneau. The smoked salmon packaged to go at Taku Smokeries Market Place in Juneau can also be ordered by mail. 230 S. Franklin Ave. (☎ 800/582-5122; www.takusmokeries.com).

The Double Musky, Girdwood. Try the Double Musky cake at the restaurant of the same name, with layers of pecan meringue, brownielike chocolate, chocolate mousse, and cocoa cream frosting. On Crow Creek Road in Girdwood, south of Anchorage (☎ 907/783-2822; www.doublemusky.com).

Alaska Wild Berry chocolates. Get some chocolate and check out the flowing 20-foot chocolate waterfall at the company's new Anchorage outlet. Filling options include wild rosehip, elderberry, salmonberry, high bush cranberry, and lingonberry (5225 Juneau St.; ☎ 800/280-2927; www.alaska wildberry.com).

Sourdough pancakes. You'll find sourdough pancakes almost anywhere up here, but they're especially good in **Dawson City's Midnight Sun,** at Third and Queen Street (☎ 867/993-5495). In Juneau's **Westmark Baranof Hotel,** 127 N. Franklin St. (☎ 800/544-0970; www.westmarkhotels.com), they're the size of Frisbees and accompanied by reindeer sausages, and in Tok you can camp next door to it at the **Sourdough Campground** (see "Campground Oases: Dawson to Fairbanks," later in this chapter).

WILDLIFE-WATCHING

We never got sated with **moose** sightings on our May trip, perhaps because spring is calving time. In early fall, however, plenty of them come down into the lower meadows in Denali. Pulling over to cook breakfast at a rest stop

A caribou crosses a side road off the Alaska Highway.

on the road between Denali and Anchorage, we saw a moose cow browsing at the edge of the trees and managed to snap a couple of shots before she gave us an aggrieved look and ambled back into the woods.

A close sighting of a **porcupine** in the wild, waddling up a bank with his silver-tipped quills aquiver, or a **bald eagle** in the roadway snacking on roadkill, is as exciting as seeing the big animals. Unless you're very quick or patient, or the animal is slow, your memory will be clearer than your photo.

Our first good day of wildlife spotting was on an early morning transit of the Crooked River Nature Corridor south of McLeod Lake in British Columbia, with a wolf, deer, and great blue herons spotted. We were too late in the season to catch the trumpeter swans that winter here.

Hummingbird-sized **mosquitoes**—aka Alaska's state bird—in a campground at Fort Nelson were next, too large, fortunately, to get through the window screens of the RV.

An early morning roadside sighting of a **black bear** a few miles north of Fort Nelson did not net any photographs. He spotted us first, so all we saw was his backside disappearing into the woods.

One of the best places to spot **caribou** is by the side of the road, oddly enough. They stand around morosely by signs and at road junctions as if waiting for a bus. They are, incidentally, the only type of deer in which both sexes grow horns. At Stone Mountain Park, there have been great caribou sightings right past a huge sign warning CARIBOU IN THE ROADWAY. **Mountain sheep,** too, like the roadsides. The indigenous stone sheep in Stone Mountain Park, colored cream and brown and bigger than Dall or Rocky Mountain sheep, can be glimpsed looking down from craggy rock cliffs or photographed as they gather by the roadside to lick salt deposits.

On the Road

NORTHERN BRITISH COLUMBIA

Once past Calgary on the eastern access road or Kamloops on the western access road, urbanites need to make an important mental adjustment. There are no more cities until Whitehorse, Yukon Territory, just small towns separated by as much as 8 hours of driving through gorgeous, uninhabited

Western Canada Campgrounds

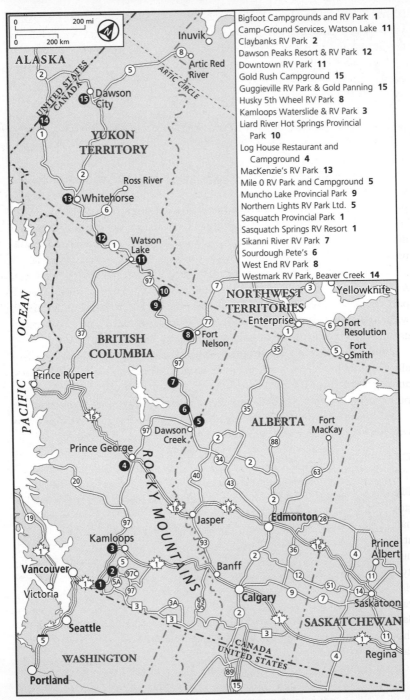

Bigfoot Campgrounds and RV Park **1**
Camp-Ground Services, Watson Lake **11**
Claybanks RV Park **2**
Dawson Peaks Resort & RV Park **12**
Downtown RV Park **11**
Gold Rush Campground **15**
Guggieville RV Park & Gold Panning **15**
Husky 5th Wheel RV Park **8**
Kamloops Waterslide & RV Park **3**
Liard River Hot Springs Provincial
     Park **10**
Log House Restaurant and
     Campground **4**
MacKenzie's RV Park **13**
Mile 0 RV Park and Campground **5**
Muncho Lake Provincial Park **9**
Northern Lights RV Park Ltd. **5**
Sasquatch Provincial Park **1**
Sasquatch Springs RV Resort **1**
Sikanni River RV Park **7**
Sourdough Pete's **6**
West End RV Park **8**
Westmark RV Park, Beaver Creek **14**

scenery. And while those places with serious names and major crossroads you've been looking at on the map all day might not be what you expect by the time you arrive, the inhabitants are generally friendly and helpful.

Dawson Creek is where most of the Alaska Highway drivers stop both coming and going to trade war stories, especially at service stations, car washes, RV parks, and the town's major drinking and dining spot, the venerable Alaska Hotel Café & Dew Drop Inn. This is where you photograph your RV in front of the Mile 0 Alaska Highway sign, take a look at one of the three competing pioneer villages, and admire the big red grain elevator that doubles as art gallery and tourist information office.

In **Fort Nelson,** as we were running out of reading and cocktail materials, we found an office supply store that had a treasure-trove of secondhand paperback books sold at half the cover price and a liquor store that had a sparse and pricy inventory. Less exciting was a highly advertised "European deli" with a meager supply of meats and cheese but doing a land-office business in microwaved burritos.

Watson Lake, on the Yukon border, has a sign forest (see "Off-the-Wall Attractions," above) and a modest supermarket. Camp-Ground Services RV park offers 140 sites, full and partial hookups, and a coin-operated car/RV wash to get rid of the top layer of road dust. Don't worry about street addresses—the whole town is laid out in a strip along the highway.

The "lodges" grandly promoted by road signs before you get there usually turn out to be basic roadside cafes with a straggle of cabins in the back and a gas tank out front, and a cashier/waitress who also sells fishing licenses, pumps gas, makes beds, and does the home cooking in her spare time.

Whatever the roadside food lacks in flavor, it more than makes up for in volume. We fussy freewheelers were glad our RV had a kitchen.

CAMPGROUND OASES: HARRISON HOT SPRINGS TO TESLIN

Bigfoot Campgrounds and RV Park. Harrison Hot Springs makes a good stopover for anyone interested in the legend of Bigfoot, who apparently hangs around this area a great deal. Perhaps it's too obvious to look for him at Bigfoot Campgrounds, where the logo is a silhouette of the 8-foot hairy humanoid. Of the 110 RV sites, all have water and 15- and 30-amp electricity, and 70 provide sewers as well. It's located on Highway 9, also Harrison Hot Springs Road, 2 miles north of the junction with Highway 7. For reservations, call ☎ **604/796-9767;** bigfoot@uniserve.com.

Sasquatch Springs RV Resort. Sasquatch, the Indian name for Bigfoot, shows up in place names around Harrison Hot Springs, so of course it's in campground names as well. Try Sasquatch Springs, 4 miles north of the junction of Highways 7 and 9 on Harrison Hot Springs Road, where 70 full hookups provide 15- and 30-amp electricity plus cable TV. Call them at ☎ **604/796-2228;** jallen@universe.com.

The world-famous Sign Post Forest at Watson Lake, B.C., on the Alaska Highway, has some 20,000 signs from all over the world.

Sasquatch Provincial Park. Located 4 miles north of Harrison Hot Springs on Rockwell Drive, with 176 campsites but no hookups (☎ **604/869-5853;** www.elp.gov.bc.ca/bcparks).

Claybanks RV Park. Claybanks is a pleasant, family-run campground at the edge of the historic little town of Merritt and near enough for an easy stroll into town. Take exit 290 from Highway 5 and follow the Sani-Dump signs along Voight Street to the campground, which has 42 full-hookup sites with 15- and 30-amp electricity. For reservations, call ☎ **250/378-6441.**

Kamloops Waterslide & RV Park. Kamloops makes a good major stop for stocking up on groceries and supplies, and a convenient place to overnight. The Kamloops Waterslide & RV Park is 12 miles east of town on Highway 1 and has plenty of holiday diversions for the whole family, including two 18-hole golf courses 5 minutes away. Some 85 sites have water and 30-amp electricity, 73 of which also include sewer connections. For reservations, call ☎ **250/573-3789;** kamwater@hotmail.com.

Log House Restaurant and Campground. This place, on Tabor Lake, near Prince George, is a clean, well-run campground with 24 sites, 30-amp electric connections, and water but no sanitary dump. There's an excellent dinner restaurant on the hill above the RV park, operated by proprietor Richard Gunther, plus a floatplane base, cottages, and fishing, as well as good bird-watching. (We spent much of our stay transfixed by the antics of a pet Canada goose and her wild boyfriend who flies in for the summer, and two pair of horned grebes.) Reservations accepted (☎ **250/963-9515**).

Mile 0 RV Park and Campground. Dawson Creek marks Mile 0, the beginning of the Alaska Highway, with a half-dozen public and private RV parks and two pioneer villages. We like the public Mile 0 RV Park and Campground, which is actually located at Mile 1½ and has 54 tree-shaded sites, 28 of them with water and 20- and 30-amp electric hookups, restrooms, showers, a sanitary dump station, laundry, and e-mail service. It's an easy stroll away from the Walter Wright Pioneer Village. Call ☎ 250/782-2590 for reservations. You'll need them because it seems as though everyone overnights in Dawson Creek to swap war stories.

Northern Lights RV Park Ltd. Located in Dawson Creek, on 97 south, a mile and a half before Mile 0, Northern Lights offers an almost intimidating list of vehicle preparations available before you set out on the Alaska Highway, with lube and oil changes, windshield repairs, bug screen installation, headlight protectors, tow-car protectors, and do-it-yourself RV wash for $5. Why you'd want to wash your RV on the way north is a mystery, but you'll certainly want to take care of it on the way back. It also has 55 sites with water and 20- and 30-amp electric hookups, 43 with full hookups (☎ 888/414-9437 or 250/782-9433; www.pris.bc.ca/rvpark/).

Sourdough Pete's. If everything in Dawson Creek is already spoken for, drive another 43 miles to Sourdough Pete's in Fort St. John, a commercial RV park in town. Sixty water and electric (15- and 30-amp) hookups, 48 full hookups, and a sanitary dump station, a modem-friendly office, and an adjacent amusement park with go-karts, miniature golf, batting cages, and driving range (☎ 800/227-8388).

Sikanni River RV Park. Sikanni River RV Park, in the British Columbia community of Sikanni Chief, offers 26 sites, 22 of them with 20-amp electricity, restrooms and showers, security, LP gas, and firewood (☎ 250/772-5400).

Husky 5th Wheel RV Park. Located in Fort Nelson, at Mile 293, Husky 5th Wheel Park provides 55 full hookups with 20- and 30-amp electricity, cable TV, laundry, groceries, RV supplies, LP gas, and a full-service truck stop. For reservations, call ☎ 250/774-7270.

West End RV Park. Also in Fort Nelson on the west side of town, the West End RV Park has 110 20- and 30-amp electric sites, 99 of which also have water and 47 of which have sewer connections (☎ 250/774-2340).

Muncho Lake Provincial Park. Between Mile 437 and 442 on the Alaska Highway in British Columbia. The lake's icy waters are a gorgeous blue and turquoise from a combination of copper in the rocks and glacial runoff. There are 30 sites, 15 in each location, with piped water, firewood, boat launch, fishing, and hiking. Caribou, moose, and sheep are sometimes seen here, and bears may frequent the area. No hookups, no reservations (☎ 250/787-3407).

Liard River Hot Springs Provincial Park. At Mile 496, this is the most popular park along the route, with its 52 sites filling up by noon (no reservations). Besides handsome, tree-shaded spots spaced well apart, the camper will find free firewood and hot springs for soaking away travel aches, but no RV hookups. Playgrounds, heated restrooms, wheelchair-accessible toilet. Bears sometimes prowl the area (☎ 250/787-3407).

Downtown RV Park. By the time you get to Watson Lake in the Yukon Territory, you and your RV will both be ready for a good bath. The Downtown RV Park throws in a free RV wash (it supplies the water, you supply the labor) when you stay overnight in one of the 71 full-hookup sites (20-amp electricity) (☎ 867/536-2646).

Camp-Ground Services, Watson Lake. Has 110 water and 20-amp electric hookups, showers, laundry, groceries, LP gas, dump station, adjacent service station, and a free RV wash (☎ 867/536-7448).

Dawson Peaks Resort & RV Park. South of Teslin at Milepost 769, Dawson Peaks Resort is famous along the route for its grilled Teslin lake trout and rhubarb pie. RVers will find 16 sites with water and 15- and 30-amp electricity (☎ 867/390-2310).

Campground Oases: Whitehorse

Whitehorse marks a dividing point in the road. From here you'll head north to Dawson City if you want to drive the Klondike Highway, then rejoin the Alaska Highway at Tok, Alaska. If you want to think about it, head for:

MacKenzie's RV Park. At Mile 922 of the Alaska Highway. Besides the usual 82 full-hookup sites with 20- and 30-amp electricity, you get cable TV, laundromat, an RV wash, and free gold panning (☎ 867/633-2337).

THE YUKON

Around Dawson City they joke, "This isn't the end of the world, but you can see it from here."

This is a destination for North Americans with a yen to wander, nagged by an insatiable restlessness to see what lies at the end of the road. It is written in the faces of men wearing rumpled plaid shirts and blue jeans as they climb out of dirty, mud-streaked RVs and 4x4s with license plates from Florida, New Brunswick, Texas, California, and Ontario. They have made it to the place where the Yukon and the Klondike rivers meet, to the fabled city of gold and the end of the infamous Trail of '98.

Coming to **Dawson City** is like meeting a childhood idol or your favorite movie star 3 or 4 decades after the fact and being surprised to find the old dear is still alive, let alone lively enough to dance a fandango and tell a couple of salty tales.

Far from being some saccharine gold rush theme park or horsehair-stuffed historical monument, Dawson is alive and kicking. Under the aegis of Parks Canada, where "money is always iffy," the town is slowly being renovated. Some buildings—like the splendid Palace Grand Theatre, the old post office, the Arctic Brotherhood Hall (now Diamond Tooth Gertie's Casino), and Madame Tremblay's store—have been restored. Others, sagging and unpainted, lean wearily against each other waiting their turn, looking as though they won't last much longer.

Alaska Campgrounds

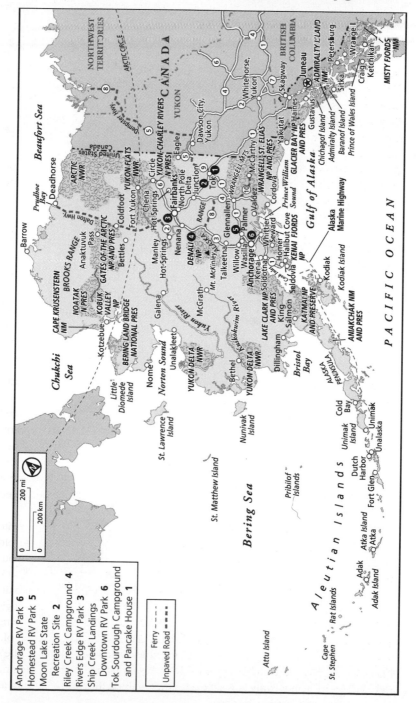

Anchorage RV Park **6**
Homestead RV Park **5**
Moon Lake State
   Recreation Site **2**
Riley Creek Campground **4**
Rivers Edge RV Park **3**
Ship Creek Landings
   Downtown RV Park **6**
Tok Sourdough Campground
and Pancake House **1**

Ferry ---------
Unpaved Road ▬ ▬ ▬ ▬

Weary buildings in Dawson City await restoration by Parks Canada.

Some of the wilder goings-on from earlier years are not in evidence lately. The "Miss Nude Yukon" contest has faded into obscurity, and the Eldorado's famous Sour Toe cocktail—a pickled human toe tossed into a beer mug of champagne—has calmed down and moved over to the Keno Lounge in the Westmark Inn. But the annual Great International Outhouse Race and Bathroom Wall Limerick Contest are still on the Labor Day weekend agenda.

Today Dawson's biggest gold mine is **Diamond Tooth Gertie's Casino,** the first legal gambling casino in the Yukon.

Campground Oases: Dawson to Fairbanks

Gold Rush Campground. The best bet in downtown Dawson City, although its main appeal is its location, at 5th Avenue and York Street, within walking distance of the sights. Some 15- and 30-amp electric connections, a sanitary dump station, and narrow parking lot–type sites are what you'll find; reserve well ahead if you want a spot in midsummer (☎ 867/993-5247).

The Guggieville RV Park & Gold Panning. Located at the south end of Dawson City, Guggieville has 72 sites with water and 15-amp electric hookups, plus gold panning, a gold nugget jewelry shop, and a laundromat (☎ 867/993-5008).

Westmark RV Park, Beaver Creek. Located at Mile 1202, the Westmark park has 67 sites with 20- and 30-amp electric and water hookups, and it's adjacent to the Westmark Inn if you want to treat yourself to a meal or two out. Lounge, laundry, gift shop, showers, wildlife display, sanitary dump. For reservations, call ☎ 867/862-7501.

Tok Sourdough Campground and Pancake House. Located in Tok, 2 miles south on the Anchorage Highway, the Tok Pancake House specializes in sourdough pancakes. The RV park adjacent has 48 sites with electric hookups (20- and 30-amp) and water, and 21 with sewer hookups. Sanitary dump station, laundry, showers, flush toilets, cafe, gift shop, walk-through museum of Alaskan artifacts, car wash. For reservations, call ☎ **907/883-5543.**

Moon Lake State Recreation Site. On the Alaska Highway at Mile 1332, west of Tok, Moon Lake has 17 campsites amid the trees by a beautiful lake. Toilets, piped water, boat launch. No hookups, no reservations (☎ **907/451-2695**).

FAIRBANKS

In 1902, when the Klondike excitement had quieted down a little, a prospector named Felix Pedro discovered gold in the Tanana Valley near present-day Fairbanks, and a new rush was on. The prospectors and gamblers from Dawson hurried west to the new boomtown, rode the crest of the newest wave, then crashed in the depression that followed.

Vestiges of those days can still be seen in **Alaskaland**—located at Airport Way and Peger Road (☎ **907/459-1087**), and not as commercial as it sounds—where the history of the gold mining days is re-created. Original cabins, a replica Indian village, the Crooked Creek & Whiskey Island railroad with its little steam engine, and the stern-wheeler Nenana, one-time star of the Yukon riverboats, are all on display. For information, call ☎ **907/459-1087.**

From Fairbanks, you can take a **paddle-wheeler day cruise** along the Chena and Tanana rivers with Alaska Riverboat Discovery (☎ **907/479-6673**), or a **motor coach excursion** along the Dalton Highway following the Trans-Alaska Oil Pipeline farther into Prudhoe Bay than private vehicles can go with the Northern Alaska Tour Company (☎ **800/474-4767**).

Feeding time at the sled dog kennels.

When in Alaska, do as the tourists do and take in a salmon bake. The **Alaska Salmon Bake** at Alaskaland can also include an after-dinner musical about life in Fairbanks at the Palace Theatre and Saloon. Call ☎ **800/ 354-7274** for the salmon bake, or 907/456-5960 for the show.

On the other hand, if you've had enough salmon, you can find a Fairbanks branch of every fast-food outlet known to man.

Campground Oases: Fairbanks

Rivers Edge RV Park. Off the Parks Highway in Fairbanks, Rivers Edge has 170 sites with full and partial 20- and 30-amp hookups, a sanitary dump station, laundry, showers, and free shuttle service to attractions such as the stern-wheeler Discovery and the Alaska Salmon Bake. On the Chena River, with fishing and boat ramp. For reservations, call ☎ **800/770-3343.**

DENALI NATIONAL PARK

Denali means "the high one" in the language of the local Athabascan people, and is both the official designation for the former Mount McKinley National Park and the original Native name for 20,320-foot Mount McKinley itself, renamed in 1917 for an assassinated president who never saw it. (The mountain is still called Denali by most Alaskans, Native and non-Native alike, although repeated attempts to change it back officially have been unsuccessful.) The 4-million-acre Denali Park, slightly bigger than the state of Massachusetts, includes a wilderness area and a national preserve; sport hunting, fishing, and trapping are allowed in the latter by state permit.

Denali State Park, southeast of the national park area, is bisected by Parks Highway, which is named for George Parks, a territorial governor in the late 1920s, not for the fact that two major parks lie along it.

With rare exceptions, you cannot drive through Denali, but must park near the visitor center and take one of the shuttle buses run by **ARAMARK/ Denali Park Resorts** (☎ **800/622-7275** or 907/272-7275; fax 907/264-4684; www.denalinationalpark.com), which takes you into the park and allows you to hop on and off at various stops to explore on foot (shuttles come by every half hour or so). The park entrance fee is $10 per family, $5 per person, and is good for 7 days. Walk-in reservations for the shuttles begin 2 days out. If it's a busy time, desirable shuttle reservations are snapped up early, and you may have to wait till the next day. On the other hand, you could get lucky, as the flow of visitors rises and falls unpredictably.

The information desk at the **Denali National Park Visitor Access Center,** Denali Park Road, a half mile from the park entrance (☎ **907/ 683-2294;** www.nps.gov/dena), is the easiest place to get Park Service information. Stop here for the park map. For advance shuttle reservations, contact ARAMARK at the number above.

Denali National Park

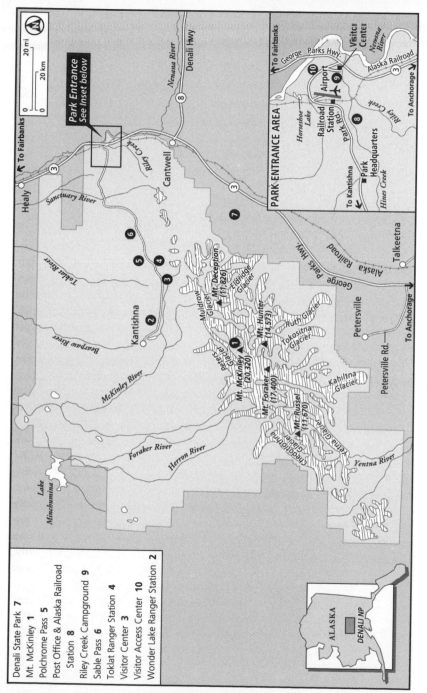

To Fairbanks

Nenana River

Denali Hwy.

PARK ENTRANCE AREA

To Fairbanks
George Parks Hwy.
Visitor Center
Nenana River
Alaska Railroad
10 Airport
9
Railroad Station
Park Rd.
To Anchorage
3
Riley Creek
8
To Kantishna
Park Headquarters
Hines Creek

Horseshoe Lake

8

Park Entrance
See Inset below

To Fairbanks
3

Healy

Sanctuary River

Riley Creek

Cantwell

3

7

6

5 **4**

3

Toklat River

Mt. Deception
(11,826)

Eldridge Glacier

Muldrow Glacier

Mt. Hunter
(14,573)

Ruth Glacier

Tokositna Glacier

Alaska Railroad

Talkeetna

2

Kantishna

Peters Glacier

Mt. McKinley
(20,320)

Mt. Foraker
(17,400)

Mt. Russel
(11,670)

Kahiltna Glacier

Petersville

George Parks Hwy.

To Anchorage

Beartpaw River

McKinley River

Foraker River

Herron River

Chedotlothna Glacier

Yentna Glacier

Yentna River

Petersville Rd.

Lake Minchumina

ALASKA

DENALI NP

Legend

Denali State Park **7**
Mt. McKinley **1**
Polchrome Pass **5**
Post Office & Alaska Railroad
  Station **8**
Riley Creek Campground **9**
Sable Pass **6**
Toklat Ranger Station **4**
Visitor Center **3**
Visitor Access Center **10**
Wonder Lake Ranger Station **2**

20 mi
20 km

Campground Oases: Denali to Anchorage

Riley Creek Campground. Riley Creek, at Denali, has 100 well-separated and tree-shaded sites not far from the railway station. Sites have flush toilets, piped water in summer, sanitary dump station, but no hookups. An overnight or two at Denali will allow time to get a spot on the park service shuttle bus. No reservations; 14-day maximum stay. After mid-June, any empty sites are usually filled the minute the previous tenant pulls out (☎ 907/683-2294).

The Homestead RV Park. In Palmer, Alaska, the Homestead is handily located in the Matanuska Valley near the junction of the Parks Highway between Denali and Anchorage and the Glenn Highway between Tok and Anchorage. With the long hours of summer, you can commute to Anchorage for dinner and get home before dark, as well as walk to trout fishing, go hiking, and take in a square dance on Thursday nights. Some 64 sites have water and electric (20- and 30-amp) hookups (☎ 907/745-6005).

ANCHORAGE

In the Bush, they like to say, "The nicest thing about Los Anchorage is that it's only 30 miles from Alaska."

People who don't know Alaska usually visualize Anchorage as being an icy outpost in the wilderness populated by moose, grizzly bears, and bush pilots. True, you will find moose and bears—most often in the Anchorage Zoo—and plenty of bush pilots taking off from and landing at Lake Hood. But the first time we arrived there, on a July day, it was warmer and sunnier than Los Angeles and bright with summer flowers. On our most recent May visit, however, it was cold and windy and socked in with fog.

Earthquake Park, on the west end of Northern Lights Boulevard, still shows graphically the results of the 9.2 earthquake on Good Friday in 1964, when two huge chunks of earth fissured and dropped 20 feet in an instant. "It looked like chocolate pudding somebody had been dragging their fingers through," one eyewitness said.

A **statue of Captain James Cook** looks out on Turnagain Arm, so named when the captain told his first mate William Bligh, later to command the *Bounty,* to turn around again when it turned out not to be the Northwest Passage he was seeking.

___DENALI TIP___

If you don't have a day or two to wait for space on the free park shuttles, advance-ticket purchases for the Wildlife Tours into Denali National Park can be made by calling Denali Park Resorts at ☎ 800/276-7234; $71 adults, $38 kids.

The fine **Anchorage Museum of History and Art,** in a stylish building
with a frieze of stylized Alaskan designs across the top, displays an excellent
collection of contemporary Alaskan and Native arts and crafts. It's located at
121 W. Seventh Ave. (☎ **907/343-4326**).

At night, head for Mr. Whitekeys' **Fly by Night Club,** on Spenard Road
south of Northern Lights Boulevard (☎ **907/279-SPAM**), where the Spam
hors d'oeuvres are free if you order a bottle of Dom Perignon champagne,
and "The Whale Fat Follies" break up the locals. The house jazz band is
called the Spamtones.

Chilkoot Charlie's Rustic Alaskan Bar says it all, and adds in its ad,
"We cheat the other guy and pass the savings onto you!" At 2435 Spenard
Rd., open 7 nights a week with live entertainment, burgers and brews
(☎ **907/272-1010;** www.koots.com).

Campground Oases in Anchorage

Anchorage RV Park. At Glenn Highway and Muldoon Road, the Anchorage
RV Park has 195 full hookups with city water and 30- and 50-amp electricity, a "welcome back" for big rigs with roof air-conditioning after long days
on the road with less amperage (☎ **800/400-PARK;** www.anchrvpark.com).
Ship Creek Landings Downtown RV Park. Close to Anchorage's downtown area at 150 N. Ingra St. at East 1st Avenue, Ship Creek Landing faces
the railroad tracks and Ship Creek. The 150 full hookups provide city water
and 20- and 30-amp electricity, and you can walk to shopping, fishing, the
farmers' market, rail, and boat and bus excursions. For reservations, call
☎ **888/778-7700** or 907/277-0877; www.alaskarv.com.

Seven Tough Side Trips & Three Easy Ones

TOUGH TRIPS

1. **The Top of the World Highway (Yukon Route 9).** The Top of the
World, from Dawson City to Eagle, is 146 miles of unpaved, white-
knuckling terror you'll talk about for years, especially if you go early in
the season when half the roadway is still covered with ice and snow.
There are no guard rails and few markers to let you know whether

you're still on the roadway or have ventured off onto a side road that peters out in the tundra. Eagle, where author John McPhee set much of his classic *Coming Into the Country,* is an optional destination at the end of the rough, narrow road. There's been a trading post here for gold miners since the 1880s, and today Eagle is populated by some 150 pioneers, curmudgeons, and refugees from urban life.

2. **The Taylor Highway.** Between Eagle to Tetlin Junction is 161 miles of rough road, with the biggest metropolis en route being the town of Chicken, population 37. There's a saloon, a cafe, a gas station, and two gift shops where you can buy T-shirts with slogans like, I GOT LAID IN CHICKEN, ALASKA. The old gold mining town is off the main road and closed to visitors except on a daily guided walking tour or gold-panning venture in summer. The original settlers wanted to name it after the ptarmigan, the plump little edible grouse that was a dietary main-stay, but since they couldn't spell it, they called the town Chicken instead.

3. **The Dalton Highway.** This road to Prudhoe Bay takes you across the Arctic Circle, the Brooks Range, and the Continental Divide, but you might have to stop a few miles short of Prudhoe Bay itself; the oil com-panies sometimes limit access. The 414-mile road was constructed to build and service the Alaska pipeline, and there are very few services available along it. Before setting out, call the Alaska Department of Transportation (☎ 907/456-7623) for a recording that will fill you in on road conditions and how far you'll be able to drive. Some years it's open only to Dietrich Camp, about halfway.

4. **Canada's 456-mile Dempster Highway.** The Dempster Highway crosses the Arctic Circle at Mile 252 after striking north from Dawson City and Klondike Highway 2. Final destination is the Northwest Territories' Inuit village of Inuvik, with 57 days of midnight sun begin-ning May 24 each year. The gravel road, with some slippery clay surface sections, also requires two ferry crossings; the most feasible time to go is between mid-June and the end of August. Black flies and mosquitoes are also a problem, so take plenty of repellent. You may spot wolves, caribou, grizzly bears, moose, eagles, and gyrfalcons. Allow 2 days in each direction to drive this tough tundra route. Government campgrounds are spotted along the road, but few services are available. Stop for gas whenever you see a station open. Experts recommend carrying at least two spare tires.

5. **Atlin Road (Yukon/BC 7).** From Jake's Corner, Mile 836, turn south for a 58-mile scenic route to Canada's Little Switzerland, with snow-capped mountains, lakes with prime fishing, and a good chance of

spotting moose or grizzly bears. The all-weather gravel road is fairly good, although winding and slippery in wet weather. The Atlin Visitors Association (☎ **250/651-7522**) can update road information for you.

6. **The Cassiar Highway (BC 37).** The Cassiar drops south from Mile 726 west of Watson Lake down to the Yellowhead Highway 16. It's also possible to use the Cassiar as an alternative to the Alaska Highway between Prince George and Watson Lake. A lot of adventuresome drivers prefer this route, which they liken to driving the Alaska Highway in the fifties and sixties. There are some stretches of gravel instead of road, and services are few and far between, but the scenery, from hanging glaciers to snow-capped mountains, is stunning. Watch out for the logging trucks. Road conditions: ☎ **250/771-3000.**

7. **Wrangell–St. Elias National Park and Preserve.** Chitina, the gateway to this 13-million-acre park, is reachable by the paved, 33-mile Edgerton Highway, running from the Richardson Highway, the route between Tok and Valdez. Only small RVs or four-wheel-drive vehicles without trailers should attempt the next 58 unpaved, steep, and sometimes slippery miles of the road into McCarthy, but the effort is worth it. The privately owned copper company town of Kennicott, now a ghost town, can be visited by hikers crossing the Kennicott River via hand-operated cable tram (wear thick gloves). Guided glacier walks, Kennicott tours, backcountry hikes, and horseback riding are available in McCarthy. Ask for road conditions in Chitina at the National Park Service Ranger Station (☎ **907/823-2205**).

EASY TRIPS

1. **Visiting Barkerville, B.C.** From Quesnel, B.C., take Route 26 over to the Cariboo gold rush town of Barkerville, in its heyday the largest city north of San Francisco and west of Chicago. More than 125 original and restored buildings, many of them occupied by costumed docents, are open, including Lung Duck Ton Chinese restaurant, Eldorado Gold Panning, The Wake-Up-Jake Restaurant, McPherson's Watchmakers Shop, and Cameron & Ames Blacksmith Shop. A historical stage stop called Cottonwood House is also on the route; the round-trip from Highway 97 is 100 miles. The best time to visit is between June 1 and Labor Day. Call the Barkerville Reception Centre at ☎ **250/994-3332.**

2. **Klondike Highway 2.** The Klondike, from Whitehorse 99 miles south to Skagway, via Carcross (short for Caribou Crossing), looks nothing like the precipitous trail, lake, and river route followed by the prospectors of '98, most of them ill-equipped cheechakos who were required by the Northwest Mounted Police to carry a ton of supplies to the gold

fields. A few had horses, a few more "sled dogs" that were usually poodles or terriers dognapped from Seattle backyards, but most had to carry the stuff on their backs, caching it along the trail and doubling back for more. Skagway, at the end of the road, is the town where sharpies like gambler Soapy Smith and his cronies fleeced the innocent. The two-lane paved road is asphalt-surfaced and fairly wide.

3. **Turnagain Arm, Alyeska & Portage Glacier.** From Anchorage, drive south along the Arm, keeping an eye out for whales, and stop at Alyeska, Alaska's top ski resort (the lifts take you sightseeing in summer), and the Portage Glacier with its self-guided nature trail to the ice worms. If time permits, keep going south to the town of Seward or take the Sterling Highway to Homer and the Kenai Peninsula.

⑦ The Dakotas: Black Hills & Buffalo Burgers

NORTH DAKOTA IS WHERE TEDDY ROOSEVELT SHOT A BUFFALO, WHERE Peggy Lee learned to sing and Lawrence Welk learned to talk (he spoke only German until he was 21), where Cream of Wheat was invented, and thin Norwegian pancakes called *lefse* are the state dish.

It's where native son Louis L'Amour learned his ABCs, and Roger Maris got to first base playing for the Fargo American Legion team as a kid, where Angie Dickinson was born, rodeo great Casey Tibbs first saddled a horse, and Sitting Bull surrendered, where the Space Aliens Grill & Bar is next door to the Kmart in Bismarck, and New York–style bagels are explained to the locals as "like bread with an attitude."

North Dakota is where the film *Fargo* didn't take place (you betcha!), and although it's the least-visited state in the union, tourism is its third largest industry. It could also be called the golf capital of America, since it boasts more golf links per capita that any other state.

South Dakota is where Kevin Costner danced with wolves, where the buffalo roam, and where cows outnumber people five to one.

It's where Wild Bill Hickok was gunned down, and where the Black Hills Motorcycle Classic in Sturgis draws as many as 300,000 bikers every August. The town also boasts the National Motorcycle Museum and Hall of Fame.

You can tour North America's largest gold mine, watch the world's biggest mountain carving under construction, reminisce at the Amateur Baseball Hall of Fame in Lake Norden, or slurp a soda at a 115-year-old marble fountain in a grocery store where Hickok's killer sought refuge.

Both states cover two time zones. South Dakota hosts the annual Lewis & Clark Cribbage Classic in July, the Sitting Bull Sailboard Regatta in August, and the Jesse James Bicycle Stampede in September; while North Dakota gets a little more down to earth with Irrigation Days in Oakes in June, Coteau Hill's Annual Beef BBQ and Cow Penning in Forbes in July, and Sauerkraut Day in Wishek in October.

North Dakota Highlights

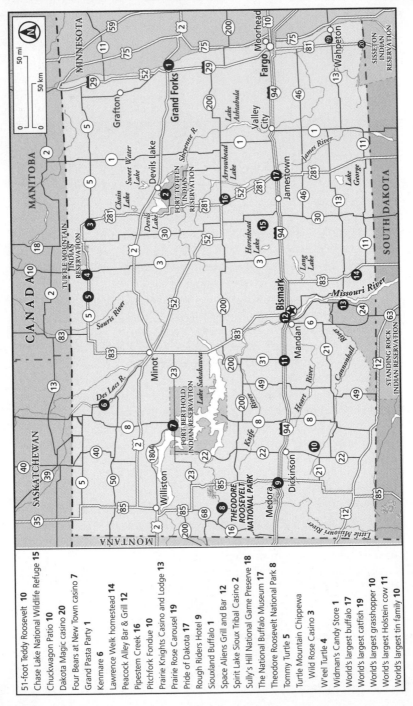

51-foot Teddy Roosevelt **10**
Chase Lake National Wildlife Refuge **15**
Chuckwagon Patio **10**
Dakota Magic casino **20**
Four Bears at New Town casino **7**
Grand Pasta Party **1**
Kenmare **6**
Lawrence Welk homestead **14**
Peacock Alley Bar & Grill **12**
Pipestem Creek **16**
Pitchfork Fondue **10**
Prairie Knights Casino and Lodge **13**
Prairie Rose Carousel **19**
Pride of Dakota **17**
Rough Riders Hotel **9**
Siouxland Buffalo **1**
Space Aliens Grill and Bar **12**
Spirit Lake Sioux Tribal Casino **2**
Sully's Hill National Game Preserve **18**
The National Buffalo Museum **17**
Theodore Roosevelt National Park **8**
Tommy Turtle **5**
Turtle Mountain Chippewa
Wild Rose Casino **3**
W'eel Turtle **4**
Widman's Candy Store **1**
World's largest buffalo **17**
World's largest catfish **19**
World's largest grasshopper **10**
World's largest Holstein cow **11**
World's largest tin family **10**

South Dakota Highlights

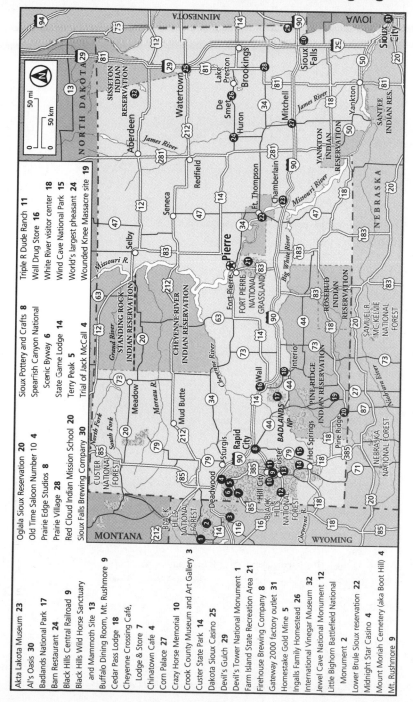

Akta Lakota Museum 23
Al's Oasis 30
Badlands National Park 17
Barn Restaurant 24
Black Hills Central Railroad 9
Black Hills Wild Horse Sanctuary and Mammoth Site 13
Buffalo Dining Room, Mt. Rushmore 9
Cedar Pass Lodge 18
Cheyenne Crossing Café, Lodge & Store 7
Chinatown Cafe 4
Corn Palace 27
Crazy Horse Memorial 10
Crook County Museum and Art Gallery 3
Custer State Park 14
Dakota Sioux Casino 25
Devil's Gulch 29
Devil's Tower National Monument 1
Farm Island State Recreation Area 21
Firehouse Brewing Company 8
Gateway 2000 factory outlet 31
Homestake Gold Mine 5
Ingalls Family Homestead 26
International Vinegar Museum 32
Jewel Cave National Monument 12
Little Bighorn Battlefield National Monument 2
Lower Brule Sioux reservation 22
Midnight Star Casino 4
Mount Moriah Cemetery (aka Boot Hill) 4
Mt. Rushmore 9

Oglala Sioux Reservation 20
Old Time Saloon Number 10 4
Prairie Edge Studios 8
Prairie Village 28
Red Cloud Indian Mission School 20
Sioux Falls Brewing Company 30

Sioux Pottery and Crafts 8
Spearfish Canyon National Scenic Byway 6
State Game Lodge 14
Terry Peak 5
Trial of Jack McCall 4

Triple R Dude Ranch 11
Wall Drug Store 16
White River visitor center 18
Wind Cave National Park 15
World's largest pheasant 24
Wounded Knee Massacre site 19

163

RVing the Dakotas

The West happens suddenly when you arrive at the Missouri River on highways rose-colored from local rock used in the paving. Tumbleweeds roll across the road, and the grasslands sway in a persistent wind.

If you pull off South Dakota's I-90 at exit 263, you can walk over to a bluff and look down at the river, which, together with the Mississippi, makes up the longest stretch of river on earth. In North Dakota you get a similar sensation on I-94 crossing the Missouri between Bismarck and Mandan.

Lewis and Clark and their 40-man expedition force traveled through these waters in their search for a waterway to the Pacific. They were paid $2,500 for their 8,000-mile, 862-day journey, and spent almost one-third of their time traversing the Dakotas.

HITTING THE HIGHLIGHTS

If you've got 2 weeks for your holiday and live on one of the coasts, you might consider flying to the Dakotas and renting an RV there (see chapter 14, "To Rent or Buy?" for a list of nationwide rental outfits). That way, you can take your time sightseeing, hiking, fishing, learning to pan gold, or watching a mountain being carved.

Mt. Rushmore itself doesn't take that long; you can drive by, take a snapshot from the parking lot, and move on. But the Black Hills and Badlands deserve more time, especially if you're interested in outdoor activities and seeing wildlife, and the Theodore Roosevelt National Park's two units should be seen.

If you have a carload of kids or your taste is jejune, you'll find more than enough gee-whiz commercial attractions around Rapid City—Bear Country USA, a drive-through wildlife park, Reptile Gardens, Evans Plunge water complex, the Flintstones Bedrock City Theme Park and Campground, the Wild West Wax Museum, Rushmore Water Slide Park, Pioneer Auto Museum, Mountain Music Show, Ghosts of Deadwood Gulch Wax Museum, Cosmos Mystery Area, Wonderland Cave, and Big Thunder Gold Mine.

There's also the 56-year-old Black Hills Passion Play in the town of Spearfish, with a cast of 250 assisted by live camels, horses, and special-effects sunsets and moon risings. The season runs from early June through August on Sundays, Tuesdays, and Thursdays, and do reserve in advance if you have your heart set on seeing it (☎ 605/642-2646).

GOING FOR THE LONG HAUL

If you want to spend more time on your Dakotas visit than 2 or 3 weeks, aim for fall and try to avoid the peak summer months. Spring is also a possibility, but the weather can be cold and rainy.

Depending on where you begin, it might take a while to get to and from the Dakotas. The side trips in this chapter are spread out around both states.

Although there's a tremendous summer demand for campsites in the Black Hills, you might be able to arrange a seasonal stay in a commercial RV park or work as a campground volunteer in one of the state or national parks or national forests in the area. (See "How to Become Campground Hosts" in chapter 3, "Where to Sleep: Campgrounds & RV Parks.")

If time and money are no problem, you might consider adding on a trail ride with a packhorse or hiking the 111-mile Centennial Trail. See "Five Active Adventures," later in this chapter.

Winter camping in the area, while not for everyone, could include plenty of cross-country or downhill skiing. Terry Peak near Lead is South Dakota's leading ski area, while North Dakota's Turtle River State Park is open in winter for sledding and cross-country skiing.

Travel Essentials

WHEN TO GO

The ideal time is late August, September, and early October, when the trees are changing color but the sun still warms the air. Early August is when motorcyclists head for Sturgis, and all summer long the South Dakota campgrounds and attractions are crowded with tourists. On the other hand, North Dakota isn't crowded even on the Fourth of July. Late spring and early summer would be almost as good, but can be cool and rainy.

WHAT TO TAKE

Bring hiking boots, cameras and film, binoculars, a gold pan if you're planning to camp in the Black Hills National Forest, and fishing tackle for dry-fly trout fishing or lake bass fishing.

WHAT TO WEAR

Summers can be very hot, but in spring and fall the temperature is cool in early morning and at night, so dress in layers. Nowhere, including Deadwood's casinos, is very dressy, so camping and RV attire will fit in anywhere.

TRIMMING COSTS ON THE ROAD

Once you get to the admittedly remote Dakotas, you'll find prices modest. And if hearty Midwestern home cooking is to your taste, restaurant fare is inexpensive all over both states.

If you can visit the casinos and avoid gambling, meals are especially cheap there. If you're traveling with children, beware the commercial attractions, no matter how "educational" they purport to be, because you'll end up spending more than you'd like.

In heavily touristed Rapid City, skip the big commercial attractions, and instead ask for the city tour brochure listing 10 free family attractions. Start at the Rushmore Plaza Civic Center (☎ 800/487-3223), 444 Mount Rushmore Rd. North, where the **Visitor Information Center** has directions on following the city circle tour, marked by buffalo head signs. **The Dahl Fine Arts Center** at 7th and Quincy (☎ 605/394-4101) features work by local Indian artists and a cyclorama of American history with lighted highlights and taped narration. The **Museum of Geology,** on the campus of South Dakota School of Mines at 501 E. Saint Joseph, shows the dinosaurs that once roamed the Badlands; and after the museum, head for the **Dinosaur Park** on Skyline Drive where the kids can climb aboard the outdoor dinosaurs. Adults might enjoy that too, since the park is open until 10 at night, and the city lights make a great view. Take Quincy west from its junction with West Boulevard, an extension of I-190. Quincy Street turns into Skyline Drive. The park is about 1 mile west of the intersection of Quincy and West (☎ 605/343-8687).

Staying in campgrounds without hookups when possible always saves money, but in summer they may be hard to find. Check at the local city park in many South Dakota towns, where camping is often free.

WHERE TO GET TRAVEL INFORMATION

The **South Dakota Department of Tourism,** 711 E. Wells Ave., Pierre, SD 57501, will send you a handsome free vacation guide on request, and its nine Welcome Centers at major highway entrances to the state have full stocks of all kinds of information helpful to an RVer (☎ 800/SDAKOTA; www.state. sd.us or www.travelsd.com).

You can also contact the **Black Hills, Badlands and Lakes Association,** 900 Jackson Blvd., Rapid City, SD 57702 (☎ 605/341-1462), and **North Dakota Tourism,** 604 East Blvd., Bismarck, ND 58505 (☎ 800/HELLO-ND; www.ndtourism.com).

The **Rapid City Convention and Visitors Bureau** can be contacted at ☎ 800/487-3223; www.rapidcitycvb.com.

DRIVING & CAMPING TIPS

- **Rent a taped narration.** Drivers entering South Dakota can rent an audiocassette about the state from the tourist information offices at the border for $20; $15 is refunded when you turn it back in, or you can mail it back. In exchange, you get a series of anecdotes, songs, and histories about the state timed for each stretch of the roadway.

- **Watch for low and narrow passes.** The narrow roads and tunnels in the Black Hills might present problems for extra-wide or long RVs. The maximum RV size that can safely negotiate Iron Mountain Road, Route 16A, is 12 feet 6 inches high and 8 feet 6 inches wide. On State 87 around Sylvan Lake, anything larger than 10 feet 8 inches high or 8 feet 7 inches wide can't make it through the tunnels; on Needles Highway, the limit is 11 feet 5 inches high and 8 feet 7 inches wide. When checking your width, be sure to include the side mirrors; when checking height, don't forget the antennae and air-conditioning units on the roof.

Wall Drug Store, one of the most visited sites in South Dakota.

The Best Dakotas Sights, Tastes & Experiences

OFF-THE-WALL ATTRACTIONS

Wall Drug Store. Only the most travel-hardened curmudgeon could refuse to turn off I-90 into Wall, South Dakota, to see the richly advertised wonders of Wall Drug Store. It started small back in 1931 with road signs promising free ice water for hot, thirsty travelers, and has grown into a monumental Western-themed mall of shops, restaurants, museums, and entertainment that draws 20,000 visitors a day in summer. The ice water is still free, and a cup of coffee costs a nickel. Open daily year-round (☎ 605/279-2175).

The Corn Palace, Mitchell, South Dakota. Located at 604 N. Main St. in Mitchell, the Corn Palace is unique in the world, a Taj Mahal of chicken feed, its walls, domes, and turrets newly covered every year with elaborate murals made of corn, bushel after bushel of red, calico, and white corn, augmented with oats and prairie grass. The decoration is replaced with a new theme every September, when Corn Palace Week carries out the corn motif with concerts by performers like Myron Floren and the Stars of Lawrence Welk and a 3-day polka festival. One version or another of the Corn Palace has been here more than 100 years. Admission is free except during the Corn Palace festival. Open daily year-round plus evenings in summer (☎ 800/257-2676).

Crazy Horse Memorial, North of Custer, South Dakota. The world's largest mountain carving is so big that all four heads on Mt. Rushmore would fit inside the chief's head. Begun in 1947 by the late Polish-American sculptor Korczak Ziolkowski in response to a request from Lakota chief Henry Standing Bear, the monument is being carried on by Korczak's wife and large

The Corn Palace in Mitchell.

family with donations and private funding. The finished sculpture will be 641 feet long and 563 feet high when completed sometime this millennium. Open daily year-round in Crazy Horse, north of Custer on U.S. 385 (☎ 605/673-4681; www.crazyhorse.org).

Mount Moriah Cemetery (aka Boot Hill), Deadwood, South Dakota. This cemetery is where Calamity Jane and Wild Bill Hickok ended up side by side with matching rock mounds and white granite tombstones. Wild Bill was shot in 1876 by Crooked Nose Jack McCall; Jane died in 1903, so it looks like she called the shots for who was buried with whom. Midnight is a popular time to visit the graves. Deadwood Visitors Bureau (☎ 800/999-1876).

Old Time Saloon Number 10, Deadwood, South Dakota. Catch a reenactment of the shooting of Wild Bill Hickok, presented several times a day, as Hickok plays out the famous Deadman's Hand at the poker table: a pair of aces, a pair of eights, and the nine of diamonds (☎ 800/952-9398).

The Trial of Jack McCall, Deadwood, South Dakota. This 60-year-old audience participation performance recruits onlookers as jurors when they depict the capture and trial of the man who shot Wild Bill Hickok. A clue: McCall most often gets off, just as he did at the original trial. It happens nightly except Sundays in the old Town Hall (☎ 605/578-3583).

The Buffalo Dining Room at Mt. Rushmore. A cafeteria with a great close-up view of the carved heads and the memory of Cary Grant running amok through the tourists in Alfred Hitchcock's film *North by Northwest*. On the buffet line, the George Washington Breakfast is Continental, Teddy Roosevelt's Rough Rider breakfast consists of biscuits and gravy, Thomas Jefferson's effete fast-breaker is French toast, and Abe Lincoln's is a straightforward scrambled eggs and toast (☎ 605/574-2515).

Devil's Gulch. This is where Jesse James and his horse, hotly pursued after the failed Northfield, Minnesota, bank robbery attempt, jumped across a 20-foot-wide chasm to clear the 50-foot-deep gulch, leaving the dumbfounded posse behind. It's located near Garrotson, 10 miles north of I-90 at the first exit past the Minnesota/South Dakota border. Guided group tours from Dakota Good Times (☎ **605/594-3404**).

The world's largest pheasant. Forty feet high and weighing 22 tons, it stands by U.S. 14 in Huron, about 50 miles north of Mitchell. It proclaims Huron as the "Pheasant Capital of the World."

International Vinegar Museum, Roslyn, South Dakota, offers the chance to see vinegar in the making, observe vinegar art, taste and sniff and learn more about vinegar than you could possibly imagine. Open June through October. Admission $2 adults, $1 children (☎ **877/486-0075;** www.vinegar man.com).

The Crook County Museum and Art Gallery, Sundance, Wyoming. Located just across the border from the Black Hills in Sundance, Wyoming, the jumping-off town for Devil's Tower, the museum displays the courtroom where Harry Longabaugh was sentenced to 18 months in jail here for stealing horses. His nickname, "Sundance Kid," came from his time in this jail; the town's name came from the summer Sun Dance the Sioux performed on the mountain back of town (☎ **307/283-3666**).

Giant men and giant animals. In a burst of civic pride, North Dakota offers drivers along the interstates a gee-whiz respite from turnpike tedium—the **world's largest buffalo,** 26 feet high, 46 feet long, and 60 tons, but strangely androgynous when you take a closer look (at exit 258 off I-94 in Jamestown); the **world's largest Holstein cow,** 38 feet high and 50 feet long (at exit 124 off I-94 in Salem); the **world's largest catfish,** the Wahpeton Wahpper (off I-29 at exit 23); and the **world's largest tin family,** the **world's largest grasshopper,** and a **51-foot Teddy Roosevelt** made from livestock watering tanks, sickles, barbed wire, and other discarded scrap metal (at I-94's exit 72 along the Enchanted Highway between Gladstone and Regent).

The National Buffalo Museum. Sitting in the shadow of the world's biggest buffalo (see above), the museum protects the world's most sought-after buffalo, the rare (one birth in a billion) female albino White Cloud. Considered sacred by ancient North American tribes, the white buffalo is thought to be a sign of great things to come. The resident herd, which includes White Cloud, can sometimes be seen from the museum's deck on the hillside above the pastures. The parking lot is big enough for RVs to turn around in, and admission to the museum is $4 adults, $8 families. The adjacent Frontier Village (free) has historical buildings moved here along with a general store that sells souvenirs and North Dakota food products and a leather goods

The world's largest buffalo.

store selling locally made hats, belts, and moccasins. Open daily May through September and located at the junction of I-94 and Highway 281, exit 258 (☎ **800/22-BISON**).

Giant turtles. Turtles, too, are big in North Dakota. **Tommy Turtle** is a 33-foot-high turtle riding a snowmobile on Route 5 near the junction of Route 14 in Bottineau in the north central area, while **W'eel Turtle** is a giant crawling turtle made of 2,000 discarded tire rims at the junction of U.S. 281 and Route 3 in Dunseith. Both towns are in the Turtle Mountains near the International Peace Garden. Bottineau Chamber of Commerce: ☎ **701/228-3849**. Dunseith Chamber of Commerce: ☎ **701/244-5860**.

Prairie Rose Carousel, Wahpeton. This restored 1926 Spillman with 29 handcrafted wooden horses and two chariots is one of only 150 operating carousels in the United States. Located in Chahinkapa Park on Route 13 off I-29 at exit 23 in Wahpeton, North Dakota, in the southeast corner of the state, it's open Memorial Day to Labor Day. For information call **Wahpeton Visitors Center** (☎ **800/892-6673**).

The Lawrence Welk homestead, Strasburg. A pilgrimage site for the musically challenged, although the maestro left here the day he turned 21, carrying his accordion, a train ticket, and $3 in cash. The wood-sided sod house of the Welk family is typical of the Germans from Russia who settled North Dakota around the turn of the 20th century after fleeing first from Alsace to the Ukraine and then to America. You'll find it off I-94 at exit 182 and south on U.S. 83 to Strasburg, then west on a marked but unpaved road. Open mid-May to mid-September from 10am to 5pm; admission $3. Contact Pioneer Heritage, Inc., Strasburg, ND 58573 (☎ **701/336-7777**).

THE DAKOTAS GAMBLING SCENE
Deadwood, South Dakota

Thanks to its 80 licensed casinos dating from 1989, the long-dormant town of Deadwood looks as bustling as it must have in 1876, when 25,000 miners came looking for gold, and Calamity Jane and Wild Bill Hickok were an item. Today at least that many tourists are still looking for gold, an early lunch, or a T-shirt that reads: "My grandma went to Deadwood and all I got was this lousy T-shirt."

The casino was put in place on the premise that the gambling would generate funds to restore the deteriorating town, a National Historic Landmark. (Old-timers have some lively ongoing discussions about what is and isn't historic.) Gambling originally went on in Deadwood until 1947, its proponents pointed out, and brothels did discreet business until 1980. Gambling was restored in 1989, and now summer visitors gamble as much as a million dollars a day, which should be enough to gold plate the historic buildings in a few years. A lot of restoration has already been completed. Day and evening variety shows with cowboys and dance hall girls are plentiful, along with live music for dancing, dinner theater suitable for the whole family, and the nightly reenactment of "The Trial of Jack McCall," about the man who shot Wild Bill Hickok.

RVers will find bright green trolleys to shuttle them from the edge-of-town RV parking lots to the casinos along the main street.

Elsewhere in South Dakota

The **Lower Brule Sioux reservation** offers card games and coin slots, as well as herds of roaming buffalo and elk in the vicinity. Take exit 248 at

The old Western town of Deadwood is flourishing again.

Reliance and drive north 15 minutes to Lower Brule. For information, call The **Alliance of Tribal Tourism Advocates** at ☎ **605/964-4000.**

The **Dakota Sioux Casino** in Watertown runs blackjack, poker, poker machines, and progressive slots, along with a bar and restaurant. Watertown is 100 miles north of Sioux Falls on I-29 (☎ **800/658-4717**).

North Dakota

North Dakota has five tribal casinos: **Four Bears at New Town,** west of New Town, in northwest North Dakota at the junction of routes 8 and 23 (☎ **800/294-5454**); **Dakota Magic** off I-29, exit 2, south of Hankinson (☎ **800/325-6825**); **Spirit Lake Sioux Tribal Casino,** 6 miles south of Devils Lake on Route 57 (☎ **800/946-8328**); **Turtle Mountain Chippewa Wild Rose Casino,** at U.S. 281 and Route 5 in Belcourt (☎ **800/477-3497**); and **Prairie Knights Casino and Lodge,** 44 miles south of Mandan on Route 1806 (☎ **800/425-8277**). All feature Las Vegas–style gambling and headliner entertainment.

EIGHT SPLURGES IN THE DAKOTAS

1. **Take a helicopter tour around the Mt. Rushmore faces.** You'll get good close-up photos to wow the neighbors back home. The choppers cover only side and distant views; you won't fly into George Washington's nostril. Companies offering tours include **Rushmore Helicopters** (☎ 605/666-4461) and **Black Hills Aerial Adventures** (☎ 605/343-5058). Rides begin at $22; for $44 per person, the tour goes within a half mile of the faces and flies over them.

2. **Take a couple of days at the Triple R Dude Ranch in Keystone,** especially if you have kids older than 7 who can go with you on trail rides into the Black Elk Wilderness Area. Fishing, swimming, almost effortless game-spotting, and cookouts supplement the daily wilderness and breakfast rides. Call ☎ 605/666-4605 for details.

3. **Hop aboard the 1880 steam-engine Black Hills Central Railroad.** It's a 20-mile chug through the Black Hills along some of the steepest grades in North America. You can get aboard in Hill City or Keystone. $18 adults, $10 children 4 to 14, under 4 free. For schedule and reservations, call ☎ 605/574-2222.

4. **See five states from the top of Terry Peak.** By winter it's South Dakota's major ski area; in summer it's a chairlift ride to a fantastic view. From I-90, take exit 30 and go southwest on 14A to the turnoff 1 mile south of Lead (☎ 605/584-2165; www.terrypeak.com).

5. **Invest in museum-quality reproductions of Sioux artifacts,** such as the distinctive hand-thrown pottery with Western motifs available at **Sioux Pottery and Crafts** (☎ 800/657-4366) or **Prairie Edge Studios** in Rapid City, for reproductions of Plains Indian beadwork, supplies for beadwork, quilts, and blankets (☎ 605/342-3086).

6. **Hit the factory outlet store for Gateway 2000.** Computer geeks see black-and-white cow spots before their eyes when they see the great prices on of computer equipment, and with a big RV you can take it all back home easily. It's located right by the factory where a good factory outlet should be (instead of in suburban malls). It's at 610 Gateway Dr., North Sioux City, SD 57049 (☎ **888/888-2017**).

7. **Visit Pipestem Creek.** One of our favorite offbeat shops, Pipestem Creek creates dried floral wreaths and bird feeders from grasses and flowers grown on the family ranch. SunFeeders and SunFlorals are two of the products built around giant dried sunflower heads. Birds love them! On Route 9 south of Carrington in the center of North Dakota; open Monday through Friday from 8:30am to 4:30pm, but production slows down at lunchtime. For a catalog, call ☎ **701/652-2623.**

8. **Pick up North Dakota–made products at Pride of Dakota,** from buffalo soap and a General Custer doll to buffalo chips (potato chips dipped in milk chocolate) or chokecherry jelly. The shop is in the Buffalo Mall in Jamestown, but there's also a catalogue you can order from Buffalo Mall, Jamestown, ND 58402 (☎ **800/447-6564**).

TAKE-OUT (OR EAT-IN) TREATS
Chinatown Cafe, Deadwood. Located in Miss Kitty's Gaming Saloon, 649 Main St., in Deadwood (☎ **605/578-7778**). Funny, we don't remember ever seeing *Gunsmoke*'s Amanda Blake dishing up chop suey. Alternatively, you could look for the ever popular Chinese Opium Tunnel Museum on the Chinatown Tour.

The Firehouse Brewing Company, Rapid City. Firehouse Brewing Co., at 610 Main St., makes boutique beers while you watch, and offers homemade pub food to go with it (☎ **605/348-1915**).

Cheyenne Crossing Café, Lodge & Store, Cheyenne Crossing. Breakfasts at Cheyenne, at U.S. 85 and the Spearfish Canyon Route 14A, feature sourdough pancakes, homemade sausage and gravy, eggs and buttermilk biscuits, while lunch brings buffalo burgers and Indian tacos (☎ **605/ 584-3510**).

Barn Restaurant, Huron. For a budget break, try the hamburgers and down-home buffets at the Barn Restaurant in Huron, South Dakota, where Cheryl Ladd once worked as a waitress. It's located on South Highway 37 (☎ **605/352-9238**).

Widman's Candy Store, Grand Forks. The Red River flooded disastrously in 1997, and Widman's was one of the first downtown businesses to reopen after the waters receded. This charming candy box of a store is famous for its Widman's Chippers: Red River potatoes cut and cooked into ruffled chips, then hand-dipped in chocolate. Thicker, less salty, and more like a candy bar than the chocolate-dipped Maui potato chips from Hawaii, the Widman's

Chippers are cheaper, too, at $8 a pound. Midwestern chocolate humor dictates novelty candies such as Moo Pies, Moose Muffins, and such. The Widman family has other shops in Fargo and in Crookston, Minnesota, across the river from Grand Forks. The Grand Forks store is at 106 S. Third St., and is open Monday through Saturday (☎ 701/775-3480).

The Pitchfork Fondue, Medora. Think of the short-lived 1960s fad for beef fondue, then imagine Grant Wood's painting American Gothic, but with rib-eye steaks impaled on the tines of the farmer's pitchfork. That's the general idea of Pitchfork Fondue, a pretheater dinner buffet served at the outdoor theater before the Medora Musical in an open air pavilion with a great view on all sides. Eleven-ounce rib-eye steaks are impaled on each tine and immersed in vats of boiling oil. The buffet also includes raw vegetables with dip, fruit salad, coleslaw, rolls, butter, baked potatoes, and baked beans. It's served at 6:30pm sharp; $19.50 adults, $11 schoolchildren, free for preschoolers. It all takes place at the Burning Hills Ampitheatre on the marked drive off the west end of Pacific Avenue in Medora. Advance reservations required (☎ 701/623-4444).

The Chuckwagon Patio, downtown Medora. The Chuckwagon, at 3rd Avenue near 3rd Street, serves barbecued chicken and ribs of beef brisket from 4:30 to 7:30pm every Saturday for less than $6 to eat inside in the air-conditioning or outside at the open-air picnic tables, then sets up a Sunday brunch buffet in its cafeteria from 8am to 1:30pm (☎ 701/623-4444).

The Grand Pasta Party, Grand Forks. Bring your fork and join the party on the prairie to salute the fact that North Dakota produces most of the durum wheat that makes the world's pasta. The festival is held each year in mid-August; in September they celebrate Potato Bowl USA, with French Fryday, a potato queen, pancake breakfast, and football game. Contact the Grand Forks Convention and Visitors Center (☎ 701/746-0444).

Peacock Alley Bar & Grill, Bismarck. Despite its prestige and romantic 19th-century ambience, Bismarck's Peacock Alley Bar & Grill serves home-made dishes. Located at 422 E. Main St. (☎ 701/255-7917).

BRING ON THE BUFFALO

According to the U.S. Department of Agriculture, buffalo meat is lower in fat, calories, and cholesterol than either beef sirloin or chicken breast, with more protein per gram than beef and no growth hormones, stimulants, or antibiotics. Typical Dakota recipes for buffalo include steaks, roasts, salami, sausage, hamburger, and jerky. Here are some places to sample it or see it running around the prairie, preprocessing:

1. **The Rough Riders Hotel, Medora, North Dakota.** The hotel dining room serves a 9-ounce buffalo rib-eye steak for around $16. Located at 3rd Street and 3rd Avenue. Open 7am to 9pm from May to early September. For reservations, call ☎ 701/623-4444.

2. **Siouxland Buffalo, Grand Forks, North Dakota.** Chuckwagon buffalo burgers and a gen-u-wine Buffalo Gift Shop at the Earl Buffalo Farm, Route 2 in Grand Forks, North Dakota (☎ **701/772-1594**).

3. **Al's Oasis, outside Sioux Falls.** Buffalo burgers South Dakota–style are the big seller at Al's, located about halfway between Sioux Falls and the Black Hills, off exit 260 on I-90. Al's is also famous for homemade pie and 5¢ coffee (☎ **605/734-6054**).

4. **Wall Drug Store, Wall, South Dakota.** Wall stars buffalo burgers at the top of its tourist menu, along with hot beef sandwiches, homemade donuts, pies, cinnamon rolls, 5¢ coffee, and free ice water. Open year-round at exit 109 or 110 from I-90 (☎ **605/279-2175**).

5. **State Game Lodge, Custer State Park, South Dakota.** Spicy buffalo sausage and biscuits make a great breakfast or midmorning snack at the lodge's Pleasant Pheasant Dining Room, located on U.S. 16 east of the junction with Route 87 in southwestern South Dakota (☎ **605/ 255-4541**).

6. **Cedar Pass Lodge, Interior, South Dakota.** Indian tacos made on Sioux fry bread with buffalo meat are a house special at the Badlands' Cedar Pass Lodge. The 24-cabin lodge is run by the Oglala Sioux tribe and is located in the Badlands in southwestern South Dakota on Route 377, off I-90 at exit 131 south (☎ **605/433-5460**).

7. **Sioux Falls Brewing Company, Sioux Falls, South Dakota.** Buffalo Stout is brewed on the premises, at 431 N. Phillips Ave. The stout is a primary ingredient in Buffalo Pie, which is a meatless chocolate cheese-cake (☎ **605/332-4847**).

8. **Space Aliens Grill & Bar, Bismarck, North Dakota.** Nonplused by the 50 friendly space aliens on display, we missed the connection at first when our waitress rattled off specials like buffalo strips, buffalo pizza, and buffalo wings. "Buffalo don't have wings," we protested. "These do," she said cheerfully. Oh, *that* Buffalo. At 1304 E. Century Ave., Bismarck (☎ **701/223-6220**).

9. **Custer State Park buffalo safari, South Dakota.** Take a buffalo safari ride, which leaves from the State Game Lodge to go into the back-country to see some of the park's 1,400 bison. Located on U.S. 16 east of the junction with Route 87 in southwestern South Dakota. Admission $19 adults, $16 children (☎ **605/255-4541**).

10. **Custer State Park buffalo roundup, South Dakota.** In late September or early October, the bison are rounded up, branded, vaccinated, and sorted to separate the culls for a November auction (☎ **605/255-4515**).

DANCES WITH NATIVE AMERICANS

The worldwide success of Kevin Costner's Oscar-winning film *Dances with Wolves* brought a lot of attention to South Dakota, and visitors ever since have arrived wanting to learn more about the Lakota people and the achingly beautiful film locations. The film was shot on location in South Dakota, much of it at a private ranch near Pierre called Roy Houck's Triple U Ranch, home of the world's largest privately owned herd of bison, some 3,500 head. From the Sioux community came 150 extras, along with consultants on the Lakota language and tribal customs. At the end of the shoot, many props and costumes were auctioned to local buyers, so if you run across someone claiming to have original artifacts from the film, you can probably believe him. Props can be seen at the Akta Lakota Museum in Chamberlain (see below). Costumes are on display at the **Midnight Star Casino** in Deadwood.

Guided tours into this area are offered by **Affordable Adventures of Rapid City** (☎ 605/342-7691).

You can go on your own to the winter camp location in Little Spearfish Canyon; ask directions at **Cheyenne Crossing Store,** at the junction of 14A and U.S. 85 (☎ 605/584-3510), or at **Latchstring Village,** on U.S. 14A in Spearfish Canyon (☎ 605/584-3333), 20 minutes from Deadwood or Spearfish and famous for fresh trout and buttermilk pancakes. It's open daily 8am to 9pm, summer only.

The **Akta Lakota Museum** is a fine Lakota Sioux cultural and heritage museum; take the Chamberlain exit 263 off I-90 and drive 2 miles north into town. The museum is free and open daily in summer except Sunday mornings, and weekdays only in winter. Besides arts and artifacts, you'll find Lakota-made crafts for sale in the gift shop. St. Joseph Indian School in Chamberlain also welcomes visitors. For information, call the Chamberlain Area Chamber of Commerce (☎ 605/734-4416).

Other central and western South Dakota reservations that welcome visitors include the **Cheyenne River Sioux Tribe,** in the center of the state, which celebrates various powwows in the summer, offers tours to its 100-head bison herd, and provides hunting and fishing opportunities.

The **Crow Creek Sioux Tribe,** in the middle of the state, offers walleye fishing and a powwow and fair the third week of August. For information, call the Chamberlain Area Chamber of Commerce (☎ 605/734-4416) or the Alliance of Tribal Tourism Advocates (☎ 605/964-4000).

The reservation for the **Oglala Sioux Tribe** in southwest South Dakota near Pine Ridge is the second largest in the United States and adjoins Badlands National Park. For Sioux tourism, call Tribal Tourism (☎ 605/964-4000). The **White River visitor center** at Badlands is south of the South Unit of Badlands National Park, Route 27, about 20 miles north of Wounded Knee battlegrounds, and sells tribal crafts, and the Cuny Table Cafe sells Indian tacos. The **Red Cloud Indian Mission School** on Route 18 near Pine Ridge offers an art show representing 30 different tribes, plus a gift shop, open on weekdays. **The Oglala Fair, Rodeo and Powwow** is held the first weekend in August. Wounded Knee is also on the reservation.

In North Dakota, where the various Native American tribes are as a group commonly referred to as Sioux, visitors are welcome to help celebrate pow-wows throughout the spring and summer. You can join tribal members in dancing when the powwow announcer calls for an "intertribal" dance. One of the biggest is the **United Tribes International Pow Wow** in Bismarck just after Labor Day. For information, call ☎ **701/255-3285.** Ask the **North Dakota Tourism Department** (☎ **800/435-5663**) for a full list, or contact individual tribal groups for their own special events: **Mandan, Hidatsa,** and **Arikara,** the Three Affiliated Tribes in New Town (☎ **701/627-4781;** www.mhanation.com); **Spirit Lake Sioux Tribe** in Fort Totten (☎ **701/766-4221**); **Standing Rock Sioux Tribe** in Fort Yates (☎ **701/854-7201;** www.standingrock.org); and **Turtle Mountain Band** of Chippewa in Belcourt (☎ **701/477-8817**).

Powwow Protocol

- Take along your folding chairs from the RV to sit on since seats are at a premium.

- Stand for the grand entry, when the flags are brought in; there may be two grand entries a day. Remain standing during the opening prayer. When in doubt, do what the people around you do.

- The program generally begins with a grand entry, then come honor songs, followed by men's traditional dancing in several categories, then women's traditional dancing, then children's dancing. You're not per-mitted to film some parts of the ceremony; the announcer will tell you

North Dakota's Painted Canyon is a favorite of photographers.

when cameras are prohibited. Otherwise, you may photograph the groups of dancers in performance but should ask permission before photographing an individual not in performance.

- It is also a Native American tradition to give money or other gifts when a particular performance has stirred you; you may follow this example if you want, but should not feel compelled to do so.

FIVE ACTIVE ADVENTURES

1. **Fishing the Black Hills.** Head for one of the 14 lakes or 1,300 miles of streams in the Black Hills in pursuit of rainbow, brook, or brown trout. Lake Pactola holds state records with a 22-pound brown trout and a 15-pound lake trout. Deerfield is best for brook trout. Try fly-fishing in Rapid Creek, Spearfish Creek, Castle Creek, and French Creek in Custer State Park. Lakes in the park are stocked, but you may catch some wild trout as well. You can also snag walleyes, bass, bluegills, perch, crappies, and bullheads. Buy a license first.

2. **Dakota golfing.** Golf courses may include hazards like deer grazing on the fairway or beaver dams by the water holes. You'll find 12 courses around the Black Hills with various degrees of difficulty. Meadowbrook Municipal in Rapid City and Boulder Canyon Country Club near Sturgis are considered the toughest. For Rapid City information, call ☎ 800/487-3223; www.rapidcitycvb.com; for more information on Sturgis golfing, call the Sturgis Chamber of Commerce (☎ 605/347-2556).

3. **Horseback riding.** Riders can find more than a dozen outfitters that offer everything from hour-long rides to a 10-day pack trip on the Centennial Trail in the Black Hills. If you bring your own horse along, you'll find "horse camps" with corrals, water wells, feed bunks, picket posts, and stock trailer parking, with room for your RV as well. **JR Bar Ranch Trail Rides** in Custer (☎ 605/673-2199) can handle beginners on short rides; also in Custer, **Dakota Badland Outfitters** offers full and half-day trail rides into the Badlands (☎ 605/673-5363). **Gunsel Horse Adventures** in Rapid City runs 4-, 7-, and 10-day adventure treks into the Badlands and Black Hills (☎ 605/343-7608).

4. **Canoeing the Missouri and Sheyenne rivers.** You'll be saying proudly, "I can canoe" after a beginner's river paddling trip. Rentals and shuttle services for the Missouri River in North Dakota can be arranged at the **Lewis and Clark Café** in Washburn (☎ 701/462-3368), or at **Cross Ranch State Park,** in nearby Hensler (☎ 701/794-3731). The shyer Sheyenne can be canoed while you're camped at the **Fort Ransom State Park;** rentals are available at (☎ 701/973-4331). Always call ahead and ask about river conditions. See "Campground Oases in North Dakota," later in this chapter, for directions to the park.

5. Fishing for paddlefish. The prehistoric paddlefish, a 75- to 100-pound freshwater billfish, runs in North Dakota's Yellowstone and Missouri rivers from early May to late June. Locals promise that once you hook one of these fighting fish, you're hooked forever. Contact the North Dakota Game and Fish Department, 100 N. Bismarck Expressway, Bismarck, ND 58501 (☎ **701/328-6300;** www.state.nd.us/gnf/).

WILDLIFE-WATCHING

The Great Plains were once dark with 60 or 70 million buffalo, and while not many remain, you'll still see a surprising number of small herds, particularly in Custer State Park, where they like to graze around the State Game Lodge. Between 400 and 500 bison calves are born each spring in the park.

Also in Custer State Park, you might see bighorn sheep, mountain goats, coyotes, pronghorn antelope, white-tailed deer, mule deer, and, rarely, elk.

President Theodore Roosevelt originally set aside **Sully's Hill National Game Preserve** near North Dakota's Devils Lake in 1904 for a national park, but it was turned into a game reserve to save the endangered American bison. Now, at 2½ square miles, it's the biggest "zoo" in the Midwest, with not only bison and elk but also prairie dogs, white-tailed deer, foxes, swans, ducks, and geese, and sometimes bald and golden eagles. A 4-mile Big Game Auto Tour route is best in early morning and early evening. It's open May 1 to October 31, 12 miles south of Devils Lake on Highway 57. Admission is free. Call ☎ **701/766-4272** for information.

The largest breeding colony of white pelicans in the United States can be seen at **Chase Lake National Wildlife Refuge,** 23 miles northwest of Medina off I-94's exit 230. To see snow geese, visit **Kenmare** on U.S. 52 in northwestern North Dakota, host to hundreds of thousands of migrating snow and blue geese in the fall.

On the Road: South Dakota

SOUTH DAKOTA'S BADLANDS

Geologists and Great Plains aficionados will claim this national park got a bad rap when the first men to record their impressions, French-Canadian trappers, called the area *les mauvaises terres a traverser* ("bad lands to travel across"). But if you stand alone listening to the wind singing a solitary song and imagine yourself tracking your way across it, you'll understand.

Wind and water wreaked this erosion, delivering an endless landscape of folds and crags and gullies, canyons, spires, and pinnacles, the austerity relieved only faintly in spring with a fuzzy green outline of fresh grass, then burned down to the bone again in the summer heat.

This region was once lush grassland in the Oligocene epoch 35 million years ago, and the fossil-rich plains hold the fossilized bones of prehistoric animals. Then, after about 10 million years, volcanoes erupted to the west,

The Badlands of South Dakota.

in what is now Yellowstone National Park, and covered the rich lands with layers of white ash. Rains lessened, and dry winds from the north continued the sculpting. But life forms adapted. In recent years, the bison and Rocky Mountain bighorn sheep were reintroduced.

If the loneliness begins to get you down, forge ahead on the Badlands Loop Road and take the Creek Rim Road northwest for 5 miles toward **Roberts Prairie Dog Town,** 5 miles beyond the 240 turnoff to Wall. These social, short-tailed rodents seem tremendously busy as they go about their daily chores, ignoring the occasional hungry coyote or badger that stands by

Dakota prairie dog.

waiting to pounce. They pop up from a hole, stand on their hind legs and look around, emitting a sharp barking cry as if to signal their friends below.

LITTLE BIGHORN & WOUNDED KNEE

The **Little Bighorn Battlefield National Monument,** on I-90 286 miles from the Rapid City area at the town of Crow Agency, Wyoming (open June–Sept only), commemorates the battle that lasted less than an hour on a hot June day in 1876, when a force of 1,500 Sioux and Cheyenne warriors led by Sitting Bull wiped out Custer's troops while two other battalions of the regiment were on a distant ridge. Custer, underestimating the Plains Indian forces, had decided to divide his 600 troops into thirds to create a pincers action, then attacked without waiting for the others.

The battlefield is a riveting spot, still haunted, still mysterious. From a visitor center you walk uphill to a fenced cemetery with tombstones naming the soldiers and where each was believed to have fallen, insofar as the names were known. A mass grave under a hilltop monument contains whatever remains were not removed later by relatives. It is debated whether the bones exhumed in 1877 and reburied at West Point are actually those of Custer.

Although eyewitness accounts vary widely, it is thought perhaps 150 braves at the most died in the battle.

Signs on the site caution visitors to watch out for rattlesnakes; one wonders if the snakes were there the day of the battle.

The **Wounded Knee Massacre site** is south of the Black Hills on Route 27, a few miles north of the Nebraska border on the Pine Ridge reservation, headquarters for the Oglala Sioux. In 1889, with growing pressure from

The gravestones at Little Bighorn.

Little Bighorn Battlefield National Monument

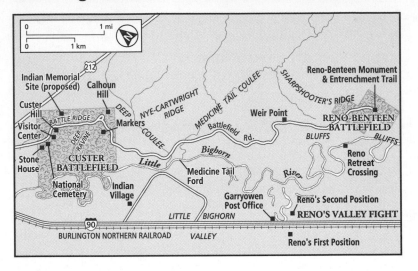

occupying military forces, Native Americans, with their traditional Sun Dance banned, began to turn more and more to spiritual movements, including the use of peyote cactus tips to induce visions. The Ghost Dance ritual, introduced by a Paiute mystic, promised that whites would be eliminated in a flood, vanished game and all their dead kin would come back, and Indians would return to the old ways if they just kept on dancing.

Troops were ordered in to stop the dances, and on December 15, 1890, Chief Sitting Bull was shot while troops were attempting to arrest him. Three hundred and fifty Sioux under the command of Big Foot were among the

THE CUSTER CONNECTION

The last big gold rush in the contiguous United States was set off by the discovery of gold in French Creek by a civilian prospector tagging along with Lt. Colonel George Armstrong Custer in 1874. (A major general during the Civil War, Custer was reappointed a lieutenant colonel after the war.) The flamboyant Custer, dressed in buckskins, rode at the head of a 1,000-man company of soldiers, scientists, newspaper correspondents, and miners, ostensibly surveying for a railroad but actually checking out the possibility of gold in the Black Hills. The area had been designated part of the Great Sioux Reservation only 6 years earlier by the Treaty of Laramie, presumably before rumors of gold in the area had reached Washington.

There was also one woman in the group, Sally Campbell, the cook for sutler John Smith. She stayed in the Black Hills, staking a gold claim and, in her later years, enjoyed telling stories about her adventures. As a non–Native American, she has gone down in history as "the first white woman in South Dakota," despite her African roots.

GOLD PANNING COURTESY

Don't pan for gold anywhere except in the streams of the Black Hills National Forest or at commercial attractions that promote it. Otherwise, you run the risk of trespassing or claim-jumping— "there's still gold in them thar hills."

last groups to be caught by the 500 cavalrymen; they were led to a military camp at Wounded Knee Creek. A medicine man called for the young warriors to resist being disarmed; fighting broke out and cannon and carbines tore the camp apart. More than 150 of the Sioux, many of them women and children, were killed on the spot, and 44 more did not recover from their wounds.

The battlefield at Wounded Knee was the scene of demonstrations in the 1970s when 200 Indian militants fought off law-enforcement officers and occupied the village for 70 days.

MT. RUSHMORE & THE CRAZY HORSE MONUMENT

The best time to see **Mt. Rushmore** is in early morning, and the best vantage points are the carved rock tunnels that frame the mountain from Alternate U.S. 16 heading north, also called Iron Mountain Road. The 17-mile route is narrow with pigtail bridges and one-way tunnels, some of them a tight fit for big RVs. If you're early enough, you may glimpse deer, bighorn sheep, raccoons, and some buffalo on the drive through Custer State Park.

The mountain itself got its name by accident, when a gold miner in a claim litigation was riding past with his recently arrived eastern lawyer, who was named Rushmore. The lawyer asked the name of that mountain, and the miner, as a joke, said, "It's Mt. Rushmore." And so it became.

Sculptor Gutzon Borglum, who started work on Mt. Rushmore in 1927 when he was 60, was a man of boundless energy, a prolific sculptor (175 of his works are in the Cathedral of St. John the Divine in New York City), and

SOUTH DAKOTA NIGHTLIFE

If the ruckus in Deadwood doesn't appeal to you, you can go to **Mt. Rushmore** to sing the national anthem and watch the lights come on the presidents' heads (that doesn't take long, but it doesn't cost anything), hit a campfire program at one of the parks, attend a free Thursday night **band concert** in Rapid City (☎ 800/487-3223), catch **free movies** in Hot Springs' Centennial Park (☎ 800/325-6991), peruse the parading **fife and drum corps** on Mondays in Hill City (☎ 800/888-1798), or catch the **Black Hills Playhouse** productions of vintage Broadway shows (☎ 605/255-4141). 🚐

a controversial and argumentative character. He charmed President Calvin Coolidge and his wife, who stayed in the State Game Lodge on their 1927 visit to dedicate the sculpture, by hiring a small plane, flying over the lodge, and swooping down to drop a bouquet of wildflowers to Mrs. C.

Borglum wanted to add a Hall of Records on the mountainside so that future archaeologists wouldn't think the Americans of the mid–20th century worshipped giant stone figures. He even persuaded Coolidge to write a text for a Hall of Records dedication, but then sat down and rewrote it to his own taste and released it to the newspapers as the president's work, infuriating the taciturn Coolidge.

It was also on his agenda to finish the figures as busts, carved down to the waist, and to remove the stone rubble to build an amphitheater, but shortly after he died in 1941, work ceased on the project.

Korczak Zielkowski, the sculptor of the nearby **Crazy Horse Monument,** worked for a while with Borglum at Rushmore, but the two men did not always get along. Zielkowski began his work in 1947, and since his death in 1982, his wife and 10 children have continued the project, working from private donations and the monies collected by admissions to the site with its museum, shop, and restaurant. It's located on U.S. 385 north of Custer.

Campground Oases in South Dakota

Mt. Rushmore/Hill City KOA. The closest campground to Mt. Rushmore offers free shuttle service to the evening lighting ceremonies at Rushmore and Crazy Horse. Some 235 RV sites have full hookups, flush toilets, showers, fire grates, swimming pool, sanitary dump, restaurant, playground, and pond with trout fishing. Sites are close together in parking-lot style, although

Mt. Rushmore is a favorite destination for RVers.

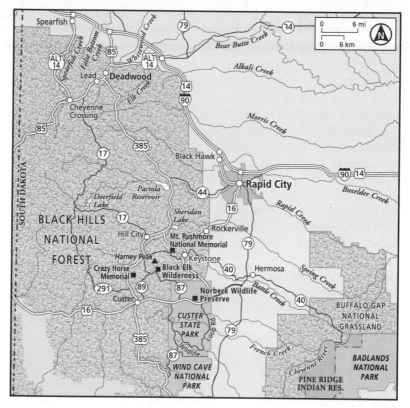

some have trees and/or grass. The campground is on Route 244 between Hill City and the Four Faces, reached from U.S. 16 at State Road 244, then 3 miles east. It's modem-friendly, provides cable TV, and has horses and cars for rent, a water slide (fee), hayrides, movies, and Indian dances (☎ 800/KOA-8503 or 605/574-2525; www.koa.com).

Mystery Mountain Resort. Next to Bear Country USA on the road to Mt. Rushmore Road at 13752 Highway 16, Mystery Mountain should please families looking for lots to do. A playground, heated 50-foot pool, hot tub, shade trees, and hiking trails are at the resort, plus 35 tree-shaded, full-hookup sites (30- and 50-amp electric) and a modem-friendly office (☎ 800/658-CAMP for reservations; www.blackhillsresorts.com).

Lazy J RV Park and Campground. The Lazy J in Rapid City offers view sites and terraced camping, daily bus tours of the region, car rentals available on the premises, and a big new heated pool and spa. Water and 30- and 50-amp electric hookups are available at 110 sites, sewer hookups at 64 of them, and there is plenty of room for big rigs. It's located at 4110 South Highway 16, accessed from exit 57 of Route 90, then driving south 4 miles (☎ 605/342-2751 for reservations; www.rvparksusa.com/sd/lazyj.htm).

Cedar Pass Campground. Located near the Ben Rifel Visitor Center in the Badlands National Park on Route 240, Cedar Pass has 100 sites with flush toilets, piped water (in summer), and sewage disposal station. A fee is charged in summer but not in winter when water is off. No hookups, no reservations (☎ 605/433-5361; www.reserveusa.com).

The Black Hills National Forest Campgrounds. Six campgrounds offer a total of 321 sites suitable for RVs, most with piped water, picnic tables, fire grates, and pit or flush toilets but no hookups or disposal stations. Closest to Mt. Rushmore and most popular is Horsethief Lake with 28 sites. From Rapid City, take Highway 16 south to Hill City. Take 16/385 south to Custer (☎ 877/444-6777 or 605/574-2534 for reservations).

Big Pine Campground. Two miles west of Custer on Route 16W, Big Pine has 70 sites with 30-amp electricity and water, 40 with full hookups, pine-shaded, and fairly well spaced. Flush toilets, showers, sanitary dump, laundry, playground, and limited groceries (☎ 800/235-3981 or 605/673-4054 for reservations).

Rafter J Bar Ranch Campground. Located in Hill City, the grounds have 130 sites, most with full hookups, in 80 acres of ponderosa pines. You can choose a campsite near the pool and playground or a more secluded spot back in the trees. Supervised pony rides for kids, flush toilets, showers, sanitary dump, laundry, satellite TV, groceries, and RV supplies. And a trout stream runs through it. Take 16 south to Hill City; go 3 miles and follow the signs (☎ 888/RAFTERV or 605/574-2527 for reservations; www.rafterv.com).

Custer State Park. Custer Park has some first-come, first-served spaces in each of its seven campgrounds. The areas most accessible to larger RVs are Game Lodge Campground with 65 sites, Legion Lake with 25, and Stockade Lake with 68. Paved camping pads, fire grates, and picnic tables are supplied, and there's a dump station at Game Lodge. None have hookups. From Rapid City, take Highway 79 to Highway 36; 36 turns into Route 16A in Custer Park. The park accepts some campsite reservations (☎ 605/255-4515).

Custer/Mt. Rushmore KOA. Three miles west of Custer on Route 16, this KOA has 103 sites, most of them shaded by pine trees, all with electricity and water and 32 with sewer. Flush toilets, showers, sanitary dump, laundry, groceries, heated swimming pool, optional chuckwagon breakfasts and barbecue buffalo dinners, and car rental (☎ 800/KOA-5828 or 605/673-7304; www.koa.com).

Berry Patch Campground. Located in Rapid City at the junction of I-90 and exit 60, Berry Patch has 113 RV sites with water and 30- and 50-amp electricity, of which 64 also have sewers. Flush toilets, showers, sanitary dump, heated pool, laundry, playground. Daily bus tours around the area, free movies, and you can camp every sixth and seventh nights free. Open April through October (☎ 800/658-4566 or 605/341-5588).

South Dakota Campgrounds

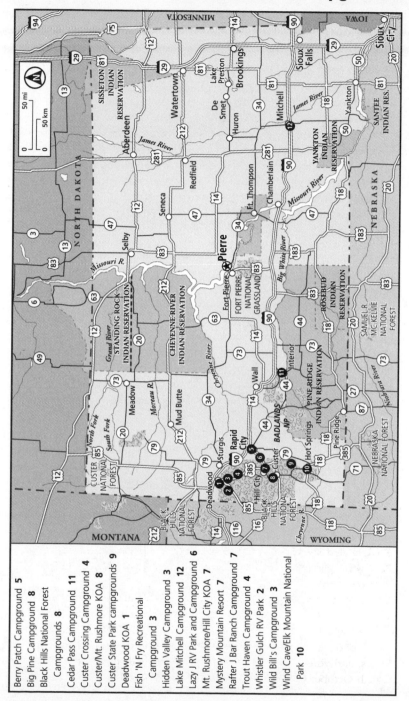

Berry Patch Campground **5**
Big Pine Campground **8**
Black Hills National Forest
  Campgrounds **8**
Cedar Pass Campground **11**
Custer Crossing Campground **4**
Custer/Mt. Rushmore KOA **8**
Custer State Park campgrounds **9**
Deadwood KOA **1**
Fish 'N Fry Recreational
  Campground **3**
Hidden Valley Campground **3**
Lake Mitchell Campground **12**
Lazy J RV Park and Campground **6**
Mt. Rushmore/Hill City KOA **7**
Mystery Mountain Resort **7**
Rafter J Bar Ranch Campground **7**
Trout Haven Campground **4**
Whistler Gulch RV Park **2**
Wild Bill's Campground **3**
Wind Cave/Elk Mountain National
  Park **10**

BEGGING BURROS

A road hazard or an irresistible attraction, depending on your point of view, are the begging burros along Iron Mountain Road that will poke their heads inside your car window looking for something to eat. Originally brought in during the 1950s to carry tourists to the top of Harney Peak, they now roam freely and panhandle. They'll accept and eat almost anything, but bread, cookies, and crackers are their favorites. These are the only animals in the park that visitors are permitted to feed. Don't think you can feed the buffalo! They are large, dangerous animals and should not be approached, even in a vehicle.

Wind Cave/Elk Mountain National Park. Located in Hot Springs, south of Custer State Park, Wind Cave Park has a year-round campground with no hookups and no reservations. Flush toilets and piped water are available in summer. Hiking, wildlife viewing, and guided tours of the caves are among the appeals, as well as a popular ranger-led "night prowl" every evening after the campfire programs. Tents and RVs with slide-outs are not permitted, and there are pet restrictions. From Rapid City, take Route 79 south to Hot Springs. Take 385 north directly into the park (☎ 605/745-4600).

Deadwood KOA. The closest campground to the gambling casinos offers a free shuttle bus to town and gold panning in Deadwood Creek, if you want to kill two urges with one stop. The terraced campground is on the side of a hill, but the entrance road has been improved and shouldn't hamper a big rig, although sites large enough for them are limited. The KOA has 51 sites with 30-amp electric, 48 of them with water and 26 with sewer, plus a heated pool, playground, grocery, laundry, and dump station. From the junction of U.S. 85 and U.S. 14A (in Deadwood), head west 1 mile on 14A (☎ 800/KOA-0846 or 605/578-3830; www.koa.com).

Other Deadwood campgrounds: Other campgrounds in the Deadwood area include Custer Crossing Campground, 15 miles south of Deadwood on U.S. 385 (☎ 605/584-1009); Fish 'N Fry Recreational Campground, 6 miles south of Deadwood on U.S. 385 (☎ 605/578-2150); Hidden Valley Campground, 7 miles south on U.S. 385 (☎ 605/578-1342); Trout Haven Campground, 20 miles south on U.S. 385 (☎ 605/341-4440); Whistler Gulch RV Park, 3 miles south of the U.S. 85/U.S. 14A junction on U.S. 85 (☎ 605/578-2092); and Wild Bill's Campground, 5.2 miles south on U.S. 385 (☎ 605/578-2800).

Lake Mitchell Campground. Located in Mitchell, only a mile or so from the Corn Palace (see "Off-the-Wall Attractions," earlier in this chapter), this campground offers 70 shaded sites, some of them pull-throughs, with 20- and

30-amp electric and cable TV. It makes a convenient stopover in the eastern part of South Dakota. From Rapid City, take I-90 to exit 330. Turn left at the ramp to Highway 37 bypass, then left at Main Street. It's less than a mile to the campground (☎ **605/995-8457** for reservations).

On the Road: North Dakota

THEODORE ROOSEVELT NATIONAL PARK

"I have always said I would not have been president if it had not been for my experience in North Dakota," Theodore Roosevelt often said and wrote.

Remembered as the preserver of our natural resources, a founder of our national parks, and the namesake of the teddy bear, Roosevelt as a young man was dedicated to big-game hunting. He had read of the threatened extinction of the American bison and first came to North Dakota's Badlands in 1883 on a hunting trip, afraid that some other hunter would shoot the last buffalo before he could get there. He had married 5 years earlier, and took the trip west when his wife Alice was pregnant with their first child.

He and his guide struggled through more than a week of cold, rainy days, not finding any buffalo until the 10th day. Roosevelt killed the buffalo, then thrust a $100 bill into the hands of his astonished guide.

Smitten with the frontier countryside, he invested in a cattle ranching plan with two other partners at the Maltese Cross Ranch in the Badlands, then returned to New York. But on February 14, 1884, both his mother and his wife died within hours of each other, his mother from typhoid, his wife from complications of childbirth. Brokenhearted, he returned to throw himself into his ranch business, buying a second spread, the Elkhorn. He changed almost overnight from a hunter to a conservationist protecting the land and wildlife. In 1901, after he was elected president, he established the U.S. Forest Service and proclaimed 18 national monuments. He also got permission from Congress to establish five national parks and 51 wildlife refuges.

The park that honors Roosevelt was dedicated in 1978. One of the most fascinating and least visited, the park is divided into two units, a North Unit 52 miles north of I-94 and a South Unit 70 miles to the south at Medora. Both offer scenic loop drives; a mile-by-mile "Road Log Guide" for them is for sale at the visitor centers in the park for $1.50. The Elkhorn Ranch Unit 35 miles north of Medora is also part of the park but difficult to reach without fording streams. The **South Unit visitor center** is in Medora at west end of Pacific Avenue (☎ **701/623-4466**); the **North Unit visitor center** is on U.S. 85 15 miles south of Watford City (☎ **701/623-4466**; www.nps.gov/thro).

The **North Unit 30-mile scenic drive** goes past herds of buffalo and longhorns; geologic formations like slump rock, caprock, and lignite coal seams; and steeply eroded canyons in what was once grassland prairie. Less often seen are herds of wild horses, pronghorn, elk, deer, and mountain lions.

Theodore Roosevelt National Park

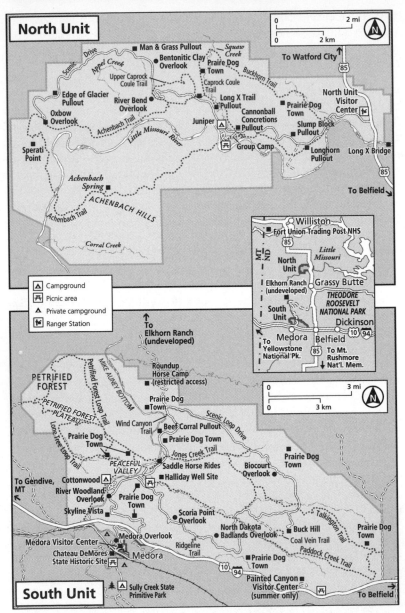

On the **South Unit 36-mile loop,** look for the Prairie Dog Town at Milepost 3.3, with adequate RV parking space; petrified tree stumps and ribbons of lignite coal in the cliffs; the Buck Hill Road overlook with a good view across the Badlands; and, of course, the buffalo, part of a herd of 400.

Don't miss the photogenic Painted Canyon turnout on I-94 and the scenery behind the visitor center. Tourists have been coming here since

1883, and the canyon was a popular tourist rest stop in the 1930s, with curio shops, caged animals on display, and a restaurant and gas station.

For more information, contact the **park headquarters** at P.O. Box 7, Medora, ND 58645 (☎ **701/623-4466**).

MEDORA

In this rustic little town of rough-sawn wood buildings, a young Theodore Roosevelt sipped iced champagne with the town's founder, the Marquis de Mores, a French business tycoon who built a meatpacking plant in 1883 and named the town for his American-born wife. The couple lived in their private railway car while building a lavish 26-room chateau on a hilltop outside town, now owned by the state and open for tours.

The meat plant ran for only 3 years, then de Mores and Medora went back to France, and the plant gradually fell into ruin, until today the site is marked only by one towering brick chimney and some random foundation stones.

The Marquis went on to even grander schemes, trying to build a railway between China and what is now Vietnam, running for French political office, and forging a Franco-Islamic alliance to drive the British from Africa until he was killed by Tuareg natives in the Sahara.

History buff Harold Shafer, owner of Gold Seal Floor Wax and Mr. Bubble, was instrumental in restoring the town in the mid-1960s.

Roosevelt's Maltese Cross cabin has been moved into the national park headquarters area here and is open for visitors on a guided tour basis only.

An annual **Cowboy Poetry Gathering** happens in Medora every spring in late May (☎ **701/225-9746**).

The Medora Musical, running nightly in a 2,900-seat amphitheater from mid-June through Labor Day, salutes Teddy with a rousing song-and-dance

Protected buffalo in Theodore Roosevelt National Park.

revue that climaxes with Roosevelt's Rough Riders at the Battle of San Juan Hill. You'll find signs directing you up the hill to the amphitheater at the west end of Pacific Avenue in Medora. Reservations (☎ **800/MEDORA-1** for reservations). While you're at it, reserve a spot at the Pitchfork Fondue—listed in "Take-Out (or Eat-In) Treats," earlier in this chapter—for dinner before the show.

Campground Oases in North Dakota

Fort Ransom State Park. One of the quietest, prettiest spots we camped in North Dakota was at remote Fort Ransom Park in the tiny Norwegian town of Fort Ransom by the Sheyenne River. Canoes are for rent, and you'll find 15 sites with electric hookups, sanitary dump, toilet facilities, and spacious pull-throughs for $11 a night. What you will have trouble finding is the park itself if you want to get there on paved roads. From I-94, take exit 288 and follow Route 1 south to Route 27, turn east for about 5 miles, and follow the Ft. Ransom turnoff north. Call ☎ **701/973-4331** for more information or the cavalry if you get lost.

Turtle River State Park. Also $11 a night with hookup, Turtle River is near Grand Forks in Arvilla, 22 miles west of Grand Forks on Highway 2, and has large pull-throughs and 70 20- and 30-amp electric connections. Open year-round for self-contained camping (the utilities are off in winter), sledding, snowshoeing, skating, and cross-country skiing (☎ **701/594-4445**).

Minot KOA. Our site at the KOA in Minot had its own resident prairie dog, something that delighted us but made our North Dakota neighbors turn up their noses at "that rodent." Some of the 66 sites are shaded and grassy; 49 of them provide 30-amp electric, and the office is modem-friendly. The campground is a little over 2 miles east of Minot at 5261 Highway 52 South (☎ **800/KOA-7421** or 701/839-7400; www.koa.com).

Four Bears RV Park. Located behind the Four Bears Casino in New Town, on Dakota 23 on the Fort Berthold Reservation, the campground is, like the casino, operated by the Three Affiliated Tribes: the Mandan, Hidatsu, and Arikara. While the 62 hookup sites with 20- and 30-amp electric are freeform rather than rigidly outlined, you can usually figure out a way to park to best access the connection. Rates are modest at $6 to $12 a night, and you can walk to the tables or to the fishing lake (☎ **701/627-4018**).

Cottonwood Campground. Located in the south unit of Theodore Roosevelt National Park, at Mile 5.6 on the Little Missouri River (14 miles west of U.S. 85), Cottonwood offers 38 sites accessible for RVs, some of them pull-throughs large enough for big rigs, but with no hookups and no reservations (☎ **701/623-4466**).

Juniper Campground (formerly Squaw Creek Campground). Located in the north unit of Theodore Roosevelt National Park, 4.6 miles off U.S. 85, opposite the Cannonball Concretions pullout, Juniper Campground has

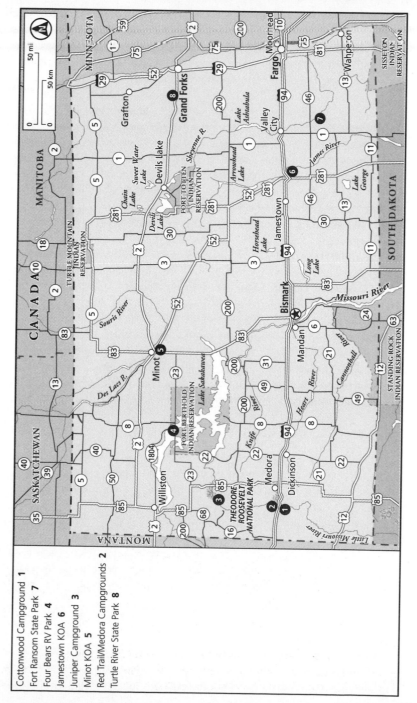

Cottonwood Campground **1**
Fort Ransom State Park **7**
Four Bears RV Park **4**
Jamestown KOA **6**
Juniper Campground **3**
Minot KOA **5**
Red Trail/Medora Campgrounds **2**
Turtle River State Park **8**

44 paved and shaded sites, none with hookups, plus a dump station and toilets. Sites are available on a first-come, first-served basis (☎ 701/842-2333).
Red Trail and Medora campgrounds. The town of Medora offers so many diversions that an interested RVer could spend a week. Unfortunately, neither of the town's two campgrounds with hookups is appealing at peak season when the crowds are there, but each has its pros and cons. Red Trail Campground, where we stayed, offers an easy walk into town and is owned and operated by a friendly family, but the campground is behind a motel and the 93 sites are fairly close together. It offers live entertainment some nights, cable TV, city water, and 30- and 50-amp hookups with a surcharge for cable and 50-amp (☎ 800/621-4317 or 701/623-4317 for reservations). Medora Campground is operated by the nonprofit Theodore Roosevelt Medora Foundation, with 185 sites closer together than those at Red Lodge. It's on the edge of town across from the road to the Medora Musical and Pitchfork Fondue Dinner (but not within walking distance, unless you want to walk uphill ¾ mile). Sites provide 20- and 30-amp electricity. Call ☎ 800/MEDORA-1 for reservations; this is also the place to buy tickets for the Pitchfork Fondue Dinner—see "Take-Out (or Eat-In) Treats," earlier in this chapter.
Jamestown KOA. This campground cooks up home-style family meals nightly between mid-June and mid-August, a boon for travelers who don't want to heat up the galley. The 48 gravel sites are shady, some adequate for big rigs, and 50-amp hookups are available. You'll also find cable TV and a modem-friendly office. It's located on the frontage road south of I-94 at exit 256 (☎ 800/KOA-6350 or 701/252-6262; www.koa.com).

A Dozen Terrific Side Trips in the Dakotas

1. **Devil's Tower National Monument.** Remember Richard Dreyfus sculpting his mashed potatoes into a flat-topped mountain in *Close Encounters of the Third Kind?* You can take a detour to that Wyoming mountain, Devil's Tower National Monument, 20 miles west on I-90, then 27 miles north via exit 185 (☎ 307/467-5283). The 867-foot core of an ancient volcano is surrounded by the pine trees of the Black Hills and has near its base one of the few protected prairie dog towns in the west. There are 51 campsites inside the park without hookups (closed in winter) and an additional 45 with 30- and 50-amp hookups outside the park gates at the Devil's Tower KOA, on the location site for the film with a fantastic view of the tower (☎ 800/562-5785 or 307/467-5395; www.koa.com). The monument is open year-round.
2. **The trail of Lewis and Clark.** Take U.S. 83 north at exit 212 for about 30 miles to visit the Farm Island State Recreation Area (☎ 605/224-5605), where a monument and interpretive center talks about their

expedition. Most of the buffalo in the fields around here were extras in the film *Dances with Wolves.*

3. **Badlands National Park.** Access is from I-90 via exit 131 from the east or 110 at Wall Drug Store from the west. A 40-mile loop on Route 240 lets you travel through a typical section of this eroded but majestic landscape brushed in watercolor pinks, soft grays, and greens—except at sunrise or sunset, when it takes on a warm burnished glow. To visit the Prairie Dog Town, continue on Route 590 along a gravel road for about 5 miles, then turn north again to Wall (☎ 605/433-5361; www.nps/badl).

4. **Spearfish Canyon National Scenic Byway.** It's a dramatically beautiful 20-mile route any time of year, but especially in early fall when the trees lining the river banks begin to change color. Take U.S. 85 southwest from Deadwood, then U.S. 14A north along the canyon. The views are better if you set out from Lead and drive north.

5. **Wildlife Loop Road in Custer State Park.** This 18-mile loop offers a chance to see pronghorn antelope, bison, white-tail and mule deer, elk, coyotes, prairie dogs, eagles, and hawks. Try to drive the loop early in the morning or very late in the afternoon for the best sightings (☎ 605/255-4515).

6. **Ingalls Family Homestead.** In tiny DeSmet, northeast of Mitchell on U.S. 14, is the Ingalls Family Homestead, the childhood home of Laura Ingalls Wilder, who wrote *Little House on the Prairie.* Her books inspired the long-running TV series. A do-it-yourself tour of 18 sites related to her stories begins at the Surveyors' House at Silver Lake. Be warned that the unpaved road to the homestead site is rough. Fans of the show will enjoy a 3-week pageant that takes place in late June and early July, with wagon rides, home-cooked meals, and an all-volunteer cast in an outdoor stage production. The homestead is marked off U.S. 14 east of town on the south side of the highway and is up an unpaved road (☎ 605/854-3383 for information).

7. **Wind Cave National Park.** South of Custer State Park via Route 87, Wind Cave has 28,000 acres of wildlife habitat aboveground for buffalo, antelope, elk, deer, and prairie dogs, as well as the 53-mile maze of tunnels underground with its unusual boxwork, frostwork, and popcorn formations (☎ 605/745-4600).

8. **Black Hills Wild Horse Sanctuary and Mammoth Site.** The Hot Springs area south of the Black Hills on U.S. 18/385 has two outstanding attractions, the Black Hills Wild Horse Sanctuary (☎ 800/252-6652), where hundreds of wild American mustangs are protected, and the Mammoth Site, where the dig goes on to excavate as many as

100 mammoths who died in a sinkhole at the springs 26,000 years ago. Bones are displayed where they were found. For information, call the Hot Springs Chamber of Commerce at ☎ 800/325-6991.

9. **Homestake Gold Mine.** If you drive over to Deadwood, add a short detour to Lead (pronounced *leed,* which means "lode") to tour the surface workings of the Homestake Gold Mine on one of their daily tours (closed in winter). The largest underground gold mine still operating in the western hemisphere was financed by George Hearst, father of William Randolph Hearst, and two California partners. From Deadwood, take Route 14A and continue on to Lead. Call the visitor's center for information (☎ 605/584-3110).

10. **Jewel Cave National Monument.** Located west of Custer on U.S. 16, Jewel Cave is the fourth largest cave in the world, with 80 miles of passageways already explored and charted. Sparkling calcite crystals and bizarre drapery, balloon, and column formations make this a favorite of cavers, who can take special tours by advance reservation (☎ 605/673-2288). Guided tours for the general public are offered on a regular schedule in summer, intermittently the rest of the year. Tours $6 adults, $3 children 6 to 16, free under 6.

11. **Prairie Village.** Located in Madison, South Dakota, Prairie Village offers considerably more than its name suggests, from an 1893 steam-driven Hershel-Spillman carousel to a Barney and Smith railway "chapel car." Chapel Car Emanuel, equipped with pews, organ, and pulpit, and a room in the back for the minister to change, was one of seven chapel cars built under the auspices of the Reverend Boston Smith, a Baptist who got the idea of sending the clergy out by rail to serve frontier settlements without churches. Today it's one of only two cars remaining. The Social Hall, now named the Lawrence Welk Opera House, originally graced the town of Oldham, South Dakota, where Welk used to play in his early days. The old church in the village is still used for Sunday morning services, and some 40 buildings are spread out over a 140-acre area with a sense of a real place and time rather than a museum collection. In August, the village holds a threshing jamboree with steam-driven farm machinery, and three coal-fired steam locomotives are fired up on occasion to offer rail excursions. It's located 2 miles west of Madison on Highway 34 (☎ 800/693-3644).

12. **Take a zigzag route from Minot to Medora.** The drive offers a good overview of North Dakota, from the farm and ranch land along Route 83 south from Minot, then west along Route 23. Both the distinctive Four Bears Bridge across the Missouri and the modern Four Bears Casino were named for a great Mandan chief, while Lake Sakakawea, a few miles to the north, is named for the young Shoshone woman also

called Sacajawea who was instrumental in helping Lewis and Clark successfully complete their mission. The Three Affiliated Tribes Museum, operated by the Mandan, Hidatsu, and Arikara people on Route 23, 4 miles west of New Town on the Fort Berthold Indian Reservation, is open daily year-round, and tells through the lives of three Mandan of the stressful adjustments Native Americans had to make to reservation life. Continue south along U.S. 85 from Wafford City, detouring to make the loop drives through the North and South Units of Theodore Roosevelt National Park (☎ **701/627-4477;** www.mhanation.com).

8
The Rio Grande Valley &
the Wilds of West Texas

ONCE INHABITED BY GIANT FLYING REPTILES WITH 50-FOOT WINGSPANS, Texas has more miles of inland lake and stream water than Minnesota, a million official road signs and markers on its highways, and, as its tourism publications frequently point out, a ranch, a military base, and two counties bigger than certain New England states.

The bottom half of Texas is where rock 'n' roll got sent out all over the universe by Wolfman Jack in the 1950s, broadcasting from a Del Rio radio station's 500,000-watt "pirate" transmitter located across the river in Mexico. The Del Rio station was built in the 1930s by "Doctor" John R. Brinkley to promote his famous goat gland surgery to restore virility.

It's where Pancho Villa and Zsa Zsa Gabor once slept (not at the same time) in El Paso's Paso del Norte Hotel, where nachos were invented by Ignacio "Nacho" Anaya at the Victory Club in Piedras Negras, and where fajitas were first served at Ninfa's restaurant in Houston on July 13, 1973.

"The sun has riz, the sun has set, And here we is, in Texas yet!"
—19th-century doggerel

John Dillinger and his gang vacationed in the sleepy little West Texas town of Balmorhea in 1934, pretending to be "Oklahoma oil men." Locals were mystified by their pastimes, things like jumping on and off the running boards of moving cars, shooting at tin cans tossed in the air, and lobbing an occasional hand grenade. Only after the gunning down of Public Enemy Number One outside a Chicago movie house a few months later did the good citizens of Balmorhea realize who their big-spending visitors really were.

South Texas Highlights

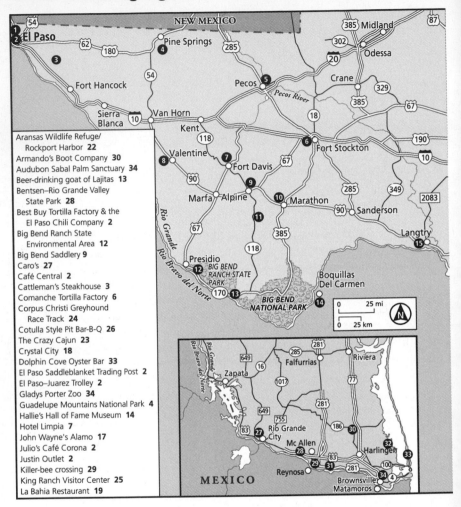

Aransas Wildlife Refuge/
   Rockport Harbor **22**
Armando's Boot Company **30**
Audubon Sabal Palm Sanctuary **34**
Beer-drinking goat of Lajitas **13**
Bentsen–Rio Grande Valley
   State Park **28**
Best Buy Tortilla Factory & the
   El Paso Chili Company **2**
Big Bend Ranch State
   Environmental Area **12**
Big Bend Saddlery **9**
Caro's **27**
Café Central **2**
Cattleman's Steakhouse **3**
Comanche Tortilla Factory **6**
Corpus Christi Greyhound
   Race Track **24**
Cotulla Style Pit Bar-B-Q **26**
The Crazy Cajun **23**
Crystal City **18**
Dolphin Cove Oyster Bar **33**
El Paso Saddleblanket Trading Post **2**
El Paso–Juarez Trolley **2**
Gladys Porter Zoo **34**
Guadelupe Mountains National Park **4**
Hallie's Hall of Fame Museum **14**
Hotel Limpia **7**
John Wayne's Alamo **17**
Julio's Café Corona **2**
Justin Outlet **2**
Killer-bee crossing **29**
King Ranch Visitor Center **25**
La Bahia Restaurant **19**

Southwest Texas is where camels were trained for combat, where Mexican revolutionary Antonio Zapata was beheaded, and where queen makers Rex Holt and Richard Guy of GuyRex Associates in El Paso became famous for grooming a string of beauty-contest winners.

RVing Along the Rio Grande

The road that follows the Rio Grande twists and turns 940 miles from the Gulf of Mexico to El Paso, laying out the border between Texas and Mexico.

It was all well and good to use the Rio Grande as the border, except that the river kept changing its course. A 600-acre piece of land called the Chamizal in El Paso/Juarez was wrangled over for 100 years until President John F. Kennedy and Mexico's Adolfo Lopes Mateos worked out a compromise. And one mission church, Nuestra Senora del Socorro, was moved back

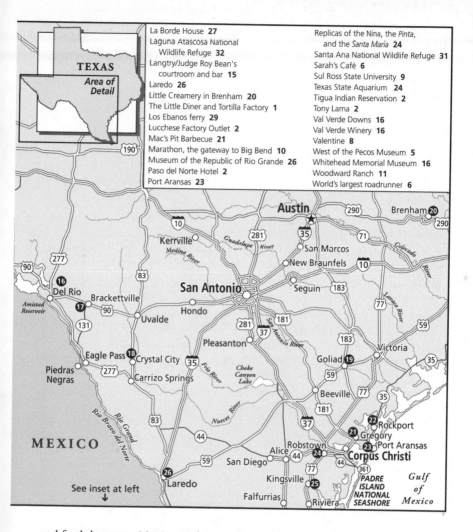

La Borde House **27**
Laguna Atascosa National
  Wildlife Refuge **32**
Langtry/Judge Roy Bean's
  courtroom and bar **15**
Laredo **26**
Little Creamery in Brenham **20**
The Little Diner and Tortilla Factory **1**
Los Ebanos ferry **29**
Lucchese Factory Outlet **2**
Mac's Pit Barbecue **21**
Marathon, the gateway to Big Bend **10**
Museum of the Republic of Rio Grande **26**
Paso del Norte Hotel **2**
Port Aransas **23**

Replicas of the Nina, the *Pinta*,
  and the *Santa Maria* **24**
Santa Ana National Wildlife Refuge **31**
Sarah's Café **6**
Sul Ross State University **9**
Texas State Aquarium **24**
Tigua Indian Reservation **2**
Tony Lama **2**
Val Verde Downs **16**
Val Verde Winery **16**
Valentine **8**
West of the Pecos Museum **5**
Whitehead Memorial Museum **16**
Woodward Ranch **11**
World's largest roadrunner **6**

and forth between Mexico and Texas by flooding a number of times without ever shifting from its foundations.

In West Texas, you can whiz through more territory in an hour in your RV than stagecoaches and wagon trains could make in 3 days. It's an easy and interesting journey, so long as you avoid the broiling hot days of summer.

Texas likes RVers a lot. Not only do many of its state parks offer hookups, but at the information centers when you drive across the border, you can usually find free booklets with lists of RV campgrounds, state parks, sanitary dump locations, and places that sell LP gas. The state also puts out a wealth of other free printed materials at all visitor information centers.

HITTING THE HIGHLIGHTS

Spend 1 night in the Corpus Christi area, visit Padre Island National Seashore but skip South Padre Island, and take the back road, Route 281, through the

Rio Grande Valley, allowing time to visit at least one bird sanctuary if you're there in winter.

If you have kids along, detour up to Bracketville for the Alamo Village theme park, then drive fairly briskly along the border, stopping in Langtry to see Judge Roy Bean's Jersey Lilly Saloon.

Spend as much time as you can spare in Big Bend and the Davis Mountains, then finish up with a day or two in El Paso.

GOING FOR THE LONG HAUL

If you want to spend the winter in the Rio Grande Valley, you'll be welcomed with open arms by the dozens of RV parks, some of them quite lavish, which dot the area between Brownsville and McAllen. The climate is semitropical, with a wide range of fresh fruits and vegetables locally grown, and prices are moderate based on the national average.

There's plenty to do, with golf courses, nearby beaches, extraordinary bird-watching, shopping in Mexican border towns, and organized activities in every community. Wanna dance? You can learn and practice tap, jazz dancing, square dancing, clog dancing, and line dancing. Some RV parks have their own dance halls and regular square or line dance programs.

Adult education classes in Spanish, art, music, local ecology, and other subjects are offered through colleges in Harlingen, McAllen, and Brownsville. Contact the Harlingen Chamber of Commerce, 311 E. Tyler St. (☎ **800/ 531-7346**); the Brownsville Visitor Information Center, at the exit to Farm Road 802 from U.S. 77/83 in North Brownsville (☎ **800/626-2639**); and the McAllen Visitors Information Center, 10 N. Broadway (☎ **800/250-2591**).

Three months is the average stay for "winter Texans," and the RV parks will give discounted rates for long stays. The state parks in the area usually limit your stay to 14 consecutive days.

Travel Essentials

WHEN TO GO

Winter is best, with mild and sunny days that cool down to crisp nights. Late fall and early spring are also comfortable. Summer is extremely hot, humid in the east and bone dry in the west, except for a few cool spots in the upper reaches of Big Bend, where roads are not suitable for large RVs or trailers, and in the Davis Mountains, where big rigs are able to maneuver.

WHAT TO TAKE

Bring camera and film, binoculars, strong sunblock and sun hat, insect repellent, stout high-topped hiking boots if you plan to hike the Big Bend and other desert terrain, and an antacid if you intend to follow the chili trail.

WHAT TO WEAR

Casual and comfortable clothing is correct all over Texas except in its biggest eastern-oriented cities, which this tour excludes. If you plan to dine out in one of the splurge restaurants (see "Five Special Splurges," later in this chapter), you might take along a slightly dressier outfit, but it's not essential.

TRIMMING COSTS ON THE ROAD

Fortunately, this part of Texas is relatively inexpensive for the RV traveler, even if you eat out more often than in. Year-round, roadside produce stands sell regional food products at low prices.

Winter Texans get rates by the month or season in most of the commercial RV parks in the Rio Grande Valley, lowering the cost somewhat.

The state of Texas permits RVers who sleep inside their vehicles to park for **rest periods** of up to 24 hours at any of the more than 1,000 highway roadside rest areas. Pitching a tent is forbidden. While we have some personal reservations about overnighting in a roadside rest area (see "Should You Sleep by the Side of the Road?" in chapter 3, "Where to Sleep: Campgrounds & RV Parks"), many RVers don't worry about it. And you would be able to save a lot of campground fees.

Gas is less expensive in this oil-producing state but not much. It tends to get cheaper as you travel eastward.

WHERE TO GET INFORMATION

The **Texas Department of Commerce, Tourist Division,** offers a free Texas travel guide (☎ 800/888-8-TEX, ext. 728; www.traveltex.com). The **Texas Travel Information Centers** (☎ 800/452-9292) can provide information. Call the latter for free booklets on public and private RV parks and campgrounds and road conditions.

DRIVING & CAMPING TIPS

- **Stock up on gas.** Particularly in West Texas, where stretches between gas stations may be long, top off your tank whenever convenient. Never let the needle drop below half.

- **Winter in the tropics.** Winter Texans head for the Texas Tropics when snow starts blowing around in the Midwest. For new RVers, and wannabe snowbirds, these Tropics can be found in the Rio Grande Valley between Brownsville and Mission, which is thick with RV parks offering rates by the week, month, or season.

- **Camp in state park campgrounds.** Many Texas state park campgrounds have RV hookups and take reservations. Seniors, too, get free park entrance and a price break on camping if they apply for a special state park windshield sticker at any Texas state park.

- **Beware of spring break.** Avoid Padre Island, Corpus Christi, and Port Aransas during "spring break" days in late March and early April unless you like to be inundated with rowdy crowds of party-hearty college students.

- **BYOB?** Each of Texas's 254 counties rules individually on the if, when, what, and how of alcohol sales. Liquor stores are closed on Sundays and holidays throughout the state.

- *Habla Español?* If you drive U.S. 281 along the Rio Grande between Brownsville and Hidalgo, be careful not to cross any bridges unless you want to find yourself in Mexico. You can also walk across. (See "Six Special Side Trips," later in this chapter, for some border crossing tips—applicable whether you go on purpose or by accident.)

The Best Sights, Tastes & Experiences of the Rio Grande

OFF-THE-WALL ATTRACTIONS

The beer-drinking goat of Lajitas. At Lajitas Trading Post, a funky combination of authentic old and ersatz new West Texas, you'll find Mayor Clay Henry Jr., the beer-drinking goat. The original goat, we are sure, has long since succumbed to cirrhosis, but judging from the dozing goats and empty beer cans we saw in the goat pen, he has worthy successors. Lajitas is 100 miles south of Alpine, Texas. Take Highway 118 to Terlingua, then take Farm Road 170, 17 miles (☎ 800/944-9907; www.lajitas.com).

Hallie's Hall of Fame Museum, Boquillas. The late Hallie Stillwell was a genuine pioneer who arrived here at the age of 12, ran a ranch, taught school, and carried a gun. Her ranch near Boquillas now contains a museum in tribute to her. It's free, and open daily. Located 46 miles southeast of Marathon. Call ahead for directions and museum hours (☎ 915/376-2244).

Replicas of the *Nina*, the *Pinta*, and the *Santa Maria*, Corpus Christi. You'll find them moored in town, along with the authentic World War II aircraft carrier *Lexington,* which is now a naval museum. Call the Lexington Museum at ☎ 800/LADY-LEX; www.lexington.com.

The killer-bee crossing, Hidalgo. On the border just west of Brownsville, a frequently photographed $20,000, 20-foot fiberglass-and-steel bee stands by the city offices at 704 E. Texano, commemorating the first crossing of the Africanized honeybees into the United States at this point in 1990.

The town of Valentine. Valentine gets very busy every February postmarking heart-shaped cards for romantics everywhere. You can drop off your cards anytime in person at the town's only post office, or mail them in before February 14 to Postmaster, Valentine, TX 79854.

The world's largest roadrunner, Fort Stockton. It's Paisano Pete, 11 feet tall and 22 feet long. Find him on U.S. 290 at Main Street.

Crystal City, former home of the of the U.S. spinach capital. Don't tell any of the Texans they're passé; they still have their Popeye statue in place on the main street. The town is 11 miles north of the U.S. 277 junction with U.S. 83 on U.S. 83.

The world's largest roadrunner, Paisano Pete.

Laredo, capital of the Republic of the Rio Grande. Adding to the usual Six Flags Over Texas (Spain, France, Mexico, the Republic of Texas, the Confederacy, and the United States), Laredo can claim one more: It was the capital of the short-lived Republic of the Rio Grande. See the flags at the Republic of the Rio Grande Museum, 1000 Zaragoza St. (☎ **956/727-3480**). And Fredonia didn't start with the Marx Brothers; the Republic of Fredonia was founded in East Texas by disgruntled settlers in the 1820s.

Val Verde Winery, Del Rio. Val Verde, the oldest licensed winery in Texas, founded by Italian immigrants, offers free tours and tastings. Their tawny port is a local favorite; they also produce a so-so cabernet sauvignon, a Johannisberg Riesling, and a Rio Grande blush. Open Monday through Saturday, 100 Qualia Dr., Del Rio (☎ **830/775-9714**).

The Marfa ghost lights, Marfa. The mysterious lights have been seen almost nightly since 1883. After it gets dark, drive west of town on Route 90/87 for 8 miles, and you'll see the sign for the "official viewing area." Look southwest toward the mountains, and you may or may not see a series of shimmering white balls of light. No one has been able to determine what causes them, but our favorite try was the expert who said they are bats with radioactive dust on their wings. Marfa is at the junction of U.S. 67 and U.S. 90, northwest of Big Bend. Chamber of Commerce (☎ **915/729-4942**).

TEN TERRIBLY TEXAS THINGS TO DO

1. **Pick up fresh shrimp in Aransas Pass.** Aransas Pass is the shrimp capital of Texas. The seafood shacks around the ferry landing sometimes offer 5 pounds for $15 or $20. Another place to buy from is Peoples Street T-Head at the marina in Corpus Christi. Also here: Landry's Seafood, 600 N. Shoreline (☎ **361/882-6666**), sells early bird special shrimp and oysters at happy hour, starting at 4:30pm.

DRIFTIN' ALONG WITH THE TUMBLIN' TUMBLEWEED

We used to think tumbleweeds were quintessentially Texan. Turns out they're really Russian and were introduced in 1873 when a few tumbleweed seeds arrived in a shipment of flax seed.

2. **Stare down a shark at the Texas State Aquarium, Corpus Christi.** You'll also see sting rays, barracuda, giant grouper, and tropical fish swimming around an artificial reef created from an oil derrick. Open daily except Christmas. Located at 2710 N. Shoreline (☎ **800/477-GULF;** www.texasstateaquarium.com).

3. **Join a jalapeño-eating contest.** Enter the one at the Brownsville-Matamoros Charro Days during Mardi Gras, when parades, carnivals, and costume balls highlight the festivities. Or hit the streets of Laredo, where the jalapeño-downing derby happens every February at George Washington's birthday party celebration. (Don't ask what chiles have to do with George's birthday; the town combined two festivals into one.) The winner is crowned King Chile and may even get a spicy kiss from Miss Jalapeño. Brownsville Visitor Information (☎ **800/626-2639**).

4. **Go fishing.** Dam fishing, for instance, at Amistad Lake near Del Rio, or saltwater sport fishing at Corpus Christi, or join in the big daddy of them all, the Texas International Fishing Tournament (TIFT), in Port Isabel in early August. For details, call ☎ **956/943-8438.**

5. **River raft along the Rio Grande.** Various companies offer 1-day trips into Santa Elena and Colorado Canyons in Big Bend National Park year-round when water flow permits. No previous experience is necessary, but reservations are required. Contact **Far Flung Adventures** in Terlingua (☎ **800/359-4138**) or **Big Bend River Tours** in Lajitas (☎ **915/371-2771**).

6. **See the stars at family "star parties," Fort Davis.** Fort Davis's McDonald Observatory in the Davis Mountains hosts stargazing parties on Tuesday, Friday and Saturday nights, no reservations required. Dress warmly and bring binoculars. Located on Route 118 northwest of the town of Fort Davis. Tours are conducted daily, $4 adults, $3 children 6 to 12. Call for times and information (☎ **915/426-3640**).

7. **Go prospecting outside Alpine.** At Woodward Ranch, 16 miles south of Alpine on Route 118, you can find red plume agate, precious opal, and other minerals and gemstones, and they'll help you identify what you've got (and charge per pound for the rocks you keep). Call the Woodward Ranch for information (☎ **915/364-2271**).

8. **Catch a game of cowboy polo.** It's sometimes featured at professional rodeos or at arenas in towns with National Cowboy Polo Association teams. The season runs March through August, and players are required to wear jeans and Western shirts and ride Western saddle, never English. Headgear is optional; many play in cowboy hats. The cowboy polo field is smaller than in English polo, and the ball is made of rubber rather than wood. The audience is a bit rowdier, too. Top Texas NRA teams include San Angelo in West Texas and San Jacinto, near Houston. Most matches during the season (from Mar–Aug) are held in rodeo arenas. San Angelo's Visitor Information Center can supply current events information (☎ **800/375-1206;** www.sanangelo.com).

9. **Check out the rodeo classes at Sul Ross State University, Alpine.** It's considered the best school for wannabe professional saddle bronco riders, ropers, rodeo clowns, barrel racers, and steer wrestlers. Call the school for a visit and tour at ☎ **915/837-8059;** www.sulross.edu.

"I SEE BY YOUR OUTFIT THAT YOU ARE A COWBOY ..."

Care to do some shopping? Here are a few places to gear up.

Saddles
King Ranch Running W saddles from the ranch's own saddle shop at the Ragland Building, 6th and Kleberg, in Kingsville (☎ **800/282-KING**).

Saddle Blankets
El Paso Saddleblanket Trading Post has hand-woven saddle blankets and rugs in southwestern designs. 601 North Oregon, El Paso (☎ **915/544-1000**).

Boots
When trying on a ready-made Western boot, be sure the heel slips a bit when you walk. When the sole gets more flexible, the slippage will stop. If it doesn't slip, it's too tight and will give you blisters. The instep should be snug, the boot shank long enough to cover your arch fully, and the ball of the foot should fit into the widest part of the boot, not sit forward or back of it.

You can get boots in El Paso at the **Justin Outlet,** 7100 Gateway East, I-10 at Hawkins (☎ **915/779-5465**); **Tony Lama,** 7156 Gate-way East just off I-10 (☎ **915/772-4327**); **Lucchese Factory Outlet,** 6601 Montana (☎ **915/778-8060**). Go to **Armando's Boot Company** in Raymondville (on Route 77 near Harlingen), for custom-made boots (☎ **361/689-3521**).

Wrangler Cowboy Cut Jeans
The VF Factory Outlet, the best place to buy bargain jeans of the brand most working cowboys wear, has branches in Corsicana, Hempstead, Livingston, Mineral Wells, San Marcos, and Sulphur Springs (☎ **800/772-8336**).

Custom-Crafted, Working-Cowboy Leather Accessories
Bandanas, hats, belts, belt buckles, and everything else for the well turned-out cowboy can be had in Alpine at the Big Bend Saddlery, East Highway 90 (☎ **800/634-4502**). 🚐

10. **Take the trolley to Mexico.** The El Paso–Juarez Trolley makes hourly trips in the daytime year-round from the Convention Center Plaza Terminal on Santa Fe Street; fare is $12 adults, $4 children. In Juarez, the trolley stops at Pueblito Mexicana, a shopping village; Sanborn's Department Store; Chihuahua Charlie's Bar & Grill; the colorful city market; and other points of interest. For reservations, call ☎ **915/544-0062.**

FIVE SPECIAL SPLURGES

1. **Visit Marathon, the gateway to Big Bend.** Allow some time and/or money for the little town of Marathon, whose antiques shops have cornered the market on Georgia O'Keeffe–type cow skulls, and where the vintage Gage Hotel from 1927 (☎ **800/884-GAGE**) has been gentrified only to the extent it had to be (if you ignore the motel-like annex with pool next door). In early March the town hosts the Texas Cowboy Poetry Gathering. Marathon was named by a retired sea captain who said it reminded him of Marathon, Greece. (Funny, it doesn't remind us of Marathon, Greece.) Marathon Chamber of Commerce: ☎ **915/386-4516.**

2. **Drop into the old Paso del Norte Hotel for a drink.** The Dome Bar at El Paso's former Paso del Norte Hotel (now the Camino Real) is the original lobby of the hotel, with its Tiffany stained-glass dome ceiling and marble walls and floor. Who knows? You might glimpse Zsa Zsa Gabor. At 101 S. El Paso St. (☎ **800/769-4300** or 915/534-3000).

3. **Chow down on a steak at Cattleman's Steakhouse at Indian Cliffs Ranch.** The restaurant serves huge steaks that *People* magazine called the best in the country, plus side orders from ranch beans to homemade bread. Located 33 miles southwest of El Paso to the I-10 Fabens exit, then north 5 miles on Route 793. Call ☎ **915/544-3200** for a reservation. Open Monday through Saturday 4 to 9pm, Sundays noon to 9pm. Your dinner reservation also gives free admission to the ranch's Western-style attractions, which kids particularly enjoy.

4. **Go cowboy.** Grab yourself some cowboy garb, a Stetson, some hand-tooled boots, or a saddle. See "I See by Your Outfit That You Are a Cowboy . . .," above, for suggested shops and outlets.

5. **Check out the beautifully restored La Borde House in Rio Grande City.** Designed in France and built by a turn-of-the-20th-century French merchant, the New Orleans–style mansion is now a sedate hotel and restaurant with a modern annex at the back. 601 E. Main St., west of McAllen on U.S. 83. For reservations, call ☎ **956/487-5101.**

TAKE-OUT (OR EAT-IN) TREATS

La Bahia Restaurant, Goliad. The 1749 Presidio La Bahia in Goliad is still used for church services as well as a museum, but time your visit for lunchtime because next door is La Bahia Restaurant. Family run for more than 30 years, the friendly restaurant serves chile con queso on homemade tortillas, chicken enchiladas with green tomatillo sauce, and beef fajitas in

West Texas cowboy at Indian Cliffs ranch.

soft tacos. For $16 we got more than we could eat, and we made another meal from the leftovers. From Highway 59, make a right on Highway 77-S. It is a little over 2 miles on Highway 77 (☎ **361/645-3651**).

The Crazy Cajun, Port Aransas. Try a shrimp and crawfish boil at The Crazy Cajun restaurant in Port Aransas on Mustang Island; take the free 24-hour ferry over from the end of Highway 361 in Aransas Pass. A sort of southern clambake, the boil includes shrimp, crawfish, stone-crab claws, smoked sausage, potatoes, and corn on the cob, served on butcher paper. On Alister Street Square. Closed Mondays (☎ **512/749-5069**).

Mac's Pit Barbecue, Gregory. In tiny Gregory, north of Corpus Christi on Highway 35 just north of 181, Mac's Pit Barbecue serves old-fashioned Texas barbecue cooked over mesquite wood. Feast on beef brisket, beef finger ribs, pork ribs, ham, chicken, or Polish sausage. Mac's has been in business for 30 years at his Rockport location at 815 Market St., open daily. The other location, in Gregory, is closed Sundays (☎ **361/729-9388**).

Grapefruit and onions. The ruby red grapefruit of the Lower Rio Grande Valley is justifiably famous. Hit the late January to early February Citrus Fiesta in Mission and buy a bagful, or find an orchard that lets you pick your own. Don't forget the mild Supersweet 1015 onions you can bite into like an apple. Both are on sale at Bell's Farm to Market in McAllen at 116 S. Ware Rd. and Business 83 (☎ **800/798-0424**).

Cotulla Style Pit Bar-B-Q, Laredo. In the streets of Laredo, 4502 McPherson, to be exact, feast on Cotulla pit-style barbecue (like Mexico's carne asada) and side dishes. There's a separate take-out area to the right of the restaurant. We noticed the locals all call their orders in ahead of time on weekends, and it's ready to pick up when they get there. Otherwise, lines can be long. You might also want to try two unique Laredo dishes: the mariachi, a fiery version of a breakfast taco, and panchos, which are nachos with beef layered in alongside the cheese and jalapeños (☎ **956/724-5747**).

Blue Bell Creameries, Brenham, Texas.

Blue Bell ice cream. Some ice cream aficionados swear by Texas's Blue Bell brand, once not available outside Texas. *Time* magazine went on record saying it was the best in the United States. The old-fashioned "Little Creamery in Brenham" (on Route 290 about halfway between Austin and Houston) keeps its small-town image and its logo, a girl and a cow, but you can find the brand now in seven states. Top flavor is vanilla, but strawberry, rocky road, pistachio almond, and chocolate chip also scoop up compliments. If you want to tour the plant (but never on Wed), reserve ahead at ☎ **800/327-8135.** You get a free sample at the end of the tour.

Dolphin Cove Oyster Bar, South Padre Island. Dolphin Cove Oyster Bar serves up fresh oysters, and you-peel-'em shrimp from a grass shack in Isla Blanca Park. Open Tuesday through Sunday noon to 9pm (☎ **956/761-2850**).

Café Central, El Paso. El Paso's most romantic restaurant, meaning it doesn't have saddles and horseshoes, the Café Central is elegant with piano music during cocktails and dinner. The menu changes daily but is a combination of Continental and contemporary cuisine. It's across from the Camino Real Hotel at 109 N. Oregon in the Texas Court (☎ **915/545-2233**).

Sarah's Café, Fort Stockton. Just down the street from the restored fort, Sarah's is filled with locals, not tourists, and open for lunch and dinner daily except Sundays and holidays. Chile rellenos with green sauce are a house specialty, but everything is good. Ask the owners to show you old menus from the 1940s when things were really cheap. Even in the 1960s you could buy a Mexican combination plate for around 50¢. Sarah's is located at 106 S. Nelson in Fort Stockton (☎ **915/336-7700**). The Comanche Tortilla Factory is across the street, open on weekdays only.

Caro's, Rio Grand City. Caro's is a small, traditional Northern Mexico/ Tex-Mex Café that's famous around these parts for freshly ground corn tortillas and freshly ground seasonings, as well as their puffed taco, stuffed with cooked ground beef, fresh tomato, and lettuce, and then fried. Their combination plate for hearty eaters includes an enchilada, rice and beans, guacamole, a 4-ounce rib-eye steak, and a grilled chicken breast. For dessert, pick up one of their homemade candies heaped by the cash register. Located at 205 N. Garcia. Opens at 11am every day for lunch and dinner, lunch only on Sundays (☎ 956/487-2255).

Tigua Indian Reservation, El Paso. The green chili at El Paso's Tigua Indian Reservation is fiery enough to sear, and the red chili is only slightly less incendiary. "White-eyes don't know how to make chili," one of the Tigua told us once. The casual cafeteria is open at lunchtime; the prettier, more formal restaurant, called Wyngs, is open in the evening, and both will dish up take-out portions if you bring your own dishes. Homemade bread baked in an outdoor adobe oven is sold in the cafe and gift shop area as well. Take Avenue of the Americas exit off I-10 south to Ysleta. Wyngs (☎ 915/859-3916); Tigua Cultural Center (☎ 915/859-5287).

Hotel Limpia, Fort Davis. On the town square in Fort Davis, the pink limestone Hotel Limpia features dishes you would have expected to find in 1912, the year it was built, including buttermilk pies, chicken-fried steak, fried chicken, and fresh catfish. They also serve the only alcohol in town, but you have to join a club to get it (☎ 800/622-5517 or 915/426-3237).

The Little Diner and Tortilla Factory, Canutillo. Try the gorditas—deep-fried masa patties filled with chunks of pork in a red chile sauce, or, as some prefer, ground beef with chopped lettuce and tomatoes. They're about a dollar apiece. Homemade thick corn tortillas are 50¢ a dozen and thin corn tortillas, 40¢. For a salad, order avocado tapatia, chopped lettuce, and guacamole on a crisply fried tortilla, and sample the chile rellenos if you're still not full. Canutillo is just north of El Paso. Take exit 6 off I-10 and follow the signs in Canutillo to 7209 7th St. (☎ 915/877-2176).

Julio's Café Corona, El Paso. Julio's originated in Juarez but also has a branch in El Paso at 8050 Gateway East, just off I-10 at the Yarborough exit on the south side. The house specialty is a dish from Zacatecas, Mexico, called salpicon, a cold shredded beef brisket with cubes of white cheese and chile chipotle served with sliced tomatoes, chopped lettuce, and sliced avocados—sort of a Mexican version of a Thai beef salad. Hot flour tortillas are served on the side (☎ 915/591-7676).

Best Buy Tortilla Factory & the El Paso Chili Company, El Paso. Best Buy is southeast of town, just off I-10 at 1110 Pendale Rd., open daily except Sundays from early morning until 5pm weekdays, 2pm Saturdays (☎ 915/595-6650). To top them off, stop by the El Paso Chili Company, at 100 Ruhlin Court in downtown El Paso next to the river (☎ 915/544-3434), for terrific cactus salsa, chile con queso, chile beans, or fajita marinade, all in jars to take away with you.

WILDLIFE-WATCHING

Birds are a primary reason to travel the Rio Grande Valley, especially in winter. The **Santa Ana National Wildlife Refuge** near the town of Alamo claims the national record for the most bird sightings in a single day, and famed naturalist Roger Tory Peterson ranks it in the top 12 birding areas in the United States. To date, 390 species have been recorded on the 2,088 acres. Between Thanksgiving and Easter, a tram travels through the refuge on Thursdays through Mondays, making birding easy. You can catch it from the visitor center when you first enter the refuge. For the tram's schedule, call ☎ 956/787-3079; www.wildtexas.com.

A diligent searcher in the refuge may even glimpse endangered **wildcats.** Four of the only five remaining wildcat species in the United States still live in the valley—cougars, bobcats, ocelots, and jaguarundi. Two other species, the jaguar and the margay cat, have disappeared during the past half-century.

Laguna Atascosa National Wildlife Refuge, east of Harlingen on the lagoon inside Padre Island, hosts as many as 394 bird species, notably in fall and winter when Canada geese, snow geese, and sandhill cranes can be seen, along with the great blue heron. On the mammal side, inhabitants include bats, armadillos, coyotes, foxes, mountain lions, ocelots, jaguarundis, bobcats, javalinas, and white-tailed deer. Both driving and walking tours can be taken. For information, call ☎ 956/748-3607; www.wildtexas.com.

HORSES, DOGS, BULLS & GOATS

Horse racing with pari-mutuel betting can be found at Sunland Park Race Track in El Paso (☎ 505/589-1131), where the season runs from October through May, and at Val Verde Downs, at the County Fairgrounds on 14th Street in Del Rio (call the Del Rio Chamber of Commerce at ☎ 830/775-3551 for current information about its 9-month season). In Nuevo Laredo, across the river from Laredo, off-track betting on live transmissions of horse and greyhound races is available at the Nuevo Laredo Turf Club, 1 block left from the international bridge, at Bravo and Ocampo streets (☎ 956/726-0549).

If you prefer going to the dogs, the Corpus Christi Greyhound Race Track, 5302 Leopard Ave., usually includes discount tickets in a packet of coupons available at area visitor centers (☎ 800/580-RACE).

Bullfights are held seasonally across the river in the border towns of Mexico, particularly in Juarez, Piedras, Negras, and Reynosa. Those in Juarez take place most Sunday afternoons between April and October at the Playa del Toros on Avenida del Charro. Call El Paso Tourism for information (☎ 800/351-6024). Piedras Negras, across from Eagle Pass, Texas, occasionally holds bullfights during summer. Call Eagle Pass at ☎ 830/773-3224. Reynosa is across from Hidalgo, Texas. The McAllen Chamber of Commerce has Reynosa information (☎ 800/250-2591).

If all other entertainment fails, you could head for the goat compound in Lajitas and share a beer with Mayor Clay Henry Jr. (see "Off-the-Wall Attractions," earlier in this chapter).

The rare and distinctive 5-foot-tall **whooping crane** winters at Aransas National Wildlife Refuge north of Corpus Christi, but you may also see roseate spoonbills, ibis, egrets, herons, Canada geese, and diving ducks. We came across dozens of alligators sunning themselves by the edges of the water. Indigenous armadillos and javalinas can also be seen there.

The whole Rio Grande River Valley is dotted with wildlife refuges that celebrate the unique bird, plant, and animal life here. **Bentsen–Rio Grande Valley State Park,** 2 miles south of Farm Market Road 2062, near Mission is a good place to see green jays, gold-fronted woodpeckers, white-winged doves, crested caracaras, and the omnipresent chachalacas (☎ **956/585-1107**; www.tpwd.state.tx.us). At **Audubon Sabal Palm Sanctuary,** 5 miles east of Brownsville (take Farm Market Road 1419), you can walk through the last remaining grove of native Texas palm trees, *Sabal texana*. Take your binoculars (and insect repellent) on the nature trail walk from the visitor center and maybe you'll glimpse a green jay, black-bellied whistling duck, or hummingbirds (☎ **956/541-8034**).

On the Road

PADRE ISLAND NATIONAL SEASHORE

The only entrance to the paved road to the park is at North Padre Island outside Corpus Christi, and the paving ends in the parking lot of the Malaquite Visitor Center. The vast center of the island is accessible only to hikers and four-wheel-drive vehicles. No driving or camping is permitted on the sand dunes or in the sea grass.

South Padre Island, entered from Port Isabel in the Brownsville area, has 34 miles of broad sandy beaches, the southernmost 5 miles adjacent to low- and high-rise hotels, condominium towers, and restaurants. The road, Park 100, is paved for 15 miles, but the northern end is mostly undeveloped.

South Padre Island also has, according to local legend, some $62,000 worth of 19th-century gold coins and jewelry buried there by John Singer of the sewing machine family when the Civil War broke out. He and his wife, who lived in a driftwood house on the island about 25 miles north of the southern end, buried their valuables in the sand dunes, but when they came back after the war, the dunes had shifted, and the gold was never found. In spite of, or perhaps because of, these rumors (and others about gold-laden Spanish ships running aground and sinking off Padre Island), the use of metal detectors or any other treasure-hunting devices is banned.

Today, tenacious wildflowers cling to the dunes, sea grasses blow in the winds from the gulf, and collector-quality seashells sweep in with each tide—along with an assortment of litter from Gulf of Mexico shipping.

An automobile may be driven 5 miles past the end of the paved road in the park on the beach when conditions allow—don't try this in your motor home—and only four-wheel-drive vehicles are permitted past the Milepost 5 sign.

South Texas Campgrounds

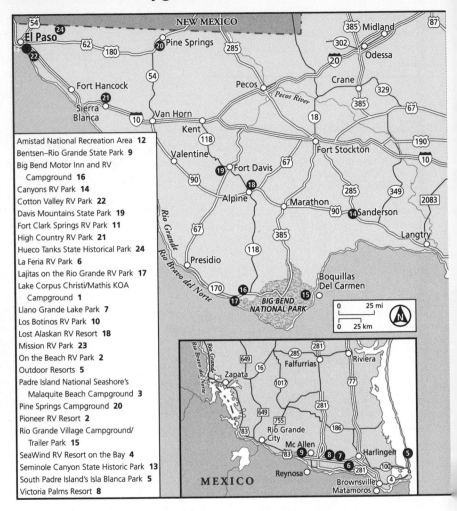

Amistad National Recreation Area **12**
Bentsen–Rio Grande State Park **9**
Big Bend Motor Inn and RV
  Campground **16**
Canyons RV Park **14**
Cotton Valley RV Park **22**
Davis Mountains State Park **19**
Fort Clark Springs RV Park **11**
High Country RV Park **21**
Hueco Tanks State Historical Park **24**
La Feria RV Park **6**
Lajitas on the Rio Grande RV Park **17**
Lake Corpus Christi/Mathis KOA
  Campground **1**
Llano Grande Lake Park **7**
Los Botinos RV Park **10**
Lost Alaskan RV Resort **18**
Mission RV Park **23**
On the Beach RV Park **2**
Outdoor Resorts **5**
Padre Island National Seashore's
  Malaquite Beach Campground **3**
Pine Springs Campground **20**
Pioneer RV Resort **2**
Rio Grande Village Campground/
  Trailer Park **15**
SeaWind RV Resort on the Bay **4**
Seminole Canyon State Historic Park **13**
South Padre Island's Isla Blanca Park **5**
Victoria Palms Resort **8**

RVers without a tow vehicle would be wise to leave the rig in the parking lot and set out on foot. Stories abound of overambitious drivers miring down in the sand, and the park's newspaper cautions that, "There are no services or means to contact anyone for help should you need it. The park service does not monitor CB radio, nor will it attempt to tow vehicles. Wreckers, when they can be induced to travel down island, cost hundreds of dollars."

No vehicles are permitted on the dunes, mud flats, or grasslands.

The seashore has an ongoing program to protect endangered sea turtle species found in the Gulf of Mexico—the Kemp's Ridley, loggerhead, hawksbill, leatherback, and green. If you see a sea turtle alive or dead along the beach, notify a park ranger rather than approaching the turtle yourself.

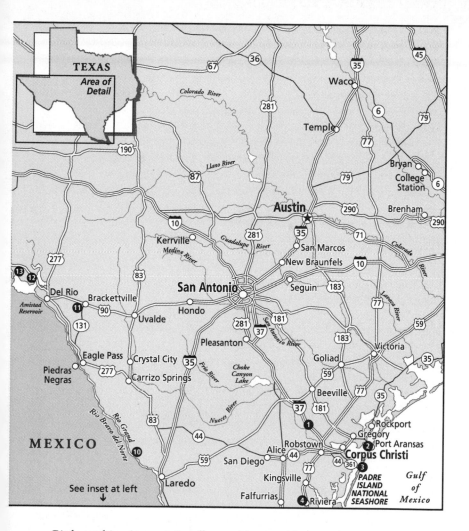

Bird-watching is exceptionally good here, with more than 350 species of seasonal and year-round residents.

Portuguese man-of-war jellyfish sometimes wash up on the beaches here. Give them a wide berth because their sting is extremely painful.

For park information, call ☎ **361/949-8068.**

Campground Oases on Padre Island National Seashore

Padre Island National Seashore's Malaquite Beach Campground. With 50 paved parallel parking or back-in sites along the beach, the campground is ¾ mile south of the ranger station visitor center along the island's one road, and has picnic tables, toilets, cold showers, and a sanitary dump. No hookups, no reservations, and a 14-day maximum stay. Weekend ranger programs and ranger-led beach walks. Ask about the weather conditions, which may vary from the mainland weather (☎ 361/949-8068).

South Padre Island's Isla Blanca Park. Operated by Cameron County, the park is located on a 1-mile white-sand beach on the Gulf of Mexico and has 396 full-hookup sites (30-amp electric), flush toilets, showers, and laundry, as well as bike trails, a marina, water park, swimming pool, and grocery store (☎ 956/761-5493).

Outdoor Resorts. Outdoor Resorts, 900 Garcia St. on South Padre Island, is a lavish, full-service RV resort where some 200 condo spaces (out of 898) are made available by their owners to overnighters. The big-rig sites offer landscaping, cable TV, 30- and 50-amp electric, pool, spa, and boating activities. Rates are $25 to $30, about twice what some local parks charge, but in this world, you get what you pay for (☎ 956/943-6449).

THE TEXAS RIVIERA

The balmy Gulf Coast likes to call itself "the Texas Riviera," but don't expect to find *Lifestyles of the Rich and Famous.* There's more Bubba-and-barbecue than Bardot-and-bouillabaisse.

Because of consistent moderate to high winds and expanses of open water, the **Corpus Christi** area has been named one of the world's 10 best windsurfing destinations. It's not a bad place to fly a kite, either. And Corpus Christi—locals call it Corpus—has become one of the top snowbird (or "winter Texan") winter resorts.

Jean Lafitte and his pirates hung around the area in the early 19th century, and General Zachary Taylor and his troops grouped here to invade Mexico in 1846. The oldest house, built in 1848, is called the Centennial House and has foundations made of shellcrete, cement made from oyster shells. Gutzon Borglum, who went on to create Mt. Rushmore, built the city's sculptured 14-foot-high seawall after a 1919 hurricane. The handsome wall is broken up with stairs down to the beach that open up the view of the sea beyond.

If you take the free ferry over to **Port Aransas** on Mustang Island from Route 361 east of Aransas Pass, watch for the bottlenose dolphins that usually swim along with the boat.

Brownsville was the site of the last shots fired in the Civil War, a full month after Lee surrendered to Grant at Appomattox. But then the city always had problems. It was taken over briefly in 1859 by Juan Cortina, either a Mexican bandit or a folk hero, depending on which side you were on; then occupied by the Confederates during the Civil War, after which it was taken by the Union, then the Confederates again.

Campground Oases on the Texas Riviera

Lake Corpus Christi/Mathis KOA Campground. The campground is open year-round by a lake near a 47-acre wildlife reserve, and isn't far from the King Ranch by Texas standards. Ninety-nine of the 137 sites have full

TEXAS TALK

Blue norther: A fast-moving cold front in fall or winter that can cause temperatures to drop 50°F in half an hour.

Down island: The roadless part of Padre Island, where two-wheel-drive vehicles, especially RVs, can't go. If they try anyway, no tow trucks will come to pull them out for less than $500 or so.

Dry whiskey: Peyote cactus, also called mescal, which contains a variety of psychoactive alkaloids; it grows wild in Big Bend and is illegal to harvest or possess.

Maverick: An unbranded cow, named for Sam Maverick, who refused to brand his cattle so he could claim any unbranded animal on the range.

Tejas: A group of Indian tribes for whom Texas was named; regarded as friendly by the Spanish invaders until the Spanish wore out their welcome.

Texas ironwood: The mesquite tree, its wood used for barbecuing and smoking meats or making furniture, its long bean pods used for animal feed, flour, beer, or wine.

Texas strawberries: Pickled jalapeño peppers held by the stem and eaten whole in one bite.

Texas turkeys: Armadillos, used for food during hard times like the Depression; also sometimes used in chili, but not legally unless the animal has died from natural causes or been hit by a car.

Tinajas: Rock cavities that trap rainwater, a good place to look for game after a rainstorm in Big Bend.

Whoopers: Short for whooping cranes, the endangered species that winters in Aransas National Wildlife Refuge.

Winter Texans: RVers from colder climates, many of whom spend winter in the Lower Rio Grande Valley.

hookups with 30- and 50-amp electric and all sorts of fishing and boating activities. To get there, take exit 47 if southbound or exit 40 if northbound from I-37 and follow the signs. It's on Route 3024, which parallels the interstate. For reservations, call ☎ **800/KOA-8601** or 361/547-5201; www.koa.com.

Pioneer RV Resort. Located in Port Aransas, the Pioneer resort is the top-rated campground on the coastal bend, 14 acres of resort-style niceties, from a clubhouse with kitchen to fish-cleaning facilities. The 211 full-hookup sites offer 30- and 50-amp electric, big-rig pull-throughs, and easy beach access for fishing and swimming in the Gulf of Mexico. It's south of Port Aransas on Route 361. For reservations, call ☎ **888/480-3246** or 361/7496248; www.gocampingamerica.com/pioneerrv.

On the Beach RV Park. Also in Port Aransas, On the Beach is not as highly rated as Pioneer but it is, as the name has it, on the beach south of town at 907 Beach Access Road 1A. Some 53 of the 59 sites are pull-throughs adequate for big rigs, and they offer cable TV, 30-amp electrical, and city water. For reservations, call ☎ **800/932-6337** or 361/749-4909.

THE COMANCHE MOON

Old-timers on both sides of the Rio Grande call the first full moon of autumn the Comanche moon because that was when bands of Comanches would go out on raids into northern Mexico. They rode through Big Bend on what came to be called the Comanche War Trail, burning, pillaging, and taking anything they could use or sell, including hostages. After receiving the inadvertent gift of horses from the Spanish, they became perhaps the greatest horsemen the world has ever seen.

The only way the U.S. Army could figure out how to get rid of the Comanches was to decimate the tribe's basic food supply, so they called in the buffalo hunters. One man could kill 1,000 or more buffalo in 3 months. He was paid well for his skills. 🚍🏕

SeaWind RV Resort on the Bay, Riviera. SeaWind is a comfortable resort with 134 wide sites, 30- and 50-amp electric, patio pads, telephone hookups, and post office boxes. Unlike most RV resorts with these features, it is a public park located in Kaufer-Hubert Memorial Park on the water at Riviera Beach, reached off Route 77 at Riviera. They offer daily, weekly, and monthly rates (☎ 361/297-5738).

THE LOWER RIO GRANDE RIVER VALLEY

A rich river delta, the 100-mile strip along the river called "the Valley" has a 340-day growing season and a new crop to harvest every month. Citrus was planted more than a century ago, and breakfast eaters cherish the area's ruby red grapefruit. Whether it's for the grapefruit or the weather, so many visitors have flocked here lately that the valley has had to add a new area code.

The town of **McAllen,** center of the winter Texan activity, was founded by a canny Scot who built a hotel here, then donated land for a railroad depot so the train would stop near his property.

Laredo is where Antonio Zapata, military leader of the self-proclaimed Republic of the Rio Grande, was captured and beheaded after 283 days of revolution against the government of Mexico's General Santa Anna. His head was displayed on a pole, which ended the dissension. Artifacts and history of that period are on display in the town's Museum of the Republic of Rio Grande, 10003 Zaragoza St. (☎ 956/727-3480).

At **Los Ebanos,** near Mission, you'll find the last remaining hand-drawn ferry crossing the Rio Grande.

The town of **Alice** lights up for the entire month of December with more than 280,000 Christmas lights in a 2-block area in the middle of town.

Campground Oases in the Lower Rio Grande River Valley

Bentsen-Rio Grande State Park. This spot, on the river southwest of Mission down Route 2062, offers great camping for birders because of the

TRAVEL TIP

If you want to venture into any of the Mexican border towns along the Rio Grande, park your RV on the U.S. side and walk across to go shopping or dining.

variety that frequent the campground—the loudmouth chachalacas, green jays, and black-bellied whistling ducks. Bring your own firewood and insect repellent. There are 77 full-hookup sites with 30- and 50-amp electric and a sanitary dump station, picnic tables, and barbecue pits. The entrance to the park is at the end of Route 2062 (☎ **956/585-1107;** www.tpwd.state.tx.us). **La Feria RV Park.** Located at 450 E. Frontage Rd. in La Feria, this park is gated and has 152 full hookups with 30-amp electricity and fairly wide sites, plus lots of planned activities. Tents are not permitted (☎ **956/797-1043**). **Victoria Palms Resort, Donna.** A huge RV resort with more than 1,000 sites aimed at retirees and winter Texans. There are usually 500 available with full hookups, 30- and 50-amp electric, wide pull-throughs, city water, and satellite TV. Gilding the lily are an activities director, computer club, dance floor, heated therapy pools, full-service restaurant, post office, beauty and barber shops, free cable TV, card rooms, library, billiards rooms, live dance bands, ceramic shop, exercise room, and card rooms—and even motel suites if you're expecting visitors. Victoria Palms is located at 602 N. Victoria Rd. in Donna (☎ **800/551-5303** or 956/464-7801). **Llano Grande Lake Park.** Adjacent to the Llano Grande Golf Course in Mercedes, the park offers many of the same enticements to retirees as Victoria Palms, but is slightly smaller with only 805 sites, 338 of them with full hookups (30- and 50-amp). Bingo, movies, square and ballroom dancing, a rock shop, exercise and aquacize classes, and photo and art instruction could certainly fill the day. Located at Mile 2 west in Mercedes. From 83 west, exit at Mile 2 west; turn left at light to entrance (☎ **956/565-2638**).

THE SOUNDS OF THE RIO GRANDE

All along the Rio Grande, listen for the unique local music called variously conjunto, norteno, tejano, or Tex-Mex, an odd mix of eastern European accordion, Mexican 12-string guitar, string bass, and trap drums, with electric bass and guitar, keyboards, and alto saxophone sometimes laid in. The sound is influenced by the polka, Mexican ballads, country/western, and salsa. The border towns between Brownsville and Laredo are good places to hear it.

A little up the Gulf coast, you'll find zydeco alive and well in Corpus Christi, where the Texas Jazz Festival takes place every year in early July.

Los Botines RV Park. Northwest of Laredo at Los Botines, the park has 14 paved pull-through sites with patios and full hookups with 30- and 50-amp electric. The office is modem-friendly. It's located off I-35 at U.S. 83, exit 18, then north 2½ miles on 83 (☎ **956/417-4141**).

Campground Oases on the Road to West Texas
Fort Clark Springs RV Park. A private park near Bracketville's Alamo Village Movie Location and historic Fort Clark, with 84 full hookups, 30- and 50-amp electric, cable TV, flush toilets, showers, and laundry. Just off U.S. 90 at Route 674 (☎ **800/937-1590** or 830/563-2493; www.fortclark.com).

Amistad National Recreation Area. At Amistad, a sprawling 85-mile-long man-made lake jointly owned by the United States and Mexico, two park campgrounds have a total of 36 sites suitable for RVs, with chemical toilets and cooking grills but no piped water or hookups. Year-round fishing; some shotgun and bow-and-arrow hunting are permitted, and there's scuba diving in the lake, with the best visibility in winter and early spring. It's located west of Del Rio on U.S. 90 (☎ **830/775-7491**; www.nps.gov/amis).

Seminole Canyon State Historic Park. The home of ancient Indian pictographs and paintings on canyon walls. Those in Fate Bell Shelter are believed to have been painted 5,000 years ago; visitors can enter the area only with a ranger. Guided tours are offered year-round Wednesdays through Sundays at 10am and 3pm. The hike is moderately strenuous. Some 27 campsites with water and electric hookups (20- and 30-amp) and sanitary dumps are available, as well as hiking and bike trails. Reservations are advised, especially March through June. Call at least 4 weeks in advance. It's near Comstock, 30 miles northwest of Del Rio on U.S. 90, 8.6 miles west of the junction with 163 (☎ **915/292-4464**; www.tpwd.state.tx.us). Call for reservations at least 4 weeks in advance to Austin office (☎ **512/389-8900**).

Canyons RV Park. Canyons is the only game in town in Sanderson, Texas, so if you're looking for an overnight hookup between the Del Rio area and Big Bend, this is pretty much it. It offers full hookups with cable TV, long pull-throughs, and a beauty shop (just the thing after a long dusty day in West Texas). It's right on Highway 90, 1½ miles east of the junction with Route 285, so you can't miss it. (Anytime anyone tells us that, we miss it.) Call ☎ **915/345-2916** for reservations or in case you miss it.

BIG BEND NATIONAL PARK
A huge but lightly visited park because of a relatively inaccessible location, Big Bend (www.nps.gov/bibe) sprawls over 1,250 miles of varied terrain, with mountains, desert, river flood plains, and rocky canyons bisected by a sometimes-turbulent Rio Grande.

The local Indians say this is where the Great Spirit put all the leftover rocks after he created the earth. The Big Bend pterodactyl, with its 51-foot wingspan, the largest flying creature known, lived here 65 million years ago.

Big Bend National Park

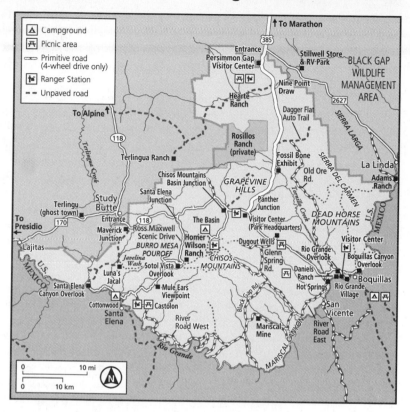

While the park is home to 1,100 plant species, 75 mammal species, 6 amphibian and reptile species, and 400 species of birds, you'll see mostly roadrunners and jackrabbits, creosote bush, and ocotillo if you don't take a hike or spend some time searching them out. We photographed some exquisite beavertail cactus in vivid fuchsia bloom on a December visit. The dagger-tipped lechaguilla is a unique local plant you'll see; it's a favored food for the javalina, or collared peccary, a wild pig found throughout the park. Endangered peregrine falcons are still found as well, protected during nesting season, when rafting through the canyons is forbidden.

Watch out for scorpions and centipedes, both nocturnal, that might be inside your shoes if you leave them outside overnight. Rattlesnakes and copperheads also inhabit the area, so wear high boots when hiking off the usual tourist trails. While mountain lions are rarely seen, there have been two attacks in recent years. If you encounter one, park rangers advise you to stay where you are, waving your arms, shouting, and throwing rocks. Never run.

There are two unusual industries that used to be in Big Bend—the second-largest cinnabar mine in the world, which produced liquid mercury until the veins ran out before World War II, and the unique candlelilla plant, whose wax was used for candles, chewing gum, and phonograph records until 1950. It's now illegal to gather it in the park.

RVers headed for Big Bend National Park should fill up their gas tanks before leaving U.S. 90 at Marathon or Marfa. There is a service station in the park, but hours of operation are limited.

A breathtaking drive that should not be missed by travelers with smaller RVs is the route through the **Big Bend Ranch State Environmental Area** along Route 170 between Presidio and Study (pronounced *stewdy*) Butte. Some guidebooks discourage RVers from this route because of a 1-mile-long 15% grade between Lajitas and Redford, although we had no problem driving it in our 27-foot motor home. Roadside rests along the way sport individual teepee shelters housing picnic tables and grills.

Primitive hiking and backpacking, rafting, and canoeing are available in the area. For information on them, plus the occasional 10-hour bus tours offered through the park's outback, visit the **Warnock Environmental Education Center,** 1 mile before Lajitas on FM 170 (☎ **915/424-3327**).

Campground Oases Around Big Bend National Park

Rio Grande Village Campground. In Big Bend National Park, 20 miles southeast of the park's Panther Junction headquarters on the river. Adjacent to the 100 tree-shaded sites without hookups is a general store and a large parking lot with 25 hookups (30-amp) that is called Rio Grande Village Store and Trailer Park. Stay here if hookups are essential. Otherwise, the campground is a much nicer place, with sites laid out in a circle like pioneer wagons. Hiking trails set out from here, and there are flush toilets, pay showers, and a sanitary dump station. The campgrounds are on Route 118, 20 miles east of Panther Junction. Park concessionaire: ☎ **915/477-2291;** park rangers: ☎ **915/477-2251.**

Teepees are roadside picnic spots in West Texas.

CAMPGROUND TIP

While the **Rio Grande Village Trailer Park** in Big Bend has 25 paved, full-hookup spaces that are booked on a first-come, first-served basis inside the adjacent village store, it is basically a parking lot with electricity and plumbing. If you can go self-contained for a couple of days, consider staying instead at the nearby **Rio Grande Village Campground** (see text above).

Lajitas on the Rio Grande RV Park. Part of the old Western town complex that includes a resort and golf course, as well as a beer-drinking goat (see "Off-the-Wall Attractions," earlier in this chapter), Lajitas on the Rio Grande has 78 full hookups with 30-amps, flush toilets, showers, and laundry. It's on Route 170, east of Terlingua and Big Bend (☎ 915/424-3467).

Big Bend Motor Inn and RV Campground. This Terlingua campground offers a big dollop of civilization among the back roads of West Texas, with 126 full hookups, 30- and 50-amp electricity, satellite RV, laundry, groceries, food service, motel units, horseback riding, river rafting, and bird-watching. Located at the junction of 118 and Farm Road 170. Reserve well ahead for the chili cook-off weekend in early November (☎ 800/848-BEND).

THE WILDS OF WEST TEXAS

"Not a stone, not a bit of rising ground, not a tree, not a shrub, nor anything to go by," Coronado is said to have sighed as he passed through West Texas en route to the seven cities of Cíbola, where he expected to find gold. He didn't realize what wonders he was missing en route.

One of our favorite West Texas towns is **Marfa,** site of the famous "Marfa ghost lights" (see "Off-the-Wall Attractions," earlier in this chapter). It was

INSIDER TIP

In Big Bend National Park, the 7-mile, dead-end **Green Gulch Road** to Chisos Basin is limited to RVs under 24 feet or 20-foot travel trailers pulled by trucks or autos. The same is true for the **Ross Maxwell drive** between the Sotol Overlook and Castolon. If you have questions about which roads may be inaccessible for your RV, ask the rangers at the Panther Junction Visitor Center, in the park at the junction of U.S. 385 and 118 (☎ 915/477-2251). A road guide booklet sold at the center is also helpful.

also the primary location for the 1956 blockbuster film *Giant*. The El Paisano Hotel, listed on the National Register of Historic Places, has a photo display in the lobby with photographs of James Dean, Elizabeth Taylor, and Rock Hudson. The town was also the setting for the play and film *Come Back to the Five and Dime, Jimmy Dean, Jimmy Dean,* about the effect the filming of *Giant* had on the town. To complete the trio of trivia lore, Marfa also boasts the highest golf course in Texas, at a 4,882-foot elevation.

Another of our favorites is **Langtry,** perhaps the most famous of all the tumbleweed-tossed, one-horse Texas towns. Here Judge Roy Bean ruled as "the law west of the Pecos" and indulged in his admiration of British actress Lillie Langtry by naming his combination saloon and courtroom The Jersey Lilly [sic] and claiming he had also named the town for her. Railroad records of the time show it was actually named for a construction foreman named Langtry, so the wily Bean probably cashed in on the coincidence.

Although often invited to visit by the judge, who knew her only from photographs in the popular press, the actress never got to Langtry until a few months after the judge's death in 1904, when she was welcomed effusively

FIVE WAYS TO ENTER TERLINGUA'S INTERNATIONAL CHILI COOK-OFF

Terlingua, west of Big Bend National Park on Route 170, is the birthplace of the chili cook-off competition, founded in 1967 by humorists Wick Fowler and H. Allen Smith. A later rivalry split the ranks of chili-heads, and now there are two annual cook-offs in Terlingua, on the first Saturday of each November, attracting more than 5,000 people. Here are a few ways to enter.

1. Enter a sanctioned CASI (Chili Appreciation Society International) cook-off and win one of the top three prizes. Contact Renee Moore, P.O. Box 5834, Gulf Shores, AL 36547 (☎ 251/949-7000; www.bigbend.com/casi/).

2. Accumulate 12 points at these cook-offs during the chili year (Oct 1–Sept 30) for placing among the top 12 at each.

3. Show up in Terlingua on the first Sunday in November and see if one of the competing qualifying teams needs an extra helper at the CASI cook-off. On the Saturday before the cook-off there is a "Beans, Wings and Salsa" competition that anyone can enter.

4. Cook your chili anyhow. While the judges will ignore you, you might get some attention from the chili-heads. Remember, no beans are allowed!

5. Look for the rival Terlingua cook-off, labeled the Original and held the same weekend behind Arturo White's store on Highway 170. It claims to be the original version and has less rigid rules. Call ☎ 903/874-5601 for a nitty-gritty rundown.

In early February, Terlingua holds a Cookie Chilloff—a competition for no-bake desserts—to raise funds for the Terlingua Foundation. 🚐

The interior of Judge Roy Bean's combination courtroom and bar in Langtry.

by his son and other locals. A nicely restored version of his Jersey Lilly saloon, where a defendant after a trial would be ordered to buy a round of drinks for the judge and jury, tells the whole story. Also here are a museum with dioramas and recorded tales of the judge, a visitor center, and a short nature trail through a cactus garden with area trees and plants labeled.

There are two replicas of the Jersey Lilly, one in the **Whitehead Memorial Museum,** 1301 S. Main St., Del Rio (☎ **830/774-7568**), where the judge and his son are buried on the museum grounds, the other in Pecos in the **West of the Pecos Museum,** 120 E. First St. (☎ **915/445-5076**).

Cary Grant slept in **Van Horn,** they say, at the old El Capitan Hotel, now the Van Horn State Bank. **Shafter,** a ghost of a town on U.S. 67 between Presidio and Marfa, was once the silver mining capital of Texas.

Presidio's original town name was Nuevo Real Presidio de Nuestra Senora de Betlena y Santiago de Las Amarillas de La Junta de Los Rios Norte y Conchos. It is also known as "The Hottest Town in Texas" and "The Onion Capital of the World."

Camels were trained for combat at **Fort Davis** in the Davis Mountains after an idea introduced in the pre–Civil War days by Jefferson Davis, then secretary of war, whom the fort was named for. The camels worked out much better than mules in the desert terrain, except for an unfortunate tendency for the males to bite each other in the legs if left untended. When the Civil War started, the fort was abandoned, then taken over by the Confederates briefly before it was burned by the Mescalero Apaches. Although the U.S. Army rebuilt the fort after the war, they never followed up on the combat camel idea because Davis, having served as president of the Confederacy during the war, was considered a traitor.

INSIDER TIP

In Juarez, the sign LADIES BAR does not designate a drinking spot that welcomes female tourists; it is rather a spot where male tourists will find women who want to meet them.

Campground Oases in West Texas

The Lost Alaskan RV Resort. Mush, you Huskies! The Lost Alaskan is in the West Texas town of Alpine, about 4,000 miles south of Alaska but with plenty of year-round sunshine. With 71 full-hookup sites (30- and 50-amps), lots of shade trees, cable TV, bird-watching, and a modem-friendly office, it offers almost everything the average Alaska RV park might except fishing. It's north of town just past the junction of 223 (☎ 800/837-3604).

Davis Mountains State Park. Located on Route 118 west of the town of Fort Davis, the park has 27 full hookups, 61 with electricity (30- and 50-amps), and 88 with water. Spacious and well laid out, most are shaded by oak trees. There are flush toilets, showers, a sanitary dump station, and a playground. You may be visited in late afternoon by a family of mule deer or see a resident longhorn herd. The weather is comfortable for camping year-round. For reservations, call ☎ 915/426-3337; www.tpwd.state.tx.us. The Fort Davis National Historic Site nearby has been beautifully restored and offers a living history program in summer.

High Country RV Park. Located in Sierra Blanca at I-10's exit 107 off Business Loop 10, High Country RV Park has 35 full-hookup sites with 30- and 50-amp electric, cable TV, modem access at your site and in the office, food service, and laundry (☎ 915/369-2212).

GUADELUPE MOUNTAINS NATIONAL PARK

One of our least-known national parks, this dramatic mountain range contains Guadalupe Peak, at 8,749 feet the highest mountain in Texas. The surrounding countryside is so wild that many of the peaks in the range are still unnamed.

Camping here is at **Pine Springs Campground** (see below), where the area is divided into tent camping sites in natural terrain with space for a tent and car parking and RV camping sites in a paved area like a parking lot with double-sized sites marked off and numbered. Some sites have a little dirt beside them and a chained-down picnic table, others are just wide parking sites. Hikers are cautioned not to park in the numbered RV sites, but sometimes they do anyhow. There are no hookups, and camping is $7 a night, half-price for seniors with national park passes.

From the camping areas, some 80 miles of trails set out into the backcountry, but the rugged terrain should not be attempted by anyone except experienced backpackers. Permits are required for overnight trips; they can be obtained at the headquarters visitor center, 4200 Smith School Rd., Austin. There is also a short, dramatic slide show about the park and its geologic and human history. The ruins of a **Butterfield Stage Station** and a museum of man's encroachment into this area at the Frijoles Ranch and Museum are other sights in the park.

A Campground Oasis at Guadelupe Mountains National Park
Pine Springs Campground. Located in Guadelupe Mountains National Park, 110 miles east of El Paso on Route 62/180. There are paved pull-through sites in the parking-lot style with restrooms and hiking trails, but no hookups. They do not accept reservations, and pets are not permitted. For information, call ☎ **915/828-3251;** www.nps.gov/gumo.

EL PASO
Originally named El Paso del Norte by Juan de Oñate, the rich grandson-in-law of Cortes, the pass here was the main route between Mexico and the missions in San Antonio and East Texas.

The local Tigua Indians, many of them Christianized by the Spanish in the 17th century, settled at Ysleta when a mission was established there in 1680. Today the town, completely surrounded by El Paso, is the oldest continuously occupied settlement in Texas.

El Paso del Norte was eventually divided into the two border towns that are today called Juarez and El Paso.

Together in one compact area you'll find the handsome 1910 **Paso del Norte Hotel,** now the Camino Real, with its Tiffany stained-glass dome on Mills and El Paso; the **Plaza Theater** on West Mills Avenue, built in 1930, with a ceiling full of twinkling stars and a cloud machine; and the site of the old **Acme Saloon** on San Antonio, where outlaw John Wesley Hardin, considered the fastest gun in the West, was shot (some say in the back of the head) in 1895. Both Hardin and his killer, lawman John Selman, are buried in the city's Concordia Cemetery, just north of I-10 at the U.S. 54 interchange on Yandel Drive. Hardin's grave is in the Boot Hill section of the graveyard near the gate to the walled Chinese section. He claimed to have shot 40 men. A newspaper of the time reported, "except for being dead, Hardin looked remarkably well."

The city's wild and woolly gunslinging era ran from around 1880 to 1916, with everyone from Texas Rangers to Mexican revolutionaries engaging in brawls and shootouts. Neither of its most famous marshals, Bat Masterson and Wyatt Earp, were able to tame El Paso. One marshal, Dallas Stoudenmire, saw four men gunned down in 5 seconds (he killed three of them) a block away from the spot where he would be shot dead a year later.

The **San Jacinto Plaza** in downtown El Paso was donated to the city in 1873 by a city parks commissioner who stocked a small pond in it with alligators; some of these reptiles continued to live there until the 1960s.

The **El Paso Museum of History** at 12901 Gateway West, is a good place to get filled in on local history with exhibits and dioramas. The museum is located in an easily accessible area just off I-10 with a parking area big enough for RVs (☎ **915/858-1928**).

The distinctive architecture of the **University of Texas at El Paso** was inspired by a *National Geographic* magazine photograph of a Bhutan lamasery because the Himalayas in the background reminded the first dean's wife of El Paso's mountains.

Fort Bliss, we are reminded, is bigger than the state of Rhode Island. It has three different military-related museums, The Museum of the Noncommissioned Officer, in Building 11331 at Barksdale and 5th streets in Biggs Army Airfield; The Air Defense Artillery Museum, in Building 5000 on Pleasanton Road near Robert E. Lee Road; and the Fort Bliss Museum, on Pleasanton Road and Sheridan Drive. All are free; for information, call ☎ **915/568-5412** or 915/568-4518.

El Paso is also home to a classic Spanish drama festival, an international rodeo, a balloon festival, and a holiday tour of lights. Call the **El Paso Convention and Visitors' Bureau** at ☎ **800/351-6024.**

Campground Oases Around El Paso

Hueco Tanks State Historical Park. Located 32 miles east of El Paso on Road 2775 just north of U.S. 62/180, the park has 17 campsites with water and electric hookups and a sanitary dump station on the premises, as well as flush toilets, showers, a pond, and a playground. The huecos, or natural rock basins to trap water, have aided travelers in this arid terrain for centuries, and many, from prehistoric hunters and gatherers to '49ers on their way to the California Gold Rush, repaid the hospitality with primitive rock drawings and initials. Ruins from a stage stop from the old Butterfield Overland Mail stagecoach have also been moved here. Rock climbing is a major activity except during summer, when the rocks are too hot to handle. For reservations, call ☎ **915/857-1135;** www.tpwd.state.tx.us.

Mission RV Park. We'd like to be more enthusiastic about Mission RV Park in El Paso since it is usually our first choice when we overnight there, but it's just off I-10 and below the flight path of El Paso International Airport. We've tried all the other local campgrounds—great in winter, hot in summer, and dust-blown on windy days—and Mission gets the nod for location if you want easy access to downtown, the Tigua Reservation, or Juarez. It's at I-10 exit 34 on the north side next door to the El Paso Museum of History and offers 188 full hookups with 30- and 50-amp electricity, city water, cable TV, and a modem-friendly office (☎ **800/447-3795** or 915/859-1133).

Cotton Valley RV Park. If you're in El Paso to enjoy the great steak dinners at Cattleman's Steakhouse (listed under "Five Special Splurges," earlier in this chapter), you'd do well to choose this place, 10 minutes away in Clint at I-10, exit 42. It offers 30- and 50-amp electricity, and paved interior roads make it a good choice for big rigs, despite blowing sand on windy days (☎ **915/851-2137**).

Six Special Side Trips

1. **Stop in at the King Ranch, Kingsville.** Southwest of Corpus Christi, the King Ranch covers more than 825,000 acres and is three times bigger than the state of Rhode Island. It developed the Santa Gertrudis cattle breed. The visitor center, on the western edge of Kingsville off West Highway 141, showcases a small museum and conducts bus tours around the ranch daily. Open between 9am and 4pm Monday through Saturday, noon to 5pm on Sunday (☎ **361/592-8055**).

2. **See the whooping cranes at Aransas Wildlife Refuge.** The flock of endangered 5-foot-tall cranes that winters here has grown from 18 in 1937, to some 140 today. Local boats take you out from Rockport Harbor to see them, weather permitting. The season runs from December through March. Call ☎ **800/782-BIRD;** www.wildtexas.com/park/anwr.htm for daily boat tours in season; $30 adults, $20 children. Other operators are at ☎ **800/338-4551** and 800/245-9324. Call for reservations for boat tours at various prices.

3. **Visit the no-bars Gladys Porter Zoo in Brownsville.** Endangered species from all over the world make up the population. Ranked as one of the top American zoos, it's at Ringgold and Sixth streets, open daily from 9am to 5pm and wheelchair accessible. Call ☎ **956/546-2177.**

4. **Visit John Wayne's Alamo.** Why fight traffic to get to San Antonio's Alamo when you could visit John Wayne's Alamo, the one built near Bracketville for his 1960 movie of the same name? The kids will like the imitation better because there are daily shootouts staged during summer. The village has 28 buildings, including a John Wayne Museum and a working ranch. Parts of the TV miniseries *Lonesome Dove* were also shot here. You'll find Alamo Village 7 miles north of town on Route 674. Open daily except Christmas week. $7 adults, $3.50 children (☎ **830/563-2580**).

INSIDER TIP

Sign the King Ranch Visitor Center guest register and you too may get a Christmas card that reads, "The grass is short, the range is dry/Good prospects ain't a half inch high/The cows ain't fat, this verse ain't clever/But Merry Christmas, same as ever."

WALKING TO MEXICO

Even if you decide to walk across one of the bridges into a
Mexican border town for a few hours, you'll still need to have
proof of citizenship with you—a birth certificate or passport. A
driver's license is not considered adequate proof of citizenship.

5. **Head 'em off at the canyon like the cavalry tried with the
   Apaches.** Fort Davis National Historic Site is a re-creation of a 19th-
   century fort in a spectacular box canyon setting. It was home of the
   U.S. Ninth Cavalry "Buffalo Soldiers," African-American troops nicknamed that by the Apaches for their courage and their dark curly hair.
   The fort presents a living history program in summer with costumed
   inhabitants, as well as Black History events in February. Most evocative
   of all if you're standing on the empty parade ground is the recording
   they play at regular intervals of bugle calls and the sound of cavalry
   troops with jingling spurs and hoofbeats. Open daily, 8am to 5pm
   except national holidays, the fort has a museum and gift shop on the
   premises. In the Davis Mountains south of I-10 on Route 17. The **Fort
   Davis Chamber of Commerce** (☎ **800/524-3015** or 915/426-3015)
   can answer questions about the area.

6. **Hop the border into Mexico.** Bridges off U.S. 281 along the Rio
   Grande between Brownsville and Hidalgo will take you into Mexico.
   Here are some tips courtesy of the *Big Bend Area Travel Guide:*

   • North Americans usually don't need a passport to go 15 miles or
     less into Mexico, but you will need proof of citizenship (such as an
     original birth certificate), plus a bit of traveler's Spanish.

   • If you drive across an international bridge, your driver's insurance
     from home is good for only 15 miles into Mexico.

   • Time zones in Mexican border cities do not always match those
     across the Rio Grande in Texas.

   • Never, ever, under any circumstances, carry a gun into Mexico no
     matter where you hide it in your vehicle; it is against Mexican law,
     and you will be jailed immediately with no questions asked.

   • If you have any questions about what you can legally bring back
     from Mexico, call U.S. Customs at ☎ **915/229-3349.**

9

In the Heart of the Heartland: Iowa, Illinois & Indiana

FOR RESIDENTS OF BOTH COASTS, THE HEART OF AMERICA IS A mysterious checkered terrain seen from a plane window on a clear day, but for anyone who takes the time to visit, there's a wonderful world of surprises.

Iowa, Illinois, and Indiana are where pop culture icons were born and popcorn grows, where corn on the cob (and in grain elevators) is a commodity and the pork tenderloin sandwich a food group.

Anyone who thinks **Iowa** isn't sexy didn't see *The Bridges of Madison County* or *Field of Dreams,* doesn't read America's leading advice to the lovelorn columnists, both Iowa-born, and perhaps doesn't realize this is where Oscar winners John Wayne and Donna Reed and singer Andy Williams came from. Iowa is also designated the official birthplace of Captain James T. Kirk, of the Starship *Enterprise,* who will be born in 2282.

Properly respectful when entering **Illinois,** home of Abraham Lincoln, birthplace of Carl Sandburg and Ronald Reagan, and the beginning of historic Route 66, we dissolved into giggles when we learned it was also the birthplace of Popeye, Tarzan, and Dick Tracy and the home of Superman.

Indiana made us giddy, promising museums dedicated to America's Most Wanted (gangster John Dillinger in Hammond), the Wizard of Oz (The Yellow Brick Road in Chesterton) and an almost-forgotten vice president (Dan Quayle Center and Museum, Huntington). It's where the Duncan yo-yo, the Louisville Slugger, and cinnamon red-hot candies are made.

Indiana is where movie icon James Dean, pop music icon Michael Jackson, and gangster John Dillinger were born, where Garfield the Cat and Raggedy Andy were created, where Johnny Appleseed and Larry Bird retired, and where factories in a 20 mile-radius turned out the only 481 Duesenbergs ever made and today's best pickles and potato chips.

Indiana was where Bloomington-born Hoagy Carmichael first recorded "Stardust" in the Gennett Studios, a major recording center in the 1930s. It's where local boy Red Skelton made good when he ran away from his home in Vincennes to join the Hagenbeck Circus in nearby Peru, and the birthplace of Colonel Harland Sanders of Kentucky Fried Chicken fame. And while Cole Porter never penned songs like "Gary, Indiana" (that was written by Iowa's Meredith Willson), he always kept his hometown of Peru in mind by ordering nine pounds of chocolate fudge from Arnold's Candies shipped to wherever he was in the world every month of his adult life.

Illinois is where a character created by Popeye cartoonist Elzie Segar gave his name Jeep to the army's first all-terrain vehicle, where Orson Welles and Paul Newman made their theatrical debuts, and where a blacksmith named John Deere started making steel plows in 1837.

Musician Miles Davis was from the river town of Alton, feminist Betty Friedan and comedian Richard Pryor came out of Peoria, Carl Sandburg from Galesburg and Ernest Hemingway from Oak Park. Walt Disney was born in Chicago, Ray Bradbury in Waukegan, and Charlton Heston in Evanston. Tampico's Ronald Reagan would have remained the only Illinois-born president to date. Only William Jennings Bryan, born in the southern Illinois town of Salem, who ran unsuccessfully for president in 1896, 1900, and 1904, could have upstaged the actor-president as first Illinois-born chief executive.

One Illinois city, Danville, claims five native sons who made good, and all of them came home in 1988 to be photographed together—Bobby Short, Donald O'Connor, Dick and Jerry Van Dyke, and Gene Hackman.

The 1854 Kathryn Beich candy factory in Bloomington is still turning out Bit-O-Honey and Laffy Taffy, and a fast food shrine to McDonald's in Des Plaines is now a museum. Bloomington/Normal's Shirk Products is the sole producer of Beer Nuts.

Iowa is where American icons John Wayne of *Red River,* Andy Williams of "Moon River," and Glenn Miller of "Moonlight Serenade" were born, where Clint Eastwood wooed Meryl Streep on the covered bridges of Madison County, and where a chartered plane carrying Buddy Holly, Richie Valens, and J. P. Richardson, the Big Bopper, crashed in the snow, killing all three on "the Day the Music Died."

The world's most famous advice columnists, twins Ann Landers and "Dear Abby" Abigail Van Buren, were born in Sioux City, jazz great Bix Beiderbecke came from the opposite side of the state in Davenport, and the thriller *Twister* was filmed in an RV park in Eldora. (Just kidding; actually an RV park was built and operated for a while on the location in 1998.)

The heartland is where you go to tour RV plants, ride antique carousels, visit pioneer towns and historic farms, eat dinner at an earlier hour than you thought possible (some restaurants close at 8pm), and rediscover yourself in a friendly, easygoing atmosphere where life is simpler and richer.

RVing in the Heartland

This part of the Midwest is generally RV-friendly, in part because many of the biggest brand names—Winnebago, Jayco, Coachmen, Gulf Stream,

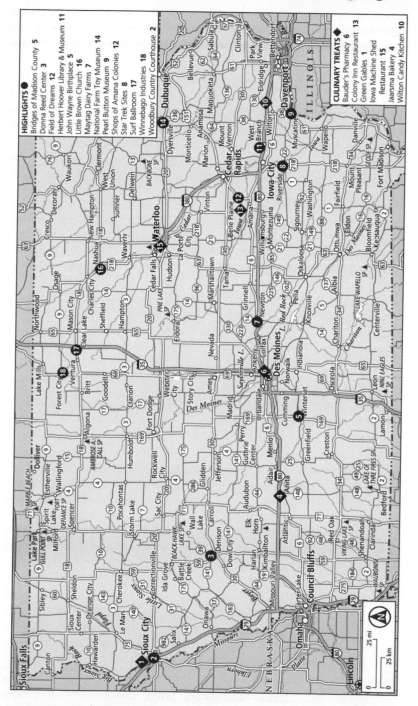

Holiday Rambler, Newmar, Shasta, Damon, and Forest River—are manufactured here. Back roads are usually well marked with a fairly good surface, except in Iowa, where many of the county roads are still unpaved.

While we'd hesitate to call Midwestern drivers slow, some of them do move more deliberately than East Coast and West Coast drivers. This does not refer to the drivers in greater Chicago, who, faced with heavy traffic on rough, often potholed highways (and these are the interstates!) sometimes indicate their displeasure at sharing their roadways with RVs.

Chicago makes a central starting point for this tour, especially if you plan to fly in and rent an RV locally, but you could also begin to the southeast in Indianapolis or to the west in Sioux City or Omaha.

HITTING THE HIGHLIGHTS

If you only have 2 weeks to explore this part of the heartland, you'll have to make a choice between sticking to a leisurely pace through one or two of the states or a quick drive through all three.

The latter offers an overview, but you may miss some of the fascinating footnotes along the way. From Chicago, head west through Rockford and Galena to Dubuque and *Field of Dreams* country, then west to Waterloo and Cedar Falls and south to Des Moines and Madison County. From here head east again through Iowa City and the Amana Colonies, then to the Quad Cities, where you reenter Illinois. Drop south to Peoria and Springfield, then east to Indianapolis. From here it's a short drive to the Fort Wayne area, then north again to Chicago. You'll have covered a minimum of about 1,200 miles, plus added detours.

GOING FOR THE LONG HAUL

A tour of Iowa might begin in Sioux City, follow the Missouri River south to Council Bluffs, then east to Madison County, home of the famous bridges, through Des Moines and north to Story City and Clear Lake. From here, travel east to Mason City, *The Music Man* town, then south through Cedar Falls to the Dubuque area and the *Field of Dreams* location. After that, zag west through Anamosa and the Grant Wood country, to Iowa City and the Amana Colonies, then east to the Quad Cities of Davenport, Moline, Bettendorf, and Rock Island. You'll cover roughly 1,000 miles, more if you take some scenic detours.

From the Quad Cities, head east into Illinois, then south through Peoria to New Salem and Springfield's Lincoln Country. If you have time, detour west to Hannibal and the Great River Road along the Mississippi. South of St. Louis you'll find Chester, home of Popeye, and still further south, at the bottom of the state, Metropolis, hometown of Superman. From Metropolis, head east to Shawneetown, on the Indiana border, then cross into southern Indiana at New Harmony. This Illinois itinerary covers about 750 miles.

From New Harmony, Indiana, drive northeast toward Indianapolis, pausing in Brown County at Nashville and nearby Columbus, then head northwest

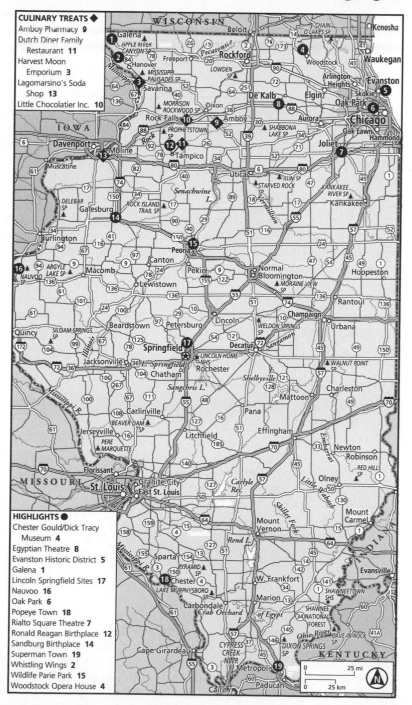

CULINARY TREATS ◆
Amboy Pharmacy **9**
Dutch Diner Family
  Restaurant **11**
Harvest Moon
  Emporium **3**
Lagomarsino's Soda
  Shop **13**
Little Chocolatier Inc. **10**

HIGHLIGHTS ●
Chester Gould/Dick Tracy
  Museum **4**
Egyptian Theatre **8**
Evanston Historic District **5**
Galena **1**
Lincoln Springfield Sites **17**
Nauvoo **16**
Oak Park **6**
Popeye Town **18**
Rialto Square Theatre **7**
Ronald Reagan Birthplace **12**
Sandburg Birthplace **14**
Superman Town **19**
Whistling Wings **2**
Wildlife Parie Park **15**
Woodstock Opera House **4**

on I-74 from the capital to Crawfordsville. From here drive north to Battle Ground, then east to Peru and then southeast to Fairmount. After paying your respects to James Dean, continue southeast to Muncie and Richmond. This southern Indiana itinerary covers some 500 miles.

Head north from Richmond to Fort Wayne, then detour to Grabill, St. Joe and Auburn for special surprises. From Auburn, head for the Amish country at Shipshewana and the nearby RV country around Elkhart and South Bend. Follow the Indiana Turnpike with detours to Indiana Dunes, Chesterton, Valparaiso, and Hammond, then drive on into Chicago, detouring over to Joliet to see the magnificent opera house. This rambling itinerary through northern Indiana covers less than 500 miles.

Travel Essentials

WHEN TO GO

Summer months are the prime season here, but that's also when the locals go driving, camping, and sightseeing. We've traveled the area in May, when there is a chance of rain some days but temperatures are mild, and in late September and October, which is practically perfect. We once had a lovely RV trip through northern Indiana and Illinois in early March, marred by a sudden snowstorm over northern Indiana. Freak weather conditions called "the lake effect" can create unusual snow and ice storms, especially in autumn, in the lakeshore areas.

WHAT TO TAKE

If you've packed your RV properly with walking shoes, binoculars, raincoat, and camera, you should have everything you need for the Heartland. We have also flown into St. Louis and rented a Rialta camping van locally, then pulled into a bargain-priced variety store and bought inexpensive bedding, reusable plastic dishes, and a couple of pots and pans.

WHAT TO WEAR

Clean and decent is the rule for summer clothing. Modest shorts and T-shirts pass muster for the whole family on a hot day, but if you stop to go to a local church or a nice restaurant, you might want a light cotton dress and lightweight long pants. When the fashion police aren't around, the male half of this duo may don a lightweight, short-sleeved jumpsuit on driving days.

TRIMMING COSTS ON THE ROAD

Restaurant portions are generous, so when we pick up a meal to go, we often buy one to share between the two of us if we don't want leftovers later.

Gas prices vary from state to state, so it's a good idea to exchange price information with fellow RVers who have just driven through the state you're headed for. We carry binoculars within reach to scan gas station price signs ahead so we can get in the correct lane to turn if we find a cheap price.

Indiana Highlights

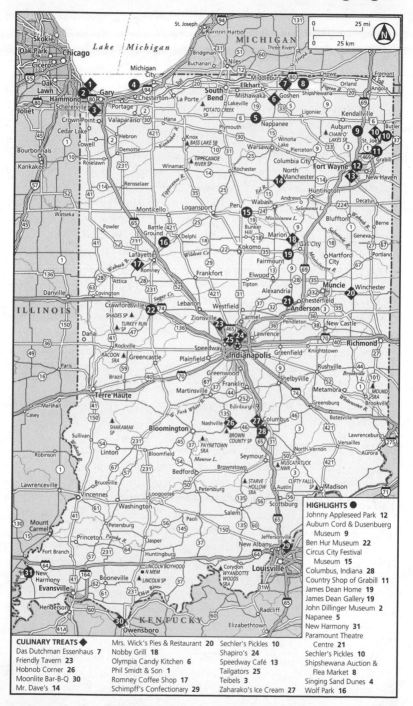

HIGHLIGHTS ●
Johnny Appleseed Park **12**
Auburn Cord & Dusenburg
    Museum **9**
Ben Hur Museum **22**
Circus City Festival
    Museum **15**
Columbus, Indiana **28**
Country Shop of Grabill **11**
James Dean Home **19**
James Dean Gallery **19**
John Dillinger Museum **2**
Napanee **5**
New Harmony **31**
Paramount Theatre
    Centre **21**
Sechler's Pickles **10**
Shipshewana Auction &
    Flea Market **8**
Singing Sand Dunes **4**
Wolf Park **16**

CULINARY TREATS ◆
Das Dutchman Essenhaus **7**
Friendly Tavern **23**
Hobnob Corner **26**
Moonlite Bar-B-Q **30**
Mr. Dave's **14**

Mrs. Wick's Pies & Restaurant **20**
Nobby Grill **18**
Olympia Candy Kitchen **6**
Phil Smidt & Son **1**
Romney Coffee Shop **17**
Schimpff's Confectionary **29**

Sechler's Pickles **10**
Shapiro's **24**
Speedway Café **13**
Tailgators **25**
Teibels **3**
Zaharako's Ice Cream **27**

Farmers' markets and roadside produce stands offer great buys on local fruits and vegetables in season.

WHERE TO GET TRAVEL INFORMATION

Stop at state tourist information offices located on interstate highways near the state borders. A blue tourist information sign is usually posted shortly after the signs welcoming visitors to the state. You can pick up armloads of free brochures from open racks.

Iowa has an attractive welcome center outside the Quad Cities at LeClaire, exit 306 near the I-80 crossing for the Mississippi River. Styled like a riverboat captain's house overlooking the river, it showcases a museum of famous Iowans (John Wayne, Mamie Eisenhower, Herbert Hoover, and Buffalo Bill). In addition to the free maps, booklets, and brochures, they offer gift shop items made in the state, including jellies from the Amana Colonies and crunchy peanut brittle from Brittles Candy Company in Clinton.

Illinois led all states for the year 2000 in its expenditures on tourism materials and advertising, so you can expect a lot of information from them.

If you want to amass material ahead of time so you can study it, contact the following state government tourist information offices:

- **Illinois Bureau of Tourism,** 620 East Adams St., Springfield, IL 62701 (☎ 880/226-6632; www.enjoyillinois.com).

- **Indiana Department of Commerce,** Tourism Development Division, 1 N. Capitol Ave., Suite 700, Indianapolis, IN 46204 (☎ 888/365-6946, 800/289-6646, or 317/232-8860; www.enjoyindiana.com).

- **Iowa Division of Tourism,** 200 E. Grand Ave., Des Moines, IA 50309 (☎ 800/345-4692 or 515/242-4705; www.traveliowa.com).

DRIVING & CAMPING TIPS

Be cautious about **weather.** In tornado season, local TV stations usually run tornado warnings by county at the bottom of the screen, so look up the name of the county you're in and the counties nearby when you stop for the night. If an alarm sounds, leave your motor home and proceed to the campground's designated shelter and remain until the alert is over.

The first time we ran into this on a dark and windy spring night in Bowling Green, Kentucky, we were having a candlelight dinner and listening to CDs. We saw our fellow campers hurrying in singles and pairs toward the recreation center, and figured there was a bingo game or ice cream social. Not until the next morning did we realize there had been a tornado warning.

You can also run into heavy driving **rain** so powerful you should pull over (well off the roadway) at the first opportunity and wait it out.

On secondary and rural roads, particularly when they are narrow, **exercise caution** and drive slowly, because you may round a turn and find a large tractor, a horse-drawn Amish carriage, or even a herd of dairy cattle crossing from the pasture to the barn in front of you. These roads are also famous for making sudden left or right turns at a property boundary.

A random observation: There's nothing an Iowan loves better than laying down a good cloud of dust from a motor vehicle, be it tractor, car, or pickup. Also bear in mind that Indiana observes two different time zones. Most of the state is on **eastern standard time** year-round except for a few counties that observe **daylight saving time.** The extreme northwest corner of Indiana, from west of South Bend to the Illinois border and south on a zigzag line down to where U.S. 24 crosses, and the extreme southwestern fringe that includes Evansville and New Harmony are on **central standard time.** The Indiana Toll Road commission explains it as follows: In summer, when it's noon in most of Indiana, it's also noon in Chicago and all of Illinois but 1pm in Ohio and Michigan. In winter, when it's noon in most of Indiana, it's also noon in Ohio and Michigan but 11am in Chicago and all of Illinois. Does that help?

On second thought, maybe it's best just to go along with that easygoing Midwestern pace and not worry about what time it is.

The Best Heartland Sights, Tastes & Experiences

OFF-THE-WALL ATTRACTIONS

James Dean's Hometown, Fairmount, Indiana. Not one but two museums in Fairmount, Indiana, are dedicated to the moody movie icon of the 1950s who died in an automobile crash in 1955 at 24. Although he was born in nearby Marion, he spent all but four of his first 18 years in Fairmount. At the Fairmount Historical Museum, 203 E. Washington St. (donation requested, closed Nov–Mar) are high school papers of Dean's, as well as his favorite motorcycle, an address book, clothing, and film costumes. It also sells souvenirs; you can buy James Dean's mug on ashtrays, T-shirts, belt buckles, calendars, coffee cups, and place mats.

The James Dean Gallery, admission $3.75, open daily 9am to 6pm except holidays, is in a Victorian house at 425 N. Main St. and shows memorabilia as well as film clips and videos from early appearances. An **annual Remembering James Dean Festival** takes place in Fairmount every September; call either museum for details. Fairmount is about halfway between Indianapolis and Fort Wayne; take state Route 26 west off I-69 and drive 5 miles into Fairmount. For information, call the Fairmount Historical Museum at ☎ **765/948-4555;** James Dean Gallery ☎ **765/948-3326.**

The Surf Ballroom, Clear Lake, Iowa. It's still a concert site as well as the historic location where rock stars Buddy Holly, Richie Valens and J. P. Richardson (the Big Bopper) made their last appearances before dying in the crash of a chartered aircraft taking off from Clear Lake. Photographs and memorabilia of the musicians are displayed. Also playing in the concert that night of February 3, 1959, were Dion and the Belmonts, as well as Waylon

The James Dean Gallery in Fairmount, Indiana.

Jennings, who let Richardson, sick with a cold, take his place on the ill-fated plane. The ballroom, open to the public between 9am and 4pm on Monday through Friday (small fee) when the box office is open or a staff member is around, is in downtown Clear Lake, Iowa, at 460 North Shore Dr. on the lakefront. Take the U.S. 18 exit from I-35 and drive west to Buddy Holly Place. The ballroom is just beyond it on the left (☎ **641/357-6151**).

John Dillinger Museum, Hammond, Indiana. A great collection of memorabilia, including life-sized wax figures and bullet-scarred automobiles, is in this museum in the original criminal courts building, the place where Dillinger was arraigned after one capture. "I don't smoke much and drink very little," Dillinger told a reporter in 1934. "I guess my only bad habit is robbing banks." He used dummy guns whittled from wood or soap and blacked with shoe polish to escape various jails. Open weekdays 8am to 6pm, and weekends 9am to 6pm, it's at 7770 Corinne Dr., Hammond, IN 46323, off I-80/94 at the Kennedy Avenue exit. Admission $4 adults, $3 seniors and children 6 to 12 (☎ **219/989-7770**).

Pearl Button Museum, Muscatine, Iowa. The world's only pearl button museum can be found in—where else?—the world's pearl button capital. In 1910, this Iowa town produced more than a third of the world's pearl buttons, cutting them from clamshells from the Mississippi River. The whole process is spelled out in the museum. Today the town has several plastic factories that turn out buttons. The Japanese came into the business in the 1920s, a curator told us, just about the time they were depleting the river's clam supply. It's at 117 W. 2nd St., open Tuesday through Saturday 1 to 4pm. Admission is free, but a donation is appreciated (☎ **563/263-1052**).

Indiana's Singing Sand Dunes. At Indiana Dunes National Lakeshore, north of I-94 between Michigan City and Gary, you can walk on the sands and hear them sing. One of the rare beaches where this phenomenon occurs, the sand's sounds are caused by the wind whistling through quartz crystals combined with moisture, pressure, and friction from walking feet. Look for access signs to the **National Lakeshore** from Route 12 (☎ 219/926-7561).

The Bridges of Madison County, Winterset, Iowa. Six covered bridges more than a century old are located within 15 miles of town, most on unpaved roads. The one featured most prominently in the Clint Eastwood/Meryl Streep film is Roseman; you may not recognize it with its coat of red paint, since it was artificially aged for the film. Get a map from the Winterset Chamber of Commerce (☎ 800/298-6119; www.madisoncounty.com).

Superman's Hometown, Metropolis, Illinois. In 1972 the only town in America named Metropolis decided to promote itself as Superman's Metropolis, and put a 9-foot bronze statue of the Man of Steel in the town square, then added a Super Museum, Superman billboards, even a water tower honoring the superhero. An official Superman phone booth lets you talk to him when you lift the receiver, and you can pick up the local newspaper, which is called *The Daily Planet.* In the spring of 2001, the actor who portrays Superman for Metropolis donned his costume and married his fiancée by the statue in the square (☎ 800/949-5740 for information, or 618/524-5518 for museum).

Dances with Wolves at Wolf Park, Battle Ground, Indiana. You can have a howling good time every Saturday night by joining the wolves at 75-acre Wolf Park in a few choruses. Open year-round for the Saturday night howls, the park also welcomes the public between May and November for Friday night howls and Tuesday through Sunday daytime visits 1 to 5pm. Howls start at 7:30 and last until 9pm (when the neighbors start complaining?). Admission $6 adults, $4 ages 6 to 13. The park is 2 miles north of Battle Ground; follow the signs (☎ 765/463-1715).

It's a bird, it's a plane, it's . . . Superman!

John Wayne's Birthplace, Winterset, Iowa. The simple four-room house has been restored to 1907, the year Wayne was born, and photos and memorabilia (including his eye patch from *True Grit*) trace his career. Guided tours are $2.50 adults, $2.25 seniors, $1 children; open daily 10am to 4:30pm (☎ 515/462-1044; www.johnwaynebirthplace.org).

SPECIAL SPLURGES: OFFBEAT SHOPPING OPS

The Country Shops of Grabill, Indiana. Well off the beaten track, this charming Amish town is also home to 30,000 square feet of antiques. The shops are open daily from 9am to 5pm, and you can break for lunch at Elias Ruff Restaurant in the complex, sampling barbecued pork on corn bread, thick-sliced corned beef, ham on rye, fried sweet potatoes, sweet Dutch slaw or their exclusive Moo-Oink sandwich, equal parts of ground beef and pork sausage with chopped onion, barbecue sauce, and pickles. For shop information, call ☎ 219/627-6315. For restaurant reservations, call ☎ 219/627-6312.

Shops of the Amana Colonies, Amana, Iowa. For beautiful country crafts such as quilts, hand-crafted wood furniture, woolens, homemade jams, sweet fruit and berry wines, and handmade baskets, browse through the colorful stone houses-turned-shops in the seven villages of the Amana Colonies (☎ 800/579-2294; www.amanacolonies.com).

Shipshewana Auction & Flea Market, Shipshewana, Indiana. More than 1,000 vendors sell everything from quilts to copper kettles, while a dozen auctioneers simultaneously take bids on live horses and cows. While the auction takes place only on Tuesdays and Wednesdays, the town's shops are open every day except Sunday year-round. For information, call the Elkhart county Convention & Visitors Bureau at ☎ 800/262-8161.

Blackhawk Chocolate Trail, Blackhawk Waterways area, Illinois. This toothsome trail takes you through four counties in northwestern Illinois—Carroll, Ogle, Lee, and Whiteside—to hand-dipped chocolates from the **Harvest Moon Emporium** in Savanna and Rock Falls' **Little Chocolatier, Inc.,** hot fudge sundaes in **Amboy's** old-fashioned soda fountain (see "Seven Candy Kitchens, Soda Fountains & Ice Cream Parlors," below), and Oreo flurries from **Tampico's Dutch Diner Family Restaurant.** For Chocolate Trail details, call ☎ 800/2CONNECT; www.enjoyillinois.com.

THREE FABULOUS FACTORY TOURS

Winnebago Industries, Forest City, Iowa. It was a tour through this factory's assembly line, plus a good experience with a leased RV, that convinced us to buy a motor home. The world's largest production plant has a catwalk that allows visitors to watch the manufacturing operation (no photos allowed). The plant is located at 1416 S. 4th St. Get there by taking the Highway 9 West exit from I-35, drive west on Highway 9 to Highway 69 and turn south. When you get into Forest City, turn right on 4th Street. Tours are offered daily between April and October except for holidays and 1 week in July. Call ahead for times (☎ 641/582-6936; www.winnebagoind.com).

Sechler's Pickles, 5686 SR1, St. Joe, Indiana. This tour starts out back where huge vats of cucumbers are pickling in brine from 10 weeks to 18 months, so you can see what a serious business it is. Then you go inside and watch the workers processing and packing the pickles; not every kind is produced every day. Afterward visit the showroom, where you can sample and purchase any of the varieties Sechler's (pronounced *seck*-lers) makes. Tours are offered on weekdays from April 1 to October 31 every half hour from 9 to 11am and again between 12:30 and 2pm (☎ **800/332-5461** or 219/337-5461; www.gourmetpickles.com).

Maytag Dairy Farms, Newton, Iowa. A member of the family that developed Maytag washing machines in 1907 gave his name to America's most famous blue cheese. Frederik Maytag founded the washing machine company, his son Elmer assembled a herd of Holstein cows in the 1920s, and Elmer's son Fred Maytag II built a cheese-making plant in 1941. The rich, full flavor of this exceptionally good cheese comes from a longer curing process. Maytag blue is cured in salt and aged for 1 month in a cave, then coated in wax and aged 5 months in a second cave. Free tours of the dairy are available Monday through Friday 9am to 5pm, Saturdays 9am to 1pm. There's also a shop where you can buy the cheese, or it can be shipped. Call to place orders or to get directions to the farm (☎ **800/247-2458**).

EIGHT TAKE-OUT (OR EAT-IN) TREATS

1. **Green Gables Restaurant, Sioux City, Iowa.** The epitome of a town's "nice" restaurant, this eatery is run by family members. We got two delicious take-out lunches for $10 and change: stuffed peppers with mashed potatoes, and fried chicken. Feeding Sioux City since 1929, the Green Gables is open every day except Christmas from 11am to 10pm, 11pm on Saturdays. It's at 1800 Pierce St., at the corner of 18th, half a mile north of downtown (☎ **712/258-4246**).

2. **Phil Smidt & Son, Hammond, Indiana.** This family spot has been preparing frog legs for more than 80 years. Originally the delicacies came from Lake Michigan, but these days most originate in Bangladesh. Quietly elegant, the restaurant is a surprise in its industrial surroundings, and very popular. The frog legs are tasty and so is the lake perch. The meal begins with a complimentary first course, a déjà vu for anyone who remembers the 1950s appetizer lazy Susans in Midwestern restaurants: sliced beets, cottage cheese, potato salad, sweet coleslaw, and kidney bean salad. Like the ladies from the Sondheim Musical "Follies," they're still here. You can get your favorites in combinations: Perch 'n Frog, Frog 'n Frog (some legs deep-fried and some sautéed), Perch 'n Chicken, and so on. The parking lot is huge, with room for motor homes. Open for lunch and dinner daily except Sundays; 1205 N. Calumet Ave. (which is also U.S. 41) in Hammond (☎ **219/659-0025**).

3. **Jaarsma Bakery, Pella, Iowa.** Dutch letters are flaky pastries filled with marzipan (almond paste), shaped like letters of the alphabet, sometimes sprinkled with sugar. We tasted them first at the Des Moines Farmers Market, but learned they were made in Pella, a town influenced by early Dutch settlers. The bakery, which began back in 1898, is on Franklin Street on the south side of the town square in a building with a brick façade that will remind you of Amsterdam. While you're nibbling on a letter, you can see the Klokkenspel (glockenspiel) animated clock half a block to the east. The figures perform daily at 11am and 1, 3, 5, and 9pm (☎ 641/628-2940).

4. **Shapiro's, Indianapolis, Indiana.** It may not look like your favorite neighborhood deli, but one sniff when you get inside this sprawling cafeteria/restaurant will correct any false impressions. At 808 S. Meridian St. (also State Road 135), this is the place for early breakfasts, fresh baked rye bread and bagels, towering corned beef and pastrami sandwiches, pickled herring, and strawberry cheesecake. Open daily year-round from 6:45am to 8pm (☎ 317/631-4041).

5. **The Iowa Machine Shed Restaurant, Davenport, Iowa.** A favorite Sunday-lunch spot for locals, this sprawling eatery is decorated with carved pigs and tractors outside, old farm implements, calendars, seed brochures, and sunbonnets inside. Our takeout here scored some pluses (a baked potato soup with sour cream, chives, and grated yellow cheese, yummy fried chicken, and a giant apple dumpling) and one big minus (a breaded pork tenderloin sandwich that was made out of—ugh—chopped pork instead of a juicy, tender slice of pounded tenderloin). It's at 7250 Northwest Blvd., just off I-80 (☎ 319/391-2427).

6. **Mrs. Wick's Pies & Restaurant, Winchester, Indiana.** Located at 100 Cherry St., on the corner of U.S. 32 and Cherry Street, Mrs. Wick's shop is adjacent to a pie factory, and sells fresh and frozen pies in 31 varieties, plus soups, sandwiches, and salads. Her sugar cream pie, called Indiana farm pie, is delicious and long-lasting when refrigerated. It costs $1.50 a slice, $3.50 a pie. Open weekdays 6am to 7pm (until 8pm Fri) and Saturdays from 6am to 2pm (☎ 317/584-7437).

7. **Colony Inn Restaurant, the Amana Colonies, Amana, Iowa.** If you're really hungry, you'll love the cooking at the family-style restaurants around the Amanas; what it can lack in finesse, it makes up for in quantity. Since we never want seconds and were tired from traveling, we wanted to get take-out food and relax over a bottle of wine in our motor home, but only the genial folks at the Colony Inn Restaurant, the third place we tried, were kind enough to let us do that. We sampled bratwurst and sauerkraut, fried chicken, and strawberry-rhubarb pie, all of it well worth taking home (☎ 319/622-6270).

8. **Teibels, Schererville, Indiana.** At the busy intersection of U.S. 30 and U.S. 41, this sprawling restaurant covers an area the size of an airplane hanger with banquet rooms, dinner restaurant, and coffee shop. There's plenty of room for RVs in the parking lot. On a midday Saturday, we joined a small cluster of people waiting for a table in the coffee shop, a room that had all the charm of a dentist's office without the magazines, so we opted for takeout. For less than $15 we carried away a quarter of a crunchy fried chicken, a heap of delicate boned and buttered lake perch, french fries, rice pilaf, coleslaw, hot rolls, melted butter, and tartar sauce for the fish (☎ 219/865-2000).

SEVEN CANDY KITCHENS, SODA FOUNTAINS & ICE CREAM PARLORS

1. **Olympia Candy Kitchen, Goshen, Indiana.** This Greek family business is busy all day, from breakfast coffee to olive burgers with homemade mayonnaise for lunch and hand-dipped chocolates, caramel turtles, chocolate-covered cherries, and handmade candy canes all day (except Sun, when it closes after lunch). At 136 N. Main St. since 1912, Olympia Candy Kitchen will ship candies (☎ 219/533-5040).

2. **Zaharako's Ice Cream Parlor, Columbus, Indiana.** Started in 1900, this marble-countered soda shop at 329 Washington St. still has a pair of vintage soda fountains brought back from the St. Louis Exposition in 1905 by the Greek brothers who owned it (☎ 812/379-9329).

3. **Amboy Pharmacy & Soda Fountain, Amboy, Illinois.** Chocolate phosphates and hot fudge sundaes top the menu in this nostalgic soda fountain at 50 N. East Ave., open daily in summer, closed Sundays in winter (☎ 815/857-2323).

4. **Schimpff's Confectionary, Jeffersonville, Indiana.** This 1891 family confectionary features the original tin ceiling, a soda fountain, antique memorabilia, and yummy candies like cinnamon red hots, which they ship all over. In the Historic Downtown Business District at 347 Spring St., it's open weekdays 10am to 5pm, Saturdays 10am to 3pm, closed Sundays and major holidays (☎ 812/283-8367).

5. **Lagomarsino's Soda Shop, Moline, Illinois.** This simple candy store and soda shop, founded in 1908 in a Victorian brick building at 1455 5th Ave., smells like heaven because of the homemade ice cream, hot fudge sauce, and handmade chocolates (☎ 309/764-9548).

6. **Bauder's Pharmacy, Des Moines, Iowa.** Established in 1922, this is the place for homemade ice cream, turtle sundaes (with caramel, nuts, and chocolate), phosphates, and cherry Cokes. At 3802 Ingersoll Ave. (☎ 515/255-1124).

7. **Wilton Candy Kitchen, Wilton, Iowa.** In an 1856 structure on the main street is a family-owned soda fountain, sandwich shop, and ice cream parlor that may be the oldest in the country. When we last visited, it was still operated by George Nopoulos, son of Gus Nopoulos, a Greek immigrant who bought the business in 1910. The family likes to say Gus invented the banana split when he had too many ripe bananas. It's a wonderfully evocative soda fountain that still makes malts, phosphates, cherry Cokes, exotic sundaes, and grilled ham-and-cheese sandwiches. Open daily 7am to 5pm with a 2-hour closing on Sundays between noon and 2pm (☎ 319/732-2278).

WILDLIFE-WATCHING

Except for birding, the Midwest is light on wildlife viewing compared to some of the other destinations in this book. However, Council Bluffs, Iowa, has a lot of **black squirrels** that are so popular they're protected by a city ordinance that makes it illegal to annoy, worry, maim, injure, or kill one.

White squirrels are the mascots of Olney, Illinois, pink-eyed and bushy-tailed, most easily seen in the Olney City Park.

Every Fourth of July, the city of Roachdale, Indiana, schedules a **cockroach race** with contestants from around the world. Starters hold eager contestants at the gate with flypaper until an official calls out, "Gentlemen and ladies, start your cockroaches!"

America's largest concentration of **ring-billed gulls** visits Lake Erie's western basin each fall.

In Peoria, Illinois, the **Wildlife Prairie Park** displays animals you might have seen in Illinois 200 years ago—wolves, bison, black bear, elk, cougar, otter, and waterfowl. The park is 10 miles west of downtown on Route 8 at Taylor Road; it can easily be reached from I-74, exit 82; signage is posted. Open daily except mid-December through February, admission $5 adults, $4 seniors, $3 ages 3 to 12 (☎ 309/676-0998; www.wildlifepark.org).

ON THE ROAD

THE WILDS OF WEST IOWA

The state of Iowa is bisected by I-35 as it runs north-south from border to border, so we'll call all of the state west of I-35 West Iowa. Sioux City on the Missouri River is one of those places where the west truly begins. If you come into town from the south or east, the **Sergeant Floyd Monument** looms from a hilltop, marking the final resting place of the only member of the Lewis and Clark Expedition to die on the journey. He fell ill suddenly and expired, probably from appendicitis, on August 20, 1804. In town, the richly ornamented and extraordinary Woodbury County Courthouse, designed in 1918 by three associates of Louis Sullivan in that Chicago master's style, signals the last vestige of the Midwest before the West begins.

About 80 miles east of Sioux City is the town of Wall Lake, where singer Andy Williams was born in a simple house with a sign out front to let you know this is the place. It's open between 2 and 4pm on Saturday and Sunday summer afternoons or by appointment (☎ 712/664-2119).

Oscar-winning Donna Reed (best supporting actress for *From Here to Eternity*) is remembered with a more stately monument in her hometown of Denison, 30 miles southwest of Wall Lake at the junctions of U.S. 30 and U.S. 59. The brick **Donna Reed Center for Performing Arts** displays her Oscar, awards scholarships in performing arts, and holds an annual 9-day festival with acting workshops led by Hollywood professionals every June. The Donna Reed Theater, built as an opera house in 1914, was restored by the foundation named for the actress. Because she also starred in a perennial Christmas favorite with Jimmy Stewart, the city of Denison uses its title, "It's A Wonderful Life," as a community slogan. A miniature model of the town of Bedford Falls is on display in the Center, and a turn-of-the-20th-century soda shop and candy store is part of the complex (☎ 800/336-4692).

Some 30 miles south of Dennison as the crow flies are the Danish villages of **Elk Horn** and **Kimballton,** the former with a Danish windmill, the latter with a replica fountain of Copenhagen's Little Mermaid and both chockablock with folk dancers, Scandinavian gift shops, and bakeries.

The little town of **Adair** at I-80's exit 86 displays a locomotive wheel and a plaque noting an 1873 landmark—the world's first robbery of a moving train, committed when Jesse James and his gang held up a train on this spot.

The **Winterset** area in Madison County, southwest of Des Moines where U.S. 169 intersects Iowa 92, has turned into the state's most visited area because of Robert Waller's book and Clint Eastwood's film *The Bridges of Madison County*. Pick up a map to the six bridges from the chamber of commerce at 73 West Jefferson St. in Winterset (☎ 515/462-1185).

In the town of **Cumming,** south of Des Moines and east of I-35 at exit 5, is the film location now called Francesca's House (the former Bell farm). It's open for tours daily between 10am and 5:30pm from May 1 through mid-October, $5 adults, $4 seniors, and $3 children (☎ 515/981-5268).

John Wayne's birthplace, also open daily, is in downtown Winterset at 224 S. 2nd St. (See "Off-the-Wall Attractions," earlier in this chapter.)

If you're around Des Moines on a summer Saturday morning, check out the downtown farmers' market on Court Street near 4th. In addition to Iowa corn and tomatoes, you'll find Asian specialty vegetables, freshly cooked samosas, and plenty of cut flowers. It runs May through October, and parking is free in the vicinity (☎ 515/243-6625).

One of the rare Herschell-Spillman antique carousels still operating is less than 50 miles north of Des Moines in **Story City.** Take exit 124 from I-35 and drive 2 miles west. The carousel resides in the town's North Park, which will be on the right as you drive into town. The hand-carved animals include 20 horses, two chickens, two pigs, several dogs, and a "whirling lovers tub."

FARM FACTS

A single Iowa farm produces enough food to feed 279 people. Iowa wouldn't be Iowa without its farm country. Walk through the state's history and chat with costumed interpreters from five different eras at **Living History Farms** in Urbandale, a suburb of Des Moines. Open daily May 1 through the third Sunday in October, the collection of farms and villages includes a 1700 Ioway Indian village, an 1850 pioneer farm, an 1875 frontier town, and a 1900 farm. Admission is $10 adults, $9 seniors, $5 children; plan to spend the day. It's at 2600 NW 11th St.; use exit 125 from I-35 (☎ 515/278-5286; www.lhf.org).

At the top are painted canvas murals and carved gargoyles, and a 1936 Wurlitzer Military Band Organ provides the music. The carousel operates daily from noon to 6pm on Mondays, Tuesdays, and Thursdays, until 9pm the other days of the week. It's open weekends only, noon to 8pm in May and September, $1 a ride (☎ **515/733-4214**).

"The Day the Music Died" was February 3, 1959, when Buddy Holly, Richie Valens, and J. D. Richardson (the Big Bopper) died in a plane crash just outside **Clear Lake, Iowa.** They had appeared that evening at the Surf Ballroom, still home to rock-and-roll and big bands and open during weekday office hours for fans who want to visit. (See "The Surf Ballroom" in "Off-the-Wall Attractions," above.) A dedicated fan can pick up a map to the crash site at the ballroom or the Clear Lake Chamber of Commerce, 205 Main Ave.

If you really want to get "bummed" out, drive another 25 miles west of Clear Lake on U.S. 18 to **Britt,** home of the annual **National Hobo Convention** in early August. If younger readers wonder what a hobo is, the

Urbandale, Iowa, is the site of the Living History Farms.

dictionary definition is "a tramp or vagrant," but a more romantic explanation might be "a man (or woman) who spends his life traveling from place to place without a ticket, most often by rail." This legendary gathering started in 1900, picked up again in 1933 when the Great Depression caused many people to hit the road. The history of the convention and its annually elected kings and queens (Box Car Myrtle, Iowa Blackie, Ohio Ned, Blue Moon, and New York Maggie among them) are on display weekday mornings 8am to noon at the Hobo Museum, 51 Main Ave. South (☎ **641/843-3867**).

About 15 miles northeast of Britt is another tribute to life on the road, albeit a much more comfortable one. **Forest City** is the home of Winnebago Industries, the world's first assembly-line recreation vehicle plant. The 60-acre facility also has a visitor center, and factory tours are available; see "Three Fabulous Factory Tours," earlier in this chapter.

Campground Oases in Western Iowa

Sioux City North KOA campground is across the river in South Dakota but only a few miles from Sioux City, Iowa. Open May 1 to October 15, the prettily landscaped park offers level, shady pull-throughs, ice cream socials, a store, and hot food service, as well as a computer connection for e-mail. It's just off I-29 at exit 2; the address is 601 Streeter St., North Sioux City, SD 57049 (☎ **800/562-9865** or 605/232-45129 for reservations; www.koa.com).

Lake Anita State Park, is off I-80 at exit 70, then south on Iowa 148, 4½ miles. This large park with trees and grass at some sites offers fishing, swimming, and boating in the lake, and 20-amp electric hookups, water, dump, and toilets with showers. No reservations (☎ **712/762-3564** information; www.state.ia.us/parks).

Des Moines West KOA, 17 miles west of Des Moines on I-80, exit 106, at 3418 L Ave. in Adel (follow the signs). With a great location, this park is in the heart of corn country—there's an all-you-can-eat corn-on-the-cob festival in Adel every summer. It's near the Living History Farms and the bridges of Madison County. Open all year, the park provides pull-throughs and full hookups with electric connections up to 50 amps, LP gas service, and free fishing (☎ **800/562-2181** or 515/834-2729, www.koa.com).

MOONLIGHT SERENADE

Bandleader and arranger Glenn Miller was born March 1, 1904, in Clarinda, near the Missouri border in the southwestern corner of Iowa near the junction of U.S. 17 and Iowa 2. His hometown salutes him every June with a festival that usually features the Glenn Miller Orchestra, along with other military and dance bands, plus a parade. Glenn Miller Birthplace Society, P.O. Box 61, Clarinda, IA 51632 (☎ **712/542-246**).

Clear Lake State Park, west of Clear Lake. From I-35, use exit 193 and travel west 1 mile on Route 106, then turn south on Route 107 and travel 2 miles to Route B-35. The park is half a mile west, with electrical hookups (30-amp) on 95 sites, a dump, pay showers, and lake fishing (☎ 614/357-4212; www.state.ia.us/parks).

Prairie Rose State Park, west of Elk Horn on Route M47, offers back-in sites with 20- to 30-amp electric hookups, a dump, access for wheelchairs, freshwater swimming, and boating. No reservations (☎ 712/773-2701 for information; www.state.ia.us/parks).

A SENTIMENTAL JOURNEY THROUGH EASTERN IOWA

Eastern Iowa makes us think of wistful love songs like Rodgers and Hammerstein's Oscar-winning "It Might As Well Be Spring" from the film *State Fair,* about a farm family's adventures at the Iowa state fair, and "Good Night My Someone" from Meredith Willson's *The Music Man.* The latter is set in the real-life River City, Willson's home town of Mason City. You'll find it in north-central Iowa 8 miles east of Clear Lake on U.S. 18.

Willson's boyhood home at 314 S. Pennsylvania Ave. is open on Friday, Saturday, and Sunday afternoons from 1 to 4pm from May to October. "The Music Man" footbridge across Willow Creek on 2nd Street SE was named in honor of the musical and its composer.

Remember TV's *Kukla, Fran and Ollie?* In another look back, you can visit the Bil Baird marionettes and puppets at Mason **City's Charles H. MacNider Museum,** next door to the footbridge at 303 2nd St. SE, open daily except Mondays and Sunday mornings (☎ 641/421-3666).

Readers of a certain age may even remember the Little Brown Church in the Vale, immortalized in the hymn "The Church in the Wildwood." The song was written in 1857 by a young music teacher who came to Iowa to visit his fiancée and was entranced by a place on the Little Cedar River that he thought would be ideal for a church. In 1864, he came back to find a church at that spot. Today the Congregational church, which serves primarily as a wedding chapel, is open to the public every day; it's located 2 miles east of **Nashua** on Highway 346.

Dyersville, the location for the Kevin Costner film *Field of Dreams,* its farmhouse, cornfields, and baseball field intact, is 26 miles west of Dubuque. To get to the site, follow 3rd Avenue NE north from Dyersville (there are directional signs) to 28963 Lansing Rd. There, the only commercial aspect of the area, open between April and November, are two separate (and rival) souvenir stands selling baseball memorabilia and logo items like T-shirts. The baseball field itself overlaps two farm properties owned by two different families that have differing views on how (and whether to) develop the area further. The farmhouse used in the film is not open to the public.

On the way to or from the *Field of Dreams* site, stop by the **National Farm Toy Museum** at 1110 16th Ave. SE (it's on the right as you drive

Iowa Campgrounds

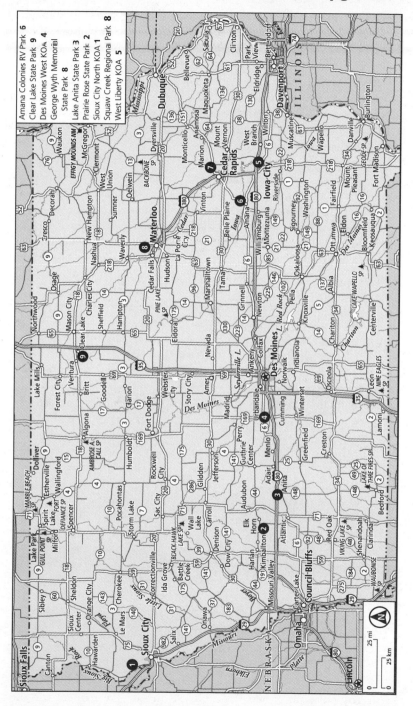

Amana Colonies RV Park **6**
Clear Lake State Park **9**
Des Moines West KOA **4**
George Wyth Memorial
State Park **8**
Lake Anita State Park **3**
Prairie Rose State Park **2**
Sioux City North KOA **1**
Squaw Creek Regional Park **8**
West Liberty KOA **5**

toward the baseball field) to look over some of the 30,000 farm toys that fill two huge floors of displays. Dyersville is a major manufacturing area for farm toys; ask about factory outlet stores in the area if you know any collectors. Open daily 8am to 7pm (☎ 319/875-2727).

Cedar Rapids has a colorful (and recently gentrified) 2-block Czech Village of bakeries, meat markets, gift shops, breweries, and restaurants, plus a new museum of Czech and Slovak Heritage, on 16th Avenue SW between C Street and Cedar River, just east of I-380 at exit 18. You can also get a good look at the famous Quaker Oats plant from I-380.

The much-visited **Amana Colonies** lie southwest of Cedar Rapids off U.S. 152, strung along Route 220. There are seven communal religious villages founded by German immigrants in the 1850s—Amana, Middle Amana, High Amana, East Amana, West Amana, South Amana, and Homestead. The society practiced the crafts of their Old World towns, handing down techniques from one generation to another. In 1932, the communities decided to separate church and state, and reorganized The Amana Society as a for-profit enterprise. The most famous product, the Amana refrigerator/freezer, is still crafted here, but the company now has outside ownership.

Today visitors can shop in the woolen mill, furniture shop, cooper shop, broom and basket shop, bakeries, meat markets, and quilt shops, but most people spend their spare time eating the rib-sticking German cooking that is served family style, dishes like *rouladen* (beef rolls stuffed with pickles, onions, and carrots), *sauerbraten* (vinegar-marinated roast beef), and locally made bratwurst with sauerkraut. Be prepared for big crowds in summer, especially on the weekends.

Forget about driving in the villages; just find a spot to park your RV (there's usually space around The Woolen Mill or you could check into the Amana Colonies RV Park) and take a walk. Streets are lined with lovely stone houses, the gardens are filled with flowers, and quilts and other crafts hang outdoors to entice shoppers. For more information, call the Amana Colonies Welcome Center (☎ 800-245-5465; www.amanacolonies.com).

About 15 miles south of Iowa City, a mile west off U.S. 218 on Route 22, is the future birthplace of *Star Trek* leader Captain James T. Kirk. He's scheduled to be born in 2282, according to the plaque. It seems the town of **Riverside** was trying to come up with something to draw a few tourists, and somebody remembered reading an interview with *Star Trek* creator Gene Roddenberry in which he said Kirk "was born in a small town in Iowa." Armed with that offhand comment, city fathers approached Roddenberry with their idea, and he gave them permission to be Kirk's future birthplace.

In the little park in the center of town is a 20-foot replica of the Starship *Enterprise* and the memorial plaque. We were even more amused with a big sign in the window at the Senior Citizens Meal Services, which read, "Come in and share a meal with the ancestors of Captain Kirk."

Some 25 miles due east of Riverside on Route 22 is the town of **Muscatine,** where the world's only pearl button museum is located. (See "Off-the-Wall Attractions," above.) After the museum, if melons are in season, buy one of the local cantaloupes or watermelons at a fruit stand.

Ten miles east of Iowa City off U.S. 6 is **West Branch,** where Herbert Hoover, the 31st president, was born in 1867. Historical exhibits, the presidential library, a museum, his birthplace, and schoolhouse are all part of the complex, which is open daily 9am to 5pm. The Presidential Library and Museum: ☎ **319/643-5301.** The National Historic Site: ☎ **319/643-2541.**

The Quad Cities—Davenport and Bettendorf, Iowa, and Moline and Rock Island, Illinois—are river towns where fur trading was established in 1812. The first railroad bridge across the Mississippi was built in Davenport in 1856, and a young lawyer named Abraham Lincoln, representing the railroad, argued a subsequent lawsuit between river traders and the railroad.

CAMPING OASES IN EASTERN IOWA

George Wyth Memorial State Park lies between Cedar Falls and Waterloo, and is quite rustic for its location, with an expanse of grass and trees with back-in sites and 30-amp electrical hookups. Off I-380 at George Wyth Park exit. No reservations (☎ **319/232-5505;** www.state.ia.us/parks).

Amana Colonies RV Park is located half a mile south of Amana on State Road 220. A big grassy field with 400 full-hookup sites, this RV park is in moderate walking distance of Amana, the main tourist center. It's a good idea to reserve ahead since they often have groups in residence. It's closed in winter. For reservations, call ☎ **319/622-7616.**

Squaw Creek Regional Park, Marion, just outside Cedar Rapids in Marion, offers big grassy sites, spaced well apart, as well as 45 sites with 30- and 50-amp electrical hookups and a sanitary dump. To get there, take exit 24A from I-380 and go west on Route 100 to the junction with State Road 13, then turn right to the marked entrance of the park. It's closed in winter, and they don't take reservations (☎ **319/398-3505**).

YOUNG MAN WITH A HORN

Bix Beiderbecke, the influential jazz musician, was born in Davenport, Iowa, in 1903. Many may know the romanticized version of him as the "Young Man with a Horn" in a 1938 Dorothy Baker novel and later depicted by Kirk Douglas in the 1950 film. Harry James dubbed Bix's licks in that flick. Every year in late July, Davenport celebrates the Bix Beiderbecke Memorial Jazz Festival, competing with the State Fair as Iowa's most popular event. The 100th birthday celebration in 2003 should really swing! For information, call ☎ **888/BIX-LIVS.**

CLASSIC AMERICANA

Iowa artist Grant Wood created one of the most reproduced (and parodied) paintings since *Whistler's Mother* with *American Gothic* in 1930 showing his sister Nan and his dentist Dr. B. H. McKeeby in front of a Gothic farmhouse with a pitchfork. The house is on American Gothic Street in the town of **Eldon** in southeastern Iowa, 16 miles southeast of Ottumwa on Route 16, and visitors are permitted to photograph the outside of the building but not to go inside. Wood was born in **Anamosa,** 20 miles west of Cedar Rapids via U.S. 151, where the largest collection of *American Gothic* parodies and a film about Wood can be seen in the Grant Wood Tourism Center and Gallery, open daily at 124 E. Main St. (☎ 319/462-4267).

The most complete collection of Wood's works is in the **Cedar Rapids Museum of Art,** 410 3rd Ave. SE, open daily except Mondays, admission $4 adults, $3 seniors and youths (☎ 319/366-7503). More Wood paintings including a self-portrait are in the **Davenport Museum of Art** at 12th and Davison streets in Davenport, open daily except Mondays (☎ 319/326-7804; www.qconline.com/arts/dma). 🚐

West Liberty KOA, 15 miles east of Iowa City off I-80 at exit 259 South, is close to the Herbert Hoover National Historic Site, not far from the Amana Colonies and convenient to Riverside, Wilton, and the riverboat gambling in Council Bluffs. It's open all year with pull-throughs and full hookups with electrical connections up to 50 amps. For reservations, call ☎ 800/562-7624 or 319/627-2676; www.koa.com.

NORTHERN ILLINOIS: U. S. GRANT TO RONALD REAGAN

Galena in the northwestern corner of Illinois is one of the prettiest historic hill towns anywhere, but not easy to maneuver a motor home through; we'd suggest finding a parking space on the edge of town and taking a steep, challenging walk. **Ulysses S. Grant** is the big name in town; he worked here as a clerk before the Civil War, returned afterward to accept a splendid brick house as a gift from the town, and stayed there during the summer and fall of 1868 when he was running for president. He returned in 1879 after his two-term presidency was clouded with scandal. But Galena won't hear any trash talk about Grant, even if he didn't spend a lot of his retirement in residence.

LONG BEFORE OK CORRAL

The peripatetic Wyatt Earp grew up in Pella, Iowa; his house is preserved at 507 Franklin St. He ran away to join the Union Army when he was 15 but was discovered and brought back. In 1864, the Earps and 40 other Iowans went by wagon train to California.

HISTORY IN BLOOM(ERS)

New York–born Amelia Jenks Bloomer of the eponymous women's fashion item, full trousers under a short skirt, moved to Iowa in 1855 and helped establish that state's equal rights legislation in 1873.

Twenty miles south of Galena along U.S. 20, then south on Route 84, is **Hanover,** home of **Whistling Wings,** the largest mallard hatchery in the world. A gift shop at 113 Washington St., on the right as you drive south, sells frozen and smoked ducks, plus live ducks, duck eggs, and duck guano, as well as mallard sweatshirts and T-shirts. The cooked, smoked ducks are delicious. They also ship some merchandise (☎ 815/591-3512).

Across the top of the state is **Woodstock,** on U.S. 14 about 20 miles west of Rockford as the crow flies, with a lot of pop culture heritage for its modest size. The 1993 Bill Murray film *Groundhog Day* was filmed here, with the town standing in for Punxatawney, Pennsylvania. The restored 1890 **Woodstock Opera House** on the town square is where Orson Welles and Paul Newman, both of whom attended school here, made their theatrical debuts, and the **Chester Gould/Dick Tracy Museum** is in the Old Courthouse Arts Center. Although Gould was born in Oklahoma, his first major success was with Hearst's Chicago newspaper, *The American,* in 1921, and he created the square-jawed detective with the wristwatch telephone in 1931. For information, call the Woodstock Chamber of Commerce at ☎ 815/338-2436.

Southeast in **DeKalb** is another impeccably restored period theater, an Egyptian Revival–style movie house called the **Egyptian,** on North 2nd Street near Lincoln Highway. If you're there in August for the Sweet Corn Festival, you'll sample free corn on the cob.

Heading west again to **Dixon,** Ronald Reagan admirers can see both the birthplace (a six-room apartment above a bakery in nearby **Tampico** on Main Street) and the boyhood home (a restored two-story white frame house in Dixon at 816 S. Hennepin Ave.) of the 40th president and film star.

Joliet, southwest of Chicago near where I-80 and I-55 intersect, has taken the 1926 **Rialto Square Theatre** and restored it to its grand days as a vaudeville movie palace. With interior details inspired by the Hall of Mirrors at Versailles, Paris's Arc de Triomphe, and Rome's Pantheon, the awesome building shows off a hundred crystal chandeliers in a block-long lobby and glitters with ornate gilded trim in the 2,000-seat auditorium. The original Barton Grande Theatre Pipe Organ, which accompanied silent films and vaudeville shows with music and sound effects, is still played.

When the Rialto reopened in 1981, flamboyant pianist Liberace, one of its first headliners, quipped, "At last! A theater to match my wardrobe!"

Joliet's Rialto Square Theatre is one of the last surviving vaudeville palaces.

To the southwest lies the legendary city of **Peoria,** where the Rock Island Line used to chug into the depot by the river. When we last visited, the chugs were more like chug-a-lugs, because the restored station had been turned into a railroad-themed bar and restaurant complex. Now we hear the place that saluted the golden days of dining cars has closed, yielding to a trendy new Italian restaurant. Maybe trains don't play in Peoria.

Everyone from Richard Nixon to native son Richard Pryor weighed in on whether (or why) something does "play in Peoria," but the longest-running drama in the city's history was a strike against the local Caterpillar company.

Between Peoria and Galesburg, 50 miles northwest, lies **Spoon River,** the setting for Edgar Lee Masters's evocative poems that bring alive the people of Lewiston, Illinois. In his book *Spoon River Anthology,* he let them talk about as though speaking from the grave. The only problem was that locals said Masters didn't disguise the local individuals well enough in their sad histories and worst traits. He was so disliked that the book, published in 1915, was still banned in the local schools and public library 40 years later.

Today all is forgiven as the town celebrates his fame with an annual festival during which two dozen costumed residents read the poems at the Oak Hill Cemetery. Masters himself is buried in Oakland Cemetery in Petersburg, near New Salem State Historic Site, not far from the graves of Vachel Lindsay, who died in 1931, and of Ann Rutledge, Abraham Lincoln's fiancée in New Salem, who died in 1835 at the age of 19. Her tombstone was carved posthumously with a quote from a Masters poem: "I am Ann Rutledge who sleep beneath these weeds/Beloved in life of Abraham Lincoln/...Bloom forever, O Republic, from the dust of my bosom."

Galesburg is a pretty town from another era, proud of its 19th-century architecture. The home at 331 E. 3rd St. where poet Carl Sandburg was born in 1878 is also his burial spot; his ashes are buried under Remembrance Rock (named for his only novel) in the park behind the house. Signs throughout town point to the birthplace, open daily year-round except holidays. Suggested donation: $2 adults, $1 children (☎ 309/342-2361).

Over on the Mississippi River, on Route 96 along the Great River Road, the historic town of **Nauvoo** recalls the strife-filled story of the Mormons. Today it's mostly a museum town staffed with costumed interpreters who tell the story of Mormon prophet Joseph Smith and his brother Hyrum, chased along with their followers first from New York and then from Missouri to this place on the Mississippi. By 1842, the town had a population of 15,000 Mormons, making it the largest town then in Illinois.

In 1844, after introducing the custom of polygamy into the faith, Smith announced that he would run for president. When a local newspaper criticized his leadership, he and Hyrum destroyed the presses. For this, the brothers were imprisoned in nearby Carthage, where a mob broke into the jail and shot them. After this, the Mormons, led by Brigham Young, migrated to Utah in 1846, leaving the town abandoned for several years until a French community called the Icarians arrived to set up wine and cheese production.

By 1856, the French too were gone, but a German group came in to continue the cheese tradition, and today you can sample delectable **Nauvoo Blue cheese** in local shops as you tour the town. The buildings are open year-round, and between April and November, the Tourist Reception Center is open daily from 9am to 4:30pm with maps and a self-guided cassette tape tour available (☎ 217/453-6648).

Campground Oases in Northern Illinois

Starved Rock State Park near Utica is a 2,630-acre preserve around a sandstone bluff where a band of Illiniwek Indians starved while besieged by their enemies below. The campground has 133 level back-in sites with 20- and 30-amp electricity and water hookups. A sanitary dump, restrooms, and showers are also in the campground. To get there, take Route 178 off I-80, go south 4 miles, and then turn east on Route 71 for 2 miles. For information, call ☎ 815/667-4726; http://dnr.state.il.us/lands/landmgt/parks/ilstate.htm.

Chicago Northwest KOA Campground at Marengo is not really near Chicago—no campground is—but it's in an attractive site with its own false-front strip of antiques shops next door and near the Illinois Railroad Museum. Exit I-90 at Marengo-Hampshire West on Route 20 and drive 4½ miles to South Union Road, where you'll turn right. Follow signs to Wild West Town. For reservations, call ☎ 800/562-2827 or 815/923-4206; www.koa.com.

Nauvoo State Park, south of the historic Mormon town on Route 96, offers both pull-through and back-in sites with 30-amp electric hookups and a sanitary dump. No reservations. For information, call ☎ 217/453-2512; http://dnr.state.il.us/lands/landmgt/parks/ilstate.htm.

Northern Illinois Campgrounds

Chicago NW KOA **1**
Lena KOA **2**
Morrison-Rockwood
   State Park **3**
Nauvoo State Park **4**
Starved Rock State Park **5**

Lena KOA at Lena, 35 miles west of Galena, is a good location for sightseeing in Lena and visiting Whistling Wings in Hanover and the Lena Cheese Factory Outlet Store on U.S. 20, 5 miles west of Lena. The campground is open May 1 through November 1 with a swimming pool and double tube slide, full hookups up to 50 amps of electricity and pull-throughs. It's located on U.S. 20 about ¼ mile east of the intersection with state 73. For reservations, call ☎ **800/562-5361** or 815/369-2612; www.koa.com.

Morrison-Rockwood State Park is at the edge of Morrison, just across the Mississippi from Clinton, Iowa. From U.S. 30 in Morrison, take State Road 78 north 1 mile to Damien Road, then go 1½ miles east to Crosby Road, then ½ mile north to the park. It's easier to get there than it sounds; signage is good, so you shouldn't get lost. Some 92 gravel sites, most shaded, have 30-amp electrical hookups, and there's a dump. Food service, fishing, swimming, and boating are available, but reservations are not accepted. For information, call ☎ **815/772-4708;** http://dnr.state.il.us/lands/landmgt/parks/ilstate.htm.

LINCOLN LAND

Kentucky-born Abraham Lincoln is linked forever with Illinois. The only home he ever owned is restored and open for visitors in Springfield. Some

17 miles northwest, the historically preserved village of New Salem, where Lincoln served as postmaster, merchant, surveyor, and captain of the town's militia, is a park open daily year-round except for holidays and Tuesdays and Wednesdays in winter. As militia captain, Lincoln took his unit to participate in the Black Hawk War where, he liked to say, they fought only mosquitoes.

When he was 25, while still studying law, he won a seat in the Illinois legislature. Two years later, he was elected to a second term, and, when he passed the bar exam, spent half of each year as a circuit-riding attorney and judge in the 11,000-square-mile Eighth Judicial Circuit.

The town of Lincoln, off I-55 at exit 133, was the first to be named for Abe, in 1853 when he was still riding the circuit. The townspeople called for him to christen it, and he picked up a ripe watermelon, broke it open, and sprinkled the juice on the site.

Perhaps the most famous of the courthouses where he practiced was in Beardstown, 46 miles northwest of Springfield via Route 125. Here Lincoln defended a New Salem friend on a charge of murder. After a witness testified he saw the fatal fight break out in the light of a high moon after a revival camp meeting, Lincoln produced an 1857 almanac showing that the moon had set before midnight that night. His client was acquitted.

Lincoln is buried in Springfield's Oak Ridge Cemetery beside Mary Todd, Tad, Eddie, and Willie Lincoln. His memory is also recalled at the **family home** at 8th and Jackson streets; the law offices at 6th and Adams streets where he practiced from 1843 until he left for Washington; at the **Old State Capitol** in the Downtown Mall where he said, "A house divided against itself cannot stand"; at **Bank One,** 6th and Washington streets, where his Springfield Marine and Fire Insurance Company ledger is on display; and at the **Lincoln Depot,** 10th and Monroe streets, where he said goodbye to Springfield after being elected president.

Log cabin in the Illinois village of New Salem.

SPRINGFIELD & RVS DON'T MIX!

We'd be remiss if we failed to caution fellow RVers that Springfield is a city doesn't seem to like us. The last time we were there, the parking lot at the Lincoln home was only big enough for cars, and for blocks in every direction around the historic sites, NO PARKING FOR VANS AND RVS signs were posted. If you're pulling a tow car, use that to visit the sites; if not, we'd suggest leaving your RV at the campground and taking a bus or cab into the historic district.

Springfield's Vachel Lindsay could be called Lincoln's poet, and Galesburg's Carl Sandburg, also a poet, won the Pulitzer Prize for his six-volume biography of Lincoln. Both volumes provide valuable insight into the late president.

Campground Oases in Lincoln Land

Mr. Lincoln's Campground, Springfield, Illinois. Convenient to all the Lincoln historical sites, this in-town campground is at exit 94 off I-55, then 1 mile west on Stevenson Drive and a right turn on Stanton into the campground. Clean and well run, with 15 pull-throughs, 42 full-hookup sites (30/50 amps), and cable TV connections, the campground is open year-round (☎ 800/657-1414 for reservations).

Springfield KOA, Rochester, Illinois. Take exit 94 off I-55, then travel east 5 miles on Stevenson Road and follow the KOA signs for 2 more miles. It's in a quiet area with swimming, and golf and fishing are nearby (☎ 800/562-7212 or 217/498-7002. www.koa.com).

Lincoln's New Salem State Historic Site and Campground, Petersburg, Illinois. Open April 1 to November 1, this simple campground is adjacent to the village where Lincoln lived for 6 years, and has back-in sites with 20- and 30-amp electricity, restrooms, and dump. No reservations (☎ 217/632-4003 for information; http://dnr.state.il.us/lands/landmgt/parks/ilstate.htm).

SOUTHERN ILLINOIS: THE PIASA BIRD TO THE MAN OF STEEL

The Great River Road follows the Mississippi River along a meandering 2,350-mile journey from its birth in Lake Itasca, Minnesota, to New Orleans. Dramatically different from the farmlands of northern Illinois, the southern part of the state has forests and lakes, craggy sandstone formations and cypress swamps, ancient Indian mounds, and early European settlements that still carry the imprint of their founders.

Starting in **Kampsville** on the Illinois River, take Route 100 to **Grafton** where the Illinois meets the Mississippi. They don't merge here, but run side

Lincolnland Campgrounds

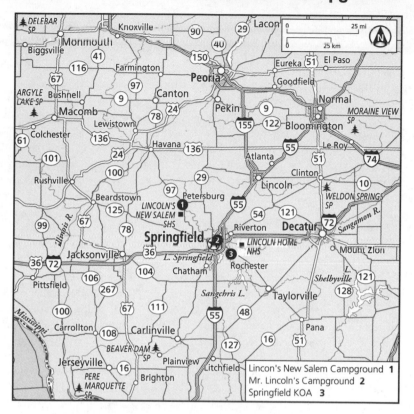

Lincon's New Salem Campground **1**
Mr. Lincoln's Campground **2**
Springfield KOA **3**

by side for several miles, the Illinois clear and the Mississippi muddy. At Alton, Route 100 becomes Route 3 and meanders south to **Cairo,** where the Mississippi and the Ohio converge with a similar dramatic color difference.

The old river towns carry their own distinctive ambience. **Elsah** is particularly charming with its parallel one-way streets and little limestone and clapboard cottages. The entire town is on the National Register of Historic Places. Don't try to drive in here with a large motor home (we found it touch-and-go in a Rialta van). Try to find a spot at the parking lot by the river at the entrance to town, or, if you're carrying your bicycles on your RV, park in Alton and take the 15-mile paved Senator **Vadalabene Bike Trail** back to Elsah. If you do visit Elsah, note little Principia College, where actor Robert Duvall is an alumnus.

The painting of the fierce **Piasa** (pronounced *Pie*-a-saw) monster-bird said to eat men was remarked on by French explorers Jacques Marquette and Louis Jolliet on the bluffs near Alton and, in a re-creation, can still be seen today. But the town itself makes one wonder what constitutes greatness. A life-sized statue of Alton-born 8-foot, 11½-inch Robert Wadlow, the world's tallest man, is on display, but nowhere could we find a tribute to native son Miles Davis, one of America's greatest jazz musicians. His family left Alton when Miles was 4, and he grew up in East St. Louis, Illinois. Alton also gives an easy access to St. Louis, across the river, if you want to explore that city.

On the Illinois side of greater St. Louis is one of the great archaeological sites of the Midwest, the **Cahokia Mounds,** believed to have been the first and largest of the great towns constructed by the Mississipian Culture Native Americans and the largest prehistoric city north of Mexico City. Some 100 earthen mounds were built here between 900 and 1250, of which some 40 remain, but the site was abandoned by 1500.

An arrangement of wooden posts in the ground suggests a horizon calendar, and so the area has been dubbed Woodhenge, after England's Stonehenge. To get to Cahokia Mounds State Park from Highway 3, drive south to I-55/70 and take the interstate east to exit 6, turn south and then almost at once east on Collinsville Road, Route 7850, to the park. There are directional signs. The outdoor park is open daily except major holidays.

Continue south on Route 3 to **Chester,** home of Elzie Segar, the cartoonist who created Popeye, his girlfriend Olive Oyl, Wimpy, Swee'pea, Bluto, and all those other characters after taking a $20 correspondence school course in cartooning. Less known is an earlier character called Eugene the Jeep with a bright-red nose and a long tail, that kept moving over any kind of terrain; after Segar's death in 1938, the Army named its new all-terrain vehicle, also called a G.P. for General Purpose Vehicle, after the cartoon character.

In Chester you'll find antiques shops and statuary that depict Segar's characters, but the most famous Popeye statue is on the west side of town in a park named for his creator on the road to the Chester Bridge, which crosses the Mississippi. Since there are so many trees in the vicinity, look to the left for the statue if you're headed toward the Mississippi, to the right if you're headed away from it. Route 3 continues south along the Mississippi

This Chester, Illinois, store celebrates the spinach-eating hero, Popeye.

Southern Illinois Campgrounds

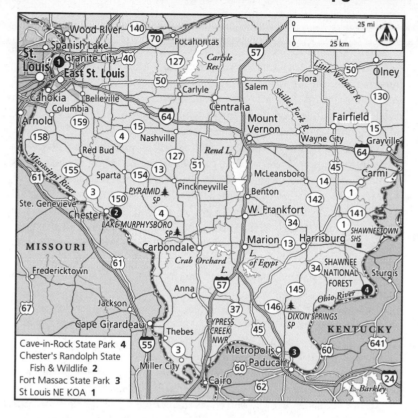

Cave-in-Rock State Park **4**
Chester's Randolph State
  Fish & Wildlife **2**
Fort Massac State Park **3**
St Louis NE KOA **1**

through some beautiful scenery. If you accidentally crossed the Mississippi into Missouri in your quest for the Popeye statue, try to turn around and come back to Chester to follow Route 3 south. The next bridge across the river isn't until Cape Girardeau, 41 miles south.

Fragrant Fields, an herb farm and tea room in Dongola, at exit 24 off I-57, sells specialty herbs, geraniums, and other fragrant plants from its gardens and greenhouses and serves an elegant afternoon tea. There's also a shop where you can buy potpourri in a dozen different fragrances. It's at 102 S. Garden St. (☎ **618-827-3677**).

Superman's town of **Metropolis** is on the Mississippi at the southern tip of Illinois, at exit 37 from I-24. The whole town has been turned over to The Man of Steel. He welcomes you from a billboard when you drive into town, signals from the water tower that looms over the town, and comes into his own in the town square, where a 9-foot bronze statue poses heroically, a perfect spot for a Kodak moment. There's a phone booth where you can change clothes or pick up the receiver and listen to Superman. Across the street is **Super Museum** with the planet's largest collection of Superman memorabilia, including the costume worn by George Reeve, TV's first superman, props from Superman films, rare toys, and comic books. Open daily 9am to 6pm, admission $3 adults, children $2 (☎ 618/524-5518).

Some savvy city fathers back in 1972 realized they lived in the only incorporated city in the United States named Metropolis, so who's to say this isn't Superman's town? They even named the local paper *The Daily Planet,* and in the spring of 2001, the actor who depicts Superman got married in his costume to his real-life sweetheart in the town square by the statue.

A jog north on Route 145 connects with Route 146, you can follow along the scenic Ohio River. Two miles south from its junction with Route 1 is **Cave-in-Rock State Park,** named for a cave with a 55-foot-wide opening overlooking the Ohio River, where outlaws hid to rob and kill unsuspecting river travelers. The cave headquarters was used from 1797 to the mid-1800s.

A cutoff via Route 13 can take you to Old Shawneetown and the **Shawneetown Historic Site,** today almost deserted. Once it was the gateway to the west for settlers traveling the Ohio River on their way to Manifest Destiny. The brick-and-sandstone First State Bank of Illinois was built in 1839; the John Marshall Bank and Home, built in 1818, served as the first bank in Illinois.

If you continue north on Route 1, you can make a convenient detour to New Harmony, Indiana (see "Back Home Again in Indiana: Southern Indiana," below) via Route 14.

Fans of Heath candy bars may want to continue north to **Robinson,** 3 miles west of Route 1 on Route 33. The crunchy, chocolate-covered toffee bar was developed here in 1915, and the factory is still here.

We're not sure the candy served as inspiration or writer fuel for **James Jones,** also born in Robinson 6 years later in 1921, but we're glad he began writing his novel *From Here to Eternity* here. Robinson's third claim to fame is the grave of the only woman ever hanged in Illinois. Elizabeth Betsey Reed was executed in 1845 after a jury found her guilt of poisoning her husband with arsenic-laced sassafras tea. While jailed in nearby Palestine, she tried to escape by setting the jail on fire; she was then moved to the Lawrence County Jail. They say some 20,000 people showed up to watch the hanging. She's buried next to her husband in Baker Cemetery near Heathsville on Route 33. For information on everything in Robinson, contact the chamber of commerce at ☎ 618/546-1557.

Campground Oases in Southern Illinois

Cave-in-Rock State Park is in a town called Cave In Rock on Route 1, 2 miles south of its junction with Route 146. There are 34 paved, back-in sites with 30-amp electrical connections, a dump, food service, swimming, and fishing. No reservations (☎ 618/289-4325 for information; http://dnr.state.il.us/lands/landmgt/parks/ilstate.htm).

Chester's Randolph State Fish & Wildlife Area offers camping without hookups but with a dump station, toilets, and food service. Some 95 narrow pull-through and back-in grass sites are available on a first-come, first-served basis. To get there, go east 3 miles on Route 150 from its junction with Route 3 and follow the signs (☎ **618/826-3706** for information).

Fort Massac State Park near Metropolis has 50 narrow back-in sites with 30- and 50-amp electrical hookups. Take exit 37 from I-24 and follow U.S. 45 for 2½ miles west toward town; the park is on the left (☎ **618/524-4712** for information; http://dnr.state.il.us/lands/landmgt/parks/ilstate.htm).

St. Louis Northeast/I-270/Granite City KOA. In Granite City, Illinois, across the river from St. Louis, the Northeast St. Louis KOA is convenient to Alton and the northern river towns, as well as the Cahokia Mounds. Take exit 3 off I-270 and drive south ²⁄₁₀ mile to Chain of Rocks Road, then turn east for ½ mile to 3157 West Chain of Rocks Rd. The campground has pull-throughs, a dataport for e-mail, and electric connections up to 50 amps. It's closed from November 1 to March 15 (☎ **800/562-5861** or 618/931-5160 for reservations; www.koa.com).

BACK HOME AGAIN IN INDIANA: SOUTHERN INDIANA

Some of our best friends are from Indiana—actors, writers, publishers, public relations executives—and they go home as often as possible. The state is near the top of our list for favorite RV destinations, because we can count on finding something weird or wonderful, often both, on our visits there.

Indiana is a treasure trove of home cooking, food festivals and food producers, offbeat museums, and some eccentric slices of Americana. Take the **breaded tenderloin sandwich,** that uniquely Hoosier snack that's little-known outside the state. Hoosier hogs are appreciated in a wide variety of guises, but nowhere more so than when they're turned into the breaded tenderloin sandwich, a hot, crunchy, Frisbee-sized circle of lean, juicy pork pounded paper-thin, then breaded and deep-fried. Finally, at its crispy peak, it's gently lifted out of the pan and nestled into a warm, supersized hamburger-style bun with garnishes such as lettuce, tomatoes, sliced raw onions, pickles, mustard, and mayonnaise.

New Harmony, at the junction of State Highways 66 and 69 and 7 miles due south of I-64's exit 4, is a good place to start a tour of southern Indiana, especially if you're going or coming from southern Illinois. The first settlers in what they called Harmonie were a German communal group called Harmonists or Rappites (after their leader, George Rapp) who arrived in 1814 with followers from Pennsylvania to settle along the Wabash River. Their aim was to practice perfectionism and celibacy in anticipation of the second coming of Christ. The community was one of the first planned towns in America, and for 10 years it flourished in farming, manufacturing, and commerce. Although they were abstemious, they made beer and whiskey to sell as far away as New Orleans. Their best-known export was a fine-quality flannel marked with a golden rose, as were all the New Harmony goods.

But the settlers were troubled by malaria, a nationwide depression that reduced the demand for their goods and the nonappearance of Christ, so they moved back to Pennsylvania and founded a new town named Economy.

In 1825 a Scottish textile magnate named Robert Owen bought New Harmony from Rapp and brought his family, along with a group of Scottish scientists and intellectuals, to establish a utopian community. It failed in 2 years, but Owen's sons stayed on to continue their father's ideas—free public schools, public libraries, equal education for boys and girls, and kindergarten for young children—and wound up establishing the Smithsonian Institution.

Today the town is a photogenic community of unpainted wood houses from the early 1800s, picket fences, a row of handsome brick and sandstone buildings along Main Street filled with charming shops and boutiques, a modern "roofless" church designed by Philip Johnson, and the postmodern Atheneum designed by Richard Meier in 1979. You can wander around on your own, if you like, or start at the Atheneum with a short film, a museum display of town models and a guided tour (☎ 800/231-2168).

The prettiest town along the Ohio River is **Madison** in southeastern Indiana. In the 19th century it was a major river port and meatpacking center; by midcentury it was the state's largest city. But when in 1847 it became the terminus of the first railroad in Indiana, other towns began siphoning off its business, and Madison declined into a sleepy town with gracious houses designed by architect Francis Costigan. The Shrewsbury House, 301 W. 1st St., is a good example of his Greek Revival structures with its three-story freestanding spiral staircase. Historic Madison can provide information for self-guided tours and arrange conducted tours (☎ 812/265-2967).

North of Madison about 50 miles as the crow flies is **Metamora,** site of the other Whitewater Scandal. In 1836, long before the world ever heard of Bill and Hillary Clinton, the Indiana legislature decided to build a 76-mile canal between Hagerstown and Lawrenceburg with 56 locks and seven dams, plus an aqueduct that would carry the canal 16 feet above Duck Creek, a waterway that flowed through Metamora. The canal was a washout, literally, from frequent floods, and the arrival of the railroad before construction was completed cinched the expensive failure, which drove the state into bankruptcy. A harried legislature passed regulations that prohibit the state of Indiana from ever contracting debt again, regulations that live today.

ON THE BARBECUE TRAIL

You can follow the Ohio River around Indiana's southern border, pausing, perhaps, in Evansville to pick up some barbecue at Wolf's, 6600 1st Ave. (☎ 812/424-8891). You could even detour south across the Kentucky border to Owensboro's **Moonlite Bar-B-Q Inn** for barbecued mutton (delicious!) and Kentucky burgoo (a thick tomato-based stew). The location, 2840 W. Parrish Ave., is also U.S. 56; it's open 9am to 9pm Monday through Saturday, 10am to 3pm on Sunday (☎ 270/684-8143).

The restored Whitewater Canal project in Metamora, Indiana.

After World War II, restoration began on the Metamora lock, an old grist-mill from 1845 and the Duck Creek Aqueduct, believed to be the only one of its kind left. By the 1960s, gentrification added craft shops, antiques stores and galleries, and a sightseeing boat along the canal. Today visitors can take a canal cruise on a horse-drawn boat, wander the streets of the town, and explore some 100 shops and cafes in 19th-century wooden buildings. For information, call the Whitewater Canal State Historic Site (☎ **765/647-6512**).

Brown County in south-central Indiana is a favorite weekend getaway for Hoosiers to see dogwood and redbud in spring and to shop for antiques and taste treats in a trio of towns around the junction of State Routes 46 and 135. Parking for large motor homes is scarce on summer Sundays, but we found a spot in the high school parking lot and walked into **Nashville.** Potters, painters, and quilt makers share storefronts with fudge and cookie makers, country stores, and antiques shops. The most famous eatery is in the Nashville House at the corner of Main and Van Buren, which earned its renown by deep-frying biscuits and serving them with baked apple butter.

The hamlet of **Gnaw Bone,** 6 miles east of Nashville on Route 46, makes sorghum, a sort of molasses, at the Brown County Sorghum Mill every September through November.

Nearby **Bean Blossom,** 5 miles north of Nashville on Route 135, is home of the annual Bill Monroe Bluegrass Festival, along with a museum devoted to the music. For information, call the Brown County Convention and Visitors Bureau (☎ **800/753-3255**).

Southern Indiana has plenty of appealing towns on the "country-cute" side like Metamora and Bean Blossom, Gnaw Bone and Nashville, but the class act is **Columbus,** a blend of award-winning architecture and small-town charm. South of Indianapolis off I-35 at exit 68, this town of 34,000 seems an unlikely location for a major collection of public and commercial buildings by the leading contemporary architects of the world.

The city's architectural legacy began back in 1942 when controversial Finnish architect Eliel Saarinen was commissioned to design the First Christian Church. It was one of the first modern churches built in the United States and is said to have influenced American church design ever since.

In 1957, the town's leading industry, Cummins Engine Company (the people who put the diesel into diesel pushers) made an offer to pay architectural fees for new school building designs if the school used an architect from a list of major international designers. Later it established a foundation to establish the same policy for all public buildings in town.

Whose work can you see? **I. M. Pei** designed the town library with its Henry Moore sculpture in front; **Eero Saarinen,** Eliel's equally famous son, designed the Irwin Union Bank and Trust Company; **Edward Larrabee Barnes** and **Richard Meier** each designed an elementary school; and **Robert Venturi** designed a firehouse. Allow 2½ to 5½ hours to cover the city's more than 50 sites; see "Architecture Watch," later in this chapter, for information. Take a break for tea at the elegant little Columbus Inn at 445 5th St. or at Zaharako's classic ice cream parlor and soda fountain at 329 Washington St.

Campground Oases in Southern Indiana

Harmonie State Park is 4 miles south of New Harmony on Indiana 69 and then west 1 mile on State Road 269. There are 200 pull-through and back-in sites, all fairly narrow, with 20- and 30-amp electrical hookups, a sanitation dump, and restrooms with showers. No reservations (☎ **812/682-4821** for information).

Maclyn Campground, Metamora, Indiana, is easy to find; it's across Highway 52 from the entrance to the town and park. It's in a field behind the Hickory Lane Smorgasbord Restaurant, which has a parking lot capable of handling big rigs. Maclyn offers hookups, back-ins, and pull-throughs (☎ **765/647-2541**).

Bill Monroe Memorial Music Park & Campground, Bean Blossom, Indiana, is on State Road 135, with 237 back-in sites, 30-amp electrical hookups, restrooms, showers, and dump (☎ **812/988-6422** for reservations).

Brown County State Park, Nashville, Tennessee, is 2 miles southwest of town on State Road 46W, with 407 narrow back-in sites offering 30-amp electrical hookups, restrooms, showers, and dump (☎ **812/988-6406** for information).

Louisville Metro KOA, Clarksville, Indiana, is across the Ohio River from Louisville. Open year-round with full hookups and electrical connections up to 50 amps, the campground also offers dataports for collecting e-mail, sells LP gas, provides cable TV and miniature golf, food service, and fishing (☎ **800/562-4771** or 812/282-4474 for reservations; www.koa.com).

Southern Indiana Campgrounds

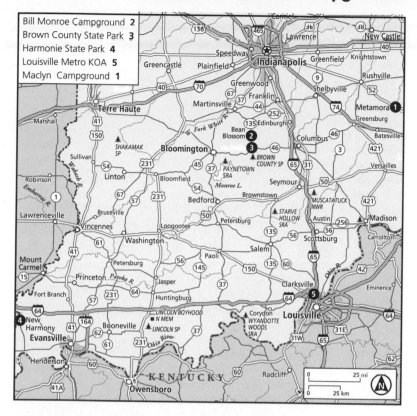

Bill Monroe Campground **2**
Brown County State Park **3**
Harmonie State Park **4**
Louisville Metro KOA **5**
Maclyn Campground **1**

NORTHERN INDIANA: BEN HUR'S CHARIOT, THE INDY 500 & THE '47 STUDEBAKER

Revered by auto racing fans as the home of the Indianapolis Motor Speedway, **Indianapolis** is also remembered as the home of folksy poet James Whitcomb Riley (although probably not by the same folks). Riley spent the last 23 years of his life with longtime friends Major and Mrs. Charles Holstein at 528 Lockerbie St. (of which he wrote, "Such a dear little street it is"); ironically, his benefactors have been forgotten, and the majestic brick home is called the James Whitcomb Riley house.

The Indianapolis 500 in May for Indy cars, dating from 1911, and the Brickyard 400 in August for stock cars pack the town with racing fans. The rest of the year you can visit a museum with racing cars from the 1920s, or take a tour bus ride around the oval track at a slow-pokey 35 miles an hour. Our own favorite sight in Indianapolis is the ornate 1901 Beaux-Arts Soldiers' and Sailors' Monument in Monument Circle, in the heart of the city. Alexander Ralston, an assistant of Pierre Charles L'Enfant, who created the street layout in Washington, D.C., designed the hub-and-spoke street pattern in the downtown area. The **Indiana Statehouse** and the **Circle Theatre** are

TEN TENDER TENDERLOINS

Mr. Dave's in North Manchester, 40 miles west of Fort Wayne on State Route 114, serves an award-winning classic, crisp but modest in size, and served with pickles only; also vends frozen ready-to-fry breaded tenderloins to take home (☎ 219/982-4769).

Das Dutchman Essenhaus, Middlebury, east of Elkhart on U.S. 20, an Amish-style restaurant complex the size of an airplane hanger with all-you-can-eat fried chicken dinners, large tenderloin sandwiches, and 27 varieties of pie (☎ 800/455-9471).

Romney Coffee Shop, on U.S. 231 north of Romney at the junction of State Route 28, serves scrumptious tenderloin and big country breakfasts (☎ 765/538-3133).

Hobnob Corner, Nashville, Indiana. This popular Brown County eatery serves tenderloin sandwiches along with strawberry sodas and a variety of soups and sandwiches. The former dry goods store is located at 17 W. Main St. This inexpensive spot has wooden booths and plank floors (☎ 812/988-4114).

Speedway Café, Fort Wayne, at 4429 Lima Rd. NW, is famous for big, big tenderloins (☎ 219/484-7013).

Tailgator's, Indianapolis, 373 S. Illinois St., sells sandwiches so big it takes two hands to handle them (☎ 317/756-7254).

Nobby Grill, 213 E. 4th St. in Marion, 45 miles southwest of Fort Wayne off I-69, exit 64, serves superlative, two-fisted tenderloin sandwiches 24 hours a day, 7 days a week (☎ 765/651-9600).

The Friendly Tavern, Zionsville, just outside Indianapolis, is a longtime Hoosier favorite for tenderloin sandwiches (☎ 317/873-5772).

Mrs. Wick's Pies & Restaurant, at 100 Cherry St. in Winchester, east of Muncie, is famous for pies, but also turns out two versions of a tenderloin sandwich, breaded or grilled (☎ 317/584-7437).

Carver's Family Dining, Richmond, Indiana, is open daily with breakfast, lunch, and dinner specials, plus popular pork tenderloin sandwiches. It's at 2270 Chester Blvd. (☎ 765/966-8565).

worth a visit, as is the Art Deco **Madam Walker Theatre Center,** honoring the first female self-made millionaire in America. Madam Walker manufactured beauty products for African-American women. Call Indianapolis information at ☎ **800/238-INDY.**

Northeast of the city is **Connor Prairie,** a living history museum that re-creates an 1836 village with costumed guides who demonstrate life in early Indiana. It's open May through October at 13400 Allisonville Rd., 4 miles south of Noblesville off Route 19 (☎ 317/776-6000).

Iowa isn't the only state famous for covered bridges. Indiana's **Parke County,** west of Indianapolis almost to the Illinois border, boasts 32 of them, some said to be haunted. An annual October Covered Bridge Festival funds bridge upkeep. For information and a site map, call ☎ 765/569-5226.

A state historical site dedicated to a beloved World War II figure, war correspondent Ernie Pyle, is just west of Parke County in Vermillion County, off U.S. 36 in his hometown of **Dana,** near the Illinois border. A Quonset hut visitor center displays memorabilia (☎ **765/665-3633**).

Northeast of Dana in **Crawfordsville** another Indiana writer is remembered with more pomp and ceremony—General Lew Wallace, author of *Ben Hur,* who wrote the first part of the book in Indiana, then finished it when he was territorial governor in New Mexico. The popular book has never been out of print since it appeared in 1880. Wallace's home, the study where he wrote, a *Ben Hur* museum, and annual chariot races staged in October are all here 2 miles south of I-74 at exit 34. For information, call the Crawfordsville Convention & Visitors Bureau (☎ **800/866-3973**).

Anderson, 25 miles northeast of Indianapolis, is home to the spectacular **Paramount Theatre Centre and Ballroom,** a rare "atmospheric" theater with a rose and blue sky and Moorish balconies that re-create a midsummer evening in Spain. Besides special evening performances and concerts, the theater is open weekdays 9am to 5pm for visitors (☎ **800/523-4658**).

Seances and evoked ectoplasms are everyday occurrences at Camp Chesterfield, a spiritualist compound in **Chesterfield,** off I-69 at Highway 32 near Anderson. This is one of several centers for spiritualism in the United States; others are Lily Dale, New York, and Cassadega, Florida. Open to the public from 9am to 5pm, the camp has lodgings, a cafeteria, an art gallery, a bookstore, and a museum. Consultations by appointment can be scheduled with the mediums of Chesterfield, who are said to go into trances, cause spirits to materialize, and predict the future (☎ **765/378-0235**).

Another once-popular author from Indiana is Gene Stratton-Porter, who wrote *A Girl in the Limberlost* and other sentimental novels with nature lore about Loblolly Marsh near her home town of **Geneva.** Also a naturalist and photographer, she lived at 200 E. 6th St., 1 block east of U.S. 27, in a rustic log home that is open to visitors; her moth collection is on display inside. Geneva is 35 miles south of Fort Wayne at the junction of U.S. 27 and Highway 116 (☎ **219/368-7248**).

Peru, Indiana, was the birthplace of Cole Porter. His home on East 3rd Street and grave site in Mount Hope Cemetery can be visited, as well as the Miami County Museum where his black 1955 Cadillac is on display. The car, which appeared in *The Godfather,* was shipped back and forth six times from New York to the French Riviera, where the composer used to spend his summers. For information, call the Miami County Museum at ☎ **765/473-9183.**

Every month, Porter had a standing order for 9 pounds of chocolate fudge to be shipped to him by **Arnold's Candies.** The confectionary, now located at 288 E. Main St., still uses the same recipe.

The **Circus City Festival Museum,** at 154 N. Broadway, commemorates with artifacts and historic photographs the days when Peru was winter headquarters for many world-famous circuses (☎ **765/472-7553**).

An old circus wagon at the Peru Circus City Festival Museum.

From the Circus Museum, it's 14 miles west to **Logansport,** where one of only three working models of a Gustav Dentzell carousel still operates between Memorial Day and Labor Day on summer weekends and weekday evenings for 50¢ a ride. Climb aboard one of the 29 hand-carved wooden horses or a goat, reindeer, giraffe, lion, or tiger in the town's Riverside Park on Riverside Drive. Call the Cass County Carousel at ☎ **219/753-8725.**

The grave of John Chapman, also known as Johnny Appleseed, can be found in **Fort Wayne's Johnny Appleseed Park** at Coliseum Boulevard and Parnell Avenue off I-69 at exit 111.

Anyone who likes antique cars, especially highly polished expensive ones, should not miss the **Auburn Cord Duesenberg Museum** in Auburn, 17 miles north of Fort Wayne and 2 miles off I-69 at exit 129, in town at 1600 S. Wayne St. Open daily except major holidays, the museum displays more than 100 classic automobiles manufactured in Indiana between 1900 and 1937. The moderately priced Auburn, later the stylish Cord, and the legendary Duesenberg, the most expensive car on the market in the 1930s, were produced here. The phrase "it's a doozy," meaning something extraordinary, may well originally have been, "It's a Deusy," the museum curators suggest (☎ **219/925-1444**).

Northern Indiana's Amish country, the nation's third largest Amish settlement, lies east of Elkhart; the towns of **Shipshewana** and **Middlebury** are particularly colorful. Amish farmers drive horse-drawn black buggies along country lanes and, to a lesser extent, highways, so watch your speed, and Amish restaurants serve mind-boggling amounts of food family style, so watch your diet. Handmade copper utensils, horses and cows, quilts, home-baked bread, and exotic popcorns are all for sale. The **Deutsch Kase House** (German Cheese House), with an Amish staff, has samples of the cheeses it makes, including baby Swiss, Colby, and hot pepper cheese at modest prices.

The **Shipshewana Flea Market and Auction** is world-famous with its 1,000 vendors, livestock auctions, and Amish-Mennonite foods (☎ 219/768-4129).

In **Elkhart,** you can visit vintage RVs at the RV/MH Heritage Foundation at 801 Benham Ave., 9am to 5pm weekdays (☎ 219/293-2344). If you want to take a factory tour and see how some brands are manufactured, you'll find Coachmen, Jayco, and Shasta Industries in Middlebury, Carriage in Millerburg, Damon and Forest City in Elkhart, Holiday Rambler in Wakarusa, and Newmar in Nappanee.

The farm home at Amish Acres in **Napanee,** 15 miles south of Elkhart on Highway 19, 1 mile west of the junction with U.S. 6, is on the National Register of Historic Places. **The Restaurant Barn** serves up the award-winning Threshers Dinner of ham, beef, chicken, and turkey, plus countless side dishes and desserts daily from 11am to 7pm, 6pm on Sundays, plus a summer-only Bountiful Breakfast Buffet. In the Round Barn Theatre, the Amish musical *Plain and Fancy* that was a Broadway hit in the 1950s is presented during summer. Call Amish Acres information at ☎ 800/800-4942.

Nearby **South Bend,** about 15 miles west of Elkhart, is home to Notre Dame of "Win this one for the Gipper" fame, one of Ronald Reagan's cinematic golden moments. The Golden Dome atop the university's main building is the symbol for this whole area, discovered by French explorer LaSalle in 1681 and again by Norwegian athlete Knute Rockne in 1918 when the alumnus and star player became football coach.

The **Studebaker Museum** is engrossing, even for nonmotor-heads, a collection of machinery dating from Henry Studebaker's wooden wheelbarrow, which he sold in vast quantities to miners in the California Gold Rush. Henry was one of five Studebaker brothers, and the $8,000 he brought back from California set the family up in a blacksmith shop. They made supply wagons

Many of Indiana's Amish community still use horse-drawn buggies.

for the Union Army in the Civil War, then went into carriages (one of them took Abraham Lincoln to Ford's Theater the night he was assassinated), and then into horseless carriages. Perhaps their most famous was the 1947 Studebaker, designed by Raymond Loewy, a packaging expert, with a front and rear end that were exactly the same shape. A favorite joke at the time was that you couldn't tell whether it was coming or going.

An interesting prototype was the Packard Prediction, built for the 1956 Chicago World's Fair, which forecast tail fins, sliding glass car roofs, and many other details. The only one ever built is in the museum, located at 525 S. Main St. next door to Covelski Stadium. For information for Notre Dame and the museum, call the South Bend Visitors Bureau at ☎ 800/882-7881.

Chesterton, 4 miles north of I-80/90, the Indiana Turnpike, at exit 31, ranks as a first-rate discovery for trivia nuts, film fans, Americana buffs, and literary detectives, because it was in this pretty town that L. Frank Baum and family spent their summers while he was working on *The Wizard of Oz*. He was writing for a magazine for interior decorators in Chicago, and the Indiana dunes town was close enough for a getaway. His son founded the International Wizard of Oz Club in this area, and today the town salutes the Wizard and all denizens of Oz, particularly the few surviving Munchkins who are feted at celebrity parties and gala dinners every September. The Yellow Brick Road shop–cum-museum sells memorabilia from the film. **Indiana Dunes State Park,** inside the national lakeshore of the same name, is north of here on State Route 49. For information, call the Porter County Visitor Information Center at ☎ 800/283-8687.

Campground Oases in Northern Indiana

Johnny Appleseed Campground, Fort Wayne. In Johnny Appleseed Park (see above), this grassy, tree-shaded campground has 36 sites with 30-amp electrical connections and some haphazardly arranged water connections that may require a long hose. There's also a dump station. The campground is closed during the annual mid-September Johnny Appleseed Festival. No reservations (☎ 219/427-6720 for information).

Crawfordsville KOA, Crawfordsville. On U.S. 231, 1 mile south of I-74 at exit 34, this campground is adjacent to a commercial strip of restaurants, motels, and malls, with large pull-through sites with up to 50 amps in electrical hookups, cable TV, and dataports for retrieving and sending e-mail (☎ 800/562-4191 or 765/362-4190 for reservations; www.koa.com).

Turkey Run State Park, Marshall. This scenic recreation area in the middle of Parke County's covered bridge country provides excellent hiking, canoeing and horseback riding on rental horses. The campground offers 235 large back-in and pull-through sites with 30-amp electrical hookups and wheelchair access. An hour west of Indianapolis and convenient to both the Ernie Pyle and Lew Wallace historic sites, the park is located on State Road 47, 2 miles east of its junction with U.S. 41 (☎ 765/597-2635).

Northern Indiana Campgrounds

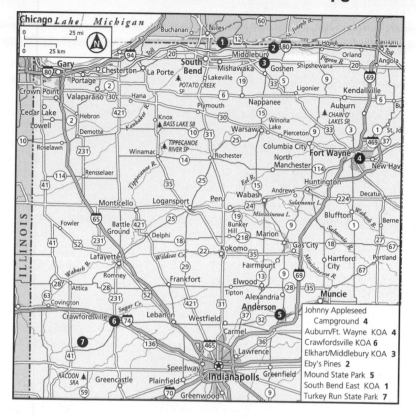

Johnny Appleseed
    Campground **4**
Auburn/Ft. Wayne KOA **4**
Crawfordsville KOA **6**
Elkhart/Middlebury KOA **3**
Eby's Pines **2**
Mound State Park **5**
South Bend East KOA **1**
Turkey Run State Park **7**

South Bend East KOA, Granger. Handy for RV tours and South Bend sight-seeing, this campground offers full hookups up to 50 amps electrical, along with dataports, cable TV, and miniature golf. Take exit 83 from I-80/90 and go north 2 miles on State Road 23; turn left onto Princess Way at Burger King. For reservations, call ☎ **800/562-2470** or 219-277-1335; www.koa.com.

Mound State Park, Anderson. East of town 2½ miles on Route 232, the park has 75 narrow campsites that are pull-throughs and back-ins with 30-amp electrical hookups. Closed in winter (☎ **765/642-6627**).

Elkhart/Middlebury KOA, Middlebury. In the heart of Amish country, this campground is 4 miles north of Middlebury on State Road 13, and from I-80/90, 1½ miles south via exit 107. A heated pool, petting zoo, electrical connections up to 50 amps, dataports, and Amish country tours leaving from the campground. For reservations, call ☎ **800/562-5892** or 219/825-5932; www.koa.com.

Eby's Pines, Bristol. Also convenient to Amish country, this family campground lined with pine trees used to be open year-round; we've stayed there comfortably in the snow. Now, however, it's open from mid-April through mid-October only. There are 250 pull-through and back-in sites with 30-amp electricity in mostly side-by-side hookups. There are a lot of activities and a store with limited supplies. Take the Bristol exit 101 from I-80/90, go south on Route 15 for about a mile, then east 3 miles on State Road 120. For reservations, call ☎ **219/848-4583.**

Auburn/Fort Wayne KOA, Auburn. Close to the Auburn Cord Duesenberg Museum and the St. Joe pickle factory, the campground provides full hookups up to 50 amps, long pull-throughs, heated swimming pool, basketball and volleyball courts, and a playground. It's located just south of Auburn off I-69, exit 126 and west on County Road 11A. For reservations, call ☎ **800/ 562-7518** or 219/925-6747; www.koa.com.

ARCHITECTURE WATCH

The American Institute of Architects ranks **Columbus, Indiana,** sixth in the United States for architectural innovation and quality of design in public and private buildings. From Eliel Saarinen's **First Christian Church** from 1942 to the 1994 Pritzger Award–winning remodeling of an 1864 Victorian house into the city's **new visitor center,** the city is chockablock with fine architecture. Information for guided tour tickets and do-it-yourself driving tours is at the visitor center at 506 5th St. (☎ **812/372-1954**).

In **Sioux City, Iowa,** the elaborately decorated **Woodman County Courthouse** is a strikingly original work of art created by three students of Chicago architect Louis Sullivan and worth a detour for avid photographers. William Steele with Purcell & Elmslie created the structure, which was finished in 1918. The courthouse, downtown at 7th and Douglas streets, is still in use and open to the public during normal business hours.

Galena, Illinois, is a dictionary of 19th-century architectural styles from Federal, Greek Revival, Steamboat Gothic, and Italianate to Second Empire, Gothic Revival, Romanesque Revival, and Queen Anne. You can pick up a walking tour map at the Historical Society on Bench Street; more than 90% of the town's buildings are on the National Register of Historic Places.

Frank Lloyd Wright's Dana-Thomas House in Springfield, Illinois.

Springfield, Illinois, is home to Frank Lloyd Wright's **Dana-Thomas house,** built in 1904 but still fresh and contemporary-looking today. It's been described as Wright's first "blank check" commission. Wright designed all the furniture, windows, and lighting fixtures, and pieces of pottery and sculpture still sit exactly where Wright specified they should go. In the library, Wright designed art-glass doors on all the cabinets so that the books with their irregular shapes and colors wouldn't clutter up his design. His client, socialite Susan Lawrence Dana, paid the architect the then-grand sum of $60,000. At 301 E. Lawrence St., the house is open for free tours Wednesday through Sunday 9am to 4pm (☎ 217/782-6776).

A BOX OF POPCORN

According to the U.S. Popcorn Board, the average American eats about 68 quarts of popcorn a year, most consumed while watching movies or TV. The oldest ears of popcorn ever found were 5,600 years old and were discovered in a bat cave in New Mexico in 1948. Columbus and his crew were offered popcorn as a trade good when they first arrived in the West Indies.

Popcorn was the first "puffed cereal" in America; colonial housewives served it with sugar and cream for breakfast.

The American love affair with popcorn got a major boost during World War II when sugar was sent overseas for U.S. troops, reducing the amount of candy available, so per capita consumption for popcorn tripled.

Many Americans buy microwave ovens just so they can make popcorn at home, but few realize popcorn was instrumental in the invention of the microwave. Percy Spencer discovered in 1945 that popcorn would pop when placed under microwave energy. He then experimented with other foods, which led to the invention of the microwave oven.

Popcorn is a celebrated agricultural product in the Heartland.

Valpariso, Indiana, honors Orville Redenbacher with a popcorn festival every Labor Day weekend Saturday downtown (☎ 219/464-8332). **Yoder's Popcorn Shop,** 4 miles south of Shipshewana, Indiana, on Route 200S, sells a variety of popcorn, including black jewel. For information and orders, call ☎ 800/892-2170.

The best place to admire popcorn as a work of art is outside Dublin, Indiana, where artist Malcolm Cochran's **"Field of Corn (with Osage Orange Trees)"** symbolizes the town's farming history and memorializes rural landscape that is being consumed by development. The outdoor artwork displays 109 white concrete ears of corn rising 5 to 6 feet out of the ground with a background of Osage orange trees, which once provided natural fencing for farmers. "Field of Corn" is located in Sam and Eulalia Frantz Park at the corner of Frantz and Rings roads. From I-70, take exit 17A, drive east on State Route 161 to Frantz Road, turn right, and continue another 2 miles. The city of Dublin has also commissioned other distinctive public artworks, including "Chief Leatherlips Monument" and "Watch House." For information, call the Dublin Convention & Visitors Bureau at ☎ 800/245-8387. 🚗

In **Evanston's Lakeshore Historic District,** the lovely Sheridan Road drive goes past mansions built between the 1880s and the 1920s, a mélange of styles including French châteaux, Tudors, Victorians, Prairie Style, and Arts and Crafts. The magnificent Baha'i House of Worship at 100 Linden Ave. in **Wilmette** and an early Frank Lloyd Wright design, 850 Sheridan in **Glencoe,** are both along the route. (William Rice Burroughs lived at 700 Linden Ave. when he published *Tarzan of the Apes.*)

Oak Park is the site of many of Wright's best works in the Prairie Style, with 20 houses that can be seen on a neighborhood walking tour with an audiotape guide. The designer's home and studio can also be toured. For information, call the Frank Lloyd Wright Foundation ☎ **708/848-1978.**

The Florida Keys (with Side Trips to the Everglades & Orlando)

KEY WEST IS "THE LAST RESORT," THE T-SHIRT CAPITAL OF THE WORLD, the place Tennessee Williams called Cocalooney Key. A sign at the end of the dock says 90 MILES TO CUBA, and a local mayor once water-skied the distance.

It's where fashion icon Calvin Klein bought a million-dollar Bird Cage, where "tea dancing" doesn't call for white gloves, and where Presidents Truman, Kennedy, Nixon, and Bush all lodged at the same upscale fishing lodge, Cheeca Lodge, though not at the same time.

The Keys are where the famous 1948 film noir *Key Largo* with Humphrey Bogart and Lauren Bacall was not filmed, although the Key Largo tourist office implies it was. The 1955 movie *The Rose Tattoo* with Burt Lancaster and Anna Magnani was filmed here, much of it in author Tennessee Williams's own house, a fact hardly (if ever) mentioned in Key West.

It's where buccaneers swashbuckled, where Harry S. Truman played poker, where ice from the frozen lakes of Maine was delivered by ship until well into the 20th century, where Anna Pavlova danced with the Russian Ballet, and Truman Capote danced with Tennessee Williams.

RVing the Keys

The first overland transportation to Key West was an extension of Henry M. Flagler's railroad, called "Flagler's Folly" or "the railroad that went to sea," which covered 25 miles of the distance on land, 75 miles over water.

The aging tycoon's railway began in 1896 when Flagler, content in north Florida's St. Augustine until the freeze of 1894–95 destroyed all the citrus and vegetables north of Palm Beach, decided to move south to get warm. The indomitable Julia Tuttle, a dowager bent on bringing attention to south Florida, sent a bouquet of fresh orange blossoms to Flagler from her farm, along with an offer to share the land the Tuttles and their neighbors owned, in exchange for Flagler extending his railway to their village on the banks of the Miami River. He did, she did, and the rest is history.

From 1905 to 1912, Flagler took his rail line even farther south along the Florida Keys despite the naysayers, running 150 miles of track that connected the Florida mainland with the southern islands. He died shortly after it was finished, secure that his biggest accomplishment, the famous Seven Mile Bridge, would also be his lasting monument. Although many of the railroad tracks were uprooted by a hurricane in 1935, the bridge remained.

Engineers used the old railroad pilings to support the 43 bridges of the Overseas Highway, which opened in 1938. While the original bridges and road have been widened or replaced, you can still see some of them, including the first Seven Mile Bridge. In April, the annual Seven Mile Bridge run sets out from Marathon with runners from all over the world.

For RVers, even those towing 40-foot travel trailers, these long, flat, overwater roads are good, free of curves and hills.

The drive from Miami to Key West is 3 to 4 hours each way if you don't stop—but if you don't stop, you have little reason to drive down.

HITTING THE HIGHLIGHTS

For most RVers, it's an easy matter to drive the Keys from Miami and back in 1 day, but that would defeat the best reasons for coming—a little sightseeing, a little fishing, a little beach camping, and fresh seafood (maybe some you caught yourself) for dinner.

Allow a half-day for snorkeling at one of the national or state parks. Take a detour into Everglades National Park via Route 9336 from Homestead and walk the boardwalk trails with binoculars to catch sight of herons, egrets, white ibis, and alligators (see "Two Great Side Trips," later in this chapter). Bicycle around Key West for a day and catch the highlights.

Who knows? You still might have time left over to take the kids to Disney World on the way back home (see "Two Great Side Trips," later in this chapter).

GOING FOR THE LONG HAUL

If you wanted to hang around Key West for the season—and a lot of people do—you could spend some time creatively by signing up for adult courses in Spanish, bird-watching, or swamp ecology at the **Florida Keys Community College** in Key West (☎ **305/296-9081;** satellite campuses located in Key Largo ☎ **305/852-8007,** and Marathon ☎ **305/743-2133**). Other classes offered sometimes include quilting, watercolors, or puppet theater.

Or you could extend your RV trip into a full Florida tour, spending the winter covering the state (although you should bear in mind that from Orlando north it can be chilly in midwinter).

Travel Essentials

WHEN TO GO

The weather is warm year-round, but the winter months have the most comfortable temperatures for bicycling around Key West. Late spring brings

Florida Keys Highlights

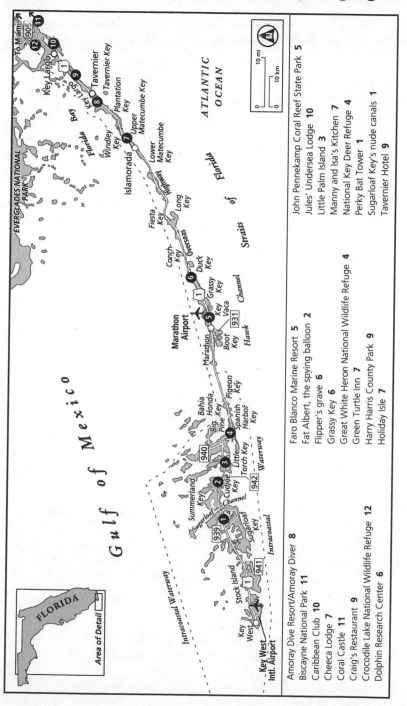

Amoray Dive Resort/Amoray Diver **8**
Biscayne National Park **11**
Caribbean Club **10**
Cheeca Lodge **7**
Coral Castle **11**
Craig's Restaurant **9**
Crocodile Lake National Wildlife Refuge **12**
Dolphin Research Center **6**

Faro Blanco Marine Resort **5**
Fat Albert, the spying balloon **2**
Flipper's grave **6**
Grassy Key **6**
Great White Heron National Wildlife Refuge **4**
Green Turtle Inn **7**
Harry Harris County Park **9**
Holiday Isle **7**

John Pennekamp Coral Reef State Park **5**
Jules' Undersea Lodge **10**
Little Palm Island **3**
Manny and Isa's Kitchen **7**
National Key Deer Refuge **4**
Perky Bat Tower **1**
Sugarloaf Key's nude canals **1**
Tavernier Hotel **9**

bright bloom to Key West's streets—bougainvillea, jacaranda, and oleander. Summer's muggy temperatures often combine with ferocious but brief thunderstorms; more rainfall comes down during fall and winter but rarely enough to bother your sightseeing. Hurricane season is early fall. Spring break can fill the streets of Key West with party-hearty college students—consider yourself forewarned. And year-round cruise ship arrivals jam Mallory Square with day-trippers.

WHAT TO TAKE

Bring binoculars, camera and film, powerful insect repellent to combat champion mosquitoes, a sun hat, and a good strong sunblock. If you've forgotten your sunblock or are running low, pick up some of the excellent locally produced Key West Aloe Sunblock at its shop/factory on Front Street.

WHAT TO WEAR

Shorts, flip-flops, and a tank top or T-shirt is the most common outfit on the streets of Key West on a hot day, but something a little more conservative is appreciated in upscale restaurants and hotels. If you splurge on a meal or overnight at Little Palm Island (see "Ten Special Splurges," below), take some casually elegant resort-type sportswear. Carry a sweater or jacket for rainy days or cool evenings in winter. If you forget anything, you can find plenty of well made, moderately priced sportswear manufactured locally.

TRIMMING COSTS ON THE ROAD

The most expensive item for RVers in the Florida Keys is a hookup site at a private campground, so if money is tight, head instead for the state parks and Everglades National Park for an overnight or two, easiest to get a site if you arrive early in the day on a weekday when public schools are in session.

Restaurant portions are very generous all over south Florida, so if you're not starving, plan to split some servings, especially the main dish. This is easiest to do tactfully as takeout. Or pick up a walk-around lunch or snack from the Cuban sandwich or conch fritter vendors.

While Key West has a number of entertaining options, we find some of the attractions overpriced. The Hemingway House is almost as interesting from the outside as it is inside, and cheaper. Unless you're a real Hemingway fan or a six-toed cat freak, we suggest you take a picture, then walk on by.

The Conch Train and Trolley tours are cute, and ideal for day-trippers off the cruise ships, but you can cover the same territory by bicycle (rentals are easy to find if you're not carrying your own) or even on foot with free walking-tour brochures from the tourist information office in Mallory Square. Since the open-air trolleys use amplified narration, you could tag along behind one on your bike and hear the same information and corny jokes the cruisers pay $20 for.

We've detailed some under-$10 attractions in Key West: See "Five Things to Do in Key West for $10 or Less," later in this chapter.

WHERE TO GET TRAVEL INFORMATION

Call ☎ 800/771-KEYS only within the Florida Keys area for a live multilingual operator who offers problem-solving assistance. The number is staffed 24 hours a day, 7 days a week. Call **Florida Keys Information** (☎ 800/ FLA-KEYS in the U.S., or 800/GO-TO-KEYS; www.fla-keys.com) to get a $9.95 video and brochure. Call **Florida State Parks** for a free state parks guidebook (☎ 850/488-9872; www.myflorida.com). **Florida RV Parks and Campgrounds** supplies Florida campground info and will, upon request, send a directory of more than 300 listings with maps and 30 campground brochures (☎ 850/562-7151; www.floridacamping.com).

DRIVING & CAMPING TIPS

- **"MM" means mile marker.** The letters MM, which you'll see throughout this chapter and on material about the Keys, stand for Mile Marker, the most commonly used address. The markers are green-and-white signs on the right shoulder of the road. Miles are measured from Key West (MM 0) to the mainland (MM 126).

- **Don't mess with the coral.** The pieces of coral and coral souvenirs you'll see for sale in the Keys come from the Philippines. The taking of any Florida coral is illegal, and snorkelers and divers who harm it or the other protected species are subject to fines and punishment.

- **Don't mess with the manchineel tree, either.** The pretty little manchineel tree growing on the beach with its green and yellow leaves makes an inviting canopy in a rain shower. But watch out—it literally drips a burning, acidlike poison from its leaves as the rain runs down them. Never touch its tiny applelike fruit, its thick milky sap, or its smooth gray trunk. Everything about it is poisonous.

- **Keep on your toes to get a campsite.** Privately owned RV parks in the Keys, particularly those that are so-called condo parks (meaning they sell memberships or timeshares), can be pricey, especially at high season, when the entire population of Canada and the upper Midwest seems to be in residence. Expect to be charged $35 or more for an overnight hookup. Even the state parks are expensive compared to other states. They make half their sites available for advance booking, but only within 60 days of your anticipated arrival. For first-come, first-served sites in the state parks, go in the morning and get your name on a waiting list if the park is full and come back in midafternoon to see if you've scored a space.

- **Call ahead about pets.** Many Florida recreation areas and state parks, as well as some private RV parks, have a hotly debated "no pets" rule. Be sure to call ahead if you're traveling with furry friends.

The Best Sights, Tastes & Experiences of the Keys

OFF-THE-WALL ATTRACTIONS

Sunset at Key West's Mallory Square. A nightly happening, with fire-eaters, jugglers, mimes, contortionists, T-shirt sellers, fortune-tellers, and uni-cyclists. There used to be a bicycling woman selling brownies with the call, "Here come the fudge!" but we didn't see her on our most recent visit.

Goofy graves, Key West. At the Key West Cemetery, seek out especially the stones of B. P. Roberts (1929–79), engraved "I Told You I Was Sick" (at the end of Seventh Street); another that says, "A Devoted Fan of Singer Julio Iglesias"; the grave of Joseph "Sloppy Joe" Russell, Hemingway's favorite bar-tender, who died on a 1941 fishing trip with the author; and the famous "bound woman" on the grave of Archibald John Sheldon Yates (at the inter-section of Angela and Grinnell). Most are stone vaults raised above the impenetrable coral base and the high water table. It's open dawn to dusk.

Lots of people, lots of beer, lots of fish. If you like to hang out in crowds with people who swap fishing stories and drink beer, Holiday Isle at MM 84 on appropriately named Windley Key is mobbed on winter weekends. If you don't, consider yourself warned (☎ 800/327-7070 or 305/664-2321).

Duval Street, Key West. Key West conchs claim that Duval is the longest street in the world because it stretches from the Gulf of Mexico to the Atlantic Ocean, a distance of about 1½ miles. Late at night the pub-lined street is also the setting for "the Duval crawl."

Coral Castle, in Homestead. Located on U.S. 1 Southwest 286 Street on your way to the Keys, Coral Castle is a living testimony to "the magic and power of love." It seems a heartsick Latvian named Ed Leedskalnin was jilt-ed by the 16-year-old girl and made his way to south Florida, where he spent the next 25 years carving 1,100 tons of coral into pieces of furniture and other unwieldy artifacts, including a table shaped like the state of Florida, all in memory of her. What he did for love, or rather how he did it, is still a mystery, since he weighed only 97 pounds and did not use any heavy machinery to move the blocks of coral. (One lunatic-fringe tome suggests he had the help of aliens from flying saucers.) When the neighbors came around to look, he stopped working until they left. He died of starvation, it's said, in 1951, with thousands of dollars hidden around the coral house. There's a Psychic Fair held on the grounds on the fourth Saturday of every month, but if they know what happened, they'll never tell (☎ 305/248-6344).

Theatre des Seances, Key West. Take in some table-rapping or a message from your late great-aunt Tess in Key West's Theatre des Seances. A 19th-century parlor at Porter Mansion at 429 Caroline St. at Duvall Street is the location for Victorian-era "love and romance spirit seances." Reservations are required, at least from the world of the living, and one or more seances is scheduled each evening at 7 and 9pm for groups of 4 to 13 participants. Fee is $30 a person (☎ 305/292-2040).

Flipper's grave, Grassy Key. Yes, that Flipper, whose real name was Mitzi. A 30-foot-high monument to a mother and baby dolphin is also on the site, on U.S. 1 at MM 59 on Grassy Key, as is the Dolphin Research Center (see "Nine Watery Wonders," below) (☎ **305/289-1121**).

Fat Albert, the spying balloon, Cudjoe Key. Fat Albert bobs around 2,000 feet above Cudjoe Key (when he isn't blown off his tether) watching for drug dealers in small planes and boats heading across the Florida straits. His avoirdupois is made up of millions of bucks of electronic surveillance gear.

The Perky Bat Tower, Sugarloaf Key. Not a celebration of energetic nocturnal flying mammals, but rather an effort to lure same to devour the mosquitoes that were the scourge of the area. Built on Sugarloaf Key in 1929 by a real estate promoter named R. C. Perky, the tower was supposed to bring in bats so Perky's resort would be bug-free. Perky, his casino, cabins, and fishing resort are long-gone, but the bat tower still stands. And the mosquitoes are still flying. Located on U.S. 1 near MM 17 on the Gulf side.

Tupperware World Headquarters and Gatorland, Kissimmee. We're usually torn between the two, located near each other on Route 441 between Orlando and Kissimmee. Since Tupperware no longer gives tours, though, we now head for Gatorland with its alligators and crocodiles. You walk into the jaws of a plaster alligator, then watch live alligators leap out of the water to snag a mouthful of chicken dangling overhead in the Gator Jumparoo show. Old-time gator wrestling, an alligator breeding marsh, even a smokehouse offering tidbits of smoked gator ribs and deep-fried gator nuggets are highlights of one of the few old Florida roadside attractions remaining amid the Disney/Universal virtual world. Gatorland is at 14501 S. Orange Blossom Trail, open daily 9am to 6pm. Call ☎ **800/393-JAWS** for details.

TEN SPECIAL SPLURGES

1. **Book a stay on Little Palm Island.** Book a day or two at the most laid-back and romantic, not to mention expensive, resort in the Keys, reached by launch from Little Torch Key at MM 28.5 by guests whose reservations are in the computer. Snorkeling, bonefishing, sunset sailing, and fine dining are some of the popular activities. At night you snuggle down in one of 30 South Pacific-style ersatz grass huts that miraculously conceal a Jacuzzi tub, minibar, and queen-sized bed. Nonresident guests may reserve for lunch or dinner (☎ **800/343-8567**).

2. **Have lunch at Louie's Backyard.** In Key West's varied dining scene, most visitors regard Louie's as the obligatory dinner out, but we like lunch better, sitting at outdoor tables with a view of sailboats gliding past. A warm fried-chicken salad (spears of chicken atop greens) is a house special, and fresh grilled fish are accompanied by Cuban black beans, fried plantains, and lime wedges. Reserve well ahead at this eatery, at 700 Waddell Ave. Musician Jimmy Buffett used to eat here when he lived in the big white house next door (☎ **305/294-1061**).

TALKIN' CONCH: A KEYS GLOSSARY

Conch (konk): A native of the Keys; named for a chewy gastropod that inhabits local waters.

Eyebrow house: A house where the second-story roof overhangs the windows.

Fretsaw: Gingerbread trim on houses, much of it applied by ships' carpenters from termite-resistant hardwood.

Hardwood hammock: Not a bed slung between two posts, but a dense grove of small hardwood trees growing on a limestone reef in a marshy area at a slightly higher elevation so they form humps.

Mangrove: Small, broadleaf, evergreen tropical trees growing in marshes or tidal shores with much of their root systems exposed.

Shotgun house: A long hall you could shoot a bullet through that runs from front to back through a house.

Square grouper: What local fishermen call bales of marijuana bobbing in the water, thrown overboard by drug smugglers when the Coast Guard is near.

Stranger: Everybody on the Keys who's not a conch.

Tourist tree: The gumbo-limbo, whose peeling red-orange bark looks like the results of a bad sunburn. 🚐

3. **Shell out for a lazy open-air tour of Key West.** The colorful Conch Train and the Old Town Trolley both leave from Mallory Square and offer 90 minutes of corny, good-natured jokes aimed at the over-50 cruise ship day-trippers. You'll get good views of 60 or so must-see spots around town. Tickets for each are $18 adults, $9 children 4 to 12.

4. **Expand your imagination with a Ghost Tour of Key West.** It leaves nightly from Noah's Ark, 416 Fleming St. (☎ **305/294-9255** or 305/293-8009). You'll be led on a lantern evening stroll down Key West's shadowy lanes and discover the ghosts and legends of this haunted paradise. Tours go out year-round, but space is limited, and reservations are required. Tickets are $18 adults, $10 children under 12.

5. **Take a cat to see the coral.** The Amoray Diver, a motorized catamaran from Key Largo's Amoray Dive Resort, can take 49 snorkelers or 34 scuba divers out to the Key Largo National Marine Sanctuary for some coral reef viewing. Cost is $54.50 per person and includes tank and weights. Reservations are requested (☎ **305/451-3595**).

6. **Take a snuba tour.** A combination of diving and snorkeling in which the air source is in a surface raft and the diver goes only 20 feet down, snuba tours offer underwater sightseeing at John Pennecamp Coral Reef State Park and Key Largo National Marine Sanctuary. No dive certification is necessary. Tours ($35–$70) are 45 minutes to a half day. Call them in Key Largo at ☎ **305/451-6391.**

7. **Parasail 600 feet above Key West from a catamaran.** Anyone can do it, say the people at Fury Catamarans, promising dry takeoffs and

landings from the boat and tandem rides. Hey, enjoy, we'll be watching from the Hilton with a cold drink in our hands. Departures are from the Hilton Marina; reservations are required (☎ **305/294-8899**).

8. **Take a night off from the RV to sleep in a lighthouse or aboard a houseboat.** Faro Blanco Marine Resort in Marathon, built in the 1940s, offers both. Call ☎ **800/759-3276** for information.

9. **Drop by Cheeca Lodge for seafood.** If you want to splurge on a politically correct seafood meal, this Islamorada hotel restaurant is your kind of place. The ever-ecoaware lodge took all conch dishes off its menu several years ago because taking the mollusks in U.S. waters is illegal; therefore, all conch is imported from The Bahamas and is "neither indigenous nor fresh," says Chef Dawn Seiber, a native of the Keys. She serves Jamaican seafood soup instead of conch chowder and buys much of her fish and shellfish from seafood farms. Polish off a piece of passion-fruit pie for dessert. Located on U.S. 1 at MM 82. Call ☎ **800/ 327-2888** for reservations.

10. **Take a seaplane to Fort Jefferson.** Head to the Dry Tortugas, 68 miles west of Key West, to see the remains of the 19th-century brick fort that was the Civil War prison for Dr. Samuel Mudd, who set John Wilkes Booth's leg, broken on his jump to the stage of Fords Theater after he assassinated Abraham Lincoln. Mudd was accused of conspiring in the crime, although it is generally believed he was innocent of any knowledge of it. He was released in 1867 after a heroic stint taking care of 270 men who came down with yellow fever. While the visit itself is free, getting there costs around $179 a person for a half-day trip. You can look down into the clear water from the plane and see numerous shipwrecks below, as well as sharks and rays. The fort itself is as eerie and haunted a place as you'll ever see under a hard blue sky and dazzling sunlight. Call **Key West Air Service (☎ 888/FLY-FORT)** or **Seaplanes of Key West (☎ 305/294-0709)**.

GREAT TAKE-OUT (OR EAT-IN) TREATS

The cheeseburgers at Jimmy Buffett's Margaritaville, Key West. Those at Jimmy's restaurant are almost as famous as the song of the same name; most customers order margaritas as well. It's at 500 Duval St. (☎ **305/292-1435**).
The Key lime pie at Manny and Isa's Kitchen, Islamorada. You can buy by the slice or the pie to eat in or take out. They grow the Key limes out back. If it's mealtime, sample their Cuban black bean soup or conch fritters too. Located at MM 81.6 (☎ **305/664-5019**).
The Key lime pie at Key West Key Lime Pie Company, Key West. If the urge for Key lime pie overwhelms you, head for the Key West Key Lime Pie Company for a sublime take-out wedge of pie in a plastic container with a fork. Some eaters were so overcome, they ate it standing up right in the

shop. Other, more discreet nibblers like us, waited until we got outside. Delectable (☎ 800/872-2714 or 305/294-6567; www.keylimepiecompany.com)!

Seafood at the Half-Shell Raw Bar. A longtime local favorite, with paper plates, plastic forks, and a big turnover of tables around mealtime. It sells shrimp from the local fleet, as well as clams and oysters on the half-shell and a tasty conch chowder. The cracked conch—breaded and fried conch steak—is yummy. It's on Margaret Street in Key West (☎ **305/294-7496**).

The Sloppy Joes at Sloppy Joe's, Key West. The sandwich may or may not have originated here, but it's a good story. It serves the Original Sloppy Joe as well as the Sloppy Joe Quesadilla. The bar is hard to miss; just follow the cruise ship day-trippers to 201 Duval St. (☎ **305/294-5717**).

Weekly Thanksgiving dinner at Pepe's, Key West. Pepe's is a resoundingly local Key West eatery, there since 1909 and noted for huge breakfasts and haphazard decor that includes everything from Christmas lights to nude paintings. Every Thursday night a Thanksgiving dinner is served, along with oysters from Apalachicola Bay (safest to eat cooked). It's at 806 Caroline St. (☎ **305/294-7192**).

Cuban sandwiches at the Five Brothers Grocery, Key West. Get them to take out. Alternatively, try the hot, deep-fried cornmeal bollitos with a buchi, a Cuban coffee similar to espresso. At the corner of Southard and Grinnell (☎ **305/296-5205**).

Street food, Key West. Key West street vendors profer conch fritters, Cuban coffee, hot dogs, piña coladas, and dolphin sandwiches (no, not Flipper, but the fish Hawaiians call mahimahi).

Turtle steak, and so on, at the Green Turtle Inn, Islamorada. Years ago, the Green Turtle Inn was the first (and last) place we ever knowingly ate alligator, and, yes, it does taste sort of like chicken. These days it serves farm-raised turtle steaks and chowders, as well as its own canned conch chowder, politically correct turtle soup (they use north Florida river turtles), and Key lime pie filling to go if you want to stock up the RV. It's old-fashioned, good-natured, eclectic, and eccentric, as well as usually crowded, with only a faint whiff of tourist trap. At MM 81 (☎ **305/664-9031**).

"The world's best fish sandwiches" at Craig's Restaurant, Tavernier. The best is grouper, but sometimes they're out, and substitute catfish or dolphin (mahimahi). Messy to eat, it's on grilled whole wheat bread with cheese, tomato, lettuce, and tartar sauce. Good if you're looking for a quick and casual lunch. At MM 90.5 (☎ **305/852-9424**).

The fresh grilled seafood at Kelly's, Key West. Its full name is Kelly's Caribbean Bar, Grill and Brewery. It's on Whitehead and Caroline, just off Duval, and the grilled seafood is topped off with a boutique brew (☎ **305/293-8484**).

Traditional Native American dishes at The Miccosukee Restaurant, near Shark Valley. Located on Tamiami Trail (U.S. 41) near Shark Valley, Miccosukee serves traditional dishes like fried catfish, pumpkin bread, and

Indian fry bread (crunchy deep-fried bread dough), which can be topped with ground beef and garnishes to make an Indian taco (☎ 305/223-8380).
Fresh seafood at Disney's Boardwalk resort. The Flying Fish Café makes an evening out special with fresh seafood that's beautifully prepared and served. It's not cheap, and reservations should be made well ahead of time, but the food is so much better than the other Disney venues, perhaps because it's operated by a chef from outside the Mouseworks. Before or after, stroll along the boardwalk and pretend you're in Atlantic City. 1800 Epcot Resorts Blvd., Buena Vista, FL (☎ 407/939-5100).

NINE WATERY WONDERS

1. **John Pennekamp Coral Reef State Park.** Near Key Largo and part of the Florida Keys National Marine Sanctuary, this is a 78-square-mile underwater park made up of reefs like those that formed the Keys. The living coral colonies are endlessly fascinating for divers and snorkelers; there are underwater observation rooms and glass-bottomed boats for those who want to keep their heads above water. The reef has more than 50 forms of coral and 500 species of tropical fish, and is the only living coral reef in the continental United States. It's at MM 102.5 (☎ 305/451-1202; www.myflorida.com).

2. **Islamorada.** Islamorada is a popular fishing resort area on Upper Matecumbe Key with the Theater of the Sea offering dolphin and sea lion shows plus a shark pool and aquarium; Lignumvitae Key State Botanical Site (☎ 305/664-2540), displays rare lignum vitae trees, a dense wood that can outlast steel; and Indian Key, a formerly settled key where John James Audubon visited in 1832. The latter two are uninhabited islands that can be toured with park rangers, but you have to get there by local boat service. Robbie's charges $15 for adults, $10 for kids. Boat departures are timed to coincide with tour times (☎ 305/664-9814).

3. **Grassy Key.** Located near Marathon Shores, Grassy Key is the location of the Dolphin Research Center at MM 59, where visitors can high-five a dolphin by joining a Dolphin Splash party. Bring your bathing suit because you'll be standing on a sunken platform in the pool as they come to visit you. They get in free, you pay $70 which also includes a 2-hour tour through the facilities. If you just want to visit the center, without the splash (and without an appointment), the admission price is $15. For information and reservations, call ☎ 305/289-1121.

4. **Harry Harris County Park.** A wide expanse of sandy beach with palm trees and picnic tables facing the Atlantic, in Key Largo at MM 92. If you have your pet along, it may have to stay in the RV; check the signage (☎ 305/852-7161).

5. **Jules' Undersea Lodge.** Ever want to spend the night underwater? Then make a reservation at Jules' Undersea Lodge, the world's first

underwater hotel, with two bedrooms below the surface and a price starting around $200 a night per person for a party of four. Beginning divers and snorkelers are welcome, they say. It's located at 51 Shoreland Dr., MM 103.2, in Key Largo. Call ☎ 305/451-2353 for information. No alcohol is permitted unless you're on your honeymoon, in which case champagne is permissible. What we wonder is how can they tell if you're really on your honeymoon?

6. **Biscayne National Park.** Biscayne National Park is an aquatic park with 181,500 acres of islands and reefs. Several concessionaires offer boat tours from the park itself. Two shallow-draft, glass-bottomed Reef Rovers set out from the park's Convoy Point headquarters daily and skim lightly over the reefs. Afternoon snorkel and scuba trips (with rental equipment available) last 4 hours, departing at 1:30pm, while morning reef sightseeing tours start at 10am. Headquarters are 9 miles east of Homestead at 9700 SW 328th St. Reservations required (☎ 305/230-7275; www.nps.gov/bisc).

7. **July Underwater Music Festival, Big Pine Key.** Divers listen to an underwater symphony at Looe Key National Marine Sanctuary one Saturday in July from 10am to 4pm. For details, call ☎ 800/USA-ESCA.

8. **Bahia Honda State Park, Bahia Honda Key.** The park has one of the best sandy beaches in the Keys, allowing you the luxury of wading out into the water on sand instead of—ouch—coral. It's 12 miles south of Marathon (☎ 305/872-2353; www.myflorida.com).

9. **Dog Beach, Key West.** Dog Beach, near Louie's Backyard, is the only beach in Key West where owners and dogs can swim together, while the so-called nude canals in an abandoned real estate development on Sugarloaf Key's Sugarloaf Boulevard are where clothing-optional sunbathers gather to catch some rays between dips.

WILDLIFE-WATCHING

There are several wildlife refuges in the Keys, each named for the species that inhabits it. The **Crocodile Lake National Wildlife Refuge** on North Key Largo has the single largest population of alligators in the United States, with as many as 500 in residence. Alligators are the most obvious reptiles, and the one a casual visitor is most likely to see, if he/she is patient enough to watch a floating log in a murky pond to see if that bump on it has an eyeball.

Less frequently seen are the state's numerous nonpoisonous **snakes,** and the three poisonous ones. Most deadly is the dainty, pretty orange-and-black-banded coral snake, but as an old swamper told us once, "He's gonna have to chew on you a long time before you die." Keep your eye out for cottonmouth moccasins sunning on a stretch of boardwalk in a swampy area, or diamondback rattlesnakes in a palmetto patch or hammock.

The shyest of Florida's indigenous fauna is the **manatee**, a 1-ton, plant-eating sea mammal that is also called a "sea cow." Legend has it early sailors thought these were mermaids, but anybody who made a mistake like that must have been away from women a long, long time. The biggest threat to the dwindling manatee population is the south Florida boater with his whirring propellers that tear into the mammal's tender flesh.

The best place to see the manatee up close is at **Homosassa Springs State Wildlife Park,** where a number of them are in residence, either lazily floating around in the water or scarfing down lettuce from their underwater "salad bar." You'll also see Florida alligators and crocodiles and learn the difference between the two during one of the park's excellent Animal Encounters programs. The park is about 90 miles west of Orlando on the Gulf of Mexico off U.S. 19 (☎ 352/628-5343; www.myflorida.com).

The reclusive and beautiful **roseate spoonbill,** although rarely seen, nests in spring. They were once virtually extinct because collectors killed them and sold their wings for hats and fans, not realizing the brilliant orange and rose feathers gradually fade when the bird dies. John James Audubon didn't realize this either, apparently, as he depicted the bird's foliage as pink. He commented that they were hard to kill and their flesh was oily and bad tasting.

Especially in spring, you'll have easier sightings of **osprey,** who usually nest atop utility poles (their nests are big and klutzy looking), and **white egrets,** which stalk haughtily in marshes and ponds. We spotted several from the walkways in **Everglades National Park.** Check in at the Royal Palm Visitor Center, 3 miles past the park entrance; a campground without hookups is nearby. A number of walking trails, most of them over boardwalk, take you into the swamp.

At Big Pine Key, delicate little 30-inch **Key deer,** like miniature white-tailed deer, roam in the **National Key Deer Refuge;** go early in the morning or just before dusk for the best chance of sighting them. There are fewer than 300 left in existence. Stop off at the rangers' office at Pine Key Shopping Center (with the Winn-Dixie), near MM 30.5 off U.S. 1. They'll give you a brochure and map of the area (☎ 305/872-2239; www.southeast.fws.gov).

Also on this key is the **Great White Heron National Wildlife Refuge.** These big, graceful birds are among the most beautiful of all seabirds. Freshwater ponds on the key have led some geologists to suggest it may once have been part of the Appalachian Mountain range. The refuge is located at MM 28–31. For information, call the National Key Deer Refuge (see above).

On the Road

KEY LARGO

Key Largo, the classic 1948 Humphrey Bogart and Lauren Bacall film, was shot almost entirely on a Hollywood soundstage, but that didn't stop the town of Rock Harbor from taking the name Key Largo after clearing it with

The African Queen in Key Largo.

the U.S. Postal Service in 1952, then building a cottage industry around the film's stars, none of whom were in town during the filming. A boat that may have been used in *The African Queen* is on display at the Holiday Inn Key Largo, and, according to local tourist handouts, is "a nostalgic addition to Key Largo's unique old film atmosphere." More recently, the owner added the *Thayer IV* from *On Golden Pond*, which was shot in New Hampshire.

Ironically, the only location in town where some second-unit footage for *Key Largo* was actually shot was the funky Caribbean Club Bar at MM 104, and that was at the original, which burned down in the 1950s and was replaced with the present club.

The old **Tavernier Hotel** in the downtown district claims to be the first hotel in the Keys, and managed to survive the great, unnamed Labor Day hurricane of 1935. Back then, weathermen didn't do cute stand-ups in front of cameras, so tropical storms didn't need names.

Old hands say the upper Keys have the best fishing, especially around Marathon and Islamorada, the latter usually billed as Sportfishing Capital of the World, but visitors with visions of Hemingway dancing in their heads keep driving south to Key West before booking a boat.

Bonefish and permit are in shallow waters of mangrove islets on the Gulf of Mexico side (but not as easy to catch as they look), while marlin and sailfish are deep-water dwellers that require a captain and crew to take you out into the Atlantic. Charter boats and guides can be found at Garrison Bight Marina on Palm Avenue in Key West or at one of the charter fishing fleet companies on U.S. 1 just south on Palm Avenue.

KEY WEST
Part One: Cayo Hueso Becomes Key West

The 8-square-mile coral island used to be called *Cayo Hueso* (means "bone key"), the name deriving from piles of human bones found by early visitors. No one is quite sure where the bones came from, but they were already in place when the first non-Indians, a bunch of buccaneers, hit town. Ponce de León had probably discovered the Keys in 1513 as he worked his way north looking for the Fountain of Youth, which he found in St. Augustine.

In 1815, Cayo Hueso belonged to Juan Pablo Salas of St. Augustine under a Spanish land grant, but when Florida became part of the United States in 1821, he sold it to John Simonton, an American businessman, for $2,000. Simonton called in the U.S. Navy's Anti-Pirate Squadron, drove out the pirates, and put the place under military control. From that day forward until 1974, there was always a navy base on Key West.

By the 1830s, the island, now anglicized into Key West, was inhabited primarily by "wreckers" who made their livings from what was euphemistically known in the 1800s as the "wrecking trade," salvaging sunken ships— even perhaps, as some historians suggest, luring those same ships to wreck onto the shoals and then salvaging them. In a good season, there would be more than a ship a week run aground. The best wreckers, it's said, lived aboard their ships so they could get to a wreck even more quickly.

Most were Cockneys from The Bahamas, along with Loyalists to the British Crown after the Americans won the Revolutionary War, plus a polyglot assortment of Cubans, seafarers from New England, and, later, émigrés from the Civil War.

Old houses of Key West.

Florida Keys Campgrounds

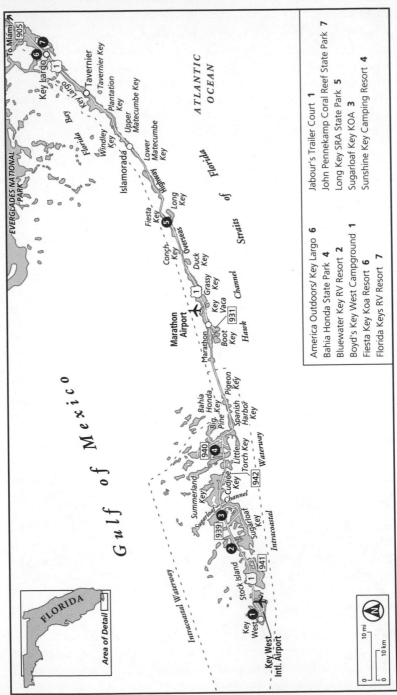

America Outdoors/ Key Largo **6**
Bahia Honda State Park **4**
Bluewater Key RV Resort **2**
Boyd's Key West Campground **1**
Fiesta Key Koa Resort **6**
Florida Keys RV Resort **7**

Jabour's Trailer Court **1**
John Pennekamp Coral Reef State Park **7**
Long Key SRA State Park **5**
Sugarloaf Key KOA **3**
Sunshine Key Camping Resort **4**

KEY LIME PIE

Key limes, which in this country grow only in the Florida Keys, are not green, but yellow fruits the size of a golf ball, with green speckles. Ergo, the filling in a genuine Key lime pie is also yellow, not green. The first Key lime pie is thought to have been whipped up in the kitchen of the Curry Mansion in Key West, now a popular Caroline Street bed-and-breakfast.

But both the buccaneers and the wreckers missed the greatest haul of loot ever recovered by American salvage hunters: **Mel Fisher's treasure trove** from the sunken Spanish galleons *Atocha* and *Santa Margarita*, millions of dollars worth of gold bars, silver coins, and emeralds. The ships sank off Key West in 1622 on their way back to Spain, laden with the riches of the New World. Some key pieces of the indescribably valuable find are on display in Fisher's museum at Whitehead and Greene streets. (On our first visit there more than a decade ago, Fisher's mother sold us the tickets and showed us around with visible maternal pride.)

At the turn of the 20th century, the city, already the richest settlement in Florida, was the cigar-producing capital of the world. Many of the 6,000 cigar makers were Cubans who flocked here to find work.

The wrecking industry bottomed out in 1921—"The navy put channel markers and buoys to warn the ships about the reef," locals said—and the cigar industry burned out when investors in Ybor City, near Tampa, lured the cigar manufacturers away with promises of fewer labor problems.

By the late 1920s, Key West had become a backwater and one of the poorest places in the United States. In 1934, with 80% of the population unemployed, the city declared bankruptcy, and the federal government sent in a New Deal administrator called Julius Stone who decided to turn the island into a tropical tourist paradise. He put people to painting and cleaning up the town and the beaches, training young women to be hotel maids, even suggesting that all the local men wear shorts to appear picturesque.

The plan was a huge success in the winter of 1934–35, but the Labor Day hurricane of 1935 swept away the railway tracks and with them all the hopes and dreams. Tourism increased again after World War II, spurred by sailors who had been stationed here.

Part Two: A Bird in the Bush
Writers and artists have always been fascinated with Key West. One of the first was **John James Audubon,** who arrived in 1832 aboard the cutter *Marion*. A crack shot, the Haitian-born painter, naturalist, and egoist had worked his way through the American south as a tutor and dancing master,

Key West Highlights & Campgrounds

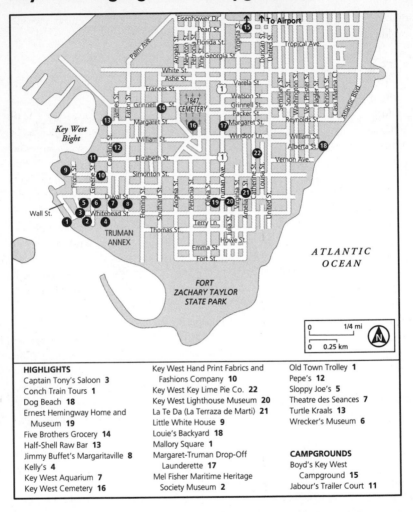

often biting the hand that fed him. His modus operandi was to kill as many birds from a species as he could because he enjoyed shooting, then mount one or two of them and arrange them in a habitat, often tree branches. While Audubon usually drew the birds himself, a young assistant—one or another always traveled with him—filled in the backgrounds. In Key West, Audubon produced two bird drawings, one of them a white-crowned pigeon perched on a branch of an orange-blossomed Geiger tree.

This type of tree was introduced from the West Indies by Captain John Geiger, who also built the house now called the Audubon House, although Audubon's connection with it is tenuous. However, there is a Geiger tree in the yard of the Whitehead Street property. The tree, by the way, was not named for the captain, and the house in its present incarnation was not at this location in 1832. The island has a long tradition of inhabitants moving buildings from one spot to another.

Part Three: The Further Adventures of Key Weird

Its detractors may sometimes refer to Key West as "Key Weird," but it's certainly a town that knows how to party.

April's **Conch Republic Days** celebrate the time not long ago (April 1982) when the Border Patrol put up roadblocks on Route 1 to look for drugs and illegal aliens. Tourists took one look and turned back, and the town's income fell off considerably. So Key West proclaimed itself the Conch Republic and seceded from the United States, then applied for foreign aid. This weeklong celebration usually involves silliness such as a bed race and a lot of drinking.

Tennessee Williams's birthday, March 25, is often an occasion for celebrating, as is the weekly **Doris Day Night** at a local gay bar, and, of course, every day at **sunset,** when there's a lot of drinking.

We're fond of the laundromat at the corner of Margaret and Truman streets, named, logically enough, the **Margaret-Truman Drop-off Launderette.**

The big brick building down by the dock was designed in 1890 as a government office building (or so a Conch tour guide told us), and the engineer had almost completed it when he died. A second engineer was sent in from up north and made them start all over again, digging a huge basement for oil-fired heating equipment, adding chimneys, and making the roofs steep enough "so the snow could slide off."

Designer-icon Calvin Klein is said to have paid a million dollars for a house locals call the **Bird Cage** or Octagon House at 712 Eaton St., only one of a group of turn-of-the-20th-century Bahamian-style wooden mansions on that street. Ship's carpenters were often the builders, and salvaged wood from wrecked ships was sometimes worked into the structures.

Kelly's Caribbean Bar, Grill and Brewery, at 301 Whitehead St. near Caroline, one of several eateries owned by actress Kelly McGillis, is in the old Pan American Airways building. Before that, it was the Pigeon House, used to raise homing pigeons sent out with boats so if the crew got into trouble at sea, the captain could release the bird, and help could be sent.

HEMINGWAY'S CATS

The six-toed cats all over the grounds of the Hemingway House are said to be descended from Hemingway's own cat. While far short of the 70 the author kept at his Cuban farm, the Key West team numbered 42 at our last visit and cost $700 a month to feed.

A sidewalk chalk drawing of one of Key West's most famous citizens.

The city's sizable gay population has done more than anyone to restore the old Conch houses, setting up a flourishing bed-and-breakfast community, and glamorizing the mainstream in this laid-back, peaceable community.

But some of the high hilarity of the 1980s softened somewhat around the millennium, in some cases to the detriment of the lounge scene. **La Te Da** (local nickname of the La Terraza de Marti, 1125 Duval St.; ☎ **305/296-6707**) and its Sunday afternoon tea dances have toned down the campiness, with no more owner-and-dog look-alike contests like the one described by Joy Williams in her guidebook *The Florida Keys*. "The Look-Alike trophy went to Frank Cicalese and his Chihuahua Sam. They appeared as identical, perfectly pink Easter bunnies in identical bunny suits, slippers, and hats, carrying matching Easter baskets. Both wore sunglasses."

Getting Around Key West

Rent a **bicycle** or **moped** from one of the shops along Truman Avenue, especially if you're traveling in a motor home without a tow vehicle (that way you can leave the rig plugged in). If you don't want to do the pedaling yourself, hail a **pedicab** and let a well-tanned and shapely young thing pedal you around. That's how they stay well tanned and shapely.

You can also hop aboard an **Old Town Trolley** or **Conch Tour Train** (tickets are sold in Mallory Square or aboard the vehicles). These open-air trams zigzag across town for 90 minutes while a friendly driver fills you in with yarns, anecdotes, and a collection of corny jokes.

Three Key West Sights

The Little White House. Where Harry and Bess Truman vacationed in winter 11 times during his presidency, beginning in 1946. Recently restored to

> ## THE PRESUNSET EVACUATION
>
> Cruise ships that call at Key West, an increasingly popular port, are encouraged to sail away at least 45 minutes before sunset so their bulky lines don't block the view from Mallory Pier.

the 1940s period with original furniture, the museum offers a guided tour and video. Open daily, it's at 111 Front St. (☎ **305/294-9911**).

The Ernest Hemingway Home and Museum. Where the author lived with his second wife, Pauline, from 1931 to 1940, is a National Historic Landmark. Self-guided or escorted tours are available through the house and the gardens, where a number of feral six-toed cats wander at will. Open daily, it's at 907 Whitehead St. (☎ **305/294-1136**).

The Key West Aquarium. You can hand-feed sharks, pet a barracuda, or reach into a touch tank to feel sea creatures. The ticket is good for several days if you want to return. Open daily (☎ **305/296-2051**).

Five Things to Do in Key West for $10 or Less

1. **Visit the Mel Fisher Maritime Heritage Society Museum.** Heft a solid gold bar and see silver bars, emeralds, and golden chalices from 17th-century Spanish galleons discovered by the late treasure hunter Mel Fisher. Open daily 9:30am to 5:30pm year-round, 200 Greene St. (☎ **305/294-2633**). Admission $6.50 adults, $2 children.

2. **Touch turtles at the old Turtle Kraals.** Kraals is a South African term for corrals. These kraals once processed turtle steaks and turtle soup, but are now the home of the Florida Marine Conservancy. Sick and injured sea turtles and birds are tended here, and there's a touch tank for kids. Free. Open daily from 11am to 1am. Land's End Village at Land's End Marina at the Turtle Kraals Restaurant & Bar (☎ **305/294-2640**).

3. **Visit the Wrecker's Museum.** Also called the Oldest House, it's where a sea captain and his nine daughters once lived. The 1829 house displays memorabilia of the wrecking business; there's also an elaborately furnished period dollhouse. Open daily year-round, 322 Duval St. (☎ **305/294-9502**).

4. **Take a free guided tour of the Key West Hand Print Fabrics and Fashions Company.** Go backstage in a former 19th-century tobacco warehouse to watch hand-printed fabrics being designed and sewn into tropical sportswear, fabric toys, bedding, place mats, and napkins. Open daily 9am to 6pm year-round, 201 Simonton St. (☎ **305/294-9535**).

5. **Climb the stairs at the Key West Lighthouse Museum.** A spiral staircase inside leads up to a panoramic view of the island from this 1847

"AND THEN I WROTE ..."

Key West claims eight Pulitzer Prize winners among its residents, and, according to a knowledgeable local, more than 100 published authors live there at present.

Writer John dos Passos passed through here in the 1920s, looked around, and recommended it to fellow writer Ernest Hemingway, who arrived in 1928, finished off *A Farewell to Arms* in a rented house on Summer Street in 1929, then bought a fine house on Whitehead Street in 1931.

To Have and Have Not, published in 1937, is what Hemingway called his Key West novel. One of the "have-nots" was Harry Morgan, a local fishing charter-boat operator reduced to rumrunning and smuggling Chinese immigrants into the United States. The author, however, was clearly one of the "haves," with a wealthy wife, a limestone mansion, the first swimming pool in Key West, and a 40-foot boat named *Pilar*.

Somewhere in the mid-1930s, while still married to his second wife, Pauline, Hemingway spotted journalist Martha Gelhorn sitting on a barstool at Sloppy Joe's. She would become his third wife in a short and tumultuous marriage after he divorced Pauline in 1940 and left Key West for good.

"You'll like Key West," Papa is reported to have written to a friend 2 decades later. "It's the St-Tropez of the poor."

---

lighthouse, which was the recipient of an award-winning restoration in 1987. Exhibits tell the history of the town and the Keys. Open daily except Christmas, 938 Whitehead St. (☎ 305/294-0012).

Key West at Night

The Keys' theme song is about wasting away in **Margaritaville,** easy enough to do at singer Jimmy Buffett's popular eatery and nightspot of the same name where you'll hear you-know-what played frequently if not incessantly. It's at 500 Duval St. (☎ 305/292-1435). If you want something more down to earth, check out the **Caribbean Club** at MM 104.5 in Key Largo, the only local location used for the eponymous movie. But don't expect Bogart/Bacall types; it's more of a redneck-and-biker bar (☎ 305/451-4466).

Hemingway's favorite bar in Key West, as everybody knows, was called **Sloppy Joe's,** and you can't miss the large bar with neon signs screaming the name at 201 Duval St. (☎ 305/294-5717). When Hemingway drank there, however, Sloppy Joe's was down the street at the present site of **Captain Tony's Saloon,** 428 Greene St. (☎ 305/294-1838), which used to be owned by Tony Tarracino, a former Key West mayoral candidate. Late one night back in 1937, Sloppy Joe Russell and his barflies moved the bar furniture from the old building over to the new building to protest a $1 raise in the rent on the former.

Then there's the famous **"Duval crawl,"** an evening spent prowling mile-long Duval Street, checking out the bars and restaurants, the attire of the natives, and the general wackiness. Once upon a time, six different taverns along this street were named Bucket of Blood.

Listen for the unique Key West style of jazz called Conchtown rhythm, a blend of New Orleans jazz and calypso.

Campground Oases in the Keys

John Pennekamp Coral Reef State Park. Located at MM 102, this park has 47 gravel sites with water and 30- and 50-amp electrical hookups, shade, flush toilets, showers, sanitary dump, swimming, fishing, and boat rentals. The reef lies several miles offshore, so you can just jump out of the RV and dive in. No pets (☎ **305/451-1202** for reservations; myflorida.com).

America Outdoors, Key Largo. Right on the Gulf of Mexico between MM 97 and 98, America Outdoors has swimming, fishing, boating, a marina, and boat rentals. Rates are $45 to $60. The 154 sites provide water and 20- and 30-amp electricity, but only 41 have sewers. There is a dump station as well, plus mobile sewer service (☎ **305/852-8054;** www.aokl.com).

Florida Keys RV Resort. At MM 106 in Key Largo, 22 miles south of Homestead, this place has 139 sites, some of them shaded and all with water and 15- and 30-amp electricity. The office is modem-friendly, and rates are $30 to $35, including cable TV (☎ **305/451-6090**).

Fiesta Key KOA Resort. Located at MM 70 on Long Key, the campground has 288 sites with full or partial hookups, 20- and 30-amp electric, flush toilets, showers, sanitary dump, laundry, groceries, heated pool and spa, adult recreation room, boat ramp, and a dock. Boat rentals available to registered campers. Pets are permitted, but rates are high—$60 to $75 a night (☎ **800/ 562-7730** or 305/664.4922; www.koa.com).

One of Florida's many giant oranges.

MIRACLE OF THE KEYS

Where Card Sound Road runs into Route 905 at North Key Largo, you'll find the Crocodile Lake National Wildlife Refuge, some 12,000 acres of hammock and mangrove wetlands that is home to six endangered species, including the alligator, the wood rat, and the cotton mouse.

It could also be called the modern-day miracle of the Keys when it replaced a proposed 2,800-unit "faux Mediterranean" housing development called Port Bougainville, which would have featured man-made lakes and canals and drive-in boat garages. Despite a series of articles in *The Miami Herald* showing a pattern of political chicanery and conflicts of interest by Monroe County officials, the project continued to plow ahead.

The proposed site was atop the most fragile ecosystem in south Florida, and the resulting "big pollution dump," as ardent environmentalist Captain Ed Davidson called it, would have ruined the living coral reefs in Everglades National Park, John Pennekamp Coral Reef State Park, and Biscayne National Underwater Park. (See "Nine Watery Wonders," earlier in this chapter.)

It would be nice to say the miracle happened solely because of the relentless battles of Captain Davidson, who operated the sightseeing boats at Biscayne National Park. But even his determined fight, which included a lawsuit he filed as president of the Florida Keys Audubon Society under the Endangered Species Act, only caused nuisance and delays. The project buckled under its own weight, due partly to the delays, and the developers went bankrupt. The property was ultimately purchased by the state of Florida, the Nature Conservancy, and the U.S. Fish and Wildlife Service. 🚐

Long Key SRA State Park, Layton. At MM 67, Long Key SRA has 60 sites with water and electrical hookups, flush toilets, showers, ocean front, fishing, and boat rentals. Most are shaded. There's a well-labeled nature walk and some good bird-watching on the flats. No pets (☎ **305/664-4815;** myflorida.com).

Bahia Honda State Park. At MM 37, Bahia Honda has a 48-site campground with water and 20- and 30-amp electrical hookups, flush toilets and showers, some shade, sanitary dump, fishing, swimming, boating, and a marina. The beach is good, and there are wading birds and a small nature trail. No pets and no slide-outs. For reservations, call ☎ **305/872-2353;** myflorida.com.

Sunshine Key Camping Resort. At MM 39, Sunshine Key has 405 sites with water and 30- and 50-amp electric, 302 with full hookups. The park permits pets, but they have to abide by a long list of rules. There's also a private beach, marina, clubhouse, pool, and waterfront sites, as well as nature trails and a bird sanctuary. Rates are $22 to $56 a night, depending on season and site location. For reservations, call ☎ **800/852-0348** or 305/872-2217.

Sugarloaf Key KOA. A private RV park north of Key West at MM 20, with 206 sites, half of them grass and half gravel. Full hookups in most with 20- and 30-amp electricity, cable TV, flush toilets, showers, laundry, groceries, fishing, and swimming pool. Some sites are shaded. Pricey at $33 to $63, it does allow pets. For reservations, call ☎ **800/KOA-7731** or 305/745-3549; www.koa.com.

Bluewater Key RV Resort. On the ocean side at MM 14.5 in Saddlebunch Keys, the resort offers 80 sites, 71 with full hookups, including 30- and 50-amp electricity as well as tiki huts, ocean swimming, heated pool, modem and phone hookups, dog walk, cable TV, and city water. Rates range from $40 to $65. For reservations, call ☎ **800/237-2266.**

Jabour's Trailer Court. If camping in downtown Key West appeals to you, Jabour's Trailer Court at 223 Elizabeth St. has 74 sites with full hookups and cable TV. Don't expect spacious or woodsy spots, but at least you'll be able to leave the rig hooked up and walk wherever you want to go. Slide-outs are not permitted. Flush toilets, showers, sanitary dump; from $40 to $60 a night. For reservations, call ☎ **305/294-5723;** www.kwcamp.com.

Boyd's Key West Campground. Boyd's promises 24-hour security and local bus service at its 6401 Maloney Ave. location. It offers 165 full hookups with 20- and 30-amp electricity, city water, cable TV, ocean swimming, and salt-water fishing, and it's modem-friendly. Some sites are on the water, and the swimming pool is resort-sized with plenty of lounging space. Expect to pay from $30 to $50 a night, and there are some pet restrictions. For reservations, call ☎ **305/294-1465;** www.gocampingamerica.com.

Two Great Side Trips

EVERGLADES NATIONAL PARK

Everglades National Park is not only the world's largest freshwater marsh but also the third largest national park in the lower 48 states, exceeded in size only by Yellowstone and Death Valley.

It is also, unfortunately, our most endangered national park because of encroaching housing developments, agricultural runoff, and several disastrous fires during the past 5 years.

The Everglades has had a human population for some 3,000 to 5,000 years. The Calusa Indians, hunters and gatherers who sometimes grew to 7 feet tall and lived off shellfish, left behind 20-foot mounds of shells, the tallest landmarks in the Everglades. Then came the Spanish with their weapons and European diseases, followed by the Creeks from Georgia and Alabama who fled south. They were called Seminoles by non–Native Americans, and ordered to move to Oklahoma.

But the Seminoles declared war on the United States Army and fought sporadically from the early 1830s to 1859. Today's Native Americans in the Everglades are descendants of the survivors and call themselves Miccosukee.

For decades, politicians fought legislation attempting to protect the Everglades and its fauna, calling it "the alligator and snake swamp bill." But in 1947, President Harry S. Truman dedicated the Everglades National Park.

Everglades National Park

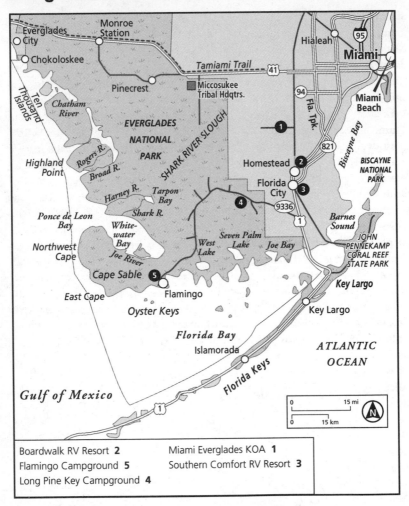

Boardwalk RV Resort **2**	Miami Everglades KOA **1**
Flamingo Campground **5**	Southern Comfort RV Resort **3**
Long Pine Key Campground **4**	

Today's visitor can go sportfishing in Florida Bay, where no commercial fishing is allowed; hike and walk on trails and on boardwalks above the marsh; rent boats, canoes, and bicycles; or take boat cruises into Florida Bay from the Flamingo Marina Store. The park's entrance is south of Homestead off the Florida Turnpike, also known as Route 1 or the Dixie Highway. Turn off onto Route 9336. The turns to the park are well marked. In the 38 miles from the entrance to the **Flamingo Visitor Center** at the southern end of the park, you pass through six different ecosystems, but the changes are so subtle you'll have to watch for them.

A second **visitor center** is at Shark Valley on the Tamiami Trail, U.S. 41, with wildlife tram tours into the sawgrass prairie. For information about the park, call ☎ **305/242-7700**; www.nps.gov/ever.

Campground Oases in the Everglades

Long Pine Key Campground. In Everglades National Park, 10 miles south of the junction of U.S. 1 and Route 9336, the campground has 108 paved sites, toilets, a sanitary dump, and bass fishing on Long Pine Key Lake; no hookups, no reservations. Some sites are shaded. Wooden overlooks and boardwalks in the park allow good bird-watching. Call Everglades National Park at ☎ **305/242-7700.**

Flamingo Campground. Also in Everglades National Park, 38 miles southwest of the park entrance on the park road, a continuation of Route 9336, Flamingo Campground has 234 paved back-in sites with no hookups and no reservations (☎ **305/242-7700**).

Southern Comfort RV Resort. Located in Florida City, Southern Comfort is adjacent to the entrance to the Everglades National Park at 345 East Palm Dr. (also 344th Street), with 350 full hookups, 30- and 50-amp electricity, optional phone hookups, planned activities (including exercise classes), special dinners, tournament shuffleboard courts, and 24-hour security. Rates of $18 to $25 are refreshingly lower that in the Keys, but there are pet restrictions. For reservations, call ☎ **888/477-6909** or 305/248-6909.

Boardwalk RV Resort. This new park at 100 NE 6th Ave. in Homestead boasts a designer clubhouse, nearby championship golf courses, a 24-hour security gate, dance floor, air-conditioned exercise facility, and 170 full-hookup sites with 30- and 50-amp electricity. Rates are $30 to $45 (☎ **888/233-WALK** or 305/248-2487).

Miami Everglades KOA. Six miles west of the junction of U.S. 1 and SW 186th Street near Monkey Jungle and the Miccosukee Indian Casino, the park has a security gate, satellite TV, shade from fruit trees, and wide pull-through sites. We spent the month of February there recently, and found it comfortable and convenient, despite a long rush hour commute into Miami. (The solution? Don't go.) What we really liked was the park's own paved 1-mile walking trail around the perimeter, and the neighboring wholesale plant nurseries and strawberry fields. Some 258 sites offer water and 20- and 30-amp electricity; there is a surcharge for 50-amp electricity. Rates are $28 to $40. For reservations, call ☎ **800/KOA-7732** or 305/233-5300; www.koa.com.

Yacht Haven Park and Marina. A good choice if you're hitting Ft. Lauderdale before or after your Everglades visit, Yacht Haven Park and Marina is off I-95 at exit 27 if you're headed south. If headed north, you have to go to the next exit and double back to access the park. There are 250 sites, mostly paved with patios, back-ins, and 30- and 50-amp hookups. The sites are narrow but deep, which allows alternating front and back sites that makes them seem wider than they are. Reserve in advance in the winter since half of Quebec comes here to escape the Canadian winter. Occasionally there will be an opening for an overnight stay. There are some pet restrictions, and Internet access. Fishing and boating from the Marina. Rates are $30 to $40, less by the week (☎ **800/581-2322** or 954/583-2322).

ORLANDO

The Orlando area offers a dizzying array of diverting, tacky, educational, glitzy, environmentally sensitive, and generally expensive attractions, which you'll be able to find on your own. In fact, given the high-pitched pitches and inescapable billboards, you can't miss them. So we offer our perspective from the point of view of a vacationer traveling by recreation vehicle.

Summer is the busiest season in Orlando, with more than 100,000 admissions a day, but with some of the worst weather, hot and muggy much of the time. If you can possibly visit during any other season, do so.

If not, start out as early in the morning as possible—some attractions are open at 7am—and budget midday time to come back to the RV and its air-conditioning or hit the water parks with a splash.

Entertainment venues are spread out all over the greater Orlando area, including the **Walt Disney World** complex at Lake Buena Vista and **Universal Studios** between Bay Hill and the turnpike. The colorful **Church Street Station,** in downtown Orlando at 129 W. Church St. (☎ 407/422-2434), is a fanciful collection of shops, restaurants, and music halls created from Orlando's railway station and filled with antiques and oddments. One admission ticket gives you access to the shows, but no tickets are needed to visit the shops and restaurants. **Kissimmee,** the world headquarters for Tupperware, is where most of the RV parks are located. It's also where you'll find **Gatorland** (☎ 407/855-5496), open daily 9am to 6pm and located on U.S. 441 next to the Tupperware plant; the **Medieval Times Dinner Tournament,** 4510 U.S. 92 (☎ 407/396-1518), nightly at 8pm (tickets $38.95); and **Xanadu,** the home of the future, located ¼ mile east of the junction of U.S. 192 and State Road 535 (☎ 407/396-1992).

If you're traveling by motor home, you'll find it easier to have a tow car along or to rent a car in the area. Prices are low, and car rental offices abound, some of them on the premises at larger RV parks.

Campground Oases in Orlando

Fort Wilderness Resort. Disney's own campground at the Disney complex (drive ¾ mile from exit 25B off I-4 to the marked entrance) combines Walt Disney World attractions with RV camping—and you don't even need an RV to do it, since it has rental RVs on the premises. There's a free shuttle to all the Disney attractions (although in summer at peak hours, it can be jam-packed) and a full restaurant and lounge on the premises. Some 695 of the 784 paved sites are full hookups with 20-, 30-, and 50-amp electricity, city water, cable TV, and a modem-friendly office. Rates range from $35 to $65. For reservations, call ☎ 407/934-7639.

Orlando-Kissimmee KOA. Located at 4471 Irlo Bronson Highway, this KOA is within driving distance of the major Orlando attractions, and also provides free transportation to certain attractions, on-site car rental, and discount ticket sales. Most of the 340 sites are paved, some are shaded, and all

Orlando/Disney Area

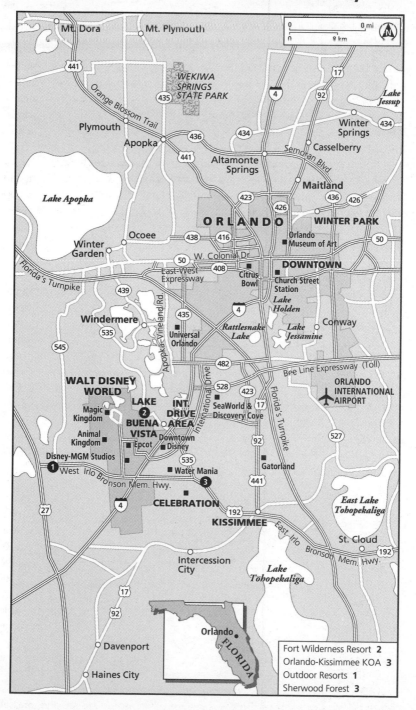

Mt. Dora   Mt. Plymouth

441

WEKIWA
SPRINGS
STATE PARK

435

Orange Blossom Trail

17

92

4

Lake
Jessup

Plymouth

436

434

Winter
Springs

434

Apopka

441

Casselberry

Altamonte
Springs

Semoran Blvd

Lake Apopka

423

426

Maitland

436   426

ORLANDO

WINTER PARK

Ocoee

438   416

Orlando
Museum of Art

50

Winter
Garden

W. Colonial Dr.

50   408

DOWNTOWN

Florida's Turnpike

East-West
Expressway

Citrus
Bowl

Church Street
Station

439

Lake
Holden

435

4

Windermere

535

Universal
Orlando

Rattlesnake
Lake

Lake
Jessamine

Conway

545

482

Bee Line Expressway (Toll)

WALT DISNEY
WORLD

528

423

ORLANDO
INTERNATIONAL
AIRPORT

LAKE 2
BUENA
VISTA

INT.
DRIVE
AREA

SeaWorld &
Discovery Cove

17

Magic
Kingdom

Downtown
Disney

92

527

Animal
Kingdom

Epcot

Gatorland

Disney-MGM Studios

1

West Irlo Bronson Mem. Hwy.

535

441

Water Mania

3

27

4

CELEBRATION

192

East Lake
Tohopekaliga

KISSIMMEE

East Irlo Bronson Mem. Hwy.

St. Cloud

192

Intercession
City

Lake
Tohopekaliga

17

92

Davenport

Orlando

FLORIDA

Fort Wilderness Resort 2
Orlando-Kissimmee KOA 3
Outdoor Resorts 1
Sherwood Forest 3

Haines City

are 30 feet wide. Rates are from $28 to $40 a night (☎ **800/562-7791** or 407/396-2400; www.koa.com).

Sherwood Forest. Located at 5300 Irlo Bronson, Sherwood Forest is just down the road from the KOA, with 362 grassy sites, most of them wide pull-throughs with 30- and 50-amp electricity. Rates are around $29. It even has park models (a sort of mobile home) for rent if you don't have an RV or have friends coming to visit (☎ **800/548-9981** or 407/396-7431).

Outdoor Resorts, Kissimmee. This excellent condo park chain offers both RV sites and RVs for rent, so it's a good place for wannabe RV owners to try out different models. Expect to pay around $30 a night for a site, more for a rental. About 100 of the 980 sites are made available for overnighters and all have full hookups, including 30- and 50-amp electricity. Stay 6 nights and get the 7th free. It's located 5 minutes west of Walt Disney World on U.S. 192 (☎ **800/531-3033;** www.outdoorresorts.com).

⑪ The Blue Ridge Parkway & Skyline Drive

VIRGINIA IS WHERE EIGHT U.S. PRESIDENTS WERE BORN, WHERE 60% OF the Civil War's battles were fought, and where "Taps" was composed, *Dirty Dancing* was filmed, and ChapStick invented. It's where George Marshall wrote his Plan, where Jerry Falwell launched the Moral Majority, and where Disney lost the Third Battle of Manassas when the company proposed to build a Civil War theme park adjacent to the battlefield, which caused such a storm of protest that The Mouse had to back off.

Country singing legend Patsy Cline, who died in a plane crash at the age of 30, was born and buried in Winchester, the Statler Brothers were born and continue to live in Staunton, and Bela Bartok dropped by Hot Springs long enough to compose his Piano Concerto No. 3.

At the Old Fiddlers Convention in Galax, Virginia, some RVing musicians get together.

Typical Blue Ridge farmhouses are restored along the Blue Ridge Parkway.

It's where John-Boy said good night to the rest of the Walton family, where Cyrus McCormick invented the first mechanical reaping machine, where a local doctor named Charles Kenneth Pepper gave his name to a soft drink, and where Rudolph Valentino's 1925 Rolls-Royce came to rest in the Historic Car and Carriage Caravan at Luray Caverns.

Ronald Reagan filmed *Brother Rat* in the cadet barracks at Virginia Military Institute (VMI), the same school where Stonewall Jackson's horse Little Sorrel was stuffed for the VMI Museum. Despite being somewhat moth-eaten, Little Sorrel is their most popular exhibit. The horse fared better than the general, who was accidentally shot by his own troops at Chancellorsville in 1863 and died a week later. The raincoat he was wearing with the bullet hole in evidence is in the same museum. Jackson is buried in two places: his arm in Wilderness Battlefield and the rest of him in Stonewall Jackson Memorial Cemetery in Lexington.

Germany's General Erwin Rommel, "the Desert Fox," came to VMI to study the military tactics of Stonewall Jackson, which he later used in his North Africa campaign against the Allies during World War II.

Western Virginia is where Henry Ford couldn't cash a check—he was on one of his famous camping trips with Thomas Edison and Harvey Firestone (see "RV History" in chapter 1, "Life on the Road: A Personal & Public History of RVing"); where John D. Rockefeller used to throw dimes into the pool by the first tee at the Homestead's Cascades golf course to watch the caddies scramble; and where the late multimillionaire treasure-hunter Mel Fisher came up from Key West to search for the mysterious Beale Treasure, now worth about $23 million (see "Off-the-Wall Attractions," later in this chapter).

Virginia Highlights

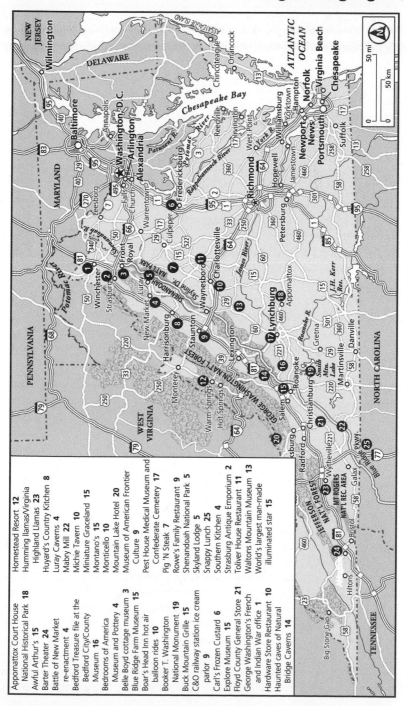

And it's where—we cannot tell a lie—a young George Washington carved his initials in one of the seven wonders of the natural world, Virginia's Natural Bridge.

In the Blue Ridge Mountains of North Carolina, Tom Dula (better known as Tom Dooley of "Hang Down Your Head" fame) was imprisoned in Wilkes County Jail in Wilkesboro after killing his sweetheart, and Frankie Silver, heroine of an even bigger ballad, became the first woman to be hanged in the state when she was tried and put to death in Morganton for murdering her two-timing lover Johnny, who "done her wrong."

RVing the Blue Ridge Parkway & Skyline Drive

The combined mileage of the Blue Ridge Parkway and Skyline Drive is 575 miles, plus any side trips you'll want to add along the route.

If you're going from north to south, Skyline Drive begins at Front Royal, Virginia, and the two-lane road snakes its way 105 miles through Shenandoah National Park, then joins up with the Blue Ridge Parkway at Rockfish Gap near Waynesboro, Virginia. The mileposts are numbered from 0.6 at Front Royal's fee entrance station to 105 at Rockfish Gap and the entrance to the Blue Ridge Parkway, which starts again at Milepost 0. While there are frequent turnouts, not all of them are long enough for a big rig.

The maximum speed limit along the parkway is 45 mph, but don't expect to maintain that, with the curving road and sightseeing traffic.

HITTING THE HIGHLIGHTS

If you diligently drive the route from Washington, D.C., to the Great Smoky Mountains, you could spend less than a week covering it by cutting down on the side trips.

While the ridge routes along Skyline Drive and the Blue Ridge Parkway are beautiful drives, do plan to drop down into parallel routes through country towns and farm communities from time to time to get a better sense of the people who live there.

Plan ahead selectively to cover some of the many battlefields, living history exhibits, and historical homes throughout the Appalachians.

GOING FOR THE LONG HAUL

If you're a craftsman or collector of antiques, you could happily and perhaps profitably spend a season or two ensconced in the Appalachians, where people are friendly and prices are modest. There are crafts courses open to the public and countless antiques shops and rural flea markets. One of the biggest and most famous is the Hillsville Flea Market every Labor Day weekend with more than 2,000 vendors on hand. It's about 8 miles north of the Blue Ridge Parkway, near Mile 200, via old Route 52 or I-77.

If you're a Civil War buff, Virginia will be endlessly fascinating, since 60% of the battles were fought there and battlefields and museums take the subject seriously.

Blue Ridge Highlights & Campgrounds

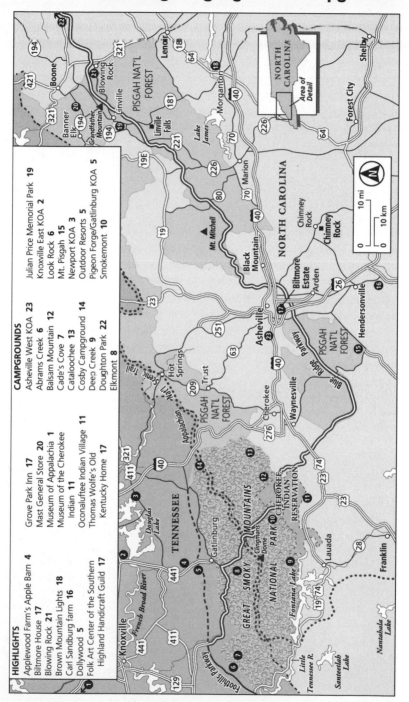

HIGHLIGHTS

Applewood Farm's Apple Barn **4**
Biltmore House **17**
Blowing Rock **21**
Brown Mountain Lights **18**
Carl Sandburg farm **16**
Dollywood **5**
Folk Art Center of the Southern
Highland Handicraft Guild **17**

Grove Park Inn **17**
Mast General Store **20**
Museum of Appalachia **1**
Museum of the Cherokee
Indian **11**
Oconaluftee Indian Village **11**
Thomas Wolfe's Old
Kentucky Home **17**

CAMPGROUNDS

Asheville West KOA **23**
Abrams Creek **6**
Balsam Mountain **12**
Cade's Cove **7**
Cataloochee **13**
Cosby Campground **14**
Deep Creek **9**
Doughton Park **22**
Elkmont **8**

Julian Price Memorial Park **19**
Knoxville East KOA **2**
Look Rock **6**
Mt. Pisgah **15**
Newport KOA **3**
Outdoor Resorts **5**
Pigeon Forge/Gatlinburg KOA **5**
Smokemont **10**

Travel Essentials

WHEN TO GO

Early spring through late fall is best. Dogwood and wildflowers begin to bloom in April. Peak time for the showiest blooms is mid-May to mid-June for flame azalea and mountain laurel, with June the best month for the vivid purple Catawba rhododendron. Craggy Gardens around Mile 365 is a particularly good place to see the latter. Autumn foliage creates another peak season as the trees turn color and begin to drop their leaves. Expect sometimes long and slow-moving lines of traffic in spring blossom, late summer, and autumn foliage seasons. Many of the facilities along the route are closed in winter. Plan early morning starts, when the air is usually clearest, and then stop in early afternoon to camp.

WHAT TO TAKE

Bring binoculars, cameras and film, hiking boots, sunscreen, mosquito repellent, detailed area maps, and fishing tackle if you want to go trout fishing. Carry a sweater or jacket even in midsummer because evenings are cool.

WHAT TO WEAR

Casual but smart sportswear is best if you plan to visit resorts or restaurants, especially in fashionable northern Virginia. Along the Blue Ridge Parkway and in North Carolina, things are a bit more casual, so your usual RV garb will pass muster almost everywhere.

TRIMMING COSTS ON THE ROAD

Shop at local fruit stands for fresh produce; you'll find fresh-from-the-farm seasonal fruits and vegetables at prices far below what supermarkets charge.

Fresh fruits and vegetables for sale along the roadsides in Virginia.

Steer clear of commercial theme parks and heavily touted roadside attractions such as Natural Bridge and Luray Caverns. Besides admission fees, they are surrounded by other attractions that seem particularly alluring to children. Instead, take a free hike to a nearby waterfall or scenic overlook.

You'll save money too, if you can **stay self-contained** with overnight stops rather than hooking up at a private campground adjacent to the Parkway. By driving every day, you'll keep the battery charged and can top off water and empty holding tanks in many of the public campgrounds.

WHERE TO GET TRAVEL INFORMATION

For a packet of **Virginia information,** call ☎ **800/VISIT-VA.** It was delivered more promptly than any other state's information in our experience. The website is www.virginia.org.

For **Shenandoah National Park information,** write Route 4, Box 348, Luray, VA 22835 (☎ **540/999-2243;** www.nps.gov/shen).

For information about the **Blue Ridge Parkway,** write 400 BB&T Building, One Pack Square, Asheville, NC 28801 (☎ **828/271-4779;** www. nps.gov/blri).

To get more information about private campgrounds and attractions, contact **Campground Association of Virginia,** 2101 Libbie Ave., Richmond, VA 23230 (☎ **804/288-3065;** www.vhta.org).

For details about state parks, contact **Virginia State Parks Department of Conservation and Recreation,** 203 Governor St., Suite 302, Richmond, VA 23219 (☎ **804/786-1712;** www.dcr.state.va.us/index/).

For reservations in a **state park campground,** call ☎ **800/933-PARK;** www.dcr.state.va.us/index/.

North Carolina Tourism is at 430 N. Salisbury St., Raleigh, NC 27611 (☎ **800/VISIT-NC;** www.visitnc.com).

Tennessee Tourism is at 320 6th Ave. N, #500, Nashville, TN 37243 (☎ **800/TENN-200;** www.state.tn.us/tourdev/).

For **Great Smoky Mountain National Park,** contact ☎ **423/436-1200;** www.nps.gov/grsm.

DRIVING TIPS

- **Check the weather.** Winter is often mild, but periods of fog or rain may make driving larger RVs along the ridge route difficult. In summer, unfortunately, increased pollution and haze along Skyline Drive have reduced visibility tremendously.

- **Don't be a road hog.** Because the two-lane roadways are heavily traveled, RVers should remember to pull out into the frequent overlooks and turnouts to let traffic behind them go past.

- **BYOB.** Southern states have local liquor-control laws governed by the city, county, or community. If you are accustomed to having wine with dinner, it's a good idea to inquire about the restaurant's policy before you go. Some permit diners to bring their own.

The Best Blue Ridge Sights, Tastes & Experiences

TEN TERRIFIC SPOTS WHERE HISTORY COMES ALIVE

1. **Museum of American Frontier Culture, Staunton, Virginia.** Shows us where many of our 18th- and 19th-century settlers came from—neat, small farms in England, Northern Ireland, and the German Rhineland—and a typical Shenandoah Valley farm that reflects the influence of all three. Costumed interpreters carry out daily and seasonal tasks from plowing to planting, spinning to gardening. From I-81, take exit 222, and then follow the signs on 250 west. It's open daily 9am to 5pm in summer, 10am to 4pm in winter. $8 adults, $7.50 seniors, $4 children 6 to 12 (☎ 540/332-7850; www.frontiermuseum.org).

2. **Appomattox Court House National Historical Park, outside Lynchburg, Virginia.** Twenty miles east of Lynchburg via Route 460 to Route 24, the Appomattox Court House has re-created the entire village as it was when Lee surrendered to Grant here. Living history exhibits in summer animate Meeks Store, Woodson Law Office, and Clover Hill Tavern, and there's a museum as well. The park is open daily except major holidays February through November, 9am to 5pm (☎ 804/352-8987; www.nps.gov/apco/index).

3. **Explore Museum, near Roanoke, Virginia.** A living history museum near Roanoke, Virginia, Explore interprets the pre–Civil War period with its Blue Ridge Settlement depicting life on the Virginia frontier in the early 1800s. Historic buildings have been reassembled on-site, including the Hofauger Farmstead, where costumed interpreters cook at the hearth, weave, spin, garden, and tend livestock. Gardens are planted in heirloom seeds, orchards grow traditional varieties of fruit, and farm animals represent breeds that were typical of the time. Open Saturdays and Sundays in April and daily through October. A gift shop sells crafts from the project. Admission adults $8, seniors $6, students $4.50. From the Parkway's Milepost 115, follow the signs to 3900 Rutrough Rd., in a residential area (☎ 800/842-9163; www.explore park.org).

4. **Battle of New Market reenactment, New Market, Virginia.** A reenactment of the 1864 Battle of New Market takes place every May 15, recalling when 247 young cadets, the entire student body of Virginia Military Institute, fought alongside Confederate soldiers against the Union Army. Ten cadets died, including a descendent of Thomas Jefferson, and 47 others lay wounded. The Hall of Valor in the New Market Battlefield Park commemorates the battle. New Market is located in the Shenandoah County of Virginia, near the intersection of I-81 and Route 211. For information, contact the New Market Chamber of Commerce at ☎ 540/740-3212; www.svta.org/New-Market.

Mabry Mill on the Blue Ridge Parkway.

5. **The Blue Ridge Farm Museum, Ferrum, Virginia.** The Farm Museum displays an 1800 German-American farm and the daily life of settlers who came here, with heirloom vegetables, vintage livestock breeds, and costumed interpreters. From Roanoke, take U.S. 220 south to Route 40. Ferrum is about 12 miles southwest off Route 40 west. Call for hours (☎ **540/365-4416;** www.blueridgeinstitute.org).

6. **Mabry Mill, near Meadows of Dan, Virginia.** At Mile 176 of the Blue Ridge Parkway, Mabry Mill is animated with craftsmen and musicians during the summer and fall. Besides the water-powered gristmill and a shop selling its stone-ground flours and meal, there's a coffee shop serving pancakes and country ham. Prepare for a queue on weekends when the locals go. Open May 1 to October 31 (☎ **540/952-2947**).

7. **Booker T. Washington National Monument.** Located where the great educator and inventor was born in 1856, the monument features demonstrations of 19th-century farming methods. The house where Washington, his mother, and two other children slept on a dirt floor has been reconstructed on the site. It's in Hardy, Virginia, 20 miles southeast of Roanoke via routes 116 south, then 122 north, near Smith Mountain Lake. Open daily (☎ **540/721-2094;** www.nps.gov/bowa).

8. **The Mast General Store, near Boone, North Carolina.** The Mast General Store was built in 1883 and is a living example of a 19th-century country store with its potbellied stove and old advertising posters. With merchandise "from cradles to caskets" and the family's 1812 log cabin and 1885 farmhouse (now an inn) nearby, it is a good example of a mountain farm complex. It's also great fun to browse

through the packed shelves of this rambling store, listed on the National Register of Historic Places. In Valle Crucis, 7 miles south of Boone on Route 194 (☎ 828/963-6511).

9. **The Museum of Appalachia, Norris, Tennessee.** A bit off the basic route, but for anyone going or coming from the Midwest or West, it could be on the way. Located 16 miles north of Knoxville at exit 122 from I-75, this living village is open daily year-round and preserves the lifestyle of the southern Appalachians as its costumed interpreters split shingles, plow fields, play fiddles, and cook meals in dirt-floored cabins. A museum displays 250,000 regional artifacts, including a Roy Acuff fiddle and Sergeant Alvin York's World War I Army jacket (☎ 865/494-0514).

10. **Oconaluftee Indian Village, Cherokee, North Carolina.** A re-created Cherokee village from 225 years ago, before many of the tribe were taken to Oklahoma on a forced relocation, still remembered as the Trail of Tears. One-fourth of them died on the 1,000-mile journey. Descendants of the 1,200 tribal members who escaped and fled into the Great Smoky Mountains in 1838 make up an 8,000-member reservation today. Costumed animators make pottery, weave baskets, sew beadwork, and build canoes in traditional fashion. The Museum of the Cherokee Indian on Route 441 (follow signs from the highway) is a remarkable exhibit of Cherokee history. The museum is open daily year-round except for major holidays; the village is open mid-May to late October. For information, contact the visitors center, ☎ 800/438-1601; www.cherokee-nc.com.

OFF-THE-WALL ATTRACTIONS

Bedrooms of America Museum and Pottery, New Market, Virginia. At the light on Congress Street (aka U.S. 11), 2 blocks from I-81, exit 264 in New Market, is a period house full of antiques, collectibles, and junk, and includes 11 bedrooms, each filled with vintage furniture and furbelows depicting a different specific period between 1650 and 1930 (☎ 540/740-3512).

The Brown Mountain Lights, Morganton, North Carolina. Mysterious ghost lights called the Brown Mountain Lights can sometimes be seen near Morganton, where Indians first noted them. In the 1950s, locals attributed the phenomenon to UFOs. A good spotting place is Beacon Heights off the Blue Ridge Parkway near Grandfather Mountain, and the best time is a clear fall night. Call Burke County and Tourism for information, ☎ 828/433-6793.

Miniature Graceland, Roanoke, Virginia. Built by the dedicated Donald and Kim Epperly in their yard on Riverland Boulevard, Miniature Graceland is a tribute to Elvis that includes an Elvis doll singing to a throng of Barbies, replicas of Graceland, Elvis's birthplace in Tupelo, and some of the theaters he performed in. Kim Epperly is also editor of an Elvis newsletter. There are no set tour schedules; visitors leave donations (☎ 540/427-4254).

The world's largest man-made illuminated star, Roanoke, Virginia. A full 88½ feet high, the star shines nightly until midnight from a mountain above Roanoke. Like a fluorescent tube, the 50-year-old-plus monument usually glows in a ghostly blue-white and hums to itself, but turns red, white, and blue on patriotic holidays and turns just plain red when there's a traffic fatality in the area. Newscaster Lowell Thomas and actor John Payne, Roanoke-born, dedicated it in 1949.

The haunted caves of Natural Bridge Caverns. A moaning female ghost lives inside the limestone formations and pipes up periodically, scaring the wits out of guides and tourists. The sound has been heard for more than a century at the caverns, on U.S. 11 near the Natural Bridge. If the ghost disappoints, there's a wax museum on the premises (☎ 540/291-2121).

The Whitetop Mountain Ramp Festival, Whitetop, Virginia. Not dedicated to freeway entrances, but to a strong-smelling wild onion of the same name. At the annual festival in mid-May you get the chance to sample ramps cooked with bear meat, with trout, in soups, and in salads. It's held at Mount Rogers Fire Hall in Whitetop, southwestern Virginia (off U.S. 58 near the VA/TN/NC borders), with bluegrass music, a crafts fair, and a quilting display (☎ 540/388-3480 or 540/388-3257).

The Pest House Medical Museum and Confederate Cemetery, Lynchburg, Virginia. The museum with the irresistible name attracts the morbid and medical-minded to Lynchburg's Old City Cemetery at 4th and Taylor streets. In the 19th century, patients ill with smallpox or measles were quarantined in the Pest House, then, when they died, were buried in the cemetery next door. The museum, at 401 Taylor St., shows curiosities such as an 1860s hypodermic needle and an early chloroform mask. Open daily dawn to dusk (☎ 804/847-1465; www.gravegarden.com).

The Belle Boyd cottage museum, Front Royal, Virginia. This is the former residence of a teenage girl who doubled as a Confederate spy. She gathered information on the Union Army by eavesdropping, then hopping on a horse and riding 15 miles in the middle of the night to take the information to Stonewall Jackson so they could defeat the Yankees at the Battle of Front Royal in 1862. The cottage, at 101 Chester St., is open variable hours, so call ahead (☎ 540/636-1446).

The mysterious Beale Treasure, Bedford, Virginia. The legend of the Beale Treasure is based on three pages of cryptically coded information in a strongbox left with a Lynchburg hotel owner in 1822. Only one of the pages has been decoded; it claims there are 2,981 pounds of gold and 5,092 pounds of silver buried in the Bedford area, worth approximately $23 million today. A group of 100 computer experts are presently working to unravel the ciphers. The late Key West treasure hunter Mel Fisher also took a crack at it without any luck. The Bedford City/County Museum houses the file, and is located at 201 E. Main St. and open Tuesday through Saturday 10am to 5pm, except January and February (☎ 540/586-4520).

Blowing Rock, North Carolina. A strong updraft at a rock ledge hanging over the Johns River Gorge usually returns items tossed over the edge. An Indian legend says a maiden prayed to the god of the winds for return of her warrior, who had fallen over; the wind blew him back. About 50 miles south, as the crow flies, Dr. Elisha Mitchell, a college professor making measurements on a mountain later named for him, had no such luck. He fell to his death over a ledge by a waterfall in 1857. On Route 321, South Blowing Rock. Call the Blowing Rock Chamber of Commerce (☎ 828/295-7851).

TEN SPECIAL SPLURGES

1. **Visit the Grove Park Inn.** Plan a meal or even an overnight in Asheville's baronial Grove Park Inn, built in 1913 by a tycoon from Tennessee. Author F. Scott Fitzgerald frequently stayed here when visiting his wife, Zelda, who spent the latter part of her life in a local mental hospital. He usually stayed in room 441, which is still decorated as it was during his visits. Check out the elevators by the huge stone fireplaces; they actually run up the chimney shafts. To get there from Greenville, North Carolina, take Highway 25 north about 55 miles. To get there from Winston-Salem, North Carolina, take I-40 west about 140 miles (☎ 800/438-5800 or 828/252-2711).

2. **Go shopping for authentic mountain handicrafts.** With an RV, you can probably find space for some split-willow baskets, a handmade broom, wooden toys, or even a hand-stitched heirloom quilt, all for sale at the Folk Art Center of the Southern Highland Handicraft Guild on the North Carolina end of the parkway at Mile 382, in Asheville. Open daily 9am to 5pm except holidays (☎ 828/298-7928).

3. **Have tea or a meal at the Homestead Resort.** Don your smartest outfits and hit the Homestead Resort at mealtime (call ahead for reservations) for a sumptuous lunch or dinner in the grand old resort tradition. Teatime with violins is also a classic pleasure here in this redbrick, Colonial-style building dating from 1892. A hotel has been on the site for 230 years because of the healing springs. At one time, the waters promised to cure such maladies as gum-boot poisoning, clergyman's throat, and a surfeit of freckles. There's a lot large enough for RV parking halfway down the hill to the hotel, but the doorman may eye your rig nervously if you drive right down to the porte-cochere. It's in Hot Springs, Virginia, on U.S. 220 near the West Virginia border. For reservations, call ☎ 800/838-1766; www.thehomestead.com.

4. **Visit America's largest private home.** The 250-room George Vanderbilt mansion on the Biltmore Estate in Asheville (see "Asheville," later in this chapter) is open daily except Thanksgiving and Christmas from 8:30am to 5pm. Admission is $29.95 for adults, $22.50 for youths 10 and over, and free for children 9 and under accompanied by a paying adult. There's also a raft of other money-making ventures there,

from gift shops to a winery, as well as seasonal and evening events. From the Blue Ridge Parkway, Biltmore is 4 miles from the Highway 25 north exit. From I-40 West, the entrance is north of exit 50B on Highway 25. From I-40 East, the entrance is north of exit 50 on Highway 25. For information, call ☎ 800/543-2961; www.biltmore.com.

5. **Go antiques-hunting in the 100-shop Strasburg Antique Emporium.** Located at 160 N. Massanutten St. in the northern Virginia town of Strasburg (near Front Royal and the beginning of Skyline Drive), the emporium has 60,000 square feet of display space, with dealers offering everything from Civil War–era buttons to Jetson lunchboxes (☎ 540/465-3711; www.waysideofva.com).

6. **Sing along with a llama.** Hit the hiking trail near Wytheville, Virginia, with some humming llamas from Virginia Highland Llamas for an all-day picnic hike on the Big Walker Mountain section of the Appalachian trail. April through October, $60 per person. You walk while the llamas carry lunch, each humming a different tone. Why do they hum? "Because they don't know the words," says their owner (☎ 540/688-4464).

7. **Cash in a chicken or ham for theater tickets at Virginia's state theater in Abingdon.** During the Depression, farmers paid for their tickets to the Barter Theater with produce. (These days you have to pay with cash or credit card!) Gregory Peck, Patricia Neal, Hume Cronyn, and George C. Scott all worked here early in their careers. The theater once paid royalties to Irish playwright and noted vegetarian George Bernard Shaw by sending him a country ham, which he returned with a note requesting spinach instead. From Highway 81, take exit 17. Follow signs to the theater, which is on Main Street (☎ 540/678-3991).

8. **Visit the Buck Mountain Grille.** If you're in the Roanoke area and looking for some trendy vegetarian dishes, or even a steak, along with a glass of wine, try this place, open daily lunch and dinner except Monday and Saturday lunch. It's at Blue Ridge Parkway, exit 121, on Route 220 south. For reservations, call ☎ 540/776-1830.

9. **Take a hot-air balloon ride.** Float over some of the Shenandoah Valley's landmarks from the lavish grounds of the Boar's Head Inn, 220 Ednam Dr. in Charlottesville (☎ 800/476-1988; www.boarsheadinn. com). It's also a top-seeded tennis resort, ranking among *Tennis Magazine's* top 50, and scene of a Merrie Olde England Christmas banquet starring a you-know-what on a silver platter.

10. **Find a mountain lodge that takes you back 30 years.** At least that's what the producers of *Dirty Dancing* thought when they used Mountain Lake Hotel to stand in for a Poconos resort in the sixties. To find it, leave I-81 at exit 118 and follow Route 460 west, bypassing Blacksburg, to road 700, then drive 7 miles up a winding road to Mountain Lake. Open May through October (☎ 800/828-0490).

GREAT TAKE-OUT (OR EAT-IN) TREATS

Carl's Frozen Custard, Fredericksburg, Virginia. Carl's turns out 120 gallons of this classic dessert (in vanilla, chocolate, and strawberry) daily in a 1940s ice cream machine. Look for the stand at the corner of Princess Anne and Hunter streets; there's no phone.

C&O railway station ice cream parlor, Staunton, Virginia. An authentic Victorian-era ice cream parlor on Middlebrook Avenue in the center of Staunton dishes up sodas and sundaes in the restored C&O railway station. (For more railway comestibles, try the crab croquettes at Charlottesville's **C&O Restaurant,** 515 E. Water St., across from the train station. Dinner, nightly; ☎ 804/971-7044.)

Toliver House Restaurant, Gordonsville, Virginia. Toliver House serves up old-fashioned fried chicken at the junction of U.S. 15, 33, and State Road 231 in the town of Gordonsville, northeast of Charlottesville (☎ 540/832-3485).

Snappy Lunch, Mt. Airy, North Carolina. Mt. Airy is the hometown of Shirley Slater, coauthor of this book, and TV star Andy Griffith, as well as the prototype of Mayberry, RFD. It's off the Blue Ridge Parkway near the VA/NC border off I-77, exit 102. Sheriff Andy often referred to the Snappy Lunch, which is an actual eatery on 125 N. Main St., notable for its pork chop sandwiches. A boneless pork chop is flattened and tenderized, dipped into batter, sizzled in hot oil, and served in a hamburger bun, dressed "all the way," with tomatoes, onion, mayonnaise, mustard, coleslaw, and chile sauce. Great (but messy) to go, but if you decided to eat in, be aware that the iced tea comes already sweetened. Open daily except Sunday from early morning through midday or whenever they run out of pork chops (☎ 336/786-4931).

Snappy Lunch patrons in Mt. Airy, North Carolina, the real Mayberry, RFD.

Huyard's Country Kitchen, Dayton, Virginia. Run by a former Mennonite missionary, Huyard's Country Kitchen is set inside the Dayton Farmer's Market south of Harrisonburg on Route 42. From I-81, use exit 240, Bridgewater, or exit 245, James Madison University. The moderately priced buffet of home cooking includes ham, chicken, beef, and vegetables. You may see horse-drawn buggies tied up outside, traditional transportation for the Old Order Mennonites who live in the area.

> *"The South is that part of America where no soft drink is ever called a soda."*
> —Reynolds Price

The Southern Kitchen, New Market, Virginia. This nonfancy place on U.S. 11 is famous for peanut soup (which we've always been fond of), along with a dish called Lloyd's Fried Chicken (☎ 540/740-3514).

The Hardware Store Restaurant, Charlottesville, Virginia. Stop in at East Main and Water streets for great gourmet sandwiches made to go amid the authentic furnishings of a turn-of-the-20th-century hardware store. Park your RV on the Water Street side (☎ 804/977-4344).

Rowe's Family Restaurant, Staunton, Virginia. Rowe's, on Route 250 in Staunton, is a longtime sanctuary for Virginia home cooking—and coincidentally where the Statler Brothers often eat. Have the fried chicken, real mashed potatoes, hot biscuits, and homemade rolls, and for dessert, traditional banana pudding. Take exit 222 off I-81 (☎ 540/886-1833).

The Pig 'N Steak, Madison, Virginia. The Pig 'N Steak is one of Virginia's top barbecue places, but also where the fictional Jason Walton from the TV series used to play the piano at the "Dew Drop Inn." Hickory pit–smoked ribs are the draw here. The restaurant is north of Charlottesville on Washington Street in Madison at the stoplight (☎ 540/948-3130).

Applewood Farm's Apple Barn, Sevierville, Tennessee. The hot fried apple pies at Applewood are prepared while you watch through a glass window. Look for Dolly Parton chocolate lollipops in the candy shop at the farm's complex of food preparation centers. Located at 230 Apple Valley Rd. (☎ 800/421-4606).

EVERYTHING YOU EVER WANTED TO KNOW ABOUT COUNTRY HAM

Yankees may invest fortunes in mail-order Smithfield hams, but the fine cured ham you'll encounter in restaurants and roadside stands throughout this drive is correctly called "country ham."

The **Smithfield ham** began in the 17th century when local farmers let their hogs run loose in the peanut fields after harvest to eat up the leftovers. They soon found they had an excellent-tasting ham with yellow fat that kept the meat from drying out, an export in great demand back in England. These

Candy Apples
Red and Plain Caramel
$ 1 39
Caramel
w/ Nuts $ 1 49 each

Delicacies at Applewood Farm.

hams are smoked and coated with black pepper. Only hams produced by peanut-fed hogs in the peanut belt and processed in Smithfield, a small town in Tidewater, Virginia, near Norfolk, can be called Smithfield hams.

Country ham, on the other hand, is a product of the Appalachians that can be either smoked or dry-cured without smoke. The fresh ham is rubbed down with a dry mix of salt, sugar, and perhaps saltpeter, and then covered for 4 to 6 weeks in a bed of salt. Then it is washed and trimmed, usually hung by the hock in a smokehouse where it sweats in hickory smoke through the summer. A total of 9 to 12 months is the minimum curing period. Some processors skip the smoking stage, saying the smoke makes little flavor difference. And some processors label their hams "sugar cured," although the sugar has no part in the curing.

The finished ham is a salty, densely textured, and intensely flavored meat that can be sliced raw and fried, or boiled whole and then baked. If you buy a country ham to take home, it will keep for a long time, up to a year, if stored in a cool, dark place. A cooked ham also keeps well under refrigeration, and a small bit of it sliced or diced can add flavor to any number of dishes.

To prepare a country ham, you need to soak it for 24 hours in a pot of cold water, then drain it, scrub off the spices and any mold from the surface, and put it in a fresh kettle of cold water to cover. Cook it at a simmer for 20 minutes per pound or until the flat bone at the butt end is loose enough to move back and forth, usually from 4 to 5 hours. Let it cool enough to handle, cut off the skin and excess fat, but leave a half-inch layer of fat to cover. Remove the loose, flat bone. Put liquid in the pan (water, wine, ginger ale, or sherry) to cover it by an inch and bake in a slow oven for an hour, covered with foil. Then remove the foil, score the fat, and cover it with any paste or glaze you wish (a mix of brown sugar, cornmeal, and a little prepared or dry mustard is good). Return it to the oven for a half hour, basting frequently. Then cool and slice it in very thin slices. It's delectable with hot biscuits.

OUTDOOR ACTIVITIES

Hikers will find plenty of trails, from 10-minute leg-stretchers to longer, more demanding walks along the way. In Shenandoah National Park, more than 500 miles of side trails set out from the ridge road (www.nps.gov/shen).

One of the most famous walking trails in America, the Appalachian Trail, stretches from Maine to Georgia across the crest of the mountains. Some of the prettiest of the trail's 500 miles in Virginia are those in Shenandoah National Park between Front Royal and Rockfish Gap. The trail also parallels the Blue Ridge Parkway for 103 miles between Rockfish Gap and Mile 103.

Canoe trips along the Shenandoah River for novices or experienced canoeists can be booked with **Downriver Canoe Company** in Bentonville, Virginia, from April to late October (☎ **800/338-1963**). If you want to paddle your own canoe, it can provide a shuttle service. **Front Royal Canoe Company** in Front Royal (☎ **800/270-8808** or 540/635-5440; www.front royalcanoe.com) can take you along the Shenandoah between mid-March and mid-November. **Shenandoah River Outfitters** in Luray is open year-round for rentals, overnight trips, and all-you-can-eat steak dinners on the trail (☎ **800/6CANOE-2**; www.Shenendoahriver.com).

Horseback riding along mountain trails is popular in the fall, and a good alternative to driving when traffic on the roadways may be bumper-to-bumper. Guided rides from **Skyland Lodge** in Shenandoah National Park leave several times a day (☎ **540/999-2210**; www.visitshenandoah.com).

Or you can spend the time happily watching a robin search for worms or marvel at the opening of a bud or the unfolding of a leaf.

WILDLIFE-WATCHING

The Blue Ridge Mountains are the stomping ground for all manner of birds and mammals, from **whitetail deer** and **black bears**, on display at the privately owned Grandfather Mountain Park, to **wild turkeys,** which we've

SOUTHERN ACCENTS: A GLOSSARY

Bald: A treeless area at about 4,000 feet covered with shrubs or grass, perhaps part of earlier Indian agricultural clearing or the product of lightning fires.
Holler: A yell of communication between farms in the days before telephones; also, a valley or "hollow."
Moonshining: Making illegal corn liquor in "dry" areas of the South; most rural areas have a few moonshiners, but you're not likely to encounter any unless you know the locals very well.
Pop: A soft drink.
Put up: To can or preserve foods for winter.

glimpsed several times from the roadway. Seldom seen but indisputably present are **bobcats,** sometimes glimpsed at night. Most commonly sighted along the roadways are woodchucks (groundhogs), chipmunks, and squirrels in the daytime; skunks, raccoons, opossums, and foxes at night. More than 100 bird species may be seen during spring migrations.

Some 300 or more **wild ponies** wander in Grayson Highlands State Park, off U.S. 58 near the point where Virginia, North Carolina, and Tennessee meet; a few of them are rounded up each fall to be auctioned off during the last week of September in the park.

On the Road

THE SHENANDOAH VALLEY

Nobody knows for sure what *Shenandoah* means. It has been translated variously as "sprucy stream," "land of the big mountains," even "daughter of the stars." One etymologist says it is the Iroquois word for "deer," animals that are still plentiful in the valley.

The fragrance of apples perfumes the valley, from the pink-and-white blossoms in spring through the harvest of the fruit in autumn, to the sweet-sour tang of apple cider in winter in the apple sheds.

History is deeply etched in the towns along the Shenandoah River, once America's western frontier. During the Civil War, the northern Virginia town of **Winchester** changed hands 72 times—and 13 times on one particularly memorable day. Pick up a walking tour map at the city's **welcome center** (1360 S. Pleasant Rd.) and see the modest log-and-limestone cabin on Braddock Street that was George Washington's office during the French and Indian War. It's now a museum (☎ **540/662-4412**). A brick house down the street was Stonewall Jackson's headquarters during the Civil War. Don't be startled to see a picture of TV star Mary Tyler Moore at the headquarters; her great-grandfather owned the house at the time and invited the general to use it. Call the Winchester Chamber of Commerce (☎ **540/662-4118**).

Virginia's **Museum of American Frontier Culture** in Staunton is a re-created village of cottages, barns, and farms that show both the farmsteads the settlers left in the Old World and the way they reinterpreted them in the New World. (See "Ten Terrific Spots Where History Comes Alive," earlier in this chapter.)

Thomas Jefferson is still very much alive in the countryside around Charlottesville, where people speak of "Mr. Jefferson" as they would a respected neighbor. **Monticello,** the dream home he designed and built, is magnificent but not overwhelming because it is built on a human scale. Meriwether Lewis and William Clark brought the moose and deer antlers in the entry hall back to Jefferson from their explorations in the West. Monticello is in the Virginia Piedmont about 2 miles southeast of Charlottesville. To get there, take I-64, exit 121 (if traveling westbound) or exit 121A

Virginia Campgrounds

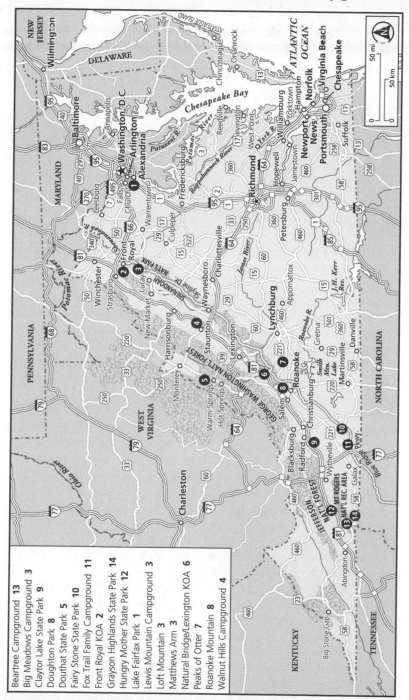

Beartree Campground **13**
Big Meadows Campground **3**
Claytor Lake State Park **9**
Doughton Park **8**
Douthat State Park **5**
Fairy Stone State Park **10**
Fox Trail Family Campground **11**
Front Royal KOA **2**
Grayson Highlands State Park **14**
Hungry Mother State Park **12**
Lake Fairfax Park **1**
Lewis Mountain Campground **3**
Loft Mountain **3**
Matthews Arm **3**
Natural Bridge/Lexington KOA **6**
Peaks of Otter **7**
Roanoke Mountain **8**
Walnut Hills Campground **4**

Re-created farm in Virginia's Museum of American Frontier Culture.

(if traveling eastbound), make a right at the first light for the **Monticello Visitor Center,** or make a left at the first light for Monticello itself (☎ 804/ 984-9822; www.monticello.org).

Jefferson was hospitable to guests, spending freely to entertain, even though he died $100,000 in debt, the equivalent of a million today. Dinner began at 4pm and often continued until dark, with fine wines the president had shipped from France accompanying the vegetables from his gardens. Dishes were prepared by one of his servants, who had trained in Paris.

Jefferson tried to establish a vineyard at Monticello, so he'd be pleased to note that today the Charlottesville area is the wine capital of Virginia, with 10 local wineries producing table vintages. Oakencraft Vineyard and Winery, Simeon Vineyards, Montdomaine Cellars, and Totier Creek Vineyard usually offer tours and tastings except in winter. Get a free wine country guide from the **Virginia Wine Marketing Program,** VDACS, Division of Marketing, P.O. Box 1163, Richmond, VA 23219 (☎ 800/828-4637).

Campground Oases in the Shenandoah Valley

Lake Fairfax Park. A Corps of Engineer Public Park in Reston, Virginia, Lake Fairfax Park is about 50 miles east of Front Royal (not actually in the Shenandoah Valley) and within commuting distance of Washington. It has 74 sites, 48 of them with 15- and 30-amp electric hookups. Toilets, showers, and a sanitary dump are provided, and there is a 7-day limit during the season, which runs from March to early December. From the junction of I-495 and Route 7, head west 6.5 miles on Route 7 to Route 606, then south 0.1 miles to Lake Fairfax Dr. Turn left into the entrance (☎ 703/471-5415).

The Front Royal KOA. Open from mid-March to late November, the Front Royal KOA has a big swimming pool and 350-foot water slide (there's a fee for the latter), hot tub, miniature golf, and stocked fishing pond. The 135 sites, while not large, are terraced and landscaped, some of them paved and some of them gravel, and the hilltop locations offer cooling breezes in summer. For sightseers who don't want to drive their RVs in Washington, D.C., the park offers a daily shuttle tour by advance reservation. Located just outside Front Royal. Take Route 81 to Route 66 east; take exit 6 onto Route 340 South. Drive through town past Shenandoah National Park on the left. The entrance is 4.5 miles past the national park, also on the left (☎ **800/KOA-9114** or 540/635-2741; www.koa.com).

Matthews Arm. The Matthews Arm in Shenandoah National Park, on Skyline Drive at Mile 22.2 (22.2 miles south of the Front Royal entrance), is open late May through October, and offers several tree-shaded loops with 180 gravel back-in sites, not all of them large enough for big RVs. There is a sewage disposal dump and toilets, but no hookups, showers, or laundry. Ranger campfire programs are presented several times a day on summer weekends, less often during the week. Camping is on a first-come, first-served basis and costs $14 a night. Designated campsites for travelers with disabilities are available (☎ **540/999-3500;** www.nps.gov/shen).

Big Meadows Campground. At Mile 51 on Skyline Drive, also in Shenandoah National Park, Big Meadows provides 227 RV sites in a designated area separate from tent campsites. Hot showers are available for a small fee, and there's a sanitary dump, laundry, and firewood for sale, but no hookups. Fees are $17 a night and ranger campfire programs are scheduled daily in summer (☎ **540/999-3500**). Most sites are paved and can be reserved in advance by calling ☎ **800/365-CAMP;** www.reservations.nps.gov.

Lewis Mountain Campground. Off Skyline Drive at Mile 57.6 in Shenandoah National Park, Lewis Mountain Campground has 31 sites, half of them tent sites and three of them pull-throughs, which in this park means a sort of curved driveway off the main road. There are no hookups and no sanitary dump, and sites are available on a first-come, first-served basis at $14 a night (☎ **540/999-3231**).

Loft Mountain. Loft Mountain is our favorite of the four sites in Shenandoah National park. Located off Skyline Drive at Mile 79.5, it has 221 paved sites, most of them shaded and more than half pull-throughs, some long enough for big rigs. Sites are available on a first-come, first-served basis at $14 a night, and there is a sanitary dump but no hookups. Ranger campfire programs are provided daily except Wednesdays in summer (☎ **540/999-3273;** www.nps.gov/shen).

THE BLUE RIDGE PARKWAY

Construction began in 1935, and the final leg of the 469-mile road was finally completed in 1987 with the spectacularly engineered Linn Cove Viaduct, which seems to float lightly around venerable Grandfather Mountain as though suspended in midair.

NIGHTLIFE ALONG THE ROAD

Things are better than they used to be. We remember visiting in North Carolina some years ago when someone suggested going out for a drink. "Where's the nearest bar?" we asked. "Washington, D.C.," our host answered dryly.

The best places in Virginia to look for nightlife are college towns like Charlottesville or gentrifying cities like Roanoke, where **Awful Arthur's**, at 108 Campbell Ave. downtown (☎ 540/344-2997), promises live entertainment Thursday nights and weekends, and **Montano's**, at 3733 Franklin Rd. SW ☎ 540/344-8960), offers jazz and a good wine list. We prefer **Floyd County General Store** at 206 S. Locust St. in the town of Floyd (6 miles off the Blue Ridge Parkway at Mile 165.2) for its Friday Night Jamboree with live country music and clog dancing and the Saturday night concerts (☎ 540/745-4563). 🚐

Skyline Drive and the Blue Ridge Parkway were among President Franklin D. Roosevelt's projects for the CCC (Civilian Conservation Corps) during the 1930s Depression. The intention was to provide drivers with a variety of untrammeled rural scenes, with the road following the landscape for scenery rather than speed, which is limited to 45 mph. The park area along the two roads averages about 1,000 feet wide, including the roadbed.

Split-rail fences, small log cabins, water-operated mills, barns, and farm fields may be glimpsed along the roadsides, as well as brilliant pink and lavender stands of wild rhododendron and mountain laurel and vivid orange splashes of flame azaleas in late spring and early summer. Arched stone bridges ornament the roads that cross over or under the parkway.

Nine visitor centers and eleven campgrounds, none with hookups but all accessible to any but the largest RV, are along the route, which passes through four national forests and the Cherokee Indian Reservation at its southern end, where it connects with Newfound Gap Road and the Great Smoky Mountains National Park.

The Appalachian Mountains were once the western frontier, and the isolated homesteads that remain—such as the **Puckett Cabin** at Mile 189, where "Aunt Orlean" Puckett gave birth to 24 children, none of whom lived past infancy, and the **Brinegar Cabin** at Mile 238, where weavers show how mountain women made fabrics—give a clearer picture than any history book of the hard and often lonely life of these fiercely independent people.

Our own favorite stop along the parkway is **Mabry Mill,** where volunteer musicians and craftspeople may hold an impromptu dulcimer concert or tell tall tales to a group of wide-eyed children. Someone's usually weaving split-willow baskets or whittling or blacksmithing. And the miller is almost always there, turning out white stone-ground cornmeal for sale by the bag. You can sample cornmeal and buckwheat pancakes at the restaurant next door, along with slabs of country ham and hot homemade biscuits. (See "Ten Terrific Spots Where History Comes Alive," earlier in this chapter.)

Animal life along the parkway is fairly sparse, except around camp-grounds and at road crossings in early morning and late afternoon. White-tailed deer, opossums, raccoons, and skunks are the most common, along with chipmunks, squirrels, and woodchucks, also called groundhogs.

NINE BLUE RIDGE THINGS TO DO

1. **Head down into Luray Caverns.** Luray is the biggest among a num-ber of cave complexes that lie like honeycombs beneath the Shenandoah Valley. It's big enough for claustrophobes to go inside to see and hear the world's only "stalacpipe" organ: tuned stalactites that are tapped with rubber-tipped hammers to make music. (How do you tune a stalactite? By grinding it down slightly.) Trivia lovers will like dis-covering the petrified fried eggs on one canyon wall and the blind albi-no shrimp in the underground river. But check out the times for the fre-quent carillon concerts, played out of the bell tower near the entrance. You don't want to be standing too near (☎ 540/743-6551).

2. **Visit Thomas Jefferson's vegetable gardens at Monticello.** The gar-dens are a re-creation of his original plantings, which he painstakingly documented in 1807. Some rare and exotic vegetables no longer pro-duced anywhere else share space with familiar favorites such as aspara-gus and artichokes, as well as 15 different varieties of English peas. Jefferson is the gardener who introduced eggplant to the United States. Open daily 8am to 5pm (☎ 804/984-9822).

LITERARY LIGHTS

Poet and Lincoln biographer **Carl Sandburg,** whose name is linked forever with Chicago, spent the last 22 years of his life on his farm at Flat Rock, near Hendersonville, North Carolina. Now a National Historic Site, the farm Sandburg called Connemara is where the two-time Pulitzer Prize winner wrote a novel, poems, a screenplay (for *The Greatest Story Ever Told*), and his autobiog-raphy, in between playing his guitar and singing folk songs. His wife Paula Steichen, sister of photographer Edward Steichen, raised prize goats; there's still a herd of them around. The farm is on Little River Road off Route 25, 3 miles south of Hendersonville, and is open daily from 9am to 5pm (☎ 828/693-4178).

Old Kentucky Home, the boardinghouse at 48 Spruce St. in Asheville where author **Thomas Wolfe** spent his childhood and which he immortalized as Dixieland in his autobiographical novel *Look Homeward, Angel,* has served in recent years as the Thomas Wolfe Memorial State Historical Site, but was dam-aged by fire and had to undergo reconstruction. Until the interiors open to the public, exterior tours of the house and visitor center at 52 North Market St. are offered. Call ☎ 828/253-8304 for information. The angel of the book title, a funeral monument sold by Wolfe's father, can be seen in Hendersonville's Oakdale Cemetery ornamenting the grave of Margaret E. Johnson. 🚐

3. **Drink a Dr. Pepper in rustic Rural Retreat, Virginia.** At exit 60 from I-81, tilt a cool one back in memory of the soda's inventor, a lovesick pharmacist's assistant who fell head over heels for his boss's daughter, was forbidden to woo her, and finally moved to Waco, Texas, where he patented and bottled his soft drink, named for his former boss and sweetheart's father, Dr. Charles Pepper.

4. **Check out far-out Floyd, Virginia.** Six miles off the Blue Ridge Parkway near Mile 165, Floyd is where New Age/neohippie handicrafts gallery New Mountain Mercantile coexists with a 75-year-old general store that holds free hoedowns every Friday. Just down the road is Blue Ridge Restaurant, with home cooking and real mashed potatoes (☎ 540/745-2147). Then there's Country Records, featuring the biggest collection of bluegrass music in the world, they say. Finally, just when you think you're getting a fix on Floyd, you run into Chateau Morrisette Winery with its jazz concerts, wine tastings, and French restaurant. At Mile 165, take State Route 8 north 5 miles into Floyd. Contact the Floyd County Chamber of Commerce for more information (☎ 540/745-4407).

5. **Lunch at Charlottesville's historic Michie Tavern.** Pronounced *Mickey,* the Michie Tavern serves traditional Southern dishes, from fried chicken and biscuits to black-eyed peas, stewed tomatoes, and cornbread plus Virginia wines. This and more is served daily 11:30am to 3pm year-round for around $10. Located at 683 Thomas Jefferson Parkway on Route 53 southeast of the city (☎ 804/977-1234).

6. **Follow the sound of fiddles to Bristol, Virginia.** The birthplace of country music has a mural commemorating Mother Maybelle Carter, matriarch of the legendary Carter Family, on State Street at Volunteer Parkway (on the side of the Lark Amusement Building, facing east). Every Saturday night at 7:30pm there's a live bluegrass show ($5 admission fee) at the Carter Family Fold in Hiltons, Virginia, off U.S. 58, 5 miles east of Kingsport, Tennessee (take Route 58—off exit 1 from Route 81—about 20 miles into Hilton; signs will show the directions to the house). Arrive early so you can browse through the displays of 78-rpm recordings, photographs, and instruments in the A. P. Carter Museum, open Saturdays only from 6 to 7:30pm (☎ 540/386-9480).

7. **Head for the Galax Moose Lodge #733 Old Fiddlers' Convention in Galax, Virginia.** Located just off the Blue Ridge Parkway via Route 97 west, Galax hosts the world's oldest and largest old-time fiddlers' contest during the second week in August, drawing musicians who play as much for their own pleasure and each other as for the audience of thousands for this 60-year-old tradition. Many musicians arrive and stay in their own RVs, so other RVers should feel right at home (☎ 540/236-8541 or 540/238-8130; www.oldfiddlersconvention.com).

Musician at the Old Fiddlers' Convention in Galax, Virginia.

8. **Visit the annual Natural Chimneys Jousting Contest.** The oldest continuously operated sporting event in the country is set against a backdrop of castlelike rock towers. The August tournament has been going on since 1821 at this site near Mount Solon, southwest of Harrisonburg on Route 607. Natural Chimneys Regional Park and its 120 RV hookup sites are nearby (☎ **540/350-2510** for jousting information or RV reservations).

9. **Run over and say "hidy" to John-Boy and his family.** The Waltons Mountain Museum in Schuyler, Virginia, on Route 617, commemorates the hometown of Earl Hamner Jr., creator of the TV series, and includes video interviews and episodes from the show, as well as re-creations of the Hollywood sets for the series. (The "real" Waltons Mountain can be found at Frazier Park near Gorman in Southern California, where location filming for the series often took place; one of this book's authors appeared occasionally on the show.) The museum is right on Route 617 at the top of a hill; open daily 10am to 4pm from early March until the end of November except for major holidays (☎ **804/831-2000**).

Campground Oases Along the Blue Ridge Parkway

Walnut Hills Campground. Near Staunton, Virginia, Walnut Hills is a good base for visiting the notable Civil War sites in the area as well as the Frontier Culture Museum. Take exit 217 from I-81 and drive west on 654 to Route 11, then south to Route 655 and follow the signs. Most of the 125 modem-friendly sites are wide and shaded, with 30- and 50-amp electric hookups

and satellite TV. It's open March 1 through mid-November. For reservations, call ☎ **800/699-2568** or 540/337-3920; www.walnuthillscampground.com.
Natural Bridge/Lexington KOA. Open year-round off I-81, exit 180, with some full hookups and pull-throughs for most of its 87 sites. Flush toilets, showers, a sanitary dump, laundry, groceries, LP gas, and dinner available nightly (☎ **800/KOA-8514** or 504/291-2770; www.koa.com).
Peaks of Otter. Peaks of Otter, on the Blue Ridge Parkway at Milepost 86 near Bedford, Virginia, has 59 paved sites, some with shade, 25 pull-throughs, flush toilets, piped water, and a sanitary dump. No hookups. Each site has a table and fireplace. Closed November through April. No reservations (☎ **540/586-4357**).
Douthat State Park. Listed on the National Register of Historic Places for the role it played in the development of parks around the United States, Douthat State Park has been a family tradition in Virginia for more than half a century. The campground has 38 gravel sites with 30-amp electric hookups, toilets, showers, and a sanitary dump station, but the area also offers lodges, cabins, a restaurant, bathhouses, boating, and fishing in a lake stocked with trout. Take exit 27 off I-64 to Route 629, then turn north for 7 miles. For reservations, call ☎ **800/933-PARK** or 540/862-8100; www.dcr.state.va.us.
Roanoke Mountain. Roanoke Mountain, near Vinton at Mile 120 of the Blue Ridge Parkway, has 105 campsites, some shaded, all paved, with flush toilets, piped water, and sanitary dump station. No hookups, no reservations, 14-day camping limit. Towed vehicles are not permitted on the Roanoke Mountain scenic loop drive. To get to the campground from Vinton, go east 2 miles on State Road 24 to Blue Ridge Parkway, then south 8 miles on the right (☎ **540/982-9242**).
Claytor Lake State Park. Claytor Lake Park, near Dublin, Virginia, has 139 sites, with water and 30-amp electric hookups, bass fishing, swimming, fishing, boating, and boat docks at the lake. Some shaded sites, some pull-throughs. Closed in winter. Located on State Road 660, 2 miles south of I-81 at exit 101. The historic Howe House features exhibits about the life of the early settlers in this region (☎ **800/933-PARK;** www.dcr.state.va.us).
Fairy Stone State Park. Fairy Stone State Park, on Route 57 between Stuart and Bassett, Virginia, is named for the little brown cross-shaped stones found in the area that legend says are the tears shed by elves and fairies when Christ was crucified. While hunting for them is permitted, don't worry if you can't find one on the ground; gift shops in the area will be glad to sell you one. There are 51 sites with water and electrical hookups (20-amps), flush toilets, showers, sanitary dump station, bass fishing, swimming, boat ramp, and rentals. Closed in fall and winter (☎ **540/930-2424**).
Fox Trail Family Campground. A quarter-mile down Route 683 off the Blue Ridge Parkway in Fancy Gap, Virginia, at Mile 199.5, Fox Trail campground is open year-round. Some of the 96 sites are shaded, and there are

19 pull-throughs; 80 are full hookup with 30-amp electric (☎ **540/728-7776;** www.foxtrailcg.com).

Hungry Mother State Park. Located near Marion, Virginia, Hungry Mother has 32 sites with electric (15- and 30-amp) and water hookups and a sanitary dump. Since some of the sites are quite narrow, it does not permit slide-outs, but a lake offers freshwater fishing, swimming, and boating. Rates are $15 to $18 a night. Take I-81's exit 47 and follow Route 11 to State Road 16, then drive north 4 miles. For reservations, call ☎ **800/933-PARK;** www. dcr.state.va.us.

Beartree Campground. Mt. Rogers National Recreation Area, near Marion, is tucked into the corner of southwestern Virginia not far from where its border touches both North Carolina and Tennessee. Beartree Campground has 91 gravel sites with flush toilets and showers, sanitary dump station, trout fishing, and swimming. No hookups, no slide-outs. Closed in winter. Seven miles east of Damascus on U.S. 58. For information, call the recreation area at ☎ **540/783-5196.**

Grayson Highlands State Park. Located near Mouth of Wilson, Virginia, Grayson Highlands Park has 73 sites with electrical hookups and sanitary dump station. The town name comes from its position at the head of Wilson Creek, famous for its trout fishing, and the campground provides good fishing access to the stream. From I-81, take exit 45 and go south on State Road 16 to Route 58, then west 8 miles. For reservations, call ☎ **800/933-PARK** or 540/579-7092; www.dcr.state.va.us.

Doughton Park, Laurel Springs, Virginia. On the Blue Ridge Parkway at Mile 238.5, Doughton Park has 26 grass sites open May 1 to November 1. Flush toilets, sanitary dump, planned activities schedule. No hookups, no reservations, no slide-outs. This is an especially good place to spot deer at dawn and dusk (☎ **336/372-8568**).

Julian Price Memorial Park. On the Blue Ridge Parkway near Mile 297, Julian Price Park has 68 paved sites, flush toilets, sanitary dump, fishing, and boating. No hookups, no reservations. Most sites shaded, some pull-throughs, 14-day maximum stay. Open May to November (☎ **828/298-0398**).

ASHEVILLE

The pretty mountain city of Asheville will be forever mingled with the memory of native son Thomas Wolfe for many readers. His thinly fictionalized story of "Altamont" and Eliza Gant's "Dixieland" boardinghouse in his novel *Look Homeward, Angel* apparently embarrassed everyone in town, including his mother, the model for the boardinghouse keeper. His books were banned by the local public library until 1935, when F. Scott Fitzgerald, shocked that the local author was not represented, bought two copies of *Look Homeward, Angel* and donated them to the library.

Later, after Wolfe's death (he died before his 38th birthday), all was forgiven, and **Old Kentucky Home,** that boardinghouse at 48 Spruce St., is today the Thomas Wolfe Memorial State Historic Site.

Another Blue Ridge author, Greensboro-born short story writer **O. Henry** (William Sydney Porter), is buried in Asheville's Riverside Cemetery, on Birch Street, not far from Thomas Wolfe's grave.

In years past, a lot of wealthy Americans liked the city's cool summer climate and clear mountain air enough to set up seasonal residence, including Henry Ford, Thomas Edison, John D. Rockefeller, Grover Cleveland, and Theodore Roosevelt. In the 1890s, George Washington Vanderbilt, grandson of the fabulously wealthy Commodore Vanderbilt, constructed **Biltmore House,** a 250-room French Renaissance mansion at the edge of Asheville. It's open daily for fairly pricy house tours, $29.95 adults, $22.50 youths 10 and over, as well as rose garden tours and wine-tasting from the Vanderbilt vineyard. If the mansion looks familiar, it was the location for the Peter Sellers film *Being There,* as well as the home of Macaulay Culkin's *Richie Rich* in the film of the same name. From the Blue Ridge Parkway, Biltmore is about 4 miles from the Highway 25 north exit. From I-40 West, the entrance is north of exit 50B on Highway 25. From I-40 East, the entrance is north of exit 50 on Highway 25 (☎ **800/543-2961**).

Besides its evocative turn-of-the-20th-century resort buildings (see Grove Park Inn under "Ten Special Splurges," earlier in this chapter), Asheville also is a treasure trove of Art Deco architecture, with a city hall and First Baptist Church (5 Oak St.) from the 1920s, as well as the handsome S&W Cafeteria on Patton Avenue.

Campground Oases Near Asheville

Mt. Pisgah. On the Blue Ridge Parkway near Mile 408, Mt. Pisgah has 70 paved campsites available with patios, some shade. Flush toilets, sanitary dump station, groceries. No hookups or reservations. Open May to November; 14-day camping limit (☎ **828/298-0398**).

Asheville West KOA, Candler, North Carolina. This pleasant campground 12 miles west of town is reached by making a loop from exit 7 off I-40 and going under the interstate, following the signs, and back under a second time. It has big level pull-throughs with cable TV, fishing and 50-amp electricity, and some hiking trails (☎ **800/562-9015** or 828/665-7015; www. koa.com).

GREAT SMOKY MOUNTAINS NATIONAL PARK

The most visited national park in the system, Great Smoky Mountains gets some eight million people a year passing through its rather garish portals, the commercial strip in **Cherokee** on the east side with its "Indian chiefs" standing by Plains Indian teepees, holding tom-toms and wearing feathered war bonnets Cherokees never used, and gaudy **Gatlinburg,** which has turned shopping, sleeping, and eating into big business.

The only place tackier than either is nearby Pigeon Forge with its flashy **Dollywood** theme park and bumper-to-bumper traffic inching its way past

Dolly Parton invites visitors to Dollywood, in Pigeon Forge, Tennessee.

wall-to-wall motels and fast-food joints. Country singer/movie star Dolly Parton, keeping abreast of the trend, has turned this formerly bucolic pottery-making village near her birthplace into a tourist town gripped with gridlock. If we didn't know better, we'd think she built it to get even with some brats who snubbed her in grammar school.

But you can get away if you try. Pay heed to any of the "Quiet Walkways" signs within the national park to take an easy and enchanting stream-side or woodland stroll. Exploring the side roads leads to special pleasures. A detour to Clingmans Dome winds past the **Indian Gap Trailhead** with its ruts well worn from the countless horse-drawn vehicles that labored along this former toll road in the 19th century. **Hiking trails,** except in the most popular months of June, July, and October, are often uncrowded, since many of the visitors are making a beeline for Gatlinburg or Pigeon Forge.

The park is an international Biosphere Reserve and a World Heritage Site, and bear sightings are fairly common, with some 850 of the furry fellows in residence. Peregrine falcons and river otters have also been seen there lately.

Campground Oases in Great Smoky Mountains National Park

There are 10 developed campgrounds in the park, none with showers or hookups. The summer camping limit is 7 days, with 14 days permitted at those that are open in winter.

Advance reservations for summer and fall camping may be made at Cades Cove, Elkmont, and Smokemont campgrounds by calling ☎ **800/365-CAMP;** reservations.nps.gov. Except during the winter, there are sewage dump stations at Smokemont, Cades Cove, Deep Creek, and Cosby campgrounds and across from the Sugarlands Visitor Center at the Gatlinburg entrance. These campgrounds are on a first-come, first-served basis. Get information at the rangers' office (☎ **365/436-1200**).

Great Smoky Mountains National Park

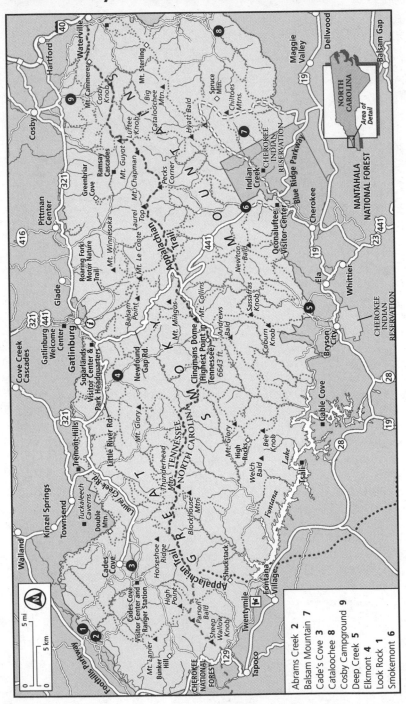

Abrams Creek. Reached by Happy Valley Road from Chilhowee, Tennessee, at the extreme western end of the park (and not accessible to any other park areas), Abrams Creek has 16 sites. No RVs over 12 feet. Open mid-March to early November; $10.

Balsam Mountain. Balsam Mountain is accessed by the Blue Ridge Parkway from Mile 458.2 and 12 miles along the Heintooga Ridge Road spur, which is paved but narrow, steep, and winding. Do not attempt to drive beyond the campground along the one-way gravel Balsam Mountain Road because motor homes and vehicles pulling trailers are prohibited. 46 sites, accommodating RVs up to 30 feet. Open late May to late September; $10.

Cades Cove. Reached by the loop road from Sugarlands Visitor Center outside Gatlinburg or from the Townsend Visitor Center entrance on Tennessee's Route 73, Cades Cove has 161 sites and allows RVs up to 35 feet. Open year-round; $12 to $15.

Cataloochee. Reached from I-40 at exit 20 along Cove Creek Road (much of it unpaved), Cataloochee has 27 sites, accommodating RVs up to 31 feet. Open mid-March to early November; $10.

Cosby Campground. Outside the bustling little town of Cosby, Tennessee, on Route 32 off U.S. 321 (or via the Foothills Parkway turnoff, exit 443 from I-40), the Cosby Campground has 175 sites accommodating RVs up to 25 feet. Open mid-March to early November; $12.

Deep Creek. On Deep Creek Road, just inside the park boundary from Bryson City, North Carolina, Deep Creek has 108 sites that take RVs up to 26 feet. Open early April to early November; $12.

Elkmont. Just off Cades Cove Road not far from Sugarlands Visitor Center at Gatlinburg, Elkmont has 220 sites accommodating RVs up to 32 feet. Open mid-March to late November; $12 to $15.

Look Rock. At the edge of the park's northwest boundaries off Foothill Parkway 10 miles northeast of Chilhowee, Look Rock offers 92 sites, taking RVs up to 35 feet. Open late May until early November; $12.

Smokemont. Along Newfound Gap Road a few miles north of Oconaluftee Visitor Center on the North Carolina side of the park, Smokemont has 140 sites accommodating RVs up to 27 feet. Open year-round; $12 to $15.

Campground Oases on the Tennessee Side of the Smokies

Pigeon Forge/Gatlinburg KOA. A great location for families that want to visit Dollywood and revel in the tourist traps of Pigeon Forge—it's only a few blocks off the main street and has trolley shuttle service to town and to Dollywood. The 181 hookup sites (30-amp) are spacious, mostly gravel surface with some paved or grass. Cable TV, shuffleboard, heated pool, and hot tub are on the premises. From the junction of U.S. 411 and Wears Valley Road (U.S. 321-S), go south 2.1 miles on U.S. 411 to Dollywood Lane, east 0.3 miles to Cedar Top Lane, north 1,000 feet, then follow the signs. Call well

GREAT SMOKIES RV SAFETY TIPS

A traffic sign just inside the park from the Gatlinburg entrance to Great Smoky Mountains National Park cautions that tunnels ahead on the highway have a clearance of only 12 feet 2 inches, a close call for many modern basement-model motor homes with roof air conditioners, TV antennae, and satellite dishes.

"I wish they had consulted with me before they put that up," said a ranger on duty at Sugarlands Visitor Center. "The 12-foot measurement is on the extreme sides of an arched tunnel that measures 17 feet in the center, and almost all the RVs get through without scraping."

When in doubt, inch toward the center when entering the tunnel, and you should clear it without a problem.

The same ranger cautioned that motor homes and vehicles pulling trailers should avoid traveling the dirt and gravel scenic drives in the park, but that the popular Cades Cove Loop is accessible to all.

About the campground limits specified in the park newspaper and listed above, he said RVs slightly larger than the limit may be able to access some sites in the campgrounds if the driver is adept.

An **Auto Touring Map** ($1) is available at the park visitor centers, mapping most of the 270 miles of roadway in the Smokies. Check at Sugarlands Visitor Center at the Gatlinburg, Tennessee, entrance; Oconaluftee Visitor Center at the Cherokee, North Carolina, entrance; and Cades Cove Visitor Center on Cades Cove Road, 2 miles south of Townsend, Tennessee. In addition, a knowledgeable ranger can recommend which routes to take and which to avoid, depending on your RV's dimensions.

in advance for summer and fall (☎ **800/KOA-7703** or 865/453-7903; www.koa.com). If Pigeon Forge is full, try Knoxville East KOA, 12 miles away off I-40 at exit 407 (☎ **800/KOA-8693** or 423/933-6393; www.koa.com); or Newport KOA on Route 27W-70, 1.6 miles west of I-40, exit 432B, half an hour from the Great Smokies National Park entrance, Pigeon Forge, Dollywood, or Gatlinburg (☎ **800/KOA-9016** or 423/623-9004; www.koa.com).

Outdoor Resorts. Like its sister resorts in Palm Springs, Outdoor Resorts, in Gatlinburg's Cobbly Nob resort area, is a "condo park," meaning the sites are owned and occupied except for 26 (in this park) that are available for transient visitors. These spacious, clean, beautifully landscaped parks are a cut above most private RV parks, and, if you're fussy about your surroundings, worth the price. Here, it's $26 to $30, about $10 a night higher than some neighboring parks. Located on 321 north out of Gatlinburg. For reservations, call ☎ **865/436-5861.**

12

The Lobster Coast: New England & the Canadian Maritimes

AS THE MAN WHO LED A LOBSTER ON A LEASH THROUGH THE GARDENS of the Palais Royal in Paris explained, "I have a liking for lobsters. They are peaceful, serious creatures. They know the secrets of the sea."

Lobsters were served at the first Thanksgiving dinner, and were so plentiful that until this century they were used for fertilizer, bait, and jail food. The largest lobster ever recorded was 48 pounds with a length of 3½ feet. They are nocturnal and generally eat fish and shellfish.

Our Lobster Land drive covers New England and Canada's Maritime provinces of New Brunswick, Prince Edward Island, and Nova Scotia.

It was along this North Atlantic coast that Alexander Graham Bell invented the telephone and Guglielmo Marconi sent out the first wireless message across the Atlantic, where Ruth Wakefield baked the first Toll House cookies, and where Sicily-born Benedetto Capalbo floated the first submarine sandwich. So popular were they during World War II that he supplied 500 a day to the submarine base in New London, Connecticut—which is how the sandwich he called a "grinder" got its new name.

New England is the birthplace of the graham cracker and the Parker House roll, where Lydia Pinkham's Vegetable Compound "for periodic female weakness" was produced and the birth control pill invented, where Lizzie Borden took an ax and the Brink's burglars took a powder, where Earl Tupper sealed up Tupperware, Clarence Birdseye flash-froze food, and the first snowmobile cranked up back in 1913.

The first Frisbees came from fun-loving Bridgeport, Connecticut, where Robert Mitchum was born and P. T. Barnum lived, only they were originally spelled "Frisbies"—pie tins from a local bakery with the name stamped on the bottom that Yale students in the twenties tossed as a fad.

Newport, Rhode Island, boasts the first traffic ordinance (1687) and the first automobile arrest—for speeding at 15 mph (1904).

Saint John, New Brunswick, is where Donald Sutherland was born, MGM's Louis B. Mayer grew up, Captain Kidd raped and pillaged, and the King of Siam's Anna Leonowens retired to found an arts academy. Benedict Arnold was burned in effigy and driven out of town—not for being a traitor (he was a hero to the Loyalists) but for nefarious business dealings.

Prince Edward Island (PEI) is where a red-haired, pigtailed orphan named Anne of Green Gables, born in a book by Lucy Maud Montgomery back in 1908, is a cottage industry, where *supper* is usually preceded by *lobster,* and potatoes have their own museum. If Malpeque oysters and seaweed pie are on the menu and Seaman's soft drinks (birch beer, ginger brew, root beer, lime rickey) close at hand, you can be sure you're on PEI.

Nova Scotia is where ice hockey was born (in Windsor around 1830), Alexander Graham Bell and the schooner *Bluenose* retired (Bell in Baddeck, the *Bluenose* in Lunenberg), and most of the victims of the *Titanic* were buried (in Halifax), since it was the closest landfall to the sinking.

RVing in New England & the Maritimes

The Lobster Coast route heads north along the edge of Connecticut and Rhode Island, jogs over to Cape Cod, then back up the shore to Boston, Salem, and Gloucester, the 18-mile coastline of New Hampshire, and the 3,500-mile coastline of Maine. After that, it carries on through New Brunswick's Loyalist and Acadian country to Nova Scotia. Prince Edward Island, which also has very fine lobsters, was once accessible only by plane or ferry, inconvenient but not impossible for RVers, but now has the 7.9 mile Confederation Bridge from New Brunswick. The whole route one way is approximately 1,200 miles, more if you dip into all Maine's picturesque coves and make a loop around Nova Scotia, and explore inland.

Canada's Maritimes offer good driving in most areas for freewheelers, but maneuvering an RV through New England is not always easy. Roads are narrow and often crowded with traffic, especially in summer around Cape Cod or Kennebunkport, and there are not a lot of pullover spots spacious enough for a big rig. The best way to explore most of the towns and villages along the Lobster Coast is to park your RV and set out on foot.

HITTING THE HIGHLIGHTS

If 2 weeks is the maximum time you have for a Lobster Land vacation, you'll be able to make the coastal drive to Nova Scotia and back from a New York or Connecticut starting point, as well as the journey around Cape Cod, but you might have to miss islands like Nantucket, Martha's Vineyard, and Prince Edward Island. Allow a week for New England, the second week for Canada's Maritimes. June is less crowded than July and August and the autumn, but some of the campgrounds and attractions may not be open yet.

Highlights of the New England Coast

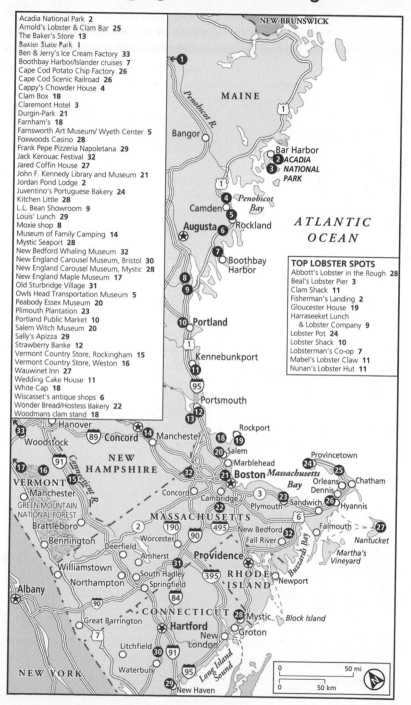

GOING FOR THE LONG HAUL

If you want to spend more than 2 or 3 weeks on the Lobster Coast, you'd better make your plans and arrangements well in advance for July and August. And don't expect to get reduced rates for a long stay in a private campground during the summer; one New Hampshire operator charged us double for the Fourth of July weekend, even though we were in residence for a month, because that's his peak season. As a Cape Cod friend reminded us, they have to make their profits for the whole year in only a few short months.

The only time more popular in New England than July and August are the autumn foliage months when the "leaf peepers" arrive by the car and busload. It's the prettiest time of year, so take refuge in some off-the-beaten-track towns and villages or head north to Canada to wait out the invasion. New Brunswick is filled with great discoveries and is uncrowded year-round; you could spend a month exploring there. While Nova Scotia and Prince Edward Island tend to be busier in summer, you can still find some space.

Travel Essentials

WHEN TO GO

Summer and fall is prime lobster season, and also when the weather is best. That's also when everyone goes. If you go too early in June, you'll encounter the mosquitoes, black flies, and no-see-ums. Autumn is crowded with leaf peepers, who go for the fall foliage. They travel in groups, often by tour bus.

WHAT TO TAKE

Bring binoculars, film and camera, rain gear, hiking boots, sun hat, sunscreen, and insect repellent. To enter Canada, you should have proof of citizenship, such as a passport, birth certificate, or voter registration card because a driver's license is not acceptable. (Some Canadian border guards let people through with only a license, but it's not technically legal. Better safe than sorry.)

WHAT TO WEAR

If you want to mingle at the posher purlieus of New England like Bar Harbor, Nantucket, and Martha's Vineyard, wear anything from the L. L. Bean, J. Crew, or Land's End catalogs, Topsiders without socks, plaid or khaki Bermuda shorts, Oxford cloth shirts, and pastel sweaters tied around your neck. Otherwise, don your usual RV garb, and you'll fit in almost everywhere.

Always have a sweater or jacket handy. The Maine coastal weather on a summer day is described by Frances FitzGerald as Baked Alaska, a simultaneous sensation of hot sun and cool breeze. And Nova Scotia residents were nicknamed "Bluenoses" for bearing up under the cold winters.

TRIMMING COSTS ON THE ROAD

First of all, never eat your lobster in a restaurant. You can pick it up at a lobster pound live or cooked. Take a live lobster back to the RV and cook it or

Canadian Maritime Highlights

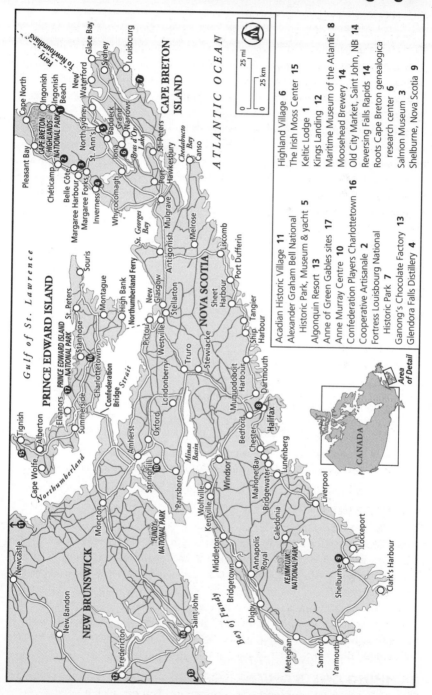

Highland Village **6**
The Irish Moss Center **15**
Keltic Lodge **1**
Kings Landing **12**
Maritime Museum of the Atlantic **8**
Moosehead Brewery **14**
Old City Market, Saint John, NB **14**
Reversing Falls Rapids **14**
Roots Cape Breton genealogica
  research center **6**
Salmon Museum **3**
Shelburne, Nova Scotia **9**

Acadian Historic Village **11**
Alexander Graham Bell National
  Historic Park, Museum & yacht **5**
Algonquin Resort **13**
Anne of Green Gables sites **17**
Anne Murray Centre **10**
Confederation Players Charlottetown **16**
Cooperative Artisanale **2**
Fortress Louisbourg National
  Historic Park **7**
Ganong's Chocolate Factory **13**
Glendora Falls Distillery **4**

refrigerate it until later (see "Looking for Lobster in All the Right Places," later in this chapter). A hot cooked lobster can be brought back to the RV or eaten on the spot at a picnic table thoughtfully provided by the pound or the town. At many pounds, you'll be able to pick up side dishes and beverages, even beer or wine, to go with your steaming crustacean.

Even though the Canadian dollar is considerably lower in value than the U.S. dollar at this writing, don't let it go to your head.

Make the most of admission to living history parks by planning to spend the day, either taking a lunch or buying one (prices are reasonable) in the on-site restaurants. If you have children along, they'll experience new dishes and utensils so interesting they'll forget they never liked such-and-so.

Plan your beach visits for state parks or national parks like Cape Cod or Acadia; many of the beaches in the northeast are private.

WHERE TO GET TRAVEL INFORMATION

It's easy to find out what's going on in New England and the Maritimes. Stop at any tourist information spot, particularly those on main highways at the entrance to a state or province, and you can pick up campground information, times and prices for attractions, maps, and leaflets on everything from local farmer's markets to self-guided drives or walks—all free. If you want to get information and maps ahead of time, contact the following tourism offices:

- **Connecticut Department of Economic Development,** Tourism Division, 865 Brook St., Rocky Hill, CT 06067 (☎ 800/CT-BOUND; www.ctbound.org).
- **Maine Office of Tourism,** 189 State St., State House Station 59, Augusta, ME 04333 (☎ 800/533-9595; www.visitmaine.com).
- **Massachusetts Office of Travel & Tourism,** 100 Cambridge St., 13th floor, Boston, MA 02202 (☎ 800/447-6277; www.mass-vacation.com).
- **New Hampshire Office of Travel and Tourism,** Box 1856, Concord, NH 03302 (☎ 800/FUN-IN-NH, ext. 169, or 603/271-2666; www.visitnh.gov).
- **New Brunswick Tourism,** Dept. 243, P.O. Box 12345, Woodstock, NB, Canada E7M 6C3 (☎ 800/561-0123 in the U.S. and Canada outside New Brunswick; www.tourismnewbrunswick.ca, publishes a New Brunswick Travel Guide).
- **Nova Scotia Tourism,** P.O. Box 519, Halifax, NS, Canada B3J 2M7. They can also arrange reservations at hotels or campgrounds (☎ 800/565-0000; www.explorens.com).
- **Rhode Island Tourism Division,** 7 Jackson Walkway, Providence, RI 02903 (☎ 800/556-2484; www.visitrhodeisland.com).

• **Tourism Prince Edward Island,** Marketing Council Visitor Services, P.O. Box 940, Charlottetown, PEI, Canada C1A 7M5 (☎ **888/PEI-PLAY;** www.peiplay.com).

DRIVING & CAMPING TIPS

• **Watch for low and narrow passes.** On New England and Canada's old side roads, be a stickler for reading underpass and tunnel clearance signs, gauging overhead branches, and eyeballing narrow roads before you start your turn.

• **Beware of small-scale campgrounds.** Many of the RV parks and campgrounds in this region were built a couple of decades ago to accommodate mostly tent campers and small trailers or folding camping trailers. Today's large motor homes with extrawide bodies and slide-outs—as well as basement storage that means more height on top, satellite dishes, and rooftop air conditioners—may face a tight squeeze in some New England campgrounds.

• **Check ahead about power requirements.** Many older campgrounds have not added 50-amp electricity although most (not all) have 30-amp. Particularly in New England and Canadian state and provincial parks, the hookups may offer 15- or 20-amp electricity only. We found it a good idea to phone ahead and emphasize our size and amperage requirements, then reiterate it when we check in so we're not assigned a spot that doesn't fit.

• **Expect fog.** You'll probably encounter some foggy or misty patches of road along the coast, especially in the mornings, with drizzle that might go on all day.

Best Sights, Tastes & Experiences of the Lobster Coast

OFF-THE-WALL ATTRACTIONS

The New England Carousel Museum, Bristol, Connecticut. Everything you need to know about carousels and carved wooden horses. You can watch antique wooden horses being reconstructed, learn the distinctive characteristics of the different types, and see some of the band organs that cranked out the music for the carousels. Admission is $4 for adults, $2 for children. The museum is at 95 Riverside Ave., Route 72 (☎ **860/585-5411**).
The New England Maple Museum, Pittsford, Vermont. You'll meet an animatronic New England maple syrup maker, see some dioramas that show sugaring in the early 1900s, admire some maple-syrup-inspired folk art, and take a maple syrup tasting (don't knock it if you haven't tried it) that shows

the subtle flavor differences between the grades. An extensively stocked gift shop sells everything maple syrupy you can imagine and then some. The museum is north of Pittsford, on Route 7, and is open daily 8am to 5:30pm between late May and October, as well as November 1 through December 23 and late March to late May, 10am to 4pm (☎ 802/483-9414).

Vermont Country Store, Rockingham and Weston. Want to pick up some cow udder balm to keep your hands soft or supple, some almost-forgotten candies like Walnettos or Valomilk bars, or some elastic-free, all-cotton Buster Brown socks? Head for the Vermont Country Store. It has two locations, but we like the Rockingham branch with its bargain attic, really a ground-level side building full of steeply discounted items so weird they might not move even at 75% off. You can also taste and buy Vermont farm-house cheeses, including a wonderful Crowley Colby–type cheese "made just down the road," along with Vermont common crackers baked on the premises. The Rockingham store is off I-91's exit 6 on Route 103 and is open daily (☎ 802/463-2224). The main store is a few miles northwest in Weston, on Route 100 (☎ 802/824-3184). For mail order, call ☎ 802/362-8440.

Ben & Jerry's Ice Cream Factory Tours, Waterbury, Vermont. We learned the hard way not to arrive on a holiday weekend at Ben & Jerry's; every sport utility vehicle in the Northeast was unloading, and the wait for a tour time was more than an hour. Fortunately, the parking lot has a special area for RVs, or we would probably have turned around and left. Tours $2 adults, $1.75 children, depart daily year-round except major holidays every 15 to 30 minutes, depending on the season, and sign-ups are on a first-come, first-served basis. When ice cream is not being produced (Sundays and hol-idays), you see a video but still get free samples. A gift shop sells all sorts of cow logos; a scoop shop dips out your favorite flavor. It's located on Route 100 north of exit 10 from I-89. For tour information, call ☎ 802/882-1260; www.benjerry.com.

The Baker's Store, Norwich, Vermont. For anyone who loves to cook, this store stocking everything from the King Arthur Flour catalog is as enthralling as a museum. Pans, cutters, yeasts, flours, mixes for everything from pizza dough to scones, dried herbs and spices, whisks, Bundt cake pans—every-thing imaginable lines the well-stocked shelves. To gild the brioche, there's an on-premises bakery selling breads and pastries from the adjoining King Arthur kitchens. Open daily 9am to 5pm Monday through Saturday and Sunday from 11am to 4pm on Route 5, just off exit 13 from I-91 (☎ 800/827-6836).

Cape Cod Potato Chip Factory, near Hyannis, Massachusetts. Watch the chips being kettle-cooked one batch at a time at Breed's Hill Road in Independence Park near Hyannis, where they turn out 200,000 bags of the crunchy darlings every day. They'll give you a free bag as you leave. Self-guided tours year-round on weekdays only between 9am and 5pm. From Route 6, turn onto Route 132; on Route 132, take a left at the fourth traffic

Young visitors to Ben & Jerry's pose for the camera.

light onto Independence Drive, go to the second stop sign, and take a right onto Breed's Hill Road. The chip factory is on the left (☎ **888/881-CHIP;** 508/775-7253).

The Salem Witch Museum. Located in a former church by Salem Common, the museum re-creates the hysteria of the 17th-century witch hunts with satanic symbols, taped music, mimed hangings in silhouette, and other spooky silliness performed with more enthusiasm than expertise. The audience loves it. It's in downtown Salem, on Route 1A diagonally across from the commons (☎ **978/744-1692;** www.salemwitchmuseum.com).

Peabody Essex Museum, Salem, Massachusetts. Also in Salem, this classy museum on East India Square displays an astonishing collection of the curiosities local sea captains brought back home from the exotic East—shrunken heads, stuffed penguins, giant sea clams, ship models, Chinese export porcelain, Polynesian barkcloth, Japanese warrior costumes, and a huge moon bed carved from a single piece of teak. Open year-round. $10 adults, $8 children, free under 6 (☎ **800/745-4054;** www.pem.org).

Alexander Graham Bell's Yacht, Baddeck, Nova Scotia. Learn to sail aboard Alexander Graham Bell's 59-foot yacht *Elsie,* which has been cruising the Bras d'Or from Baddeck, Nova Scotia, for 80 years. You can book lessons, as well as day cruises, overnights, and cruises of up to 2 weeks between mid-June and the end of October. Call Captain Patterson at ☎ **902/ 295-7245.**

The Wedding Cake House, Kennebunk, Maine. Located on Summer Street, Route 35, Kennebunk, this is a gorgeous 19th-century house built, it is said, by a sea captain for his new bride after he went to sea without even having a taste of his own wedding cake. It's a drive-by site not open to the public.

Owls Head Transportation Museum, Owls Head, Maine. Watch the Red Baron's Fokker triplane from World War I soar into the sky or listen to the hiss of a Stanley Steamer. On summer weekends you not only see antique motorcycles, biplanes, automobiles, and farm machinery but hear them and smell them—these antique machines are all in working order and cranked up regularly. Visitors may even be offered a ride in a Model T Ford. Call ahead to see which machines are running and when. The museum is 2 miles south of Rockland on Route 73 (☎ 207/594-4418; www.ohtm.org).

Claremont Hotel, Southwest Harbor, Maine. The nine-wicket croquet tournaments at the Claremont Hotel, on the Claremont Road in Southwest Harbor, draw international attention from the croquet circuit; you can watch the action from the big front porch. Take the Maine Turnpike to Augusta, and exit to Route 3. Then take Route 3 through Ellsworth to the Trenton Bridge and Mount Desert Island. Once over the bridge, take Route 102 to Southwest Harbor. Call for dates (☎ 207/244-5036; www.acadia.net/claremont).

The Reversing Falls Rapids, Saint John, New Brunswick. The reversing rapids are produced by a phenomenon called a tidal bore. It happens twice a day when high tides in the Bay of Fundy cause the Saint John River to turn back on itself and flow upstream until the bay again drops below the river level and the river reverses itself again. Since the tides here are the highest in the world and the river bed has an underwater ledge, the boiling and surging of the water are dramatic. Best way to watch is from Fallsview Park, near the Reversing Falls Information Center (15 Market Square, St. Johns, New Brunswick). The highest tides are when the moon is full. Sea kayaking in the bay is the latest thrill around Saint John. For information, call the Saint John Visitors and Convention Bureau at ☎ 506/658-2990; www.cityofsaint john.com.

Glendora Falls Distillery, Cape Breton Island, Nova Scotia. For a real Scottish moment, head for this distillery on Highway 19 between Mabou and Inverness, where the only single-malt Scotch whiskey in North America is produced. The distillery is recent, but the whiskey is ready for drinking. You can take a tour every hour on the hour (☎ 902/258-2662).

Anne Murray Centre, Springhill, Nova Scotia. This is the most popular tourist attraction in town, dedicated to the pop singer whose recording of "Snowbird" might well be the theme song for all winter-escaping RVers. You should be able to find a copy in the gift shop, if you want to spring for the admission fee. C$5.50 adults, C$4.50 seniors, C$3 children 6 to 18, free under 5. It's at 36 Main St., Springhill, Nova Scotia (☎ 902/597-8614).

The Potato Museum, O'Leary, and Irish Moss Interpretive Center, Miminegash, Prince Edward Island. In these two museums, you'll learn about two important agricultural products. Potatoes, the economic mainstay, are lauded in pictures, videos, and exhibits (see the giant sculpted potato, visit The Amazing Potato, and taste the cooked potatoes in the kitchen). Irish moss, a seaweed better known as carrageenan, is gathered when storms loosen it, and the whole town goes down to the shore with scoops. The economically valuable carrageenan is a starchy substance that has no calories or flavor and is used to thicken dairy products, toothpaste, shampoo, cough syrup, and other products. A cafe at the center serves seaweed pie. Potato museum (☎ **902/859-3605**); Irish moss museum (☎ **902/882-4313**).

FIVE THOUGHT-PROVOKING PLACES

The John F. Kennedy Library and Museum, Dorchester, Massachusetts.
Exhibits, films, tapes, and slides trace JFK's career and that of his brother Robert. A half-hour biographical film runs regularly. The striking building design is by I. M. Pei. Located by the sea (follow directional signs from I-93) and open daily 9am to 5pm except major holidays (☎ **617/929-4501**).

Baxter State Park. Maine's 200,000-acre Baxter State Park is rugged, primitive, and guaranteed to stay pristine forever. In the 1920s, Governor Percival Proctor Baxter suggested the legislature acquire Mount Katahdin and its surroundings for a park, but the legislators balked at the expense. So Baxter spent the next 30 years buying up parcels of land himself and donating them as a park "to be maintained primarily as Wilderness . . . [and] be Forever Wild." Roads are gravel or dirt and usually narrow and winding. Self-contained RVs, motorcycles, and pets are not permitted in the park; all overnight camping is by reservation only. Backpackers and hikers will find 175 miles of wilderness trails. Even if you take a 4x4 and drive through the park, you'll have to get out and walk down a trail to see the most spectacular scenery; it's designed that way. The park can be found northwest of Millinocket off Route 11/157 via a paved private road to the park entrance or via Route 163 east from Adesque Isle to Ashland, then by private unpaved road into the park. Both access roads require a permit and fee. Call ☎ **207/723-5140** for forms for reservations that can be made only by mail.

The Maritime Museum of the Atlantic, Halifax, Nova Scotia. A deck chair and other artifacts from the *Titanic* are among the displays. As the closest port to the disaster, Halifax hosted hundreds of funerals for more than 10 days. Today the unclaimed bodies of some 150 victims are buried in three different Halifax cemeteries. Only 5 years later, the city faced its own disaster, the Halifax Explosion, when two ships, one of them carrying a half-million pounds of TNT plus other explosives, collided in the harbor, killing 2,000 people instantly and destroying much of the city. Located at 1675 Lower Water St. in Halifax, Nova Scotia. Open daily 9:30am to 5:30pm and some evenings. Admission C$6 adults, C$5 seniors, C$2 children, free for 5 and under, C$15 family (☎ **902/424-7490**; www.maritime.museum.gov.ns.ca).

New Bedford Whaling Museum, New Bedford, Massachusetts. The cobblestone streets of old New Bedford's harbor have been turned into a Whaling National Historic Park with this fine museum at its heart. Dominating the lobby is a 66-foot skeleton of a blue whale. The world's largest ship model of the whaling ship *Lagoda*, half its real size, lets you walk around the deck, while an adjacent exhibit of a whaleship fo'c'sle (fore-castle) gives you a realistic picture of life at sea on these voyages that went on for many months. Across the street is the Seaman's Bethel, the site of the sermon in Herman Melville's *Moby-Dick*. A self-guided "Moby-Dick Trail" takes you around sites mentioned in the book. The museum is at the corner of Johnny Cake Hill and William Street in the historic waterfront area of New Bedford. Open daily 9am to 5pm except major holidays. Admission $6 adults, $5 seniors, children 6 to 14 $4 (☎ **508/997-0046;** www.whalingmuseum.org).

Farnsworth Art Museum/Wyeth Center, Rockland, Maine. A thrifty New England spinster named Lucy Farnsworth, the last remaining member of her family, died at 97 in 1935, leaving a million-dollars-plus to preserve the family home and create a library and art museum in her father's memory. Today the 50-year-old museum is a complex of five buildings, four in Rockland and the fifth in nearby Cushing. The Victorian Farnsworth home and the Olson House in Cushing are open in summer only, while the museum and Wyeth Center are open daily year-round except Mondays in winter. A six-level art museum preserves the work of native Maine artists and artists who did significant works in Maine, such as the Wyeths, Winslow Homer, John Marin, George Bellows, Edward Hopper, and Rockwell Kent. The austere Wyeth Center, located in a former church adjacent to the Farnsworth home and museum, displays works by N.C. Wyeth, his son Andrew Wyeth, and Andrew's son James (Jamie) Wyeth. But most evocative of all for Andrew Wyeth fans is the Olson House, the grey farmhouse near Cushing that is seen in many of his paintings, notably *Christina's World*. Unfurnished, the house displays copies of Wyeth's works in the rooms where they were painted. The complex is at 356 Main St. in Rockland, where you can also get a map and directions to the Olson House. Admission from Memorial Day Monday through Columbus Day Monday is $9 seniors, $8 students 18 and older $5 with valid ID, ages 17 and younger, free (☎ **207/596-6457;** www. farnsworthmuseum.org, www.wyethcenter.com).

LIVING HISTORY SITES

New England and Canada's Maritimes have a plethora of "animated" villages that re-create life in earlier times. Costumed actors, also called interpreters or animators, usually portray a real person who lived in the village. Some villages are fixed permanently in a given year, and day-to-day life goes on exactly as it would have then. No one seems to mind if you come into their kitchens while they prepare a meal, poke your head in the barn, or talk to someone tending a garden or feeding the animals. They are happy to pose for pictures as well.

Mystic Seaport. Connecticut's Mystic Seaport, at exit 90 off I-95, is a restored 19th-century village with whaling ships, costumed craftsmen to chat with, and maritime artifacts. The construction of a replica of the *Amistad,* the early-19th-century schooner depicted in Steven Spielberg's film of the same name, is planned as an educational "floating classroom." Plan to spend a full day at this engrossing place, which is open daily from 9am to 5pm between April and October. Admission $17 adults, $9 youths 6 to 12, and free under 6 (☎ 888/9-SEAPORT or 860/572-5315; www.mysticseaport.org).

Plimoth Plantation. At Plimoth Plantation, near Plymouth, Massachusetts, you can talk with Pilgrims who are still living in the year 1627, tending their crops and remembering their long, cramped sea journey on the *Mayflower*. You'll hear 17 different dialects in the village, reflecting the places the Pilgrims came from. Even the livestock is authentic, "back-bred" to re-create the Pilgrims' stock. Handcrafted items you can watch being made are for sale. It's open daily 9am to 5pm between April and Thanksgiving Weekend. Accessible only from southbound Route 3. Take exit 4 to the Plimoth Plantation highway and follow the signs (☎ 508/746-1622; www.plimoth.org).

Old Sturbridge Village. Located on Route 20 in Sturbridge, Massachusetts, at the intersections of Interstates 84 and 90 (about an hour from Boston), Old Sturbridge Village has re-created rural New England life in 1830, with costumed interpreters, craftsmen, farm animals, and the beginnings of industry with shoemakers, coopers, tinners, and blacksmiths. Open daily year-round except Mondays in winter (☎ 508/347-3362; www.osv.org).

Strawberry Banke. This 10-acre historic community has 42 buildings, seven that illustrate different time periods in the area's history, plus 17th-century herb and vegetable gardens, furnished houses, and crafts shops that include weavers, coopers, cabinetmakers, potters, and boat builders. Entrance tickets are good for 2 days; you may need that to see it all. Closed November to April. Located in Portsmouth, along New Hampshire's 18 miles of coastline; take 95 to exit 7, and follow signs from the exit to a 10-acre site near the waterfront (☎ 603/433-1100; www.strawberrybank.org).

Shelburne, Nova Scotia. Once the fourth largest city in North America, Shelburne—on the southeast tip of Nova Scotia on Route 103, 60 miles southwest of Liverpool—is now a sleepy little town with a magical historical complex. In 1783, 10,000 Loyalists from the United States, protesting the American Revolution and remaining loyal to the British Crown, arrived in ships from New York City. The historic district has re-created the oldest store in America, a dory-making shop that still produces the working boats in traditional fashion, and the only remaining privately owned cooperage (barrel-making shop) in North America. The Shelburne waterfront along Dock Street was also the location for the 1994 film *The Scarlet Letter*. Some attractions are open seasonally. Ross-Thomson House and Store Museum (☎ 902/875-3141); Dory Shop Museum (☎ 902/875-3219).

Fortress Louisbourg National Historic Park. One of North America's largest historical reconstructions, Fortress Louisbourg, near Sydney, Nova Scotia, is for us the most fascinating and realistic of all. It is always the summer of 1744, and the fortress is staffed with scruffy, unruly soldiers (who were to mutiny 6 months later) and French aristocrats in exquisite houses.

Officer's wife at Fortress Louisbourg demonstrates lace-making.

Inns with pewter mugs and earthenware dishes serve 18th-century food to visitors. "A moment in time" is portrayed in remarkable detail by a cast of more than 100 in and around the 50 or so buildings. Spend at least half a day; try to arrive first thing in the morning. Buy a loaf of soldiers' bread from the bakery and some farm cheese from the Destouches House to take along on the road (but bring your own plastic bags to take them back to the RV—there was no plastic in 1744). And bring a jacket and an umbrella, as the weather can change suddenly along this coast. Open 9am to 7pm; C$12 adults, C$10 seniors, C$6 children, and free under 6. Located south of Sydney, Nova Scotia, on Route 22 just beyond the modern town of Louisbourg. Take exit 8 near Sydney (☎ **902/733-2280;** www.fortresslouisbourg.ca).

Kings Landing. This re-creation of a Loyalist settlement of the early 1800s has more than 100 costumed animators and 60 buildings—farmhouses, mills, churches, and inns. You may see Scottish dancing or caber tossing between June and mid-October, when the park is open daily 10am to 5pm. Located on the Trans-Canada Highway near Fredericton, New Brunswick, about 60 miles north of Saint John; C$12 adults, C$10 seniors, C$6 children, and free under 6 (☎ **506/363-4999;** www.kingslandingnb.ca).

Acadian Historic Village. You'll have a window into the lives of Acadians between 1780 and 1890, watching costumed residents from fur trappers to blacksmiths at work. A cafeteria and restaurant in the village serve traditional Acadian dishes, which bear no resemblance whatsoever to the food their Cajun cousins cook in Louisiana. West of Caraquet on Route 11 near Chaleur Bay on the banks of the Riviere-du-Nord, about 160 miles north of Moncton; C$12 adults, C$10 seniors, C$6 children and free under 6. Open daily in summer between June and late September (☎ **506/726-2600**).

Highland Village. Scottish Americans looking for their roots should visit the Highland Village on Route 223 in Iona, on the south shore of Cape Breton Island, Nova Scotia, which commemorates the settlement of the area by the Highland Scots. Open daily in season, the village has 10 historic structures dating from 1810 through the early 20th century, moved here and staffed with costumed interpreters doing traditional crafts and farming; C$5 adults, C$4 seniors, C$2 children 5 to 8, free under 5, and C$10 family. It's in Iona by the Bras d'Or Lake in the heart of Cape Breton Island and open early June to mid-October (☎ 902/725-2272; www.highlandvillage.ns.ca).

Also on the premises is **Roots Cape Breton,** a computerized genealogical research center with data collected from census, cemetery, birth, death, and marriage records.

Confederation Players, Charlottetown, Prince Edward Island. Costumed interpreters conduct walking tours ($3.50 adults, children under 12 free) and perform daily vignettes from 1864 when the Fathers of the Confederation met here to form a union of the colonies. These strolling players are around throughout July and August, and are happy to pose for your cameras as well as reenact history (☎ 800/955-1864; www.capitalcommission.pe.ca).

TEN SPLURGES

1. **Spend a weekend at the Wauwinet on Nantucket.** Wauwinet is an elegantly understated, gray-shingled, white-trimmed seaside inn on a remote, sandy neck of land between Nantucket Harbor and the Atlantic. The whole place looks as though it were decorated by Ralph Lauren with Martha Stewart arranging the flowers, and has sailboats, clay tennis courts, bicycles, and a 21-foot launch that's available for picnics and bay cruises. Nantucket is accessible by ferry from Hyannis, Massachusetts. For reservations, call ☎ 800/426-8718; www.wauwinet.com.

2. **Go shopping in Nantucket.** Pick up a classic Nantucket Lightship Basket purse, considered an heirloom that increases in value; prices start at around $350. Or you could choose some delectable chocolate almond buttercreams in pretty hand-painted tins at Sweet Inspirations on India Street. For some of us, that's a splurge.

3. **Take a scenic cruise aboard the *Islander*.** From Boothbay Harbor the boat takes you to a clambake at Cabbage Island, where each feaster gets fish chowder, two lobsters, steamed clams, corn on the cob, Maine potatoes, and blueberry cake ($39.95 per person; mid-May to mid-September). There's also a full-service bar. For information and reservations, call ☎ 207/633-7200.

4. **Check out the treasures in Wiscasset's antiques shops.** There are more than 20 shops within walking distance of each other, featuring everything from early American furniture to 19th-century paintings. Wiscasset is about 15 miles east of Bath on U.S. 1. Call Wiscasset Regional Business Association at ☎ 207/882-1119 for information.

5. **Take a summer whale-watching cruise.** Boats leave from Hyannis, Provincetown on Cape Cod, and Gloucester. Take cameras, binoculars, a jacket, a securely fitting hat, and sunscreen. From Provincetown: **Dolphin Fleet** (☎ 800/826-9300) and **Portuguese Princess Whale Watch** (☎ 800/442-3188), $20 adults, $17 children. From Hyannis: **Hyannis Whale Watcher Cruises** (☎ 800/287-0374), $26 adults, $21 seniors, $16 children 4 to 12. From Gloucester: **Seven Seas Whale Watch** (☎ 800/238-1776); **Yankee Whale Watch** (☎ 800/WHALING; www.yankeefleet.com); and **Cape Ann Whale Watch** (☎ 800/877-5110; www.caww.com), $28 adults, $22 seniors, $16 children. The last leaves from Rose's Wharf, Gloucester, from exit 10 off Route128, and promises plenty of parking—RVs are welcome.

6. **Have a 17th-century meal at Massachusetts's Plimoth Plantation.** Every Friday and Saturday evening a period dinner is served. Vegetables come from the plantation gardens, and you eat with your fingers and a knife (forks were not in general use at the time) and listen to madrigal singers. The museum is in Plymouth, Massachusetts, and is accessible only from southbound Route 3. Take exit 4 to the Plimoth Plantation highway and follow the signs. For reservations, call ☎ 508/746-1622.

7. **Book a dinner train ride on the vintage Cape Cod Scenic Railroad.** Enjoy a five-course meal on a 2-hour twilight ride through 42 miles of the cape. Admission is $13 adults, $9 children. There is also a morning trip. Located at 252 Main St., Hyannisport, Massachusetts (☎ 508/771-3800).

8. **Go antiques shopping along Old King's Highway on Cape Cod.** Also known as Route 6A, Old King's Highway is lined with countless antiques shops. Glass collectors must not miss the **Sandwich Glass Museum** in Sandwich, showcasing glassware made here between 1825 and 1888 with sand imported from New Jersey (Cape Cod sand has iron oxides that discolor the glass). At 129 Main St. at the Junction of Main Street and Route 130. Open daily April through December, Wednesday through Sunday February and March, closed January (☎ 508/888-0251).

9. **Take a day sail aboard a Maine windjammer out of Camden.** The *Appledore,* a windjammer that's sailed around the world, will take you out among the rocky islands of Penobscot Bay where seals sun themselves on the rocks and porpoises play in the water. Come to the dock at Bayview Landing by the Town Landing and sign up or call ahead; $25 adults, $15 children (☎ 207/236-8353).

10. **Stop off for lunch or tea at a 19th-century resort.** Relive the golden days of summer-long vacations in old-fashioned resort hotels by visiting

the half-timbered 1899 **Algonquin,** 184 Adolphus St., St. Andrews-by-the-Sea, New Brunswick, surrounded by manicured lawns, lush gardens, and a century-old golf course (☎ **506/529-8823**); or at **Keltic Lodge** (built in 1940 but looking much older) near Ingonish Beach on Nova Scotia's Cape) Breton Island. (☎ **800/565-0444**). In Bar Harbor, Maine, the **Bar Harbor Inn's** Reading Room Restaurant opened its doors in 1887. Now the re-created inn offers sumptuous (if expensive) lobster rolls and more pedestrian fare such as fish and chips and hamburgers. On the waterfront by the Municipal Pier (☎ **800/248-3351** or 207/288-3351; www.barharborinn.com).

LOOKING FOR LOBSTER IN ALL THE RIGHT PLACES
Where to Find 'em
A single-minded lobster lover along the Maine coast can cheerfully overlook Bar Harbor day-trippers and T-shirt vendors, fudge fairs, and ye olde gift shoppes to search out a lobster pound or an "early bird lobster dinner." Before 5:30 or 6pm, you can dine on a whole fresh lobster weighing around 1¼ pounds for the price of the day. You might even hit a two-for-one special, two 1-pounders on the same plate and enough for two. This is best done as a takeout, since the thrifty New England proprietors usually won't allow two to share. With a little concentration, you can hit a couple of these spots before prices go up for the evening and it's time to get ready for dinner.

How to Eat 'em
The peerless *Homarus americanus northern,* or American lobster, has meaty front claws that his warm-water cousins lack. We also think he is much more succulent.

Only when driven to desperation (or boredom) should you order lobster prepared any way other than steamed or boiled, except on a cold day, when a lobster stew goes down well, and perhaps at lunchtime, when a lobster roll fills the bill. For the uninitiated, a lobster roll is a top-sliced hot dog bun filled with chunks of cold lobster moistened with mayonnaise or melted butter or both, and sometimes a crunch of chopped celery.

Buying 'em Live
When buying a live lobster, look for the liveliest, with a good greenish-brown color. Avoid any that have turned blue. Pick a feisty one just as you would a puppy at the pound, and look for long antennae. That means he's been there less time than the ones with short antennae, which get bitten off. Lobsters can last up to 2 days out of seawater if you refrigerate them in your RV in a heavy brown paper bag with a few strands of seaweed or several layers of newspapers. Never close a lobster up in a plastic bag, where it will suffocate, or store it in a pot of cold tap water, where it will drown.

How to Cook 'em

To cook a lobster, put several inches of water—preferably seawater—in a pot, bring it to a boil, and drop the lobster in, holding him by the underside of the body to keep him from splattering the water, then cover the pot quickly. Listen for the water to boil again, then reduce the heat to keep it from boiling over. The lobster is cooked when all of its shell has turned red, usually in as little as 10 minutes for a small lobster to 20 minutes for a large one. The happy medium seems to be 13 or 14 minutes for a 1¼-pounder, adding 3 minutes for each additional quarter pound. Soft-shell lobsters, if you're lucky enough to find some, take less time. Another expert suggests that when the lobster turns bright red and floats, cook for 3 or 4 minutes longer.

The British Society for the Prevention of Cruelty to Animals suggests the most humane way to cook a lobster is to lower it into the pot head first, starting with cold water, which will put the lobster to sleep as it warms.

TOP LOBSTER SPOTS

Nunan's Lobster Hut, Cape Porpoise, Maine. At Nunan's, the crustaceans are steamed to order in a little water rather than boiled in a lot. A bag of potato chips and a hard roll with butter fill out the dinner tray. Finish off with a slice of homemade apple or blueberry pie. It's located at 11 Mills Rd. and is open evenings from 5pm. No reservations or credit cards (☎ 207/967-4362).
Beal's Lobster Pier, Southwest Harbor, Maine. Beal's serves soft-shelled lobster, steamer clams, corn on the cob, and onion rings. You sit at picnic tables at the end of the pier and feast. Located at the end of Clark Point Road (☎ 207/244-7178).
Fisherman's Landing, Bar Harbor, Maine. At Bar Harbor's waterfront, you'll find live or cooked lobster by the pound to take out, along with

Lobster pots off Boothbay Harbor, Maine.

LOBSTER TRIVIA QUIZ

The Maine Lobster Promotion Council put out a trivia quiz to test your lobster IQ. Here are some of the questions. You'll find the answers following the quiz. To learn more about lobsters, log on to www.lobster.um.maine.edu/lobster.

1. The lobster's nervous system most closely resembles the nervous system of what insect?

2. How long have lobsters been harvested in Maine?

3. What do lobsters eat?

4. What is the tomalley, the light green substance found in the lobster's carapace?

5. Why do lobsters turn red when they are cooked?

6. How fast can a lobster swim?

ANSWERS: (1) The grasshopper. (2) The first report of caught lobsters was in 1605 when early explorers caught them in a net. Commercial lobstering began in the mid-1800s. (3) Crabs, clams, mussels, starfish, sea urchins, and other lobsters. (4) The liver and pancreas of the lobster, which can contain contaminants; consumers are urged not to eat the tomalley, although some lobster aficionados relish it. The red coral eggs found inside the female lobster, on the other hand, are treasured by gourmets and used in sauces or cooking. (5) The lobster shell carries different color pigment chromatophores; when cooked, all but the red pigment called astaxanthin are masked. No matter what color the lobster shell when raw, it will turn red when cooked. (6) By flipping its tail and swimming backward, a lobster can cover 25 feet in just under a second.

wonderful lobster rolls, fried clams, and crab rolls. Of course, you don't have to take them any farther than the picnic tables outside the restaurant. Open 11:30am to 8pm daily; $8 to $10 a pound, cooked (☎ 207/288-4632).

Lobsterman's Co-op, Boothbay Harbor, Maine. On Atlantic Avenue near the aquarium you'll find a wooden pier with outdoor picnic tables and a choice of hard-shell or soft-shell lobster (defined on a hand-printed sign as SOFT SHELL = LESS MEAT, SWEETER TASTE). To that definition, we can add "easier to crack open." While fat gulls perched on the rail look on, you can devour lobsters with melted butter, a bag of potato chips, corn on the cob, onion rings, steamed or fried clams, and jug wine by the glass or pitcher. Open mid-May to Columbus Day, lunch and dinner (☎ 207/633-4900).

The Gloucester House, Gloucester, Massachusetts. At the Gloucester House, waitresses call you "dearie" and serve an inexpensive assembly line clambake with lobster, clam chowder, corn on the cob, and watermelon at long wooden tables out back. Located on Rogers Street (☎ 978/283-1812).

Harraseeket Lunch & Lobster Company, South Freeport, Maine. Harraseeket is at a pier on the harbor, and the town won't let RVs access the

Abbott's Lobster in the Rough, Noank, Connecticut.

quarter-mile residential street down to the pier. If you really want a lobster, park along South Freeport Road, send one member of the party to walk to the lobster company while the other stays with the RV in case you need to move. Go around back at the lobster company, place your order and take a number. About 20 minutes later, you'll have your freshly cooked crustaceans. If you have a legal parking space, you can both walk down and eat on the premises if you can find a seat. Open 11am to 7pm (☎ 207/865-3535).

Abbott's Lobster in the Rough, Noank, Connecticut. Abbott's serves fresh boiled lobster with coleslaw and its own label potato chips at outdoor picnic tables by the water. You can get clams on the half-shell or in chowder, or a lobster roll, if you'd rather. Weekdays are less crowded, and there is adequate RV parking. Located at 117 Pearl St. in Noank (just south of Mystic on Route 217) (☎ 860/536-7719).

The Old City Market, Saint John, New Brunswick. The Old City Market sells live or cooked lobsters to take out or ship home, as well as lobster rolls and cooked lobster tails. Everywhere you see paper bags of dark red flaky leaves, called dulse, dried seaweed that is a favored local snack and very much an acquired taste. The market dates from 1876 and is built to resemble the inverted keel of a ship. It's at 4951 Charlotte St. and is open 8am to 6pm. There's a glass-walled solarium next door if you want to eat your lobster here, or head for Billy's Seafood Company (11am–10pm) in the north corner if you favor a sit-down meal (☎ 506/672-FISH).

The Lobster Shack, Cape Elizabeth, Maine. The Lobster Shack occupies an incomparable setting by the sea at the end of Two Lights Road by the lighthouse in Cape Elizabeth. A local landmark, it encourages you to "come as you are" and offers "eat in or take-out" service. You can also choose between eating indoors or at picnic tables above the rocks at seaside. Open daily 11am to 8pm from April through mid-October (☎ 207/799-1677).

Mabel's Lobster Claw, Kennebunkport, Maine. Mabel's, where George and Barbara Bush indulge in the peanut butter ice-cream pie, has softshell lobster in season (July–Sept) and lovely lobster rolls to eat in or take out; 124 Ocean Ave. (☎ 207/967-2562).

The Clam Shack, Kennebunkport, Maine. The Clam Shack is located by the bridge. There's nowhere nearby that is big enough for an RV to park, but if a passenger hops out and the driver goes on into town and parks for a while (there's often a wait), you can get fantastic lobster rolls to go or serious baskets of fried clams. It's open around 11am to 7pm (☎ 207/967-3321).

The Lobster Pot, Provincetown, Cape Cod. This funky but pricey restaurant in a two-story clapboard house serves classic clam chowder along with local clambake dinners, and has take-out chowder and lobster. You can sit inside or out on an open deck on the upper level, called Top of the Pot, but you can't drive or park an RV in P-town. Located at 321 Commercial St. (☎ 508/487-0842).

Prince Edward Island's Famous Lobster Suppers, Prince Edward Island. All summer long, the island holds lobster suppers as fundraisers, special events, or daily occurrences. Watch for the signs as you walk, bike, or drive around. St. Ann's Church in Hope River, for instance, has served them every summer for 35 years daily except Sunday from 4 to 9pm. St. Ann's (☎ 902/621-0635). **New Glasgow Lobster Suppers** serves from its own pound on Route 258, 10km southeast of Cavendish, open daily from 4 to 8pm. (☎ 902/964-2870; www.peilobstersupper.com).

TAKE-OUT (OR EAT-IN) NONLOBSTER TREATS

Kitchen Little, Mystic Seaport, Connecticut. On Route 27, 2 blocks east of the Mystic Seaport entrance (near the Mystic Seaport Museum), is a tiny restaurant that serves breakfast and lunch, both memorable meals, especially when taken in the back garden by the water. We opted for an early lunch to miss the breakfast rush and ate a cup (served in a coffee mug) of light and unique clam chowder in a thin clear broth redolent of fresh clam, followed by a fried scallop roll and a lobster roll. The late breakfasters around us were feasting on huge omelets, pancakes with fresh strawberries, and eggs with cheese and jalapeño peppers. It's on Highway 27 (☎ 860/536-2122).

Woodmans clam stand, Essex, Massachusetts. The first clam was fried and served at Woodmans back in 1916, so they say, and today you can get clams to take out or eat in by standing at a counter and watching them fry after you order them. This style of service is called "in the rough," but the delectable clams and their companion onion rings are silky inside, crunchily crusty outside. The clam fritters aren't bad, either. In fact, we defy you to drive out of the parking lot past the giant plaster clam without succumbing to the irresistible urge to taste at least one. We've been there a number of times and

The tidy little Clam Box in Ipswich looks like a take-out box itself.

only twice has the queue to get in defeated us (during Memorial Day weekend one year, Labor Day weekend another). It's at 121 Main St. (☎ 978/768-6451).

Farnham's, Essex, Massachusetts. To continue our tale from Woodmans, above, we drove down Eastern Avenue (Route 133) toward Gloucester, and on the edge of Essex we found Farnham's, a smaller, less crowded restaurant, where, like Woodmans, diners order from the counter, then take a seat in the restaurant or wait until the takeout is ready. The fried clams are crunchy, crisp, and luscious, the fish and chips light and delicious, and the clam chowder as rich and thin as any model's dream. In a moment of weakness, we also ordered the fried onion rings (the servings are enormous), and reheated both potatoes and onion rings the next day without any loss of quality. You can call ahead for takeout; 88 Eastern Ave. (☎ 978/768-6643).

The Clam Box & The White Cap. Another pair of fried clam standbys awaits the aficionado just north of Essex in Ipswich, the center for great clam digging. The Clam Box, at 246 High St. (Route 133) on the north end of town looks a little like a take-out box itself (be prepared for a wait) (☎ 978/356-8707). The White Cap, in a strip mall at 141 High St., also fries up some tasty morsels (☎ 978/356-5276).

Durgin-Park, Boston, Massachusetts. Boston baked beans and Indian pudding are still the mainstays at Boston's Durgin-Park, now located in the gentrified confines of Faneuil Hall Market but still served at long family style tables by brusque New England matrons. No reservations, no credit cards. At the North Market Building, Faneuil Hall (☎ 617/227-2038).

Arnold's Lobster & Clam Bar, Eastham on Cape Cod, Massachusetts. The onion rings at Arnold's are extra-special, and the steamed lobster, fried clams, steamers, and mussels not bad, either. Prices are modest, and there's little decor, but the patio and picnic tables among the pines are always filled with happy eaters. Beer and wine are available. At 3580 State Hwy. (☎ 508/255-2575).

Frank Pepe Pizzeria Napoletana, New Haven, Connecticut. Frank Pepe's claims to have baked America's first pizza in 1925. They still use the original brick ovens to turn out the famous white clam pie, a tomato-free pizza. Pepe's, at 157 Wooster St, opens at 4:30pm into the evening (☎ 203/865-5762). Its pizza-making neighbor a block down the street is **Sally's Apizza** at 237 Wooster, open at 4:30pm through the evening. Sally's was a Bill Clinton favorite in his Yale days, and it makes a fresh tomato pie in summer and a broccoli-cheese pie year-round. Wooster Street, where the pizzerias are located, is in a residential area on the east edge of town (watch for signs) with adequate street parking for RVs early in the evening but not later (☎ 203/624-5271).

Louis' Lunch, New Haven, Connecticut. It was in New Haven that Louis Lassen made the first hamburger (so they say) in 1900, and four generations later Louis' Lunch on Crown Street is still serving them plain on toasted bread, no hamburger buns, ketchup, mayo, mustard, or special sauce allowed. It's at 261-263 Crown St. (downtown between Temple and College) (☎ 203/562-5507).

Portuguese *caldo verde* soup. The classic Portuguese soup, a luscious brew of potatoes, kale, and smoked garlic sausage, is one of many dishes brought to Nantucket by immigrants. One good place to sample it is the upscale **Jared Coffin House,** 29 Broad St., open 9am to noon, 1 to 5pm (☎ 508/228-2400). **Juventino's Portuguese Bakery,** at 331 Commercial St. in Provincetown, Cape Cod, is an option for takeout (☎ 508/487-1803).

Harraseeket Lunch & Lobster, Freeport, Maine. Harraseeket, on Main Street in South Freeport (for instructions about getting there, see above, under "Top Lobster Spots"), serves the famous whoopie pie, a pair of big cakelike chocolate cookies sandwiched together with fluffy marshmallow cream. It's an old Maine treat, usually homemade and always wrapped and ready to go on the cafe counter (☎ 207/865-3535).

Moxie, the first carbonated soft drink, Lisbon Falls, Maine. Sample the descendent of the first carbonated soft drink, Moxie, in its tiny Maine headquarters in Lisbon Falls, between Brunswick and Lewiston. Developed in 1876 as Beverage Moxie Nerve Food, it predated Coca-Cola by a decade, and lent its name to the slang vocabulary of the twenties, when *moxie* meant "a lot of nerve." Today the company sells memorabilia and soft drinks from the store at 2 Main St. at the junction of Route 196. You can also have it shipped by the case (☎ 207/353-8173).

Jordan Pond Lodge, Acadia National Park, Maine. Afternoon tea at Jordan Pond Lodge, on the Park Loop Road, begins at 11:30am and features popovers and strawberry jam in an old-fashioned garden filled with dahlias, sweet peas, and delphiniums. The island is called Mt. Desert but pronounced *dessert*. Think sweet thoughts, and call ahead (☎ 207/276-3316).

Cappy's Chowder House, Camden, Maine. Cappy's ladles up clam chowder by the cup or bowl to eat in or take out, as well as serving bar drinks in Mason jars. This is the town where *Peyton Place* was set. Poet Edna St. Vincent Millay worked as a waitress at the nearby Whitehall Inn during the summer of 1912 (☎ 207/236-2254).

The Portland Public Market, Portland, Maine. This indoor market also has snack bars and take-out food, heaped counters of fresh seafood, farmhouse cheeses, and butter made in Maine. Greengrocers carry more than one variety of Maine-grown potatoes. Located at 25 Preble St. on the corner of Cumberland, the market is open from 9am to 7pm, except Sundays, when it's open 10am to 5pm (☎ 207/228-2000; www.portlandmarket.com).

Ganong's Chocolate Factory, St. Stephen, New Brunswick. Just across the border from Maine, Ganong's is where the candy bar was invented when the owner wrapped some slabs of chocolate in waxed paper to take on a fishing trip. Among its unique sweets are "chicken bones," crunchy white-striped, cinnamon-flavored logs with a bittersweet chocolate center. Early August the town celebrates a 6-day chocolate festival. The Chocolatiere on Water Street sells candies by phone (☎ 506/465-5600). It has a store in town at 73 Milltown Blvd. The factory itself is located on 1 Chocolate Dr. and hosts a tour once a year, in the first week of August.

Moosehead Brewery, Saint John, New Brunswick. In summer, tour the Moosehead Brewery, sample the highly praised brew, then drop by the Moosehead Country Store on Main Street for a Moosehead cap or T-shirt. The brewery is at 89 Mainstreet West. Call for a tour appointment: ☎ 506/635-7000.

Malpeque oysters. Look for briny Malpeque oysters, a Prince Edward Island specialty, on menus throughout Canada's Maritime Provinces in season, and search out the fundraising lobster suppers offered around Prince Edward Island by churches and other community centers. You'll not only dine copiously and well, but you'll find the natives are friendly on their own turf.

WILDLIFE-WATCHING

It always comes as a surprise to New England visitors when they learn that there are still plenty of **moose** in the woods, although the only people that seem to run into them do it literally. Throughout New Hampshire, road signs give the tally of how many moose have been hit by cars during the year.

White-tailed deer are plentiful throughout New England and the Maritimes, as are **beavers, raccoons, porcupines,** and **skunks. Black bear** are occasionally spotted. The **red fox** is common in Maine's Acadia National Park but rarely seen by visitors.

With all that ocean, you'll find an abundance of marine life, especially **whales.** Humpbacks, fin whales, and occasionally rare right whales (rare because they were the "right" whale for whalers and therefore virtually decimated) may be spotted, most easily aboard a whale-watching boat. You'll also usually see **seals, porpoises,** and **dolphins.** We've seen more humpback whales off Boston than in the Arctic, Antarctic, or anywhere.

Day cruises go out from Connecticut's Waterford; Maine's Bangor, Boothbay, Lubec, Northeast Harbor, and Portland; Massachusetts's Barnstable, Boston, Gloucester, Plymouth, Provincetown, and Rockport; New Hampshire's Rye Harbor; Nova Scotia's Cheticamp, Big Bras d'Or, and Westport; and New Brunswick's Grand Manan Island, near Campobello.

Pelagic **seabirds,** those that return to land only for breeding and raising their young, are frequently sighted along the coastline. Look for storm petrels, shearwaters, gannets, guillemots, razorbills, and puffins.

The National Audubon Society and the Canadian Wildlife Service have been working on a project since 1971 to return the puffins to Seal Island off Rockland, Maine. The once-thriving colony of birds was almost wiped out around the turn of the century by hunters.

On the Road

CAPE COD

The Pilgrims landed at the tip of Cape Cod, where Provincetown is located, before they reached Plymouth Rock, on November 11, 1620. They stayed there for 36 days before crossing Cape Cod Bay to Plymouth.

The famous rock, what's left of it, is shielded under a Grecian colonnade, and a replica *Mayflower* is staffed by costumed personnel.

Things are a bit more crowded these days. Try to avoid arriving on a summer weekend—or during the months of July and August—if you want easy driving and a place to park within walking distance of kitschy little Provincetown. Autumn is a beautiful season on the cape, and you can have the beaches to yourself.

Traffic on Route 28, the southernmost highway across the cape, is very slow because the area is built up like a quaint megalopolis. A far better route for RVers is smooth-running Route 6. Route 6A is the one to take if you like a slow-moving drive through villages with antiques shops and country inns.

For 30 miles of protected and beautiful beaches, but no camping, head for **Cape Cod National Seashore.** Unfortunately, it has only six parking lots, which fill up by midmorning in summer. Those at Nauset Light Beach and Wellfleet's Marconi Beach have steep stairways leading down to the beach. Hiking trails set out from Salt Pond Visitor Center in Eastham, where there's spacious parking for RVs, and Head of the Meadow Trailhead in Truro, both off Route 6. Bicycle trails run along both sides of the Cape Cod Canal, with parking available in the Sandwich Marina area, adjacent to the National Seashore from Eastham North.

Bay-side beaches have warmer water and less turbulent surf than the ocean side. Low tide is best for beach hiking because the sand is packed; at high tide you'll be struggling through looser, deeper sand.

New England Coast Campgrounds

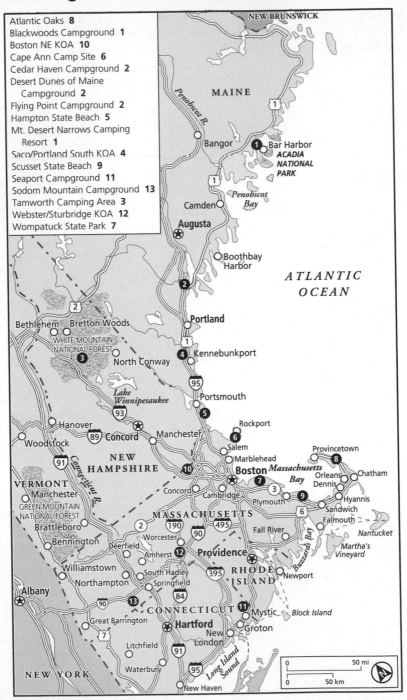

Atlantic Oaks **8**
Blackwoods Campground **1**
Boston NE KOA **10**
Cape Ann Camp Site **6**
Cedar Haven Campground **2**
Desert Dunes of Maine
    Campground **2**
Flying Point Campground **2**
Hampton State Beach **5**
Mt. Desert Narrows Camping
    Resort **1**
Saco/Portland South KOA **4**
Scusset State Beach **9**
Seaport Campground **11**
Sodom Mountain Campground **13**
Tamworth Camping Area **3**
Webster/Sturbridge KOA **12**
Wompatuck State Park **7**

INVESTING WITH THE MASHANTUCKET PEQUOTS

Foxwoods High Stakes Bingo and Casino, generally considered the biggest and most profitable casino in the United States, is in Ledyard, Connecticut, about 6 miles north of I-95's exit 92 or I-395's exit 79A near Mystic Seaport on the Mashantucket Pequot Indian Reservation. The Pequots were virtually decimated in the 17th century by settlers and militia, but since the casino opened, their numbers, once down to one surviving resident on the reservation, have been increasing (☎ 800/PLAY-BIG).

Virtually next door, you can see where the profits went, and make your own investment in the new $193 million, 100,000-square-foot **Mashantucket Pequot Museum.** This awesome museum re-creates a glacial cravasse, a computer animated caribou kill 11,000 years ago and a full-size 16th-century village of Eastern woodland Indian village life that the visitor can see, hear, and smell. Your tickets, $12 adults, $8 seniors, $8 ages 6 to 12, can be applied toward a membership (from $35) that allows free entrance in the future plus special events and discounts at the museum shop (☎ 800/411-9671; www.mashantucket.com).

Another lavish tribal resort/casino in the area with big-name headliners is the **Mohegan Sun,** also off I-395 at exit 79A, then east 1 mile on route 2A. For information, call ☎ 888/226-7711; www.mohegansun.com.

For information, contact **Cape Cod Chamber of Commerce,** 307 Main St., Hyannis, MA 02601 (☎ 888/33-CAPECOD; www.capecod.com).

NANTUCKET

Leave your RV on the mainland and take a day trip on the ferry to the island of Nantucket from Hyannis via Hy-Line Cruises (☎ 888/778-1132 or 508/778-2600), daily year-round; traditional ferry: $27 adults, $13.50 children; high-speed ferry: $58 adults, $41 children. Then rent a bicycle. The free public beaches, seafood restaurants, and bright flowers blooming in front yards everywhere make this one of New England's prettiest places; plus, there's a Whaling Museum and 11 other equally appealing little museums.

Nothing built after the 1920s gets any notice from the local guides. Walking tours meander through the main part of town looking at the shingled houses graying in the weather, the brick houses built by whaling barons, and the newer Federal and Victorian houses. In the early summer, lupine, iris, and lemon lilies grow along the walkways, old-fashioned hollyhocks, alyssum, geraniums, hydrangeas, and nasturtiums bloom in pint-sized gardens, and rosa rugosa with its big red rose hips thrives in hedges everywhere.

Guides like to point out one house occupied by a writer who had traveled twice around the world before deciding that Nantucket was the best place; he nailed two pairs of shoes by the door to show his traveling days were over.

Thomas Mayhew purchased Nantucket Island for 40£ in 1659 from Lord Sterling, who had been granted it by Charles I. After holding onto the island for 18 years, Mayhew sold it for only 30£ and two beaver hats.

JACK KEROUAC FESTIVAL

Every year at the end of September, Jack Kerouac's birthplace of Lowell, Massachusetts, celebrates the birthday of the author of *On the Road* (1957) and what he called his "spontaneous prose" about life on the highways of America. Kerouac himself hated the lack of privacy his fame cost him, and fretted that he'd lost the gift of high-speed writing during the 1960s in California. He and his wife returned to Lowell to live with his mother for several years, then he took his family to St. Petersburg, Florida, where he died in 1969 at the age of 47. He's buried in Lowell's Edson Cemetery on Gorham Street. For information, call ☎ **978/656-3127.**

The early Nantucket sailing ships always carried a crew of four young boys ages 13 or 14 in each whale boat, along with a master and a harpooner. The boys did not necessarily choose to go whaling, but in Nantucket, they would not be acceptable suitors for a bride until they had been around Cape Horn and had taken a whale.

Rules like this probably contributed to the sheer islandness that Nantucketers display, a quirky cantankerousness that dictates its idiosyncrasies. Here the world is divided into two simple camps—"on island," which is Nantucket, and "off island," which is everywhere else.

And that's where everybody else comes from, as many as 50,000 of them in summer, thronging the streets and filling the restaurants at lunchtime. So locals often partake of a midmorning meal, then splurge on a late dinner after the last of the day-trippers have taken the ferry back to the mainland.

Nantucketers claim all the young people and rock stars go to trendier Martha's Vineyard. "We're happy in Nantucket that they're happy over there," one resident told us.

For more information about Nantucket, contact **Nantucket Island Chamber of Commerce,** 48 Main St., Nantucket, MA 02554 (☎ **508/228-1700;** www.nantucketchamber.com).

Campground Oases in Connecticut, Massachusetts & New Hampshire

Seaport Campground, Mystic, Connecticut. Located 3 miles from Mystic Seaport, the campground has 130 sites and is open March through November. Sites are fairly well spaced, with water and electric hookups and sanitary dump, hot showers, flush toilets, laundry, playground, and fishing. RVs over 34 feet are not permitted. To get there, take exit 90 from I-95 to Route 184, at Old Mystic, Connecticut (☎ **860/536-4044;** www.seaportcampground.com).

Scusset State Beach, Sagamore, Massachusetts. Located at Sagamore on the Cape Cod Canal near the junction of Routes 3 and 6, the campground has 100 RV sites with 20- and 30-amp electricity and water hookups, a sanitary dump for registered guests only, a fishing pier, showers, flush toilets, and piped water. No reservations; open year-round (☎ **508/888-0859**).

Atlantic Oaks. In Eastham Massachusetts, half a mile north of the entrance to Cape Cod National Seashore on U.S. 6, Atlantic Oaks has 100 pull-through sites with 30-amp electric, dump station, and cable TV. Sites are wide for New England, but there are some pet restrictions. It's within walking distance of Arnold's Lobster & Clam Bar (☎ **800/332-2267**; www.capecamping.com).

Wompatuck State Park. Southeast of Boston at Hingham (1¾ miles on State Road 228 to Free Street, then 1 mile east to Union Street, then south 1½ miles on marked turnoff), Wompatuck has 400 grassy and shady sites, 150 of them with 30-amp electric hookups. We stayed there early in the season with few neighbors, but in July and August it can get crowded, especially on weekends. Prices are modest ($6–$8), and there are restrooms and showers, a sanitary dump station, and a 14-day camping limit. For information, call ☎ **781/749-7160.**

Boston NE KOA, Littleton, Massachusetts. A good choice if you're towing a car and want a base for jaunts into the surrounding area. You will be close to Concord and Lexington, Salem, Gloucester, Lowell, and Boston. Trust us, you do not want to take a motor home into downtown Boston. There are 100 gravel, mostly shaded sites with 17 pull-throughs, 30- and 50-amps, Internet access and all the usual KOA facilities. From exit 30 on I-495 go west on route 2A for 2½ miles to the campground (☎ **800/562-7606** or 978/772-0042; www.minutemancampground.com).

Cape Ann Camp Site. Listed under Gloucester but actually on the Cape Ann Peninsula off exit 13 from Route 128, the Cape Ann Camp has 150 sites, some with great views of the water. Water and 30- and 50-amp electric are available in all sites, but only 50 also have sewer hookups. There is a dump station. We recommend anyone with a large motor home or towing a long trailer or fifth-wheel not to drive up to the office at the top of the hill but call and let them send someone to meet you at the entrance, where some of the larger sites are located (☎ **978/283-8683**; www.cape-ann.com/campsite).

Webster/Sturbridge KOA. Near Old Sturbridge Village in the Worcester area off exit 10 from the Massachusetts Turnpike. There are 97 sites, 25 of them pull-throughs, with a lot of shade, 20- and 30-amp electric hookups, cable TV, and a modem-friendly office (☎ **800/KOA-1895** or 508/943-1895; www.koa.com).

Sodom Mountain Campground. Located in Southwick, Massachusetts, Sodom Mountain has spacious, shaded sites plus a few floored teepees where campers can unroll sleeping bags. Open early May to mid-October, the campground is located near Springfield, 3 miles west of Route 57 from the junction of 57 and routes 10/202 (☎ **413/569-3930**).

Hampton State Beach. The state of New Hampshire likes RV campers, so you can find a state park, right by the ocean in Hampton—that not only has 28 sites with full hookups (20- and 30-amps) but also imposes a 3-day minimum stay. There are some pet restrictions. It's open mid-June to late September. From the junction of I-95 and Route 101 (exit 2), go east 3 miles on Route 101 to Route 1A, then south 2 miles. The entrance is on the left. For information, call ☎ 603/926-8990; www.nhparks.state.nh.us. For reservations only (7 days in advance), call ☎ 603/271-3628.

Tamworth Camping Area. On the edge of Tamworth, New Hampshire, this is a sprawling campground on a family farm complete with barn and farm animals. Some 100 spaces include secluded tent-sized sites by the Swift River and big-rig sites in an open field with water and 15- and 30-amp electric hookups. Open mid-May to mid-October. Tamworth is a quiet New England village not far from bustling Conway and its factory outlet shopping. From the junction of highways 25-W and 16, go north half a mile on Highway 16 to Depot Road, then west 3 miles. The entrance is on the left (☎ 800/274-8031 or 603/323-8031; www.tamworthcamping.com).

MOUNT DESERT ISLAND

Maine's Mount Desert Island (pronounced des-*sert* by some, *des*-ert by others) is home to most of the serene and scenic **Acadia National Park** as well as the overcrowded summer streets of **Bar Harbor.** Even in August the climate is fresh and cool.

Landscape painters from the group called the Hudson River School came here in 1844 to paint, then sold the pictures to wealthy northeast urbanites who traveled to see the places depicted and, in typical robber baron fashion, ended up buying the real estate in their canvases to build elaborate 30-room summer "cottages" patterned after Tudor hunting lodges and Scottish castles.

Most of the grandiose cottages are gone now, victims of a 5-day fire that swept through Bar Harbor in 1947, changing the town's image considerably.

Summer residents of the island, many of them millionaires, are responsible for preserving the 35,000 acres of land in Acadia National Park and handing it

---

THE MUSEUM OF FAMILY CAMPING

Visit the Museum of Family Camping at Bear Brook State Park in Allenstown, New Hampshire, to walk through a free exhibit of the evolution of family camping from tents and bedrolls to today's modern RVs. Set indoors and out around a pine grove, the museum is open daily 10am to 4pm between Memorial Day and Columbus Day. Allenstown is located in Merrimack County on Route 28 between Epsom and Suncook, about 15 minutes from Concord. From the junction of routes 4 and 28 at the Epsom Traffic Circle, drive south 5.6 miles on Route 28 to the park entrance, then northeast 1.5 miles on Bear Brook State Park Road to the museum (☎ 603/485-3782). 🚐🚙

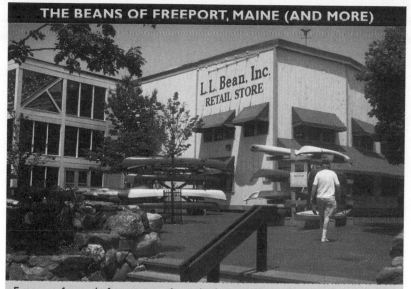

THE BEANS OF FREEPORT, MAINE (AND MORE)

Freeport, formerly famous mostly as the home of **L. L. Bean,** has turned into the factory outlet capital of New England with around 100 shops, including a vast L. L. Bean emporium open 24 hours a day, 365 days a year. There are several RV campgrounds with hookups in the vicinity if you've shopped till it's time to drop (see "Campground Oases in Maine," below). For a free visitor guide, call ☎ 800/865-1994; www.freeportusa.com. The main L. L. Bean showroom is on Main Street, and a smaller factory outlet store, adjacent to the town's RV parking lot, is open during regular business hours. 🚐

over to the government in 1916. John D. Rockefeller, who disliked automobiles and preferred driving through the parklands in a horse-drawn carriage, commissioned over 50 miles of gravel carriage roads. Today hikers, bicyclists, and bird-watchers are more in evidence than carriages in summer, and cross-country skiers use the roads in winter. The 27-mile **Park Loop Road** for automobiles is accessible for RVs.

Call Acadia National Park for more information about camping and hiking (☎ 207/288-3338; www.nps.gov/acad).

Campground Oases in Maine

Saco/Portland South KOA. A comfortable, centrally located RV park with big wooded sites and a large heated swimming pool, it also offers Belgian waffle and blueberry pancake breakfasts on summer weekends, nightly desserts that include blueberry pie, a lobster cruise along the coast, and lots of scenery and nearby shopping. It's located off exit 5 from the Maine Turnpike, then exit 2B from I-195 and north 1½ miles. There are 120 sites in a wooded park, more than half of them pull-throughs, with city water and 20- and 30-amp electric (☎ 800/KOA-1886 or 207/282-0502; www.koa.com).

Flying Point Campground. In Freeport, Maine, heaven for shoppers and lobster lovers (not necessarily in that order), we like Flying Point Campground on Casco Bay, which has 45 oceanfront campsites with 30-amp electric hookups. It's a modem-friendly campground with restrooms, pay showers, sanitary dump station, and mobile sewer service. From the junction of I-95 and U.S. 1 (exit 19), go north 1 mile on U.S. 1 to Bow/Lower Flying Point Road, then east 3¾ miles. The entrance is on the left. For reservations, call ☎ 800/798-4569 or 207/865-4569.

Cedar Haven Campground. Also in Freeport and a tad closer to the shopping is Cedar Haven Campground, which purports to be the closest campground to L. L. Bean, only 2 miles away. It's also modem-friendly, with some 50-amp electric hookups and big rig capability, cable TV, camp store, and sanitary dump station. Located at 39 Baker Rd. (☎ 800/454-3403 or 207/865-6254; www.campmaine.com/cedarhaven).

Desert Dunes of Maine Campground. In Freeport you'll find this campground, with a free shuttle into Freeport (it's 2½ miles from L. L. Bean) so some family members can go shopping while others hike around the sand dunes. There are 45 sites with water and 20- and 30-amp electric hookups, a sanitary dump, pool, store, and laundry. From the junction of I-95 and Desert Road (exit 19), go west 2 miles on Desert Road. The entrance is on the left. For reservations, call ☎ 207/865-6962; www.desertofmaine.com.

Mt. Desert Narrows Camping Resort. On Route 3 (Bar Harbor Road) in Bar Harbor, Maine, this is a resort-style park on the ocean with some grassy, tree-shaded, fairly spacious sites. There's a swimming pool, video game room, playground, laundry, hot showers, and 239 sites with full and partial hookups. They even sell Maine lobster in July and August. Closed in winter (☎ 207/288-4782; www.barharborcampgrounds.com).

Blackwoods Campground. Located in Maine's Acadia National Park, Blackwoods requires advance reservations for its 45 RV sites between June 15 and September 15. There are toilets, sanitary dump, no hookups, and 14-day maximum stay. Seawall, the park's other campground, is first-come, first-served (☎ 207/288-3338; www.nps.gov/acad).

NOVA SCOTIA'S CAPE BRETON ISLAND

Cape Breton Highlands National Park in the wild and rocky Cape Breton Islands is the northernmost thrust of Nova Scotia into the Atlantic. The poetic headlands are dashed by the surf and softened by morning mists.

A 184-mile loop begins at Baddeck, a tranquil seaside village that was the longtime summer home of Alexander Graham Bell, who is buried here. The **Alexander Graham Bell National Historic Park and Museum,** 559 Chebucto St., shows the inventor's energetic and creative mind, which ranged far beyond the telephone into work with the deaf, early aircraft, and conversion of seawater to fresh (☎ 902/295-2069).

Take the Cabot Trail, Canada Route 105, north of Baddeck in a clockwise direction for easier driving, especially if you begin in the morning, to the

Cape Breton Island near Bras d'Or.

cluster of towns along the Margaree River that are named after the river. North East Margaree is home to the unique little **Salmon Museum** with its collection of hand-tied flies, fishing tackle, poaching equipment, and a study of the life cycle of the Atlantic salmon (☎ **902/248-2848**).

Follow the river to the coast and you'll encounter a series of French Acadian villages—Belle Cote, Terre Noire, St. Joseph du Moine, Grand-Etang—whose residents still speak the 18th-century French of their Norman ancestors. The Cape Breton Acadians show off their regional cooking and handicrafts at the **Cooperative Artisanale** gift shop, 15067 Main St., Cheticamp, each summer between early May and the end of October (☎ **902/224-2170**). In the tiny downstairs restaurant, local women serve chicken *fricot,* potato pancakes, fish chowder, homemade pies, and ginger-bread with syrup. In the craft shop upstairs, you can browse among the hooked rugs, woodcarvings, hand knit sweaters, and quilts.

From Cheticamp, you enter the park itself with its dazzling vistas of beach-es and stark cliffs sculpted by the wind and sea. Except for occasional camp-grounds and picnic areas, you'll encounter no habitation until Pleasant Bay. Then the road turns inland to the sweeping grandeur of the highlands and distant vistas of the churning sea, interspersed with wooded valleys.

Note Neils Harbour, bright with colorful, painted houses and fishing boats, lobster pots, and fishnets. The cottages are usually daubed with what-ever paint is left over from the boats by thrifty fishermen.

A few miles south at Ingonish Beach, a side road leads to the splendid **Keltic Lodge** (see "Ten Splurges," earlier in this chapter; ☎ **800/565-0444**). Moody, mist-clouded Cape Smoky lies south of Ingonish Beach, with Wreck Cove, Skir Dhu (Gaelic for "Black Rock"), and North Shore, from which you

THE LOYALISTS & THE ACADIANS

By the end of the American Revolution, 40,000 Americans loyal to the British Crown had fled north to Canada. Some 14,000 arrived in what is now New Brunswick, with land grants along the Saint John River given to them by the Crown. In 1785, they incorporated their settlements into the city of Saint John.

Meanwhile, to the south in the pretty village of St. Andrews-by-the-Sea, across the Passamoquody Bay from Maine, other Loyalists put their houses on rafts and towed them over the water to Canada. Kings Landing near Fredricton re-creates a Loyalist community from the early 1800s with costumed interpreters. (See "Living History Sites," above.)

The Canadian Acadians, in an area of Nova Scotia, New Brunswick, and Maine once called Acadia, are cousins of the Louisiana Cajuns. Descended from French peasant families who were the first European settlers in Canada, the Acadians in 1755 refused to swear allegiance to the British Crown and so were ordered deported. Some fled to other parts of the North Atlantic coast, others south to French-speaking Louisiana. Henry Wadsworth Longfellow dramatized the story in his poem "Evangeline."

Today the Acadians remaining in Canada continue to speak French and to protect their cultural inheritance. The Acadian Historical Village near Caraquet re-creates their early settlements.

can sometimes see the Bird Islands, protected nesting area for cormorants, puffins, petrals, and terns. The park's Bog Trail is suitable for wheelchairs.

For more information, contact **Cape Breton Island Tourism,** P.O. Box 1448, Sydney, NS, Canada B1P 6R7 (☎ **800/565-9464;** www.cbisland.com).

Campground Oases in Canada's Maritimes

Rockwood Park. This 2,200-acre park in the city of Saint John, New Brunswick, welcomes RVers with 170 pull-through sites, 150 of them with water and 15- and 30-amp electric hookups, a dump station, flush toilets, showers, picnic tables, and fireplaces. Take exit 113 from Highway 1 westbound or exit 111 and Route 100 eastbound. With fishing, swimming, a golf course, and a zoo, the park, 5 minutes from central Saint John, makes a good stopover. No reservations (☎ **506/652-4050**).

Fundy National Park. Located near Alma, New Brunswick, Fundy National Park has campgrounds with hookups and kitchen shelters. Chignecto Campground has 127 water and 30- and 50-amp hookup sites, and Headquarters Campground has 29 full-hookup sites with 30-amp electric. To get to Headquarters, follow Route 114 for half a mile northwest; to get to Chignecto, continue on another 2 miles. For information, call ☎ **506/ 887-2000;** for reservations, call ☎ **800/414-6765.**

Canadian Maritimes Campgrounds

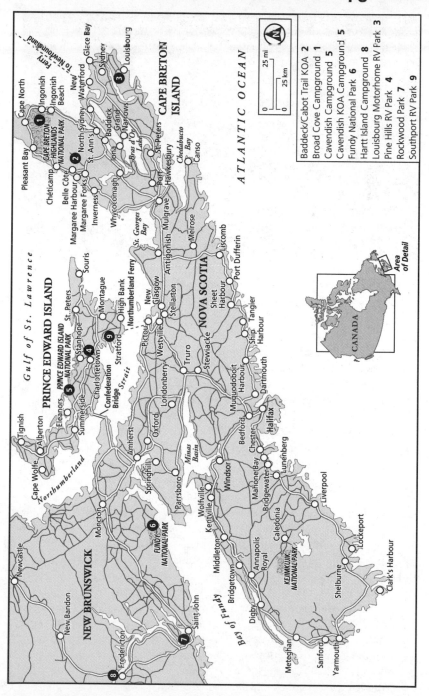

Baddeck/Cabot Trail KOA **2**
Broad Cove Campground **1**
Cavendish Campground **5**
Cavendish KOA Campground **5**
Fundy National Park **6**
Hartt Island Campground **8**
Louisbourg Motorhome RV Park **3**
Pine Hills RV Park **4**
Rockwood Park **7**
Southport RV Park **9**

Lighthouse along the New Brunswick coast.

Broad Cove Campground, Ingonish Beach, Nova Scotia. Cape Breton Highlands National Park's Broad Cove Campground has 83 full-hookup sites (15- and 30-amp) with flush toilets and showers, fishing, swimming, and a playground. There's also a fine 18-hole golf course called Highland Golf Links inside the park. No campground reservations. Located 7 miles north of the East Park entrance on Cabot Trail (☎ 902/285-2691).

Louisbourg Motorhome RV Park. Located in the town of Louisbourg, Nova Scotia, near the national historic park, the RV park has 49 sites, 36 of them with full hookups (15- and 30-amp). The park is modem-friendly. Open mid-May through mid-October. Flush toilets, showers, sanitary dump, fishing, by the ocean. From the junction of Highway 22 and Harbour Front Crescent (in the town center), go northeast 200 feet on Harbour Front Crescent. The entrance is on your left. For reservations, call ☎ 902/733-3631.

The Baddeck/Cabot Trail KOA. Sitting off Trans-Canada Highway 105 at exits 8 or 9, this KOA lets you leave your RV in camp and take off to drive the Cabot Trail with your car, truck or a rental vehicle. The campground also offers free fishing on a watery arm of the Bras d'Or Lake, access to a major 18-hole golf course, and guided tours to Fortress Louisbourg or the Cabot Trail (☎ 800/KOA-7452 or 902/295-2288, www.koa.com).

Hartt Island Campground. Near the New Brunswick capital of Fredericton on Route TCH 2, the Hartt Island Campground provides 90 campsites with water and 15- and 30-amp electric hookups. You can go freshwater fishing in the St. John River or visit King's Landing Historical Settlement. For information and reservations, call ☎ 506/451-9696; www.campingfredericton.com.

Cavendish Campground. The Prince Edward Island National Park was established to protect sand dunes, beaches, sandstone cliffs, saltwater marshes, freshwater ponds, and cultural and architectural treasures such as the Green Gables farm site and Dalvay-by-the-Sea Hotel. Its newest acquisition is the Greenwich Sand Dune System. Cavendish Campground off Route 6 on Gulf Shore Parkway provides 80 full-hookup sites, 15- and 30-amp electric. Both the park and the campground are open from late June to early September and require a national park personal use permit. For information on permits and camping reservations, call ☎ **800/213-PARK** or 902/672-6350; www.gov.pe.ca/.

Cavendish KOA Campground. Located on Route 6, near Green Gables, Cavendish Beach, and Rainbow Valley, this KOA offers a good central location for Prince Edward Island sightseeing and—good news for big-rig drivers—some 50-amp electric hookups as well as a heated swimming pool. There are 230 grass sites, all with water and 148 with 30- and 50-amp electric (☎ **800/ KOA-1879** or 902/963-2079; www.koa.com).

Pine Hills RV Park. Located between Charlottetown and Cavendish in Harrington on Route 15, Pine Hills has 112 full-hookup sites with 15- and 30-amp electric. There are free daily hayrides and movies, a swimming pool, and a playground (☎ **877/226-2267** or 902/672-2801).

Southport RV Park, Stratford, Prince Edward Island. Closest to Charlottetown at 20 Stratford Rd. on the beach, this park overlooks the Hillsborough River and offers 90 full-hookup sites with 30- and 50-amp connections. Open May 15 to October 13 (☎ **902/569-2287**).

Five Side Trips

1. **Visit Newport, Rhode Island.** Take a detour off I-95 in Rhode Island along the coast on U.S. 1, across Route 138 and over the spectacular Newport Toll Bridge into the city of Newport. This is where Jackie and Jack Kennedy got married, where Claus von Bulow's trial took place, and where various Vanderbilts, Astors, and Belmonts built 70-room "cottages," many of which are restored and open to the public. (Extra-wide and extra-long RVs and travel trailers should skip the trip into Newport since the streets can be narrow and congested with limited parking.) **Newport County Convention and Visitors Bureau,** 22 America's Cup Ave. (☎ **401/849-8048;** www.newportri.com). From here, it's an easy dash up to **Fall River, Massachusetts,** where Lizzie

> **RV TRAVEL TIP**
>
> The **Confederation Bridge** to Prince Edward Island from Cape Tormentine, New Brunswick, opens up the smallest and one of the most charming of Canada's provinces to much more vehicle traffic, increasing tourism by 51% in the first year alone. Go sooner, not later, to see this jewel of an island.

ANNE OF GREEN GABLES SITES

Anne of Green Gables, the heroine of a series of books, movies, and television shows, is a cottage industry on Prince Edward Island (PEI), because PEI has taken the unique step of trademarking the name. All summer, "Anne of Green Gables–The Musical" (seats $30–$40) runs in the Mainstage Theatre at the Charlottetown Festival, playing matinees and evenings most days, alternating on occasion with other shows (box office ☎ 800/565-0278; www.confederation centre.com).

The Lucy Maud Montgomery Birthplace, New London. This house and antiques shop at the junction of routes 6 and 20 houses Montgomery's wedding dress and other personal mementos; closed mid-October to early May. For information, call ☎ 902/886-2099.

Green Gables Post Office and the site of **Lucy Maud Montgomery's home,** Cavendish. The site of the farmhouse where the author was brought up by her strict grandparents is east of the junction of routes 6 and 13. Parking is at the Green Gables Post Office or down the gravel side road at the bookstore. A short walking trail leads to the site from both the post office and the bookstore. Admission C$2. For information, call ☎ 902/963-2231.

The Anne of Green Gables Museum at Silver Bush, Park Corner, is her aunt and uncle's big white house of at the old Campbell homestead, filled with many artifacts. Also at Park Corner on route 20 is the **Lucy Maud Montgomery Heritage Museum,** displaying family artifacts and items she wrote about in her books. Admission fees. Both closed November to May. For information, call ☎ 902/436-7329 or 902/886-2807.

Green Gables House, Cavendish. Her cousins' home, which Montgomery used as the setting for her novel, has been extensively restored, with Lovers' Lane and Haunted Wood nearby; off Route 6 just west of Route 13 and closed November to mid-May. C$45 Adults, C$4 seniors, C$12 family. For information, call ☎ 902/672-6350. For all Anne of Green Gables information, contact www.peiplay.com.

Avonlea, Cavendish. A commercial version of Anne's village of Avonlea (which was based on Cavendish) is populated with costumed characters and offers pony rides, cow milking, fiddling, storytelling, and free tastings of Anne of Green Gables chocolates and raspberry cordial throughout the summer season. Admission fee charged (☎ 902/963-3050; www.avonlea.ca).

Borden may or may not have dispatched her parents with an ax. The relics from the trial, including the alleged murder hatchet, are on display at the **Fall River Historical Society,** 451 Rock St. (☎ 508/ 679-1071; www.lizzieborden.org). Lizzie was acquitted and lived in Fall River until her death in 1927; her home is now a B&B.

2. **Follow the painters through Maine.** Maine's pristine beauty has drawn many artists over the years, including Andrew Wyeth. His famous *Christina's World* was painted at the Olson farm in Cushing, near Rockland. Winslow Homer painted at Prouts Neck, south of

Portland, and Edward Hopper's Maine was captured in his lighthouse paintings at Two Lights in Cape Elizabeth. Hopper also painted with fellow artists George Bellows and Rockwell Kent at Monhegan Island; they followed their former teacher Robert Henri there. Boat service to the island is provided by Hardy Boat Cruises in New Harbor; $27 adults, $15 children (☎ 800/2-PUFFIN; www.gwi.net/~hardy). Bear in mind that the trip can be rough. It's said Winslow Homer got so seasick on the way over that he turned around and went home without ever getting off the boat. Motor vehicles are prohibited on the island.

3. **Visit an FDR summer home.** Take the short detour from Whiting, Maine, up Route 89 and across the bridge at Lubec to Campobello Island in Canada, the summer home of Franklin D. Roosevelt, who was vacationing here in 1921 when he was stricken with polio. The garden is magnificent, the house evocative, even poignant, with FDR's austere bedroom, and the surrounding countryside has a number of wooded and beachfront walking trails where there's a chance of spotting deer, osprey, eagles, and, below the rocky ledges by the beach, seals. **Herring Cove Provincial Park,** with 91 campsites, is on the island; 40 of the sites have 30-amp electrical hookups. Take an umbrella if you go walking. Campobello walking tours (☎ 506/752-7943); Campobello park (☎ 506/752-2922); Herring Cove (☎ 506/752-2396).

4. **Visit the Acadian shore around northern New Brunswick.** Drive north from Moncton to Shediac, self-proclaimed "Lobster Capital of the World," where you can pick up a crustacean at a stall on the wharf and cook it yourself in a pot of boiling seawater, or pop into popular Fisherman's Paradise for table service. The town's annual lobster festival is in early July. Acadian towns in this region and the Acadian Historical Museum restaurants serve unique ethnic dishes like *fricots* (stews) based on potatoes and various kinds of meat. A *poulet fricot* is a chicken stew; *rapure* is a pie with pork and a potato crust. Look for children selling blueberries by the roadsides in summer. Contact Tourism New Brunswick at ☎ 800/561-0123.

5. **Take the ferry from Hyannis to Martha's Vineyard.** The ferry takes walk-on passengers and their bicycles to Martha's Vineyard, where summer weekends can see as many as 80,000 visitors and traffic and parking are nightmares. Chic shopping and fashionable restaurants give the impression of gentrification, but institutions like The Black Dog Tavern by the ferry landing, with its sought-after T-shirts, are still around. Bear in mind a couple of Vineyard peculiarities—beaches are privately owned down to the low tide mark, and Martha's Vineyard is dry except for drinks served at restaurants in Edgartown and Oak Bluff (you can take your own wine or beer when you're going out to dinner); $27 adults, $13.50 children 5 to 19 (☎ 508/778-2600).

Harry & Shirley's RV Buying & Renting Guide

Just as with permanent homes, some people are RV buyers and some are RV renters. This section will provide the information you need, whichever profile you fit.

⑬ RV Types & Terms

AT THE BEGINNING, WE TOOK SOLEMN OATHS NOT TO REFER TO OUR motor home as a "rig" (although we're not above calling her "Winnie" for Winnebago—but only in private). We also swore we'd never (a) wear visored caps (although they are handy to keep sun out of the driver's eyes), (b) display a carved wooden nameplate saying, "Hi, we're Harry and Shirley from L.A.," and (c) never refer to ourselves as "pilot" and "copilot," terms we considered unbelievably coy the first time we heard them.

However, like some New Year's resolutions, these proclamations have undergone a bit of change. "Rig" has become "vehicle" (sometimes), and "copilot" is now "navigator." But we still haven't carved out the nameplate.

Just as we had to learn certain technical terms to work as film actors, then pick up a new set of terms as professional travelers, so we've had to adopt certain accepted terms from the RV world in order to correctly describe the vehicles. This chapter gives a few of the terms you'll need to know to get along in the RV world. More glossary words will turn up in chapter 14, "To Rent or Buy?," as they become necessary. Don't worry about memorizing them yet. All will be revealed, as we say when we're stuck 5 hours in the Beijing airport or the ship we're waiting for in Ibiza never arrives or we're questioned by the Tunisian police, who suspect we're spies because we're carrying cameras.

In the section after the glossary are definitions and descriptions of the major varieties of RVs: type A motor homes, type B van campers, and type C minimotor homes (previously called Class A, B, and C), truck campers, folding camping trailers, travel trailers, and fifth-wheel travel trailers.

> *"Look, Dad, it's got a TV and everything so the driver can watch television!"*
>
> —Child's comment on seeing a van camper at the L.A. RV Show

The ABCs of RVs: A Glossary of Common RV Terms

Airbag: In RV terms, a sort of shock absorber positioned at the forward and rear axles of a motor home.

Arctic Pack: Also spelled Arctic Pac and Arctic Pak, an optional kit to insulate RVs for winter camping.

Auxiliary battery: Extra battery to run 12-volt equipment.

Basement model: An RV that uses large storage areas under a raised chassis.

Bunkhouse: An RV area containing bunk beds instead of regular beds.

Cab over: Part of a type C minimotor home overlapping the top of the vehicle's cab, usually containing a sleeping area, storage, or entertainment center.

Camper shell: Removable unit to fit in the bed of a pickup truck.

CCC (Cargo Carrying Capacity): The maximum permissible weight of all pets, personal belongings, food, tools, and other supplies you can carry in your motor home. This is the GVWR minus the UVW (see below).

Cassette toilet: Toilet with a small holding tank that can be removed from outside the vehicle in order to empty it.

Cockpit: The front of a motorized RV where the pilot (driver) and copilot (navigator) sit.

Coupler: The part of the trailer that hooks to the hitch ball.

Crosswise: A piece of furniture arranged across the RV from side to side rather than front to rear.

Curbside: The side of the RV that would be at the curb when parked.

Curb weight: The weight of an RV unit without water in the holding tanks but with automotive fluids such as fuel, oil, and radiator coolant.

Diesel pusher: A motor home with a rear diesel engine.

Drink holders: Fitted wood or plastic devices attached to the dashboard area designed to hold cups or cans steady while the RV is moving.

Dry weight or unloaded weight: Manufacturer's weight estimate with no passengers, fuel, water, or supplies.

Entry level: A price deemed attractive for first-time RV buyers.

GAWR (Gross Axle Weight Rating): The maximum permissible weight that can be carried by an axle with weight evenly distributed through the vehicle.

GCWR (Gross Combination Weight Rating): The maximum allowable weight for the combination of vehicle, tow vehicle, passengers, cargo, and all fluids (water, fuel, propane, and so on).

GTWR (Gross Trailer Weight Rating): The maximum allowable weight of a fully loaded tow vehicle.

GVW (Gross Vehicle Weight): Total weight of a fully equipped and loaded RV with passengers, gas, oil, water, and baggage; must not be greater than the vehicle's GVWR.

GVWR (Gross Vehicle Weight Rating): The amount of total loaded weight a vehicle can support; determined by the manufacturer, this amount must not be exceeded.

'RITHMETIC

In addition to the verbiage in this section, you've got to learn a few numbers to talk the RV talk since most (but not all) RV manufacturers use as model numbers an abbreviated code that can give you basic information about the vehicle—28 RQ, for instance, will often mean a 28-foot vehicle with a rear queen bed, and 34 D may mean a 34-foot diesel pusher.

Garden tub: A bathtub angled into the bathroom so plants can be put on the wide edges against the corner walls.

Gaucho: Sofa/dinette bench that converts into a sleeping unit; a term less used now than formerly.

Generator: Small engine fueled by gasoline or propane that produces 110-volt electricity, built into many RVs but also available as a portable option.

Gooseneck: A colloquial name for fifth-wheel travel trailers.

Hard-sided: RV walls made of aluminum or other hard surface.

High profile: A fifth-wheel trailer with a higher-than-normal front to allow more than 6 feet of standing room inside the raised area.

Hitch: The fastening unit that joins a movable vehicle to the vehicle that pulls it.

Hitch ratings: The maximum amount of weight the hitch can handle—Class I up to 2,000 pounds, Class II up to 3,500 pounds, Class III up to 7,500 pounds, Class IV up to 10,000 pounds, and Class V up to 14,000 pounds. A fifth-wheel hitch can handle up to 25,000 pounds.

Holding tanks: Tanks that retain waste water when the RV unit is not connected to a sewer. The gray-water tank holds waste water from the sinks and shower; the black-water tank holds sewage from the toilet.

Inverter: A unit that changes 12-volt direct current to 110-volt alternating current to allow operation of computers, TV sets, and such when an RV is not hooked up to electricity.

Island queen: Not Hawaii's Queen Liliuokalani, but a queen-sized bed with walking space on both sides.

Leveling: Positioning the RV in camp so it will be level, using ramps (also called levelers) under the wheels, built-in scissors jacks, or power leveling jacks.

Pop-up: Foldout or raised additions to an RV that add height for standing room.

Porta-Potti: Brand name for a portable plastic toilet frequently used in folding camping trailers without facilities.

Self-contained: An RV that needs no external connections to provide short-term cooking, bathing, and heating and could park overnight anywhere.

Shore cord: The external electrical cord that connects the vehicle to a campground electrical hookup.

Slide-out: A unit that slides open when the RV is parked to expand the living area.

Soft-sides: Telescoping side panels on an RV that can be raised or lowered, usually constructed of canvas or vinyl and mesh netting.

Solar panels: Battery chargers that convert sunlight to direct current electricity.

Street side: The part of the vehicle on the street side when parked.

Tail swing: The rear motion of a motor home built on a short chassis with a long rear overhang when the vehicle turns sharply; in simpler terms, the reason we knocked down that road sign when we came out of the driveway.

Telescoping: Compacting from front to back and/or top to bottom to make the living unit smaller for towing and storage.

Three-way refrigerators: Appliances that can operate on a 12-volt battery, propane, or 110-volt electrical power.

Tow car: A car towed by an RV to be used as transportation when the RV is parked in a campground; also called a dinghy.

Turning radius: The distance across the diameter of an arc in which a vehicle can turn.

UVW (Unloaded Vehicle Weight): The weight with full fuel, water, LPG, driver, and passenger weights.

Wide body: Designs that stretch RVs from the traditional 96-inch width to 100 or 102 inches.

Winterize: To prepare the RV for winter use or storage.

Types of RVs

There are two basic types of recreation vehicle based on locomotion—towable vehicles and motorized vehicles.

Towables, such as folding camping trailers, travel trailers, and fifth-wheel travel trailers, are living units that can stand alone in camp but are hitched to motor vehicles to travel. Truck campers, compact living units that travel atop the bed and cab of a pickup truck, are also part of the towable team.

Motorized vehicles include motor homes and van campers, both of which are self-contained units built on a truck or van chassis with living, sleeping, cooking, and bathroom facilities accessible from the driver's area without leaving the vehicle. More and more, the dividing line is blurred between van camper and minimotor home as more compact units fitted with all the necessities for self-contained camping appear on the market. At the present time, however, the type A motor home, the type B van camper, and the type C minimotor home are still considered three different vehicle categories.

In most models and price ranges, the buyer can choose interior colors and fabrics from samples if the models on the lot are not to his liking.

TOWABLE RVS
Folding Camping Trailers
Think of it as a modern-day covered wagon, with your own team of oxen or horses already in your garage.

Affordable, open and airy, easy to store and tow, these lightweight units are the closest thing to tent camping, will fit into a carport or garage, and can usually be towed even by compact cars. From a traveling configuration that resembles a small U-Haul trailer, the RV unfolds to standing-room height with collapsible side walls to form two screened, covered wings, each containing a double bed area.

The center section has a solid floor that supports cooking, dining, and lounging areas, some converting to provide even more sleeping space, as well as optional toilet and shower facilities. Some models are equipped with heating and air-conditioning options, and most have a gas cookstove that can be used inside the unit or plugged into outside connections.

Generally the least expensive of the RVs, folding camping trailers are priced from $3,600 to $12,000, and may sleep as many as eight. The average price is around $5,650. Whereas the original units had canvas and/or screen sides, newer models also offer the choice of vinyl or even lightweight aluminum hard siding.

Budget-minded families with small children, tent campers who seek a bit more luxury without giving up the canvas-and-campfire ambience, and even veteran RVers seeking a simpler travel lifestyle enjoy these vehicles.

Folding camping trailer ready for the road.

Erecting a folding camping trailer, Des Moines KOA campground.

Average Cost of Using a Folding Camping Trailer

In a study by the Go Camping America Committee, the vacation costs for a family of four, traveling in their personal automobile towing a folding camping trailer, staying at campgrounds and preparing the majority of their meals, came to $149 for 2 nights, $483 for 7 nights, and $889 for 14 nights.

Folding Camping Trailers: The Plus Side

- **Ease of towing, with good gas mileage and lower wind resistance.** Even a compact car can handle most, and they can go anywhere the family car can go and can be left behind in camp while the family sets out to explore the area by car.

- **Economical to purchase and operate.** These units offer many options found in more expensive RVs, such as air-conditioning, heating, bathroom facilities, three-way refrigerators, awnings, and roof racks that can carry boats or bicycles atop the folded unit. Naturally, the more options added, the more expensive the unit is.

- **Easy to store.** Garage or carport storage capability of these small units eliminates the potential problems larger RVs create. Folded, they measure from 5 to 19 feet long and are usually less than 60 inches high.

Folding Camping Trailers: The Minus Side

- **Not always convenient.** Most folding camping trailers use a hand-cranked system for raising and lowering, simple enough when the operator is fit and the weather nice, but not always pleasant in the rain when you're trying to keep the wing mattresses dry.

- **Offers limited on-road access to stored items.** The unit is not usable when underway unless you crank it open at rest stops. Some models have front storage units that are accessible when the unit is folded if you want to get to picnic items, toys, or bicycles. Access to kitchen and toilet facilities is available only when the rig is set up.

- **May mildew if left wet.** If a canvas unit is closed when wet, it has to be unfolded at home and dried out completely before storing or it can mildew. Vinyl units can simply be wiped dry.

- **Offers limited toilet facilities.** Some models do not have toilet or shower facilities or offer them only as an option. Most have a storage area for a portable toilet that must be emptied manually. When you're camping in areas that have public toilets and showers it won't be a problem, but self-contained camping is not feasible.

Truck Campers

For people who own a pickup truck, the easiest and least expensive RV addition might be a truck camper, a unit that slides onto the bed of a pickup, sometimes overhanging the cab or the rear of the vehicle. Most models sleep two to six people and cost between $4,500 and $22,000, with the average price around $13,380. Since the unit is slid on and off, the truck continues to be useful as a hauling and transportation vehicle without the camper.

Sportsmen particularly like the rugged outdoorsy capability of truck campers because they can remove the camper and set it up in camp, then use the truck to go to and from the ski area, fishing hole, or trailhead. It is also possible to tow a boat, snowmobile, horse trailer, or Jet Skis behind a truck camper, something not permitted with other towables.

Low-profile pop-up models are available, as well as units that have optional electrical systems to load and unload the camper from the truck bed. They are often equipped with bathroom and kitchen.

Truck camper.

Units range from 7 to 18 feet long, with a cab-over bed extending over the pickup's cab. Sofa or dinette built-ins may convert to form a second sleeping area, but these are usually fairly short beds. A step leads from the lower floor area up to the cab-over bed.

Buyers of truck campers should plan to spend extra time matching camper to pickup. Some dealers may not be conversant with the details that make the combination work, so it is essential to be sure the camper's weight is compatible with the truck carrying it. If an additional vehicle is being towed, the GCWR (Gross Combination Weight Rating) must also be considered.

Average Cost of Using a Truck Camper

On a cost comparison survey, a family of four with a light-duty truck and truck camper, staying in campgrounds and preparing most of their meals at campsites, spent $152 for 2 nights, $492 for 7 nights, and $916 for 14 nights.

Truck Campers: The Plus Side

- **Economical.** Cheaper to buy, maintain, and operate than most other towables, with better gas mileage.

- **Versatile.** The camper unit can be removed and stored at home or set in place at the campground, and the truck separately. With a self-contained camper and a 4WD truck, you can go almost anywhere.

- **Durable.** Most models are made to endure tougher road conditions than other towables.

- **Offers passenger convenience.** In most states (except Maine, Mississippi, New Hampshire, New Mexico, North Dakota, Pennsylvania, and Wisconsin), passengers are permitted to ride inside a truck camper. California permits passengers to ride inside only if there is communication possible with the driver and if the door can be opened from inside and outside. Several areas in Canada (Newfoundland/Labrador, Nova Scotia, Saskatchewan, and the Yukon) do not permit passengers to ride inside a truck camper.

Truck Campers: The Minus Side

- **Floor space is limited inside.** There's inadequate room for two adults to move around freely at the same time.

- **Hard to handle.** Weight distribution and higher center of gravity often mean more difficulty in handling these units on the road.

Travel Trailers

Vans, autos, or pickup trucks can tow these soft- or hard-sided RVs, depending on their weight. They sleep from two to eight people and usually contain full bathroom and kitchen facilities. They range from 10 to 40 feet long.

Models come in traditional box shape, an aerodynamic or teardrop shape, and a hard-sided telescoping travel trailer that can be lowered for towing and

Exterior of a travel trailer.

storage and raised for campground living. Prices range from $9,500 to $63,000, with an average cost of around $14,700.

"Slide-outs" that are expanded at the campsite to add more walking-around room have greatly enhanced the comfort of travel trailers and fifth-wheels. Some models may have as many as three slide-outs. There are, however, some campgrounds that prohibit RVs using slide-outs.

Travel trailers often have two doors with a sofa and dinette slide-out area, which could be made into a second sleeping area. Sometimes the bathroom is split into two sides, and both linoleum and carpet are used on the floors, the former in the kitchen and bathroom, the latter in the bedroom and living room.

Average Cost of Using a Travel Trailer

A family of four traveling in their car or light truck towing a travel trailer and staying in campgrounds where they prepare most of their meals, spends an average of $158 for 2 nights, $504 for 7 nights, and $924 for 14 nights.

Travel Trailers: The Plus Side
- **Easy to unhitch.** Travel trailers can be unhitched at the campsite, releasing the tow vehicle for local errands and touring.

INSIDER TIP

Before selecting a travel trailer to be towed with a vehicle you already own, be sure to consider how much weight you'll be adding for traveling—food, water, clothing, books, sports gear— and be sure your tow vehicle is capable of handling it.

Interior of a travel trailer.

- **Large selection of interiors.** Travel trailers come in a wide variety of floor plans, with homelike furniture, full kitchens, and bathrooms. Many models have two doors, and some offer a forward bedroom and rear bunkhouse design to sleep the whole family without converting other furniture into beds.

- **Can be pulled by most vehicles.** Today's travel trailers take a greater variety of tow package options, including 4x4s, light trucks, full and midsize cars, station wagons, and minivans.

Travel Trailers: The Minus Side

- **Can be hard to handle.** Some drivers find handling a travel trailer, especially when backing up, takes extra skill at the beginning.

- **Not always convenient and economical.** Wind resistance is greater with travel trailers, and hitching or unhitching can be a nuisance in bad weather.

- **Will cost you more in tolls.** For both travel trailers and fifth-wheels, road tolls based on axles will be higher.

Fifth-Wheel Travel Trailers

These are the most luxurious of the towables, popular with full-timers and snowbirds who cite the ease of maneuvering and towing, the generous storage areas, large living space, and homelike design. The raised forward section that fits over the truck bed allows a split-level design. This area is usually a bedroom and bathroom, but is sometimes a living room or kitchen/dining area instead. By the time basement storage and slide-outs are added, a fifth-wheel is comparable in comfort to a condo or a home in the suburbs.

There are numerous bedroom options as well as living, dining, and bathroom choices in a 36-foot fifth-wheel. The slide-out contains sofa and dining furniture, while a second optional slide-out in the bedroom area can add more room there as well. There's often space for a washer/dryer, bedroom TV, entertainment center, and large sitting area.

Fifth-wheels sell from $28,000 to $97,000 and up, with an average cost of around $25,355. They are from 22 to 40 feet long.

Average Cost of Using a Fifth-Wheel

For average expenditures on vacations, see "Travel Trailers," above.

Fifth-Wheels: The Plus Side

- **Maneuverability and towability.** These are major assets; fifth-wheels are easier to handle than a travel trailer because the hitch is in the bed of the truck, with less vehicle trailing behind. This also creates a shorter turning radius.

- **Easy to unhitch.** Like the other towables, the fifth-wheel can be unhitched and left at the campsite while the truck is available for touring or shopping in the area.

- **Allows storage in your pickup.** The truck bed can still be used for storage with the addition of a pickup bed cover.

Fifth-Wheels: The Minus Side

- **Can't carry passengers on the road.** Because a truck is the obligatory tow vehicle and passengers are not permitted to ride in the fifth-wheel in 29 states and 8 Canadian provinces, large families might find them inconvenient for long trips.

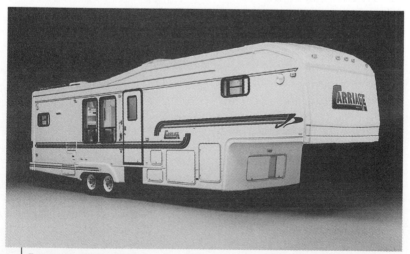

Exterior of a fifth-wheel.

Interior of a fifth-wheel.

- **Limited headroom.** In many forward bedroom models, except those labeled "high profile," there is not quite enough headroom for anyone over 6 feet tall to stand up straight.
- **No entry from towing vehicle.** As with all towables, you have to exit the towing vehicle and go outdoors to enter the RV, an inconvenience in bad weather.

MOTORIZED RVS

Type-B Van Campers

Also called type B motor homes, these conversions are built within the framework of a van, but with raised roofs or lowered floor sections to allow passengers to stand upright, at least in the center of the vehicle. Galleys, fresh-water hookups, sleeping and dining areas that convert to beds, even toilets and showers are readily available in these versatile vehicles.

Ranging from 18 to 22 feet in length, van campers sell from $35,000 to $65,000 (on the upper end comparable in price to an entry-level motor home), with an average cost of around $56,500. Most sleep two to four people, but also can carry four to six adults as a weekday commuter vehicle. They typically sleep four people, two in the overhead bunk and two on the convertible sofa. A drop-in table fits in front of the sofa for dining.

One enterprising man we met at the Los Angeles RV show was buying a camper van with four swivel passenger seats to use on weekend family trips, but hoped to pay for it by carrying weekday commuters who appreciate having a toilet, microwave, and TV set on the daily run.

Custom van conversions are available from a number of manufacturers at an average price of around $28,500. For a list of manufacturers that make van conversions, contact RVIA, P.O. Box 2999, Reston, VA 22090; www.rvia.org; no phone.

Average Cost of Using a Van Camper

A family of four using their own van camper or van conversion, staying in campgrounds and preparing most of their meals in camp, spends an average of $155 for 2 nights, $501 for 7 nights, and $924 for 14 nights.

Van Campers: The Plus Side

- **Multipurpose use.** These RVs double as a second car to use around town or for carpooling.

- **Easy to drive and park, with good gas mileage.** Van campers can go anywhere a passenger car can, including areas in national parks where larger RVs may be restricted.

- **Cozy (the good kind).** Self-contained van campers mean there's no need to leave the vehicle to use any of the facilities.

- **Easy to park.** Unlike other motorized or towable RVs, the camping van can fit into almost any spot left in a campground, so it's good for TGIF getaways and late arrivals.

Van Campers: The Minus Side

- **Cozy (the bad kind).** While most van campers can sleep four people, they'd have to be very good friends, or, more likely, a couple with one or two small children. The living area is extremely compact for a family spending a rainy day inside.

- **Susceptible to wear and tear.** Because it doubles as a second car, the greater mileage accrued by selling time may make it harder to sell or trade than a larger motor home.

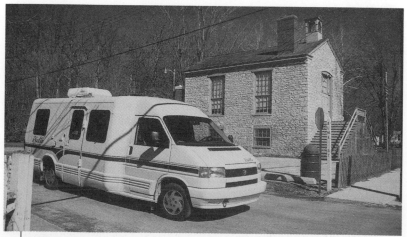

Rialta van camper.

- **Not always easy to set up.** Making up some of the optional beds in these vans could knock your back out—even before you lie down.

- **Limited storage space.** You'll have to carry fewer clothes and supplies than in other RVs, meaning more frequent laundry and grocery stops. Also the minirefrigerator may not have a freezer.

Type C Minimotor Homes

Familiar, convenient, and affordable, the type C (think cab-over bed) motor home packs a lot of living in a compact space. Also called minimotor homes, the units are built on a truck or van chassis, and usually range in length from 19 to 31 feet long. Wide-body designs up to 102 inches across and diesel engine options are available, as well as low-profile models that can be telescoped for travel and storage to less than 8 feet high. Type Cs are priced from $45,000 to $75,000 or more, with the average price around $56,700. Some models offer slide-outs that increase the usable living space.

Normally, a cab-over bed is above the driver's seat, while a sofa provides additional sleeping area. A dinette, rear galley, and bathroom complete the interior. In some models, the cab-over may be turned into an entertainment center with a double bed in back and dining on a drop-in table by the sofa.

Average Cost of Using a Type C Minimotor Home

A family of four traveling in their own motor home, staying in campgrounds and preparing most of their meals in camp, spends an average of $188 for 2 nights, $590 for 7 nights, and $1,059 for 14 nights. Compare this to a family traveling in their personal car and staying at motels or hotels and eating most of their meals in restaurants, and you find the latter spends an average of $339 for 2 nights, $1,169 for 7 nights, and $2,257 for 14 nights.

Exterior of minimotor home.

Interior of minimotor home with entertainment area replacing cab-over bed.

Minimotor Homes: The Plus Side

- **Easy to drive.** Type Cs are more maneuverable for beginning RV drivers than most type A motor homes.

- **Comfortable and compact.** Minimotor homes are as livable as larger motor homes but take up less parking and campground space.

Minimotor Homes: The Minus Side

- **So-so sleeping accommodations.** The cab-over bed is not appealing for claustrophobic adults, but kids love it. In general terms, the sleeping accommodations, except where there is a rear bedroom, are less private than in the type A motor homes when more than two are traveling together.

- **Limited driving visibility.** Because of the overhang from the "cab-over" bed, visibility is limited to a normal-sized windshield, while most type A motor homes provide larger windshields.

Type A Motor Homes

A self-propelled motor vehicle chassis with a living unit built on it, the type A motor home offers the widest range of choices in the RV fleet, from small,

---

INSIDER TIP

Despite its generally smaller size, in our experience, the type C gets no better gas mileage than a small type A, except in the models constructed of extra-lightweight materials.

Exterior of type A motor home.

22-foot, fully equipped entry-level vehicles to enormous, 45-foot, buslike wide-body coaches with slide-outs, ice makers, washer/dryers, beautiful furnishings, and marble bathrooms. They're priced from $50,000 up to $725,000 for the most deluxe models, with the average around $117,500.

Decor can vary from the old-fashioned but tough velour fabrics in slate blue or green in the lower-priced vehicles to Bluebird Wanderlodge's cushy white leather furniture, brass trim, parquet floors, and sculpted area rugs.

A standard entry-level 28-foot model will contain cockpit seats that swivel; a choice of sofa with drop-in tables or a dinette, either of which can be made into a bed; a bathroom; rear island queen bed with an option of twin beds.

Average Cost of Using a Type A Motor Home

For a cost comparison of traveling in a motor home and staying and cooking in campgrounds versus traveling in the family automobile, staying in hotels and eating in restaurants, see "Type C Minimotor Homes," above.

Type A Motor Homes: The Plus Side

- **Always accessible from the front seats without going outside.** The type A motor home lets you pull over to fix lunch, use the bathroom, or take a quick nap by the side of the road or in a parking lot.

- **Bigger windshield and windows than type C.** You'll have greater visibility when traveling and better vantage points for photographs.

- **Livability.** A big, open sense of space and luxury makes the type A the most livable of the motorized RVs for most people.

- **No setup required.** In most type As, all the living areas are ready for two people, without any additional conversion. (For sleeping more than two, however, a sofa or dinette usually has to be made up.)

Type A Motor Homes: The Minus Side

- **It's your only wheels.** Unless you're towing a car, a type A has to be unplugged and moved anytime you need to go out shopping or sightseeing away from the campground.

- **Tough to maneuver.** The larger type A motor homes can offer maneuvering problems in narrow city streets with heavy traffic, as well as parking problems almost everywhere except mall and supermarket parking lots. When street parking is feasible, remember you'll have to feed two or even three meters instead of one. Height and width limitations prohibit entering most parking garages and can present problems in clearing low overhanging roofs and narrow tunnels or bridges.

- **Low mileage.** Gas mileage is quite low, usually under 10 miles to the gallon.

- **Sometimes too big for parks and campgrounds.** Choosing a size to match your travel style is critical, since larger units cannot be accommodated in some campgrounds and are not permitted to enter certain narrow or winding roadways in national parks such as Glacier, Big Bend, and Zion.

TEN QUESTIONS TO ASK YOURSELF WHEN SELECTING AN RV

1. **How often will I use the vehicle?** Some RV owners in cold climates have to winterize and store the RV, while others use it year-round. If you think you may use it only once a year for a 2-week family vacation, it might be cheaper to rent rather than buy.

2. **Where will I store the vehicle?** City dwellers like us have to rent storage space because there's nowhere to store our motor home on our

Interior of a type A motor home.

property. But even suburbanites may face parking regulations that preclude keeping an RV in the driveway or on the street. Owners with a large garage might consider folding camping trailers, truck campers, or telescoping travel trailers that are compact enough to store inside. Some travelers who like to visit the same park or campground year after year might want to store the vehicle permanently at the vacation location.

3. **Do I already have part of an RV unit?** If you have a pickup, for example, depending on its size, you're already capable of handling a towable, such as a travel trailer, truck camper, or fifth-wheel. Most family cars can pull a small travel trailer or folding camping trailer.

4. **How much money can I spend?** Budgeters and young families often begin by buying an entry-level RV in whichever category they want. With sticker shock a strong factor these days, more and more manufacturers are offering lower-priced models in all categories. Previous RV owners often, but not always, look to buy a larger, newer, more expensive model. A few choose to downgrade for a simpler travel lifestyle. In many cases, interest paid on your loan to purchase an RV is tax deductible as a second home.

5. **How many people does the RV need to accommodate on a routine trip?** There's a big difference between a salesman's estimate of how many people a vehicle can sleep and the reality of the number it can comfortably accommodate. Some people dislike the idea of making a bed out of a sofa or dinette night after night during a vacation. Others don't want someone climbing over them in the middle of the night to go to the bathroom. A major consideration is how many seat belts are in the vehicle if it's a motorized RV. All states but New Hampshire now require that all passengers in the vehicle be secured by seat belts, and will not authorize more passengers than there are seat belts provided.

6. **How will I be using the vehicle?** People who like to stay in one place, say a private campground with swimming pools and putting greens, will want a more luxurious vehicle than campers who want to go out in the woods in a national park or forest, build a campfire, and cook outdoors. Travelers who want to stop at a different campground every night need to give priority to ease of setting up camp and fuel efficiency, while snowbirds who want to stay cheaply all winter on BLM desert lands or other self-contained camping should look for vehicles with greater capacity in water storage and holding tanks.

7. **Which is more important, generous living space in the vehicle or more flexible handling, parking, and roadway options?** In making a decision on vehicle size, 1 foot in length or 4 inches in width can make a tremendous difference. Spend a lot of time mentally moving

around in the floor plan, or even physically moving around in the vehicle at the dealer's or the RV show, to assess its livability. Know your size requirements before setting out to look at vehicles, especially if you are considering a motor home; you'll save a lot of time on the lot.

8. **How important is personal privacy?** Some types of RVs offer more solid-door privacy areas than others. In particular, the shower and toilet facilities in folding camping trailers or camping vans, when they are provided at all, may offer minimum privacy, while travel trailers, fifth-wheels, motor homes, and some truck campers provide facilities in a completely closed-off area. Sleeping facilities as well may be open or shielded with curtains rather than doors, as in many folding camping trailers, truck campers, and even type C minimotor homes.

9. **What kind of fuel do I want the vehicle to burn, gasoline or diesel?** The consensus is that diesel engines cost more on initial purchase but less in the long run to operate. One disgruntled RVer, however, has gone on record complaining about the high cost of oil and filters for diesel engines. Diesel engines usually seem quieter in the cockpit than gasoline engines because they are positioned in the rear of the vehicle.

10. **Will I be happy with a standard "off-the-rack" model RV, or do I want some special features and options?** Manufacturers are coming up with new "toys" and gimmicks for today's younger market. Hi-tech elements such as computer stations, satellite dishes, and electronic navigational systems have joined the rearview cameras and slide-outs as common optional equipment. Other design elements include slide-out patios, retractable sun roofs, roof patios, beds stored under the floor that can pop up at bedtime, voice-controlled lighting, and eye-controlled outside mirrors that can be adjusted just by looking at them.

(14)

To Rent or Buy?

FOR A FIRST-TIME RV TRAVELER, RENTING A UNIT OF THE SAME TYPE you're thinking of buying can be an invaluable help in making up your mind. Just be sure to allow enough time—a week is the minimum, 2 weeks is better—to get comfortable with the day-to-day logistics of handling it on the road and hooking it up in the campground.

Our own first RV experience was a 6-week lease on a 27-foot motor home because of a book assignment that required us to visit more than 100 remote ski areas. If we'd been renting it for only a few days, we'd probably have turned it back in and said RVing was not for us. (See chapter 1, "Life on the Road: A Personal & Public History of RVing.")

When they heard about our plans, well-meaning friends regaled us with their experiences. A West Los Angeles bookstore owner took her family out for a month, but they used the RV only for travel and sleeping. "We never cooked a single meal inside," she said. "It seemed too complicated."

A couple from San Diego had tried a rented motor home for 2 days, then, frustrated by slow road speeds, turned it back in and set out in their Mercedes 300 SL instead.

But even that's a record compared to a short-tempered lawyer and his wife, who rented an RV for a weekend and gave it up less than an hour into the trip.

Note that in none of these cases did the user give the vehicle the old college try.

Three Ways to Check Out Campground Life Without an RV

1. **Check into a Kamping Kabin or Kamping Kottage at a nearby KOA (Kampgrounds of America) campground.** Kamping Kabins, one- and two-room rustic log cabins with porches and double beds plus bunk beds, can sleep four for $20 to $30 a night. Kamping Kottages offer a kitchenette, dining area, bathroom with shower, and sleeping quarters for four, with porch swing and sometimes fireplaces

403

and air conditioners. It's a good introduction to camping, especially for families with kids. The fee includes use of the campground's toilet and shower facilities, pool, playground, laundry, and store. The Kabins do not have bathrooms, but an outdoor grill and picnic table are provided. You need to bring your own bedding, lantern, and cooking utensils. Get a full list of locations from KOA, free at any KOA campground or by sending $3 to KOA Directory, P.O. Box 30558, Billings, MT 59114. You can call its administration offices at ☎ **406/248-7444.**

2. **Call around to the campgrounds in your area** or the area you'd like to visit and ask if they have any rental RV units. Sometimes a popular area may offer RVs already in place and hooked up and available for rent by the night. See the "The Best Campground Directories," in chapter 3, "Where to Sleep: Campgrounds & RV Parks," for a listing of campground guides. **Outdoor World** has a network of 15 campgrounds on the East Coast from Maine to Florida that offers RV rental units where you can sample RV living without owning. Their website has complete details on all the campgrounds. Contact them for details and rates at P.O. Box 396, Bushkill, PA 18324 (☎ **800/446-0229;** www.resortsusa.com/outdoor.htm).

3. **Book the family into Fort Wilderness at Walt Disney World in Orlando.** Lodging is in Fleetwood park trailers with full kitchens and bathrooms, similar to travel trailers but set in place for a season or longer. Although you won't be able to road test the vehicle, you can determine how well your family fits into an RV. The cost—with air-conditioning, pool privileges, cable TV, cookware, and housekeeping services—is around $200 a night for a party of six with two adults. It's a good idea to reserve well ahead (☎ **407/934-7639** or 407/WDW-CAMP).

Renting

WHEN TO RENT RATHER THAN BUY

• When setting out on your very first RV journey.

• When considering replacing your current RV with a different type.

• When your family can only take a 2-week vacation once a year but wants to do it in an RV. That way you can test drive different models, and when you decide to buy, you'll have plenty of experience.

• When you want to travel several weeks far from home—say, in a distant part of the United States—or take a camping trip in Europe. Popular fly-and-drive packages are available from many companies.

• When you want to drive the Alaska Highway (see chapter 6, "Driving the Alaska Highway") in one direction only and/or without subjecting your own vehicle to inescapable wear and tear.

Reserve a rental RV at least a month in advance, 3 months during peak vacation time. If planning to rent in Alaska, reserve 6 to 12 months ahead.

WHERE & HOW TO RENT

A great many rental RVs are booked by European and Australian visitors to the United States who want to be able to see our national parks or drive along the coast of California.

The most common unit available for rental is the motor home, either the larger type A or the type C minimotor home, which accounts for 90% of all rentals. Prices begin at around $725 a week.

Use of the generator is not usually included in the fee. You would need it only for operating the ceiling air-conditioning, microwave, and TV in a place without electrical hookups, and the dealer will know how much time you've logged by reading the generator counter, usually located by the on/off switch.

When you find a company that rents travel trailers, you'll find they usually require that you furnish your own tow vehicle, hitch, and electrical hookups on the tow vehicle.

Some companies offer a furnishings package with bedding, towels, dishes, cooking pots, and utensils for a flat price of around $85 per trip. Other add-on kits are those containing power cords and hoses, plastic trash bags, toilet chemicals, and a troubleshooting guide.

Be sure you're provided with a full set of instruction booklets and emergency phone numbers in case of a breakdown. Best of all is to have a 24-hour emergency 800 number in case of a problem.

When in doubt, ask a fellow RVer what to do. They're always glad to help, but sometimes hesitant to offer for fear of offending. No matter how much you bustle around like you know what you're doing, the veterans in the campground can spot a goof-up a mile away.

Before setting out, be sure the dealer demonstrates all the components and systems of your unit. Take careful notes, and, just as with rental cars, check for dents and damage from prior use before leaving the lot.

To find information about RV rental companies all over the United States and Canada check out the website of Recreation Vehicle Rental Association (RVRA) (☎ **800/336-0355;** www.rvra.org). You'll find a directory that lists addresses, phone numbers, and prices for European, Canadian, and U.S. companies listed by city and state or province. There is also a companion page, ***Rental Ventures,*** with additional helpful information. Write to them at RVRA, 3930 University Dr., Fairfax, VA 22030-2525. For rental information, call ☎ **888/467-8464;** www.rvra.org.

> **INSIDER TIP**
>
> Get a detailed list of what furnishings are included in your rental so you'll know what necessary items you have to supply. It may be easier to bring things from home than spend vacation time searching for them on the road.

Your local yellow pages should also carry a listing for rentals under "Recreation Vehicle—Rentals."

Cruise America, the largest rental company with more than 100 outlets, has added budget items such as camping vans, fully equipped travel trailers, and fold-out truck campers with compact pickups to tow them, to answer the requests from European campers in America, who are responsible for one-half to two-thirds of the company's rentals. Rentals will range from $723 to $1,350 a week (☎ 800/327-7799; www.cruiseamerica.com).

Adventures Rental in Ontario, California, claims to have the largest trailer rental department in the United States, offering folding camping trailers from $350 a week and travel trailers from $550 a week. No rentals are made to anyone under 25. Renters supply tow vehicle, hitch and electrical connections, bedding, and utensils. A cleaning deposit is required and forfeited if the vehicle is not returned clean; the company has its own dump stations for holding tanks. Call them at ☎ 909/983-2567 for details.

Altman's Winnebago in Carson, California (☎ 800/400-0787 or 310/518-6182), has type A and type C new motor homes for rent. A typical rental charge for a small type C motor home would be $502 to $1,158 a week. Rental of a type A motor home would run $887 to $1,350 a week. Additional charges would be a $74 prep fee, $12 a day insurance, $6 a day generator fee, and optional charges for kitchen kit (pots, dishes, glasses, $42 per trip) and bedroom kit (bedding and towels, $26 a person per trip).

Many rental companies offer free **airport pickup** and return, if you notify them ahead of time of your flight number and estimated arrival time.

Finally, if you fall in love with your rental vehicle (as we did our first one), you might be able to negotiate a purchase price that would subtract your rental fee from the total. If the vehicle is a couple of years old, the price should be even lower, since most dealers get rid of vehicles after 2 or 3 years.

One source for low-priced **used RVs** is Cruise America's RV Depots, lots that sell previously rented units at discounted prices, along with a 12-month, 12,000-mile warranty and free emergency road assistance for a year. Call ☎ 800/327-7799 and ask for national fleet sales.

FIVE MONEY-SAVING RENTAL TIPS

1. **Check prices with several companies before making a decision.** Establish exactly what the lowest-priced rental will include, such as free miles, amenities like dishes and linens, and breakdown service.

2. **Try to plan your trip for shoulder season or off-season.** This may vary seasonally, depending on the rental area.

3. **Check in advance to see if your own automobile insurance agent will cover your rental insurance.** He can usually do it more cheaply than the rental company.

4. **Try to plan a loop trip from the area where the rental unit is based to avoid drop-off charges.** On long, major journeys such as Alaska or Baja California, you might want to pay the drop-off charge and fly back rather than repeat the arduous drive back to the beginning.

5. **Negotiate based on selection.** The more units a company has, the wider your choice, but if you're flexible about what sort of rig you rent, you may be able to negotiate a better price if the selection is limited.

TEN BIG RENTAL COMPANIES

1. **Cruise America,** 4,000 units nationwide (☎ 800/327-7799).

2. **Rent 'N Roam RV Rentals,** Shrewsburg, Massachusetts (☎ 800/842-1840).

3. **El Monte RV Center,** Orlando, Florida (☎ 800/367-2120); Santa Ana, California (☎ 800/367-2201), with 950 units.

4. **Adventures Rental,** Ontario, California (☎ 909/983-2567).

5. **Moturis, Inc.,** 300 units in Hawthorne, California, near LAX; 400 units in San Francisco and other cities in the United States. Call central reservations, toll-free, at ☎ 877/MOTURIS for all locations.

6. **Road Bear Intl.,** 100 units in Agoura Hills, California (☎ 818/865-2925).

7. **Nolan's RV Center,** 120 units in Denver, Colorado (☎ 800/232-8989).

8. **Western Motor Coach,** 95 units in Lynnwood, Washington (☎ 800/800-1181).

INSIDER TIP

Normally, **insurance on a rental RV** is not covered on your personal automobile insurance, so ask your agent for a binder that extends your coverage to the RV for the full rental period. Many dealers require the binder before renting you a vehicle.

> **INSIDER TIP**
>
> Read your instruction sheets and checklists through at least once before setting out, then daily before hooking up and unhooking until you know the whole routine. Otherwise, you may—as we did that first time—drive miles out of your way to an RV dealer to find out why your generator doesn't work, only to learn it never works when your gas level drops below one-quarter of a tank.

9. **El Monte RV,** Linden, New Jersey (☎ 800/337-3418).

10. **Altman's Winnebago,** 45 units in Carson, California, near LAX (☎ 310/518-6182).

Buying

SHOPPING AT RV SHOWS

Dozens of national and regional RV shows are held annually, most during the winter months. They make especially safe hunting grounds for three types of people: looky-loos who have no idea what they want but are not about to succumb to the first smooth-talking salesman they encounter; well-researched potential buyers who know exactly what they want and are ready to make a deal; and RV owners who want to see the latest technical and design innovations but are basically happy with their existing rig.

The action gets hot and heavy during the last day or two of a show, when it's possible to stumble across an offer you can't refuse. On the other hand, if you're susceptible to supersalesmen, tread carefully or you may be driving a brand-new rig home from the show.

Besides acres of new RVs to explore, a show usually presents seminars on how to "full-time" or where to travel, a bazaar of esoteric gadgets from no-snore pillows to salad-makers (as well as a lot of helpful and practical items), and entertainment from Dixieland or country music musicians to a walk-through virtual reality module.

For a free listing of RV shows, contact the **Recreation Vehicle Industry Association (RVIA),** Dept. SL, P.O. Box 2999, Reston, VA 22090 (☎ 703/620-6003; www.gorving.com or www.rvia.org), or watch your local newspapers for a show in your area.

SHOPPING AT RV DEALERS

Check the Yellow Pages for local RV dealers and spend an afternoon walking the lot looking at types of vehicles and mentally moving into them. The dealer can give you a brochure to take home and study, which details all the features, along with floor plans and specifics about the vehicle's features.

Every dealer has a number of previously owned vehicles it has taken in as trade-ins or RVs it is brokering for the owners. You can figure the used vehicle could be one-third to half the price of a new model. Purchasing from a reputable dealer ups the chances that the RV will be in good condition and gives you someplace to come back to if there's a problem.

Don't worry about taking up time if you're not ready to buy yet. Sooner or later you will be, and dealers are accustomed to the allure of a new and unfamiliar RV both to wannabe and veteran owners.

Expect the best buys in December and January, when dealers want to get the previous year's models off the lot to make room for the new year's models. Get on their mailing list for any sales they may have in the future.

WHERE *NOT* TO SHOP FOR AN RV

Avoid parking lot and campground "distress" sellers who give you a spiel about bad luck and desperate need for cash. A nationwide group of con artists who call themselves Travelers make a big profit selling cheaply made travel trailers, which also serve as living quarters and office headquarters for numerous other scams.

Be extremely careful buying from any private party unless you know a great deal about the RV you're considering and can make a clear-eyed evaluation of it before signing the deal. If it looks beat up and shows wear inside and out, walk away. Chances are, if the owner has treated the superficial areas badly, the systems you can't see are also flawed. Remember, with motorized vehicles, you're buying both a used car and a used house.

RV PRICES

Prices (entry, midrange, upscale, and luxury) vary according to the type of RV. Motor homes range from $50,000 at entry level to $350,000 and up for luxury. Type-C minimotor homes range from $45,000 to $75,000, fifth-wheels from $28,000 to $97,000, travel trailers from $9,500 to $63,000, van campers from $35,000 to $56,500, truck campers from $4,500 to $22,000, folding camping trailers from $3,600 to $12,000.

FINANCING

Because RV buyers are generally considered more reliable for a loan than car buyers (only 1.39% of all RV loans are delinquent), loans are easier to get. Check with banks, savings and loan associations, finance companies, credit unions, or the RV dealer. Loans for big new RVs typically range from 10 to 12 years, even 15, with many asking a 20% down payment or less. A few lenders may require a 25% down payment. Financing packages for used RVs are usually for up to 8 years. Interest on the loan is deductible as second home mortgage interest, if the unit contains basic cooking, sleeping, and toilet accommodations. To get free **IRS publications** detailing interest information, call ☎ **800/829-3676** and request Publication 936, "Home Interest Deduction," and Publication 523, "Selling Your Home." *The RV Money Book* by Bob Howells (Trailer Life Books, 1992, $29.95; also available from RVIA) offers detailed information on buying, selling, financing, and insuring RVs.

FIVE PRECAUTIONS BEFORE BUYING A USED RV

1. **Take a long test drive.** Watch gauges closely, and check all systems personally from toilet flush to water pump and heater. Look for dry rot in any areas with wood, or water stains that may be signs of leaks.

2. **Ask questions.** Ask the owner very direct and specific questions about all systems in the vehicle.

3. **Have the RV inspected.** Ask a knowledgeable friend, or better still, hire an RV mechanic to a look at the vehicle.

4. **Check the book value of the rig.** Find out the current value in a Kelley or NADA blue book; your bank loan officer should have current copies.

5. **Shop around.** Check comparable models and prices at another dealer's lot to have a price comparison.

___INSIDER TIP___

Renting your RV to others to help defray costs of ownership may appeal to you. If you decide to try it, check the costs of upgrading your insurance policy to cover any liability, and see if a local dealer might add it to his rental fleet for a share of the profits.

USEFUL RV WEBSITES

www.gorving.com. A comprehensive source of RV information by the Go RVing Coalition, a nonprofit organization.

www.rvia.org. A variety of information about manufacturers, retail shows, and clubs.

www.fmca.com. Family Motor Coach Association's online guide to that organization's events.

www.campnetamerica.com. A site to locate campgrounds, parks, clubs, and RV dealers.

www.funoutdoors.com. American Recreation Coalition's site includes outdoor activities, recreation information sources, research, and statistics.

www.funroads.com. Offers personalized RV trip planning and maps and other information.

www.gocampingamerica. From National Association of RV Parks and Campgrounds, camping information for more than 3,100 member properties.

www.gorp.com. Dedicated to outdoor recreation, scenic drives, a guide to campgrounds, and lists of information sources.

www.goodsamclub.com. Membership club with campground discounts and other RV goods and services.

www.koa.com. Kampgrounds of America list of its member parks and information about facilities.

www.motorhomemagazine.com. *Motorhome* magazine's site.

www.rvadvice.com. Created and maintained by an RV service technician featuring basic maintenance and repair information.

www.rvamerica.com. An RV sales and industry information site sponsored by *RV News* magazine.

www.rvclub.com. An Internet gathering place for RV enthusiasts.

www.rvda.org and **www.rvra.org.** How to buy and rent RVs.

www.rvdoctor.com. A source of technical information on RV maintenance.

www.rvhome.com. An independent referral service representing about 50 rental companies.

www.rvusa.com. Lists RV dealers, manufacturers, parts and accessory sources, rentals, and campgrounds.

www.trailerlife.com. From *Trailer Life* magazine.

www.woodalls.com. From Woodalls Publications, a useful site providing information about RV and tent camping, from manufacturers to destinations.

PUBLICATIONS FOR CAMPERS & RV OWNERS

Camperways, Woodall Publications Corp., 13975 W. Polo Trail Dr., Lake Forest, IL 60045 (☎ 847/362-6700).

Camping and RV Magazine, P.O. Box 458, Washburn, WI 54891 (☎ 715/373-5556).

Camp-orama, Woodall Publications Corp., 13975 W. Polo Trail Dr., Lake Forest, IL 60045 (☎ 847/362-6700).

Chevy Outdoors, 30400 Van Dyke Ave., Warren, MI 48093 (☎ 810/574-9100).

Coast to Coast, 64 Inverness Dr. E., Englewood, CO 80112 (☎ 800/368-5721).

Families on the Road, 2601 S. Minnesota Ave., Suite 105-191, Sioux Falls, SD 57105; www.familiesontheroad.com; no phone.

Family Motor Coaching, 8291 Clough Pike, Cincinnati, OH 45224 (☎ 513/474-3622).

Highways, TL Enterprises, 2575 Vista Del Mar Dr., Ventura, CA 93001 (☎ 805/667-4100).

Midwest Outdoors, 111 Shore Dr., Hinsdale, IL 60521 (☎ 630/887-7722).

Motorhome, TL Enterprises, 2575 Vista Del Mar Dr., Ventura, CA 93001 (☎ 805/667-4100).

Northeast Outdoors, 13975 W. Polo Trail Dr., Lake Forest, IL 60045 (☎ 847/362-6700).

Pop Up Times, 225 Mill St., Vienna, VA 22180 (☎ 800/938-9717).

Roads to Adventure, 2575 Vista Del Mar Dr., Ventura, CA 93001 (☎ 805/667-4100).

RV West, 3000 Northup Way, Suite 200, Bellevue, WA 98004 (☎ 800/700-6962).

Southern RV, 13975 W. Polo Trail Dr., Lake Forest, IL 60045 (☎ 847/362-6700).

The Caretaker Gazette, P.O. Box 5887, Carefree, AZ 85377 (☎ 480/488-1970).

Trailblazer, Thousand Trails, Inc., 2711 LBJ Freeway, Suite 200, Dallas, TX 75234 (☎ 800/328-6226).

Trailer Life, TL Enterprises, 2575 Vista Del Mar Dr., Ventura, CA 93001 (☎ 805/667-4100).

Travelin', P.O. Box 23005, Eugene, OR 97402 (☎ 541/485-8533).

Western RV News, 64470 Sylvan Loop, Bend, OR 97701 (☎ 541/318-8089).

Woodall's Go & Rent . . . Rent & Go, Woodall Publications Corp, 13975 W. Polo Trail Dr., Lake Forest, IL 60045 (☎ 847/362-6700).

Appendix:
Recommended Reading

AS YOU GET READY TO HIT THE ROAD, YOU MAY WISH TO FIND OUT more about the places you will be visiting. In addition to the contact information for tourist bureaus and information centers in each chapter, we've compiled a list of *Frommer's* and *Unofficial Guides* to the areas covered in this book. Frequently updated information about these destinations is also available online at Frommers.com.

Two guides that are useful wherever you travel in the United States are *Frommer's USA*, which provides an overview of major cities, resorts and national parks; and the *Unofficial Guide to the Best RV & Tent Campgrounds*, which lists detailed information about more than 10,000 sites across the country.

Chapter 4: The California Desert & Las Vegas
The Unofficial Guide to the Best RV & Tent Campgrounds in California & the West
Frommer's Great Outdoor Guide to Northern California
Frommer's California
Frommer's California's Best-Loved Driving Tours
The Unofficial Guide to California with Kids
The Unofficial Guide to Las Vegas
Frommer's Las Vegas

Chapter 5: Utah's Parks & Canyons
The Unofficial Guide to the Best RV & Tent Campgrounds in California & the West
Frommer's Zion & Bryce Canyon National Park
Frommer's Utah
Frommer's Family Vacations in the National Parks
Frommer's National Parks of the American West

Chapter 6: Driving the Alaska Highway
The Unofficial Guide to the Best RV & Tent Campgrounds in the Northwest & Great Plains
Frommer's Alaska
Frommer's Alaska Cruises & Ports of Call

Chapter 7: The Dakotas: Black Hills & Buffalo Burgers
The Unofficial Guide to the Best RV & Tent Campgrounds in the Northwest & Central Plains
Frommer's National Parks of the American West

Chapter 8: The Rio Grande Valley & the Wilds of West Texas
The Unofficial Guide to the Best RV & Tent Campgrounds in the Southwest & South Central Plains
Frommer's Texas
Frommer's National Parks of the American West

Chapter 9: In the Heart of the Heartland: Iowa, Illinois & Indiana
The Unofficial Guide to the Best RV & Tent Campgrounds in the Great Lake States
The Unofficial Guide to the Best RV & Tent Campgrounds the Northwest & Central Plains

Chapter 10: The Florida Keys (with Side Trips to the Everglades & Orlando)
The Unofficial Guide to the Best Campgrounds in the Southeast
Frommer's Florida from $70 a Day
Frommer's South Florida Including Miami & the Keys
Frommer's Walt Disney World & Orlando
The Unofficial Guide to Florida with Kids
The Unofficial Guide to South Florida Including Miami & the Keys
The Unofficial Guide to Walt Disney World

Chapter 11: The Blue Ridge Parkway & Skyline Drive
The Unofficial Guide to the Best RV & Tent Campgrounds in the Southeast
The Unofficial Guide to the Best RV & Tent Campgrounds the Mid-Atlantic
Frommer's Virginia
Frommer's the Carolinas & Georgia
Frommer's Family Vacations in the National Parks
The Unofficial Guide to the Great Smoky & Blue Ridge Region
The Unofficial Guide to the Mid-Atlantic with Kids
The Unofficial Guide to the Southeast with Kids

Chapter 12: The Lobster Coast: New England & the Canadian Maritimes
The Unofficial Guide to the Best RV & Tent Campgrounds in the Northeast
Frommer's New England

Frommer's Great Outdoor Guide to New England
Frommer's New England's Best-Loved Driving Tours
Frommer's Vermont, New Hampshire & Maine
Frommer's Cape Cod, Nantucket & Martha's Vineyard
Frommer's Nova Scotia, New Brunswick & Prince Edward Island
Frommer's Portable Maine Coast
The Unofficial Guide to New England & New York with Kids

You can find these books at your favorite bookstore, or order them online from Frommers.com.

Notes

Notes

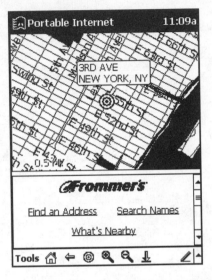

FROMMER'S® COMPLETE TRAVEL GUIDES

Alaska
Alaska Cruises & Ports of Call
Amsterdam
Argentina & Chile
Arizona
Atlanta
Australia
Austria
Bahamas
Barcelona, Madrid & Seville
Beijing
Belgium, Holland & Luxembourg
Bermuda
Boston
British Columbia & the Canadian Rockies
Budapest & the Best of Hungary
California
Canada
Cancún, Cozumel & the Yucatán
Cape Cod, Nantucket & Martha's Vineyard
Caribbean
Caribbean Cruises & Ports of Call
Caribbean Ports of Call
Carolinas & Georgia
Chicago
China
Colorado
Costa Rica
Denmark
Denver, Boulder & Colorado Springs
England
Europe
European Cruises & Ports of Call
Florida
France

Germany
Great Britain
Greece
Greek Islands
Hawaii
Hong Kong
Honolulu, Waikiki & Oahu
Ireland
Israel
Italy
Jamaica
Japan
Las Vegas
London
Los Angeles
Maryland & Delaware
Maui
Mexico
Montana & Wyoming
Montréal & Québec City
Munich & the Bavarian Alps
Nashville & Memphis
Nepal
New England
New Mexico
New Orleans
New York City
New Zealand
Nova Scotia, New Brunswick & Prince Edward Island
Oregon
Paris
Philadelphia & the Amish Country
Portugal
Prague & the Best of the Czech Republic
Provence & the Riviera

Puerto Rico
Rome
San Antonio & Austin
San Diego
San Francisco
Santa Fe, Taos & Albuquerque
Scandinavia
Scotland
Seattle & Portland
Shanghai
Singapore & Malaysia
South Africa
South America
Southeast Asia
South Florida
South Pacific
Spain
Sweden
Switzerland
Texas
Thailand
Tokyo
Toronto
Tuscany & Umbria
USA
Utah
Vancouver & Victoria
Vermont, New Hampshire & Maine
Vienna & the Danube Valley
Virgin Islands
Virginia
Walt Disney World & Orlando
Washington, D.C.
Washington State

FROMMER'S® DOLLAR-A-DAY GUIDES

Australia from $50 a Day
California from $70 a Day
Caribbean from $70 a Day
England from $75 a Day
Europe from $70 a Day

Florida from $70 a Day
Hawaii from $80 a Day
Ireland from $60 a Day
Italy from $70 a Day
London from $85 a Day

New York from $90 a Day
Paris from $80 a Day
San Francisco from $70 a Day
Washington, D.C., from $80 a Day

FROMMER'S® PORTABLE GUIDES

Acapulco, Ixtapa & Zihuatanejo
Amsterdam
Aruba
Australia's Great Barrier Reef
Bahamas
Baja & Los Cabos
Berlin
Big Island of Hawaii
Boston
California Wine Country
Cancún
Charleston & Savannah
Chicago
Disneyland

Dublin
Florence
Frankfurt
Hong Kong
Houston
Las Vegas
London
Los Angeles
Maine Coast
Maui
Miami
New Orleans
New York City
Paris

Phoenix & Scottsdale
Portland
Puerto Rico
Puerto Vallarta, Manzanillo & Guadalajara
San Diego
San Francisco
Seattle
Sydney
Tampa & St. Petersburg
Vancouver
Venice
Virgin Islands
Washington, D.C.

FROMMER'S® NATIONAL PARK GUIDES

Family Vacations in the National Parks
Grand Canyon

National Parks of the American West
Rocky Mountain
Yellowstone & Grand Teton

Yosemite & Sequoia/ Kings Canyon
Zion & Bryce Canyon

FROMMER'S® MEMORABLE WALKS

Chicago	New York	San Francisco
London	Paris	

FROMMER'S® GREAT OUTDOOR GUIDES

Arizona & New Mexico	Northern California	Vermont & New Hampshire
New England	Southern New England	

SUZY GERSHMAN'S BORN TO SHOP GUIDES

Born to Shop: France	Born to Shop: Italy	Born to Shop: New York
Born to Shop: Hong Kong,	Born to Shop: London	Born to Shop: Paris
Shanghai & Beijing		

FROMMER'S® IRREVERENT GUIDES

Amsterdam	Los Angeles	San Francisco
Boston	Manhattan	Seattle & Portland
Chicago	New Orleans	Vancouver
Las Vegas	Paris	Walt Disney World
London	Rome	Washington, D.C.

FROMMER'S® BEST-LOVED DRIVING TOURS

Britain	Germany	New England
California	Ireland	Scotland
Florida	Italy	Spain
France		

HANGING OUT™ GUIDES

Hanging Out in England	Hanging Out in France	Hanging Out in Italy
Hanging Out in Europe	Hanging Out in Ireland	Hanging Out in Spain

THE UNOFFICIAL GUIDES®

Bed & Breakfasts and Country	Florida with Kids	New Orleans
Inns in:	Golf Vacations in the	New York City
California	Eastern U.S.	Paris
New England	The Great Smoky &	San Francisco
Northwest	Blue Ridge Mountains	Skiing in the West
Rockies	Hawaii	Southeast with Kids
Southeast	Inside Disney	Walt Disney World
Beyond Disney	Las Vegas	Walt Disney World for
Branson, Missouri	London	Grown-ups
California with Kids	Mid-Atlantic with Kids	Walt Disney World for Kids
Chicago	Mini Las Vegas	Washington, D.C.
Cruises	Mini-Mickey	World's Best Diving Vacations
Disneyland	New England & New York	
	with Kids	

SPECIAL-INTEREST TITLES

Frommer's Adventure Guide to Australia & New Zealand	Frommer's Exploring America by RV
Frommer's Adventure Guide to Central America	Frommer's Gay & Lesbian Europe
Frommer's Adventure Guide to India & Pakistan	Frommer's The Moon
Frommer's Adventure Guide to South America	Frommer's New York City with Kids
Frommer's Adventure Guide to Southeast Asia	Frommer's Road Atlas Britain
Frommer's Adventure Guide to Southern Africa	Frommer's Road Atlas Europe
Frommer's Britain's Best Bed & Breakfasts and Country Inns	Frommer's Washington, D.C., with Kids
Frommer's France's Best Bed & Breakfasts and Country Inns	Frommer's What the Airlines Never Tell You
Frommer's Italy's Best Bed & Breakfasts and Country Inns	Israel Past & Present
Frommer's Caribbean Hideaways	The New York Times' Guide to Unforgettable Weekends
	Places Rated Almanac
	Retirement Places Rated